# *Reform in Education*

# Reform in Education

## ENGLAND AND THE UNITED STATES

## by James D. Koerner

A SEYMOUR LAWRENCE BOOK

DELACORTE PRESS / NEW YORK

# *Contents*

# *Foreword*

My principal aim in this book is to describe and interpret the English educational system for American readers. One must of course do this at a point in time, recognizing that change within the system not only is inevitable but at this particular time is very rapid. One searches for what is relatively changeless, for the spirit and essence of English education, only to find that these too are changing in response to inexorable social and political movements. Still, I believe that the portrait I have tried to draw of English education will remain a reasonably faithful likeness for some years to come.

But my purpose is more than descriptive. Although there is much about the English educational system that is intensely interesting in itself, most readers of this book will also be interested in how British problems relate to American; they will be interested, that is, in what we can learn from England. I hope that readers in England will also be interested, not only in how their educational system looks to a visitor who admittedly is not exactly a detached observer, but also in what England might learn from the United States. Thus my own judgments are sprinkled generously throughout the book, especially in the last two chapters, which are addressed specifically to the question of what each nation might learn from the other. I have also tried to relate both English and American education to practices and new developments in the rest of Europe. English education, after all, is far closer in organization and principle to education in France or Germany or other European countries than it is to American education, and it should not be considered wholly in isolation from the Continent.

I hope the time has come in the United States when our educational authorities are willing to look abroad for ideas. In the past those who ran our educational system were frequently imbued with a kind of isolationism that made them either indifferent or hostile to the suggestion that we might learn something by looking at what other advanced nations were doing in education. There was little in the training or experience of the average school administrator or professor of education to encourage in him any interest in education outside his own country. He feared that criticism of American standards and practices might come from the study of other school systems; and he often decided, *a priori*, that we were so far ahead of other countries educationally that there really wasn't anything they could teach us. I put these observations in the past tense because I hope and believe the situation is improving. There is still a strong strain of insularity in American education (and in English education, for that matter), but a broader and less defensive attitude than in the recent past is increasingly evident among those who call themselves professional educators. "Comparative education" as a separate field of study continues to develop, although fitfully, in both the United States and Great Britain—a vindication of the lifelong work of a very few people like I. L. Kandel, as well as the earlier efforts of such figures as Matthew Arnold, Michael Sadler, and Henry Barnard. Perhaps we have reached the point in the United States where systematic attention can be given educational developments abroad; in doing so, we have much to gain and nothing whatever to lose except perhaps the chains of our provincialism.

Having said that, I suppose I should disclaim in advance any reader's inference that we should adopt one or another foreign practice in American schools. I do not intend anywhere in the book to suggest that we can find little homilies in the educational system of England or any other nation, or that we should seek specific things in foreign systems to imitate or shun. Education everywhere is very much a native plant, with at least as many varieties as there are countries. We obviously should not merely transplant any of these varieties to American soil. Our own experience in postwar Germany ought to disabuse us of the idea that an educational system can change in any but indigenous ways. We were rightly concerned after World War II about reforming the educational system of a nation that had accepted, if not enthusiastically supported, a policy of genocide, and that had sown most of Europe and much of the world with corpses; and we naively undertook through the expenditure of many millions of dollars in the American Education Program to bring about some changes along American lines in the German educational system. Today German education remains what the Germans and not the Americans want it to be. It too is changing, as is education all over Europe, but not because of anything we have done. So let us look to England or Europe not for educational items that we can simply import, but rather

for ideas of proved worth that might throw light on our own problems
and that we might well consider adapting to our own circumstances.

I have had the general reader rather than the professional educator in
mind in organizing and writing the book. Thus I have relegated references and notes to the back of the book, even though this will inconven-
ience some readers. And I have relegated certain subjects to appendices,
where they will be out of the general reader's way but available to anyone interested in them. I have capitalized certain nouns where there was
a chance of misunderstanding by the layman—"Public Schools," for example, when I am talking about some independent schools in England,
and "Education" when I am referring to the professional study or subject
rather than to the broad field of "education." Except in some quoted
passages, I have changed English spelling to American. Quoted passages
not otherwise referenced are verbatim transcriptions from interviews.
I have often used the terms "Britain" and "England" synonymously,
although the usage is a loose one; strictly speaking, "Britain" means England, Wales, and Scotland, whereas most of this book is concerned with
only England and Wales. However, such usage is very common, and
I think the context will make clear in each case the area to which the
term "Britain" refers.

I hope the reader will bear with certain stylistic devices that can
become annoying: I am conscious of having filled these pages with
qualifying adverbs and adjectives—"few," "often," "sometimes," "most,"
"many"—the plague of educational writing. And I am conscious of having
listed too many items in too many numbered series, of setting up too
many antitheses, of using too many "buts," "althoughs," "for examples,"
"stills," and "therefores." I remember with sorrow one of Thoreau's trench-
ant *dicta* on style to the effect that a sentence should read as though its
author, had he held a plow instead of a pen, would have drawn a furrow
straight and deep to the end. Alas, few writers can plow a straight furrow
over the hills and convoluted fields of education. I must also ask the
reader's indulgence in the matter of length, for this is a long book on a
big subject. One tries to satisfy both the general reader's demands for
conciseness, which I have given first priority, and the specialist's demands
for full disclosure. If some readers still find more facts in these pages
than they want, there may be some wry comfort for them in the thought
that much was deleted or withheld that I would like to have included!

I am indebted to so many people for help in gathering the material for
this book that there is no satisfactory way of thanking them. During two
years of living and traveling in England and Europe, of visits to perhaps
two hundred educational institutions, of numberless hours at administrative centers, I took up so much of the time of so many people that I must

have made a rather negative contribution to the economies of Britain and Europe. People always gave their time cheerfully and helpfully, and I can offer them only this inadequate expression of thanks.

Special mention must be made of a number of people whose help was a good deal more than routine: Hélène Terré of the American Embassy in Paris, and her counterpart, Ursela Bodenburg in Bad Godesberg, Germany; also Joseph Majault, Deputy Director of the National Pedagogical Institute in Paris; and officials at the documentation center of the Permanent Conference of Education Ministers in Bonn. I should also like to record my debt to the many people in the Department of Education and Science in London, both in the Inspectorate of Schools and in the department proper, who helped me throughout the study in more ways than I could list. A number of people read in manuscript the material on Swedish education in Appendix A and made very useful suggestions about it: Anthony Abrahams, Director of the London Office of the Folk University of Sweden; Janet Anderson, formerly a teacher in Sweden, now of Cambridge University; Professor Carl H. Lindroth, University of Lund, Sweden; Patricia Pemberton, formerly a teacher in Sweden, now of King Alfred's College, Winchester; and E. Tennemar, a Swedish teacher on leave of absence during the 1965–66 academic year at St. Martin's College, Lancaster. This section was also read by a number of Her Majesty's Inspectors of Schools in the United Kingdom. Chapter IV and various other parts of the book were read in manuscript by Dr. James A. Petch, former Secretary of the Joint Matriculation Board, Manchester, now Director of its Research Unit. Chapter VIII was read in manuscript by H. Martin Wilson, former Chief Education Officer, Salop County Council.

A number of persons in England read and criticized, often in some detail, the entire book in manuscript. They are:

CATHERINE AVENT, Careers Advisory Officer, Youth Employment Service, Inner London Education Authority.

H. C. DENT, former Editor, *The Times Educational Supplement.*

DAVID HOUSEGO, News Editor, *The Times Educational Supplement.*

EDMUND KING, Reader in Comparative Education, University of London, King's College.

STUART MACLURE, Editor, *Education* ("The Official Organ of the Association of Education Committees").

W. R. NIBLETT, Dean, Institute of Education, University of London.

JOHN J. SULLIVAN, Her Majesty's Inspectorate of Schools.

GEORGE TAYLOR, former Chief Education Officer, Leeds.

PHILIP TAYLOR, former Head of the Research Department, Schools Council, now Professor of Education, University of Birmingham.

In the United States the entire book was read in manuscript by Professor Derek Colville, Harpur College, the State University of New York; and

Mortimer Smith, Executive Director, and George Weber, Associate Director, Council for Basic Education, Washington, D. C.

I hasten to absolve all of these people of any responsibility for the deficiencies of the book, which are wholly and obviously mine. But I want also to make it clear that individually and collectively these persons contributed enormously to whatever virtue the book has. Where I have not followed their advice I have still profited by weighing it; where I have followed their advice, as I have with great frequency, the book is stronger for it.

Some of the material used in the book appeared first in the following publications: in England in *The Daily Telegraph, Education, New Society, The Observer,* and *The Times Educational Supplement;* in the United States in *The Saturday Review.* I am grateful to these publications for permission to use the material in somewhat altered form in this book.

Finally, I would like to thank the Council for Basic Education, which sponsored and administered the project that produced this book, and the Lilly Endowment, Inc., which financed it.

J. D. K.

*August, 1966*

*Lynton Cottage, Dean Way*
*Chalfont St. Giles*
*Bucks, England*

# Introduction

BY ROBERT MAYNARD HUTCHINS

*President of the Center
for the Study of Democratic Institutions
(Fund for the Republic)*

In spite of their reputation as muddlers through, the British have given more sustained attention to education over the last twenty-five years than the people of any other country. The series of remarkable reports that they have had before them has reflected the application of first-rate minds to educational issues. They have guaranteed the discussion of education at every level. If the British have made mistakes, they have not done so carelessly. They have not simply yielded, as Americans seem inclined to do, to the strongest pressure groups in operation at the moment.

The problems are the same on both sides of the Atlantic. How can the doctrine of equality of educational opportunity be reconciled with differences in background and "ability"? Is education to serve the needs of the state, the individual, or both? What is meant by "needs"? What do we do with those who do not appear to have "academic ability"? How can we fit the young into their environment, when we do not know what the environment will be? If we cannot train them for jobs, what *can* we do with them? How do we tell which of them should go how far in education?

In the past these questions have been left to the market. Those who had the money fought or drifted through the educational system, falling into employment or vocational training when they had enough, or were told they had.

Technological change, which has reduced the opportunities for unskilled labor, makes employment for the young an unlikely option for those who do not fare well in school or who lose interest in it. Technological change defeats vocational training in school at a distance in time from entrance into an occupation. It may be worse than wasteful, for it may displace something that might be important to the student as a citizen and a man. It may even displace a kind of education that might be useful to him in entering any occupation or in shifting from one to another.

Technological change has carried with it vast social changes. Social classes are breaking up. Physical mobility has increased even more dramatically than social mobility, and each has undoubtedly contributed to the other.

Hence those who have proposed social adjustment as the aim of education, particularly for pupils who do not fit readily into an "academic" system, are in no better case than those who have sought salvation in vocational training. Mr. Koerner's critique of the Newsom Report seems irrefutable.

At the same time a mixture of motives and tendencies is leading everywhere to new insistence on education for all. Whether we think, as the Robbins Report appears to do, that everybody has a right to the fullest development of his intellectual powers, or whether we believe that the state needs that development for its own purposes, as the governments of the United States, the Soviet Union, and the industrializing countries seem to do, the result is everywhere the same. Democratic ideals and nationalistic ambitions converge in supporting universal schooling as the alternative to a market that has turned unreliable.

These changes have caught us off balance. The British have tried to think and argue their way through them. As Mr. Koerner shows, their answers to the questions that contemporary society puts to education are still tentative. His picture is one of proposal, discussion, reconsideration, revision, and a new proposal. He is far from satisfied with the results. He says, "Britain, faced with the same problem that has bedeviled American education for half a century—how to educate the mass of students who fall below the top quarter or third of ability—is going to take the same road we took and presumably make the same mistakes."

Nevertheless he insists, and documents his case, that we could learn much from British experience. "We could learn that children are capable of working in language and number earlier than they do in American schools; that they are capable in the elementary school of more systematic and sustained study in basic subjects than they generally get in American schools; that the true abilities of many children are often buried by low scores on standardized tests or by poor home conditions or by low expectations on the part of teachers; that children do not suffer from a longer school day and year than is standard in America.

"Even more important, we could learn the importance of a limited, though by no means a rigid, curriculum for students at every ability level; that schools cannot try to do everything and anything and still be schools; that they must establish some priorities thought by adults, not children, to be important; that secondary school students of modest ability can be brought further in basic subjects, including mathematics and foreign languages, than they commonly are in American schools; that students of high ability can be brought a great deal further in basic subjects than they commonly are in American schools. And we could learn that the elaborate administrative machinery which characterizes our schools and schools systems, with their plenitude of non-teaching supervisory personnel, is not visibly superior to the looser and much less grandiose system of the English (and European) schools, where the emphasis in administration is on classroom freedom, not restriction, and on the selection of part-time administrators who are respected for their ability as teachers."

This is a great deal, and there is much more in Mr. Koerner's book, so much that it is bound to command the attention of every thoughtful American.

# *Introduction*

BY SIR EDWARD BOYLE
*Former Minister of Education
under the Conservative Government,
now Opposition Spokesman for Education*

I FEEL PRIVILEGED at the invitation to contribute an Introduction to this very interesting study of English education by Dr. James D. Koerner.

Since I entered Parliament in 1950 there has been an enormous expansion in the human, physical and financial resources which have been devoted to our education service. In 1950 we had 5¼ million pupils in maintained schools, with 12½ per cent of the age group staying on till sixteen; now there are 7¼ million with 23 per cent staying on.

In 1950 there were 250,000 teachers in the schools, colleges and universities; now there are 400,000. In 1950 there were 22,000 teachers in training, mostly on a two-year course; now there are 84,000, on a three-year course. In 1950 there were 150,000 full-time students in higher education; now there are 410,000.

In 1950 public expenditure on education in the United Kingdom was 430 million pounds; now it is 1780 million pounds. In 1950 we were investing 60 million pounds in new educational buildings; in 1966 the figure was 187 million pounds. Educational expenditure as a share of Britain's Gross National Product has risen from just over 3 per cent in 1954–55 to 5½ per cent twelve years later—it has risen more rapidly than any other main block of demand on our national economic resources. Indeed, one can fairly say that educational expansion has been one of the really significant developments in Britain during the postwar period.

Dr. Koerner does not question the desirability of this expansion. "With 75% of your young people still leaving school by the time they are sixteen," he tells us, "with 4% in the universities and another 4% in other kinds of higher education, there can be little doubt that the expansion and extension of your education service is necessary if your island economy is to thrive, and the quality of life to improve." But Dr. Koerner is concerned at what he feels to be "the absence of defined objectives at the various levels of your education system." "What is it," he asks, "that you want your schools to accomplish? . . . Do you want to use [them] as primary instruments of social change . . . or do you want them to concern themselves with *developing and furnishing* the minds of future citizens who might be able to change society in whatever ways seem to *them*, [and] not necessarily to teachers or educational experts, to be most desirable?" (my italics).

I think if anyone were to ask me why we attach such importance to education in Britain today, I should give two main answers. In the first place, we recognize the tremendous significance of educational advance to any industrial nation such as our own at a time of rapid technological change. For my part, I feel one cannot overstress the need for the education service *to increase the amount of talent available* within a modern industrial community; and this requires not only an expansion of university education and of technical education, but also rising standards of general education in our primary and secondary schools. As the Plowden Report on Primary Education points out, "Good primary education will help to equip children to live and work in a rapidly changing economy. Our present society requires a highly adaptable force which is not only *more* skilled, but is better able to learn new skills, to tackle new jobs, and to face new problems."

Secondly, many of us in Britain feel that, in recent years, we have come to a much clearer understanding of the *social* purpose of the education service. It is surely right that all children should have the maximum opportunity and encouragement to develop their potential talents and abilities to the full; yet, as Lord Robbins and many others have emphasized, there is every reason to believe that "the reserves of untapped ability" in our society are still extensive. If one reads the impressive sequence of educational reports which have appeared in Britain during the last twelve years—the Report on Early Learning, Crowther, Robbins, Newsom, and now Plowden—their conclusion on one crucial point is absolutely unanimous: far too many boys and girls are still being allowed to write themselves off well below their true potential.

It was Lord James—no educational egalitarian, but an outspoken (and exceptionally persuasive) "meritocrat"—who said recently that "we have long been aware of the way in which home and environmental circumstances, whether material, intellectual or moral, affect a child's development [and] make much of our talk about equality of opportunity sound like a joke in rather bad taste. . . . We are given [in the Plowden Report] lines of practical approach to enable [the school] to make a greater contribution to the mitigation of the effects of bad material and cultural background." I do not wish to see any child entering upon adult life feeling, as it were, disinherited, and in this important sense I consider that schools can and should act as instruments of social change.

Nevertheless, I think that Dr. Koerner is right to lay the emphasis he does on the importance of our schools *also* concerning themselves with "developing and furnishing the minds of future citizens." And while I do not, myself, regret the way in which attention in Britain has recently been focussed on the *collective* purposes of education, I believe that the time has now come to think rather more about the *individual,* and the type of education most suited to his or her personal needs. Even so, I cannot imagine any adequate concept of "secondary education for all" which does not offer to all children the opportunity of a course in general science, instruction in the use of a second language, or in the rudiments of the more intellectual aspects of mathematics (e.g. algebra).

Some of Dr. Koerner's most interesting pages deal with the current controversy in Britain over secondary-school reorganization. Dr. Koerner makes it plain that he does not expect a reversal of the present trend away from the separation of children by ability, at the moment of transfer to secondary school, into different institutions. I do not think he would disagree with what I said on this subject at the 1966 Conservative Party Conference: "Sooner or later in any educational system there has got to be selection. But the question is how soon? I think the majority of opinion in Britain today, including certainly the majority of educational opinion, and also of Tory opinion, tends to feel that the age of eleven is too early in a child's life for the most decisive act of selection to be made." The trouble with the eleven-plus has always been the border-liners; whatever the percentage of selective places in a particular area, it has been very hard in practice to justify making quite different arrangements for children on either side of a narrow dividing line, especially bearing in mind the limits of reliable prediction of a child's potential at so early an age. I say this without any desire to disparage the very fine achievements of many secondary modern schools in providing for their late developers.

On this whole subject Dr. Koerner certainly makes a number of most valuable points, especially his warning against the facile assumption that "the comprehensive school . . . will bring greater equality into English life, that it will overcome social barriers and snobbery and put an end to the social divisiveness of separate schools." As he rightly says, this is "the weakest and least tenable ground upon which to base the comprehensive movement in Britain. Comprehensive schools, because they are comprehensive, serve relatively small catchment areas precisely in those parts of the country where the problems of inequality are greatest—in and around cities. . . . The social effect of such schools is to reinforce rather than combat class consciousness." He also stresses the danger that within a large comprehensive school it will be "the multitudinous average that sets the entire ethos. . . . By virtue of sheer numbers, the voice of the average becomes the dominant one." These are timely warnings, though of course "comprehensive" in Britain does not necessarily mean "all-through comprehensive"—i.e., large schools catering for the whole secondary-school age range of eleven to eighteen; quite a number of local authorities are experimenting, or planning to experiment, with "two-tier" or "three-tier" schemes—end-on schools covering the whole ability range, but with a more limited age range (for example, in the case of a three-tier scheme, five to nine, nine to thirteen, thirteen to eighteen).

I should wish to add two further points. First there is obvious danger in putting pressure on local authorities to reorganize quickly while making it plain that the money to do the job properly cannot be made available. It is not a politician but a highly respected Chief Education Officer who first drew attention to the evils of "agglomerating widely separated buildings" and calling the result a comprehensive school. Secondly, it is essential that the *sixth forms* should be strengthened, never weakened, as the result of reorganization. Indeed, any change in the institutional role of the grammar schools must not be at the cost of the academic standards and intellectual discipline long associated with these schools; in this connection I was especially pleased to note Dr. Koerner's warm commendation of the best of the Direct Grant Schools, whose future is no less important to the future of British education than that of the public schools.

I am glad that Dr. Koerner should have devoted a chapter to teacher training, on which his conclusions are, however, somewhat critical ("One of my disappointments"). No doubt he will have noted that the Plowden Report has since called for a full inquiry into this aspect of English education, and has drawn attention to certain shortcomings in the secondary-school background of many students in training: "Too many have concentrated in the sixth form on English, history and geography, too few are qualified to take college main courses in mathematics, science or music. . . . The secondary schools with their specialist tradition in teaching are not sufficiently aware of the need of the primary schools for teachers whose value lies in a marked degree in their versatility."

Dr. Koerner also provides an objective assessment of the English system of Public Examinations, containing much interesting information which will, I suspect, be new to many of his English readers. In his chapter on the universities Dr. Koerner remarks very pertinently that the Robbins Report "brought the idea of national planning in higher education, [and] of deliberate long-range policy-making for the entire field on the basis of reliable data, into public and professional consciousness." This is indeed true, and I believe there is much scope for similar exercises in "long-range policy-making" relating to other aspects of public social provision, such as national health.

Dr. Koerner's final verdict is a little somber: "Is British education as good as you thought it was before going to England? In parts, yes, mostly, no." I am not in a position to judge how far this conclusion is representative of professional educationalists from overseas. Nevertheless I think we should take seriously Dr. Koerner's injunction: "By all means try to raise the status of institutions, but by genuinely improving their quality, not by artificially lowering your best." Also, I sense throughout Dr. Koerner's book—and this is confirmed by a conversation we had together—the feeling that, in terms of intellectual effort, we are inclined to allow the center of gravity of our schools to lie at a point a little way below where it ought to be. Perhaps it is significant that the Plowden Report, though so eloquent (and convincing) in its general defense of progressive teaching methods, had little to say about the concept of a "critical learning period," and that the Newsom Report should have been so worded as to lead Dr. Koerner (and no doubt others) to doubt whether its educational objectives for children of average ability were sufficiently ambitious. At a time of rapid educational expansion, it surely cannot be stressed too strongly that excellence, almost by definition, is the "value" most worth pursuing—though this does *not* mean that only a tiny minority can make a worthwhile attempt to achieve it.

Above all, we should bear in mind what Dr. Koerner has to say about priorities: "How to get and keep first-rate teachers, in decent classrooms, with classes of reasonable size . . . for the extended schooling in fundamental subjects of all children: *that* problem will dwarf any others for a considerable time to come." These, indeed, are words that cannot be repeated too often.

## CHAPTER I

# The Educational Scene in Europe and England

A GLANCE AT THE WORLD'S MAP can be a sobering reminder to any American of how much we all owe a small corner of the earth called Western Europe. Embracing sixteen countries in an area half the size of the United States, Western Europe has originated in one way or another most of the ideas, most of the public institutions, most of the culture of most of the modern world. From Western Europe have come the political, social, and economic movements that now control or convulse both the industrialized and the underdeveloped nations. The sheer concentration of intellectual energy and achievement in Western Europe is reason enough for Americans to study the educational systems of the countries involved. Although my main concern in this book is with English education and how it compares with our own, I will touch on other countries occasionally. Hence I should like to begin with a brief discussion of the general education scene in Europe, and then turn to the present situation in Britain.

The legacy of war is, of course, much more than pain and destruction. It is often social reform, usually economic growth, and always the advancement of knowledge. In Europe the legacy of World War II has been a great deal of all three, so much so as to push the traditional problem of European nationalism into obscurity. As I write this, the Gaullist rodomontade makes a United States of Europe seem more chimerical than ever, but Gaullism will pass. Meanwhile there is an unmistakable unity developing, as a product of radical postwar change, in a great many areas of European life. The scope of the social revolution in Europe is not easy for an American or a casual visitor to grasp. Vestiges of privilege and of the old class divisions of European society remain everywhere, but they are just that, vestiges. To talk any longer about a

Marxian "class struggle" would be anachronistic nonsense. Equality and opportunity are no longer merely demanded but are on the way to being achieved through, among other things, education. Let me mention just three of the movements that are changing the face of European education.

*Planning.* The national educational planner is now ubiquitous. Before his appearance in force, which has come about mostly in the last fifteen years, the countries of Europe formed their educational policies and projections without much systematic knowledge of what was actually happening in their educational systems and certainly without any defined long-range objectives. What improvements were made were *ad hoc,* as they still are in the United States, without considering the interdependence of the various parts of an educational system. Decisions were made in ignorance of their economic consequences or their social repercussions. Now the ministries of education all over Europe are inhabited by statisticians, psychometricians, and researchers of many kinds, and they are headed by what might be called educational liberals, who are trying to plan the development over an extended period of years of their educational systems in harmony with political considerations, economic needs, and "national goals." By "educational liberals" I mean people who wish to move education, at least for large numbers of students now staying in school much longer than their parents did, away from what they regard as the restrictive, formalistic, classical tradition toward something resembling American progressive education, with a stress on permissiveness, improvisation, and practicality. I was repeatedly struck by this progressivization, so to speak, of European education. As the schools of Europe approach the quantitative scope of American schools, they encounter the same qualitative problems. As they begin to keep a steadily rising percentage of each age group in school for a steadily rising number of years, they face the insistent question we faced years ago—what to do with vast numbers of children for whom the old academic curriculum is thought to be inappropriate or irrelevant. And Europe is, unhappily, grasping at the same answers.

The acceptance of national planning as an idea in education has created an unprecedented flow of educational information and has even suggested the possibility of international planning. It has become important for one nation to look beyond its borders at what its neighbors are doing in education, if for no other reason than to use the improvements of other countries as leverage at home. Thus lines of communication among Europe's politicians and ministries concerned with education have been opened up. Every eighteen months or so there is a meeting of the European Ministers of Education, a group that maintains a secretariat, brings together people and information, and publishes surveys of current developments in planning and expenditure. The Council of

Europe, at Strasbourg, is increasingly active in education, particularly through its Council for Cultural Co-operation, which finances educational studies among member nations, sponsors conferences on educational subjects of general interest, and publishes comparative surveys of such subjects as guidance in European schools, teacher training, social studies, and language training. The Organization for Economic Co-operation and Development, in Paris, has become especially important for its work in the economics of education and in manpower studies, and most recently for its promising attempts to standardize educational terminology and statistics in its member countries. Because of its emphasis on relating education to economic considerations, a subject of paramount interest to all nations, OECD has played an influential role in educational change in Europe. Also there is the continuing work of agencies like UNESCO and the International Bureau of Education, not to mention the expanding centers of educational research in European universities, or such well-financed new agencies as the Institut fur Bildungsforschung in der Max-Planck Gesellshaft, in Berlin, or numerous other "research and documentation" centers scattered around the Continent.

All this means a steady interchange of information and statistics, as well as of people, and the beginnings of regular comparative studies. And this in turn means a larger role for the educational planner. It is entirely possible that planning may ultimately produce something that could be called a Continental system of education, one that would include Britain.

*Expansion and Reform.* The two terms are almost synonymous, because expansion and reform are reciprocal phenomena; one implies the other throughout Europe. Expansion, that is, is taking place at a dramatic rate not only because of rising populations but even more because of the drive to make secondary education universal and beyond that to make various kinds of post-secondary education available to many more people than in the past. At all levels, *l'explosion scolaire,* as the French call it, is perhaps the supreme fact of European education today. Still, the length of compulsory schooling remains less everywhere in Europe than in the United States. It therefore follows that the percentage of students completing any level of education above the legal "leaving age" is lower than with us. If we look only at the quantitative side of education, the gap between our own system and the systems of Europe is still solidly in our favor. At the risk of oversimplification, I have tried to illustrate this gap in the four diagrams on pages 4–7, along with other major elements in the educational systems of France, Germany, England, and the United States. These highly simplified charts demonstrate at a glance the main lines of movement within each system and the relative size of the groups

# THE EDUCATIONAL SYSTEM OF
# THE UNITED STATES

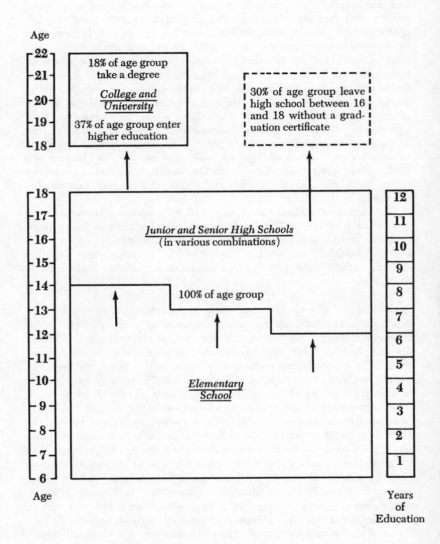

# THE STATE-SUPPORTED EDUCATIONAL SYSTEM OF ENGLAND AND WALES

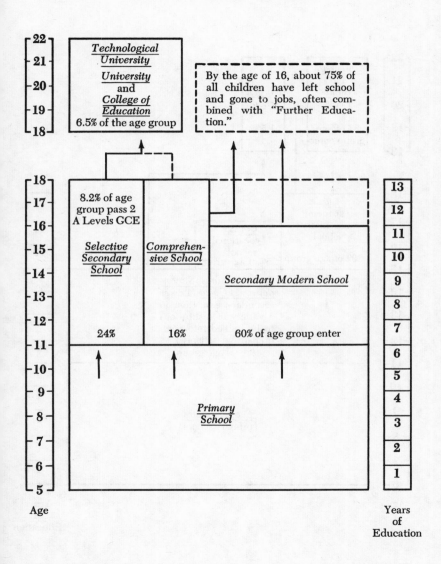

**Age**

**22**
**21**
**20**
**19**
**18**

Technological University

University and College of Education
6.5% of the age group

By the age of 16, about 75% of all children have left school and gone to jobs, often combined with "Further Education."

**18**
**17**
**16**
**15**
**14**
**13**
**12**
**11**
**10**
**9**
**8**
**7**
**6**
**5**

8.2% of age group pass 2 A Levels GCE

Selective Secondary School

Comprehensive School

Secondary Modern School

24%    16%    60% of age group enter

Primary School

**Years of Education**

13
12
11
10
9
8
7
6
5
4
3
2
1

# THE EDUCATIONAL SYSTEM OF FRANCE

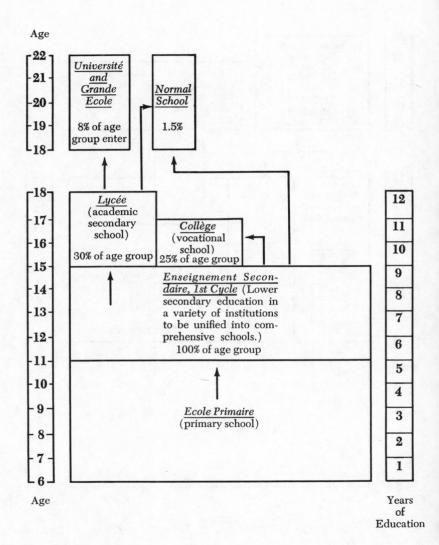

# THE EDUCATIONAL SYSTEM OF
# THE FEDERAL REPUBLIC OF GERMANY

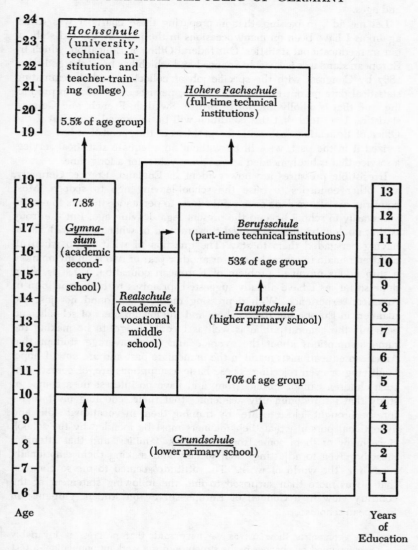

Age

Years
of
Education

involved. The percentages given are for the size of the age group *entering* each type of school; in most cases I have not tried to show percentages for those leaving the schools since students usually leave at various stages and ages.

Let me add, in passing, that in preparing these charts, I was struck again, as I have been on many occasions in the past, by the sad state of our own educational statistics. Our federal Office of Education, which by European standards is lavishly financed and which has been charged since 1867 by Congress with the specific job of collecting and disseminating statistical data on our educational system, persists even today in producing stuff that is wholly inferior to British, Swedish, French, and German statistics. I am told that this condition will be improved soon, but if the Office of Education deals with the problem at the speed that has characterized it in the past, we will be without an adequate statistical service, a service that is badly needed and of great value, for a long time.

Irresistible pressures are now evident in England, France, Germany, and other countries to raise the school-leaving age to sixteen. Most countries are also making successful efforts to persuade students to remain voluntarily in school beyond the present legal leaving age. But the irony is that no country has yet solved the problem of what to do with them, having persuaded them to stay. The question of what to do when all children remain in school by law for another year or two is, in my opinion, a stupendous unsolved problem of European education. What is being done so far, as I have already suggested, promises to be a repetition of American experience. With depressing regularity I found not just the planners in Europe but the teachers and the headmasters of schools, and certainly the general public as well as I could judge, to be making the same assumptions about the average and below-average student that American educationists made in the immediate past and are now, I hope, modifying or even rejecting. These basic assumptions are, of course, that such children cannot "profit" from, and have no interest in, a course of study that is predominantly academic; that their schooling must therefore be brought "close to life" by training them in vocational skills and avocational pursuits; that their manners must be mended by the school, since many of them come from lower-class families; and that attention must be given to adjusting them socially and making them emotionally ready for "the world of work." This attitude seemed to me so common that I was more than surprised to find the following statement of the contrary view in a Council of Europe survey on student guidance in European schools:

> The economists show us, as we have said, that progress is invariably accompanied by changes in the structure of the working population, a fact which increases uncertainty about a child's future occupation. Moreover,

it is impossible to foresee the requirements of techniques which have not yet been invented, and if we do not know in which economic sector a child will be expected to work, we cannot tell either, in the long term, what will be the requirements of that sector. For all these social and economic reasons, there is an insistence everywhere on the supreme need to teach pupils how to adapt themselves to various requirements, on the need to provide them with a basic education broad enough, and a way of thinking general enough, to leave them equipped to acquire later any specialized knowledge which they may need.[1]

Well, yes, exactly. But I can only record that I found no such "insistence everywhere" in Council of Europe countries. Quite to the contrary, most people seemed persuaded not only that a curriculum of vocational training and social adjustment was the most realistic one for average and below-average secondary students, but that it was desirable and right.

However that may be, the twin developments of expansion and reform, although general in Europe, are by no means universal. There are many backwater areas. Southern Italy, for example, is still as stubborn an economic and educational problem as ever. The planners in Rome, hardly the most imaginative on the Continent at any time, have made little progress in *Il Mezzogiorno,* where the problems of overpopulation and excessive reliance on agriculture closely limit what can be done educationally. Italy is one of the few countries of Europe with a surplus of teachers, but there is still a shortage in the south, to which nobody wants to migrate. Even in so prosperous a country as Denmark, living next door to the most reformist nation in Europe, Sweden, one finds a surprising degree of educational inaction. Paradoxically, Denmark was an educational leader in Europe when in 1814 it established a compulsory common school, the *Folkeskole,* of seven years; but a century and a half later it still had a seven-year compulsory *Folkeskole,* having failed to raise the school-leaving age in all that time! In Germany, where compulsory education under the Prussians preceded even that of Denmark, the length of compulsory schooling is still only eight years in most areas. It is also true that many parents in countries like Germany, Italy, the Netherlands, and even Switzerland are not as "education-minded" as American parents and are much more frequently content to have their children leave school at the legal age and go to work.

Nevertheless, the rapid expansion and reform of secondary education is an outstanding characteristic of the present educational scene in Europe. Even at the post-secondary and university level the ghost of Malthus seems to haunt few people these days. Not many years ago in both the United States and Europe, but particularly in Europe, the fear of "overproducing intellectuals" who would outrun the supply of jobs was very much alive. That fear seems to have been thoroughly exorcised in most of Europe.

*The Comprehensive Middle School.* A third notable movement in Europe is the conversion of lower secondary schools, "middle schools," from selective to comprehensive institutions. The reasons for this conversion are given by officials as educational and pedagogical, but the real reasons are political and social. To date the new comprehensive middle school has been adopted as the future national pattern by Italy, France, and Belgium; also by Norway and Sweden, where it is not a separate school but part of a nine-year common school. It will also be adopted widely if not universally in England, will possibly be adopted in some of the German states, and is being at least considered in most other countries. The whole movement is a natural outcome of the social revolution in Europe and the postwar drive toward equality; and it may well extend upward in the future to the senior secondary school, as indeed can already be seen in England and Sweden.

Everywhere that a comprehensive plan has been adopted, opposition has been fierce from the universities (less so, however, in England than in Europe), from teachers in selective secondary schools, often from church and independent schools, and from some undetermined percentage of the electorate. But everywhere political power has in the end overridden this opposition. In Italy the new school is a *scuola media unica,* ostensibly without tracking or ability groups; in France it is a "polyvalent" school, a *college d'enseignment secondaire,* with three basic tracks; in Sweden it is part of a *grundskola* and is afflicted with no fewer than nine different tracks; in Britain it is a "comprehensive" school and can be organized in a variety of ways. Everywhere in the unified middle schools great stress is put on personal freedom and unrestricted choice about what track students enter, but everywhere this turns out to be freedom strongly conditioned by school recommendations. The school, that is, usually decides on the basis of measured ability and achievement where the student is to go within the comprehensive school and what kind of upper school, if any, he will go to afterward. More often than not in Europe, free choice is only a nice theory.

Along with the comprehensive school have come complementary developments in curriculum and pedagogy. Progressivism, as I have mentioned, may be dead or dying in the United States or merely out of fashion for a time, but it is very much alive in the new comprehensive schools of Europe. In France, for example, experimental classes were organized after the war at the Centre International d'Études Pédagogiques, at Sèvres outside Paris, by an *avant-garde* group of theorists who were themselves influenced by American theories and by Americans during the war. These *Classes Nouvelles* made much of freedom, shunned the customary methods of the *lycée,* stressed the exploration of the student's immediate environment, and encouraged experimentation in general. They were a deliberate move away from the formalistic and hierarchical patterns of French secondary education and an attempt to demonstrate, in spite of steady opposition from *lycée* teachers, that the spirit of French education could be and needed to be transformed. Their success—at least the success claimed by those who ran them (examination results in the "new classes" were not impressive)—influenced the French decision to adopt a comprehensive middle school, the idea of which went back at least as far as the Langevin Report in 1947. No doubt the new pedagogical spirit as cultivated in the "new classes" will be a strong influence in French education as the comprehensive school becomes national. Thus France, the citadel of educational conservatism, of tough and unsentimental schooling, of respect for culture and intellect, and of a certain contempt for stupidity, is no more able than other nations to maintain the old standards or even the old priorities against the pressures of extended universal secondary education. Much the same kind of liberalization, or perhaps I should say Americanization, can be seen in the new comprehensive schools of Sweden, Italy, and England.

Many other facets of education in Europe are of interest to an American, and I will touch on them from time to time, but the three I have mentioned above seem to me the preeminent developments today—the advent of national planning, with its resultant interchange of educational influence and information; the great scope of expansion and reform to be seen in almost all the systems of the Continent; and the sociopolitical creation of the comprehensive school with its affinity for flexible curriculums and progressive pedagogy.

Though such a cursory survey of so vast a subject as European education is no doubt of limited use, I want to resist the temptation to extend it, for my principal concern is the English system. Yet a number of readers may well feel the need for a more detailed knowledge of educational developments in Europe than they might get from the foregoing discussion, if for no other reason than to put English education into a reasonable perspective. I have therefore discussed in some detail in Appendix A the present situation in Sweden, the one country of Europe that seems to me to point the way in which the rest of the Continent is likely to go in the future. Much of what is being done in Sweden today will be done elsewhere in Europe and in England tomorrow. So with the above vignette of European education in mind, and of Swedish education as discussed in Appendix A for readers interested in it, we are ready to turn to the present situation in England.

"There is a very cynical little story," said a peeress in the House of Lords during a 1965 debate on educational policy, "attributed to a celebrated politician now dead, in which he said that the Scots have a respect for education, the Welsh have a passion for it and the English have no particular objection to it." [2] The comment does not seem very cynical to me and it does have as large an element of truth as epigrams permit. Taking people as a whole, the Scots do respect education highly, the Welsh do pursue it assiduously, and the English are beginning only now to surmount their lethargy about it. Of course, middle- and upper-class families of all three groups have always taken education seriously enough. But not so the English working class, which does not seem to share the concern for education often found, especially since World War II, among lower-class American families. The English working-class man takes an approach to life different from the American. Chances are that the American takes life pretty seriously, wants to improve his lot, is, as the sociologists say, "upwardly mobile," and sees education as an important way up, perhaps the only way. The English working-class person is as much interested in increasing his share of creature comforts as anybody, but he takes a more light-hearted approach to the problem, is not preoccupied with moving into the middle class, is not devoted to the middle-class virtues of thrift and industry and planning for the future; and when confronted with the choice of staying in school in the hope of some kind of deferred benefit or of earning high wages at once in the booming British labor market, he often finds the lure of immediate money and freedom decisive. The English working classes, as Richard Hoggart puts it in his excellent book of sociological exploration, "have been cheerful existentialists for ages," [3] and they prefer to take their pleasures now. This attitude is yielding in England as in Europe to the overwhelming force of what we might call "embourgeoisment," but the process takes a much longer time in educational and cultural matters than in economic affairs. Thus the present situation in British education still reflects a history of political neglect and public apathy.

Britain now finds her general position in Europe and the world a fairly grim one. Her economic status, upon which the advancement of education and most other things depend, is precarious: She has a chronic imbalance of payments (although enjoying the highest volume of tourist trade in Europe); she competes rather poorly in international markets; she has full employment but low productivity; she has an undereducated and backward-looking labor force still proud of its scars and still fighting old Depression battles with capitalism; she has a well-educated but untrained and unenterprising managerial class; she has a lower gross national product per capita than France or Germany or other nations on the Continent with whom she trades; she is well behind the United States in computerization and automation; she has a sick currency that was saved from devaluation in 1964, 1965, and 1966 only by massive loans from American and other foreign bankers.

How much have Britain's economic problems to do with her educational system? Most people would assume a good deal, but there is no way of proving it. Like many other questions in education, the relationship between length of schooling and growth in the economy is uncertain, for the number of factors that must be taken into account is almost unlimited. Any assumption that schooling and economic growth move upward together is not supported by the recent history of some of Europe's most prosperous countries, such as Germany, Denmark, and the Netherlands, in all of which the average length of schooling is less than in Britain. The academic specialty known as the "Economics of Education" suffers from the double handicap of bringing together two of the most inexact fields of human knowledge. We all look forward to the time when the connections, if any, between these two subjects can be established on something more than supposition. Meanwhile, what we can say with reliability is that English education, whatever the state of the economy, compares well with most of Europe but is still a good deal this side of what it should be.

The present organization of English education was established by a great parliamentary reform Act that was developed during World War II by the coalition goverment. Such a major piece of legislation naturally had its roots in the past, and we need to pause long enough to examine a few of the main roots. Primary education did not become general in Britain until well after the Liberal Party with Gladstone at its head put through a very modest Elementary Education Act in 1870, which provided fee-paying education for five years for children not then being schooled in church or other private establishments. But it was some years before elementary education became universal. The Victorians were hard-headed about business and dead serious about educating middle-class children, but their attitude toward mass schooling is probably summed up in a comment made by a Victorian churchman and philosopher, Hastings Rashdall:

> To give large masses of persons an education which necessarily and inevitably awakens ambitions which cannot be satisfied, and tastes which cannot be gratified, and so to increase their discontent with that drudgery which must inevitably form a large portion of the lives of the majority . . . such a policy does seem to me, I confess, to involve a most gratuitous increase in the sum of human misery. And yet that would be the inevitable result of a logical application of the principle of equality of opportunity.[4]

Educational predestination, as it were, made good sense to the educated Victorian. Not until 1902 did Britain get anything that could be called a national system of education. In that year another landmark Act of Parliament abolished the multitudinous school boards that were then elected locally on a nonparty basis all over Britain and created politically appointed bodies in their place. The first sentence of this Act is one of the most important in English educational development: "For the purposes of this Act the council of every county and every county borough shall be the local education authority . . ." This meant, as the Act further stipulated, that each such authority, each "LEA," would appoint an "Education Committee" to which extensive powers over local education were to be given. Since the councils of each county and county borough were usually elected on political platforms, as they still are, the 1902 Act meant that education thereafter, in addition to being organized on a coordinated national basis, was to reflect the political coloration of local government.

World War I, like all British wars over the last century, produced another important education Act, this time providing, among other things, compulsory schooling for all children to age fourteen. Unfortunately, the Act was not fully enforceable because of economic difficulties. So the first real departure in secondary education came with a document prepared by a national committee in 1926 and called the Hadow Report. It is both praised and condemned in England as the inspiration for the present selective or "tripartite" system of secondary schools, although actually selective secondary education was already well established. But equally important with its recommendations about a split in secondary schools was its influence in making at least a few years of secondary education the normal and expected thing in Britain rather than the exception; and that was no small achievement. The report also supported strongly the "11-plus" selection procedure that has come into such disrepute today. In the introduction to its report, the committee found a Shakespearean metaphor the best means of making its point about separating children at age eleven:

> There is a tide which begins to rise in the veins of youth at the age of eleven or twelve. It is called by the name of adolescence. If that tide can be taken at the flood, and a new voyage begun in the strength and along the flow of the current, we think that it will "move on to fortune." We therefore propose that all children should be transferred, at the age of eleven or twelve, from the junior or primary school either to schools of the type now called secondary, or to schools (whether selective or non-selective) of the type which is now called central, or to senior and separate departments of existing elementary schools.[5]

The committee thus set the course of English secondary education by reaffirming the idea that eleven was the best age for children to leave elementary school and that they could be divided at that age on the basis of tested abilities with sufficient accuracy and justice for them to be sent on to different types of secondary schools. These were reasonable assumptions, granted the expert testimony taken at the time by the committee. A dozen years later another national committee issued a report, the Spens Report, following up strongly on the Hadow Report. It recommended that secondary education be given in three distinct types of school—academic, technical, and modern—and repeated the earlier recommendation that all children be channeled into one or the other of them at 11-plus. This tripartite system of schools was reexamined once again, and in detail, by still another national committee in 1943, the Norwood Committee, which found again that the "rough grouping" represented by this three-way division of schools was valid and necessary.

At the beginning of World War II the great majority of English children were still leaving school at fourteen, with a total of nine years of education. The war brought this system to the brink of chaos with the destruction of a great many schools, with the entry of many teachers into the armed services, and with the evacuation of children from the main cities to areas poorly equipped to manage such an influx. But the war also brought something else: a general determination to reform English life after the war—to make it more egalitarian and, as a vital step toward that goal, to reconstruct the educational system. The Conservative politician R. A. Butler, then President of the national Board of Education, supervised the development between 1941 and 1943 of what is probably the most important education Act in English history and guided it through Parliament in 1944. (Scotland had its counterpart of this Act in 1945; it repeats many of the main provisions of the English Act.) The 1944 Act is a long and complicated piece of legislation that should be read together with a commentary on it; [6] here a summary of its major provisions will serve our purposes. The title of the Act, "An Act to Reform the Law Relating to Education in England and Wales," signified in itself the national desire to effect a fundamental change. Its main provisions will apply to many matters that I will discuss in later chapters:

1. The Act created a Minister of Education and gave him a great deal of power over Local Education Authorities and education generally.

2. The Act created a "Central Advisory Council for Education" (one for England and one for Wales) to advise the Minister on important questions of theory and practice and to undertake special investigations at the request of the Minister. The Advisory Council for England has produced some extremely important reports, which I will cover in due course.

3. The Act stipulated that state education should be organized in three successive stages—primary, secondary, and "further education"—but it did not specify a tripartite system of secondary schools.

4. The Act charged each LEA (Local Education Authority) with the duty of providing education for all children between the ages of five and fifteen "offering such variety of instruction and training as may be desirable in view of their different ages, abilities, and aptitudes."

5. The Act required each LEA to submit to the Minister by April 1946 a comprehensive "development plan" covering all of primary and secondary education and setting forth detailed proposals for meeting the provisions of the Act itself.

6. In a typical demonstration of the British capacity for rational compromise and accommodation of conflicting views, the Act solved the hotly

debated issue of the place of religious and independent schools in the new Britain by expanding the national system of "dual control." Voluntary schools were thereby allowed to fit into the state system in one of several ways, yielding rights to the state in proportion to the financial help that they accepted from the state.

7. The Act raised the school-leaving age to fifteen and recommended that it be raised to sixteen as soon thereafter as possible.

8. The Act required the LEA's to make various provisions for compulsory "further education," but lack of funds has prevented this requirement from being put into effect throughout the country (though voluntary further education has grown tremendously).

9. The Act said: "It shall be the duty of the parent of every child of compulsory school age to cause him to receive efficient full-time education suitable to his age, ability, and aptitude, either by regular attendance at school *or otherwise*." I italicize the last two words to stress the admirable characteristic of English education of allowing parents as much freedom as possible. The Act also sought to protect parental freedom by stipulating that all government authorities in education "shall have regard to the general principle that, so far as is compatible with the provision of efficient instruction and training and the avoidance of unreasonable public expenditure, pupils are to be educated in accordance with the wishes of their parents."

10. The Act required all independent schools to register with the new Ministry of Education and to open themselves to inspection by state authorities.

11. One of the Act's most far-reaching provisions removed "fee-paying" from state education in England: "No fees shall be charged in respect of admission to any school maintained by a local education authority, or to any county college, or in respect if the education provided in any such school or college." The significance of this provision was that low-ability students could no longer be kept in selective secondary schools because of the ability of their parents to pay a fee; in a word, it made attendance at a state grammar school a matter of merit for all.

Considered in the light of history and the problems of English education in 1944, the Act was a tremendous achievement, and it does not deserve the harsh things said about it now by a few educationists enjoying a quarter-century of hindsight. R. A. Butler spoke of the Act in an interview in 1965 as "the most creative thing I ever did."[7] The Act was not put into effect as well or as rapidly as people supposed it would be in the euphoria of victory in 1945, but under it English education has moved a long way indeed in a short time.

Today the British educational system might be summarized, along with American comparisons where appropriate, in the following way. The figures are from the relevant statistical sources, but such data are not always reported in the way one seeks; thus the figures I have calculated are close but not precise.[8]

| | ENGLAND AND WALES | UNITED STATES |
|---|---|---|
| 1. Percent of the total population in full-time schooling, public and private: | 15% | 25% |
| 2. Percent of the total population employed: | 46% | 36% |
| 3. Percent of the gross national product spent on education: | 5.3% (U.K.) * | 5.9% |
| 4. Percent of all children aged 15–16 in full-time schooling: † | 63% | 99% |
| Percent of all children aged 14–17 in full-time schooling: | 40% | 94% |
| Percent of all children who have received at least 12 years of full-time schooling: | 13% | 70% |
| 5. Percent of secondary-school students attending selective schools (grammar schools): ‡ | 24% | |
| Percent of secondary-school students attending "modern" schools: | 60% | |
| Percent of secondary-school students attending comprehensive, technical, and other schools: | 16% | |
| 6. Percent of elementary-school pupils in independent schools (ages 5–11 or 5–13 in Britain; 6–14 in U.S.): | 7% | 15% (mostly Catholic) |
| Percent of secondary-school students in independent schools (ages 11–18 in Britain; 14–18 in U.S.): | 9% | 10% (mostly Catholic) |
| 7. Pupil-teacher ratio in all schools, national average: | 24/1 | 25/1 |
| 8. Percent of the age group who enter some kind of full-time higher education: | 6.5% | 37% |
| Percent of the age group who finish some kind of full-time higher education: | 5.5% | 18% |

* The British figure is for the United Kingdom and is for expenditures by government authorities only, thus excluding the very large expenditures of private schools; the U.S. figure includes all education, public and private.

† Note that British children begin school a year earlier than American.

‡ Note that these figures apply only to students attending state schools. If the total age group is considered, the grammar-school figures would have to be increased to include those going to independent schools—see No. 6.

Perhaps this brief profile, together with the earlier diagrams, will give the reader at least a rough idea of how the British system relates quantitatively to that of the United States. Quantitative differences of the sort shown above account in one way or another for the principal educational controversies that now fill the English air.

I think it will help, at the risk of boring the reader by continuing to number items in series, if I round out this introductory view of British education by simply listing, say, the ten most important areas of controversy—all of which will be dealt with in later chapters:

1. *The centralization of authority*—whether the growing power exercised over English education by the central government should be stopped or accelerated.

2. *Abolition of the 11-plus*—whether the selection procedure used at the end of primary school should be abolished or replaced by a different method.

3. *Streaming in the primary school*—whether children should be divided in the primary grades into tracks or "streams."

4. *Reorganization of secondary schools*—whether the "bipartite" or "tripartite" system of secondary schools should be converted to a system of comprehensive schools, and if so, how it should be done.

5. *Extension of compulsory schooling*—whether the leaving age should and can be raised to sixteen by 1971 or whether available resources can better be used in other ways.

6. *Change of status for independent schools*—whether the English "Public Schools" and other types of private and semiprivate institutions should be abolished, left alone, or "integrated" into the state system.

7. *Reduction of specialization*—whether the last two and often more years of the secondary school, the "sixth form," impose too narrow a course of study.

8. *Reform of the "GCE"*—whether the principal national leaving examination should be broadened or eased or abolished or otherwise changed.

9. *Raising the status of teachers*—whether the teacher's place in society could be improved by placing colleges of education under the control of universities, by giving degrees to teachers, or by other steps such as raising salaries beyond national guidelines.

10. *Expansion of higher education*—whether standards will fall if more people receive higher education and whether they should get a different education from the traditional one; also, the degree to which universities should be made to respond to social pressures.

I would also consider the Christian-Humanist controversy in Britain a major educational issue, for it often centers on the place of religion in the schools—whether compulsory religious observance and instruction should continue in English schools and if so whether it should be fundamentally changed. But religious education, although of supreme importance to many people in both England and the United States, is of limited relevance to our public schools. I therefore discuss the matter for interested readers in Appendix C. I pass over other, relatively minor controversies, such as those relating to an increase in coeducation, a decrease in the use of school uniforms, a change in the pattern of entry to boarding schools, and the acceptance by teachers themselves of "aides" and "auxiliaries."

Also, there are, of course, educational problems that are not controversies. For example, a great many Britishers would agree that the replacement or modernization of school buildings, especially among the primary schools, and the adequate equipping of them, are matters of urgency, perhaps the greatest urgency of all. And many others would agree that the chronic shortage of teachers is the most important problem. Thus not everything that excites people about education is an issue —only most things. Controversy, after all, is one of the strongest threads of continuity in education. And the fact that the present age is one of far greater and far faster change than any other in history makes it necessarily an age of greater controversy. A very adequate exposition of either contemporary British or American education could be written in terms of the surrounding controversies. The controversies I have listed will reappear in a variety of ways in the following chapters.

## CHAPTER II

# A Political Anatomy of
# English Education

THE EXERCISE OF AUTHORITY in education—who decides what and under what kinds of pressure—is at the heart of much educational discussion in both the United States and Britain. Unfortunately, public attention is often focused on less important matters. We talk about how a particular problem should be met, but less often about how it came to be a problem in the first place. The politics of education are of supreme importance and are surely one of the first things that should be looked at in any educational system.

The biggest difference on this point between the United States and England is in the role of party politics. In the United States, political views are often peripheral or irrelevant to the issues we debate in education. They may form the backdrop against which matters like federal aid to schools are discussed, but it seems to me that the most important controversies of the last fifteen or twenty years, such as teacher training, school curriculums, and standards of achievement, rarely fall out along political lines. A simple illustration is seen in the fact that the vast majority of college and university professors are political liberals but educational conservatives; they see no particular contradiction in this fact and manage to keep the two kinds of allegiance separated most of the time.

But in Britain there is a strong political current generated by many educational controversies. Or, perhaps more often, political convictions generate educational controversies. Either way there is sometimes a kind of polarization that takes place in public discussion. Leading people find themselves having to defend or oppose an issue in more absolute terms than they really believe simply because they have become identified with a political party and the party has taken a stand on the issue. This "injection," as many call it, of politics into education is said to be a recent phenomenon, and Britons commonly deplore it. I don't fully share their view. People often want to shield some segment of public life from the discomforts of representative government. The British Medical Association cries, "Let's keep politics out of medicine"; economists wish politicians would "Keep sterling out of the election." In education, the real problem in both countries is not to keep politics out of education, but to give it a proper role. As we saw, the 1902 Act in England was a deliberate attempt to make education subject to political influence, and one can easily argue, given the political history of Britain, that this is good. The problem is to keep political dogma and unreason out of education and to prevent the school system from being manipulated for purely partisan purposes. For example, when one British educationist can upbraid another, as one recently did in private, for publishing research findings that run counter to certain political views on the subject of streaming children in schools, that is manipulation of education by dogma. I am sorry to say that there seems to be quite a bit of this in England. Later in this chapter we will be looking in some detail at another example, an instructive one: the dominance of party politics in the movement toward comprehensive schools in Britain.

I suppose the main reason that the political content of educational debate is greater in Britain than in the United States is that British society is still split more sharply than ours. Britain may no longer be divided, as Disraeli observed, between two nations, the rich and the poor; but its two major political parties often act as though it were. Despite the rapid expansion of the middle class, the parties retain their old habits. The Labor Party remembers Aneurin Bevan with great affection, as the Tories remember Churchill. The Labor Party is still the party of militancy, reform, discontent, resentment, and is still committed to the general proposition that whatever is is wrong and must be changed in the interests of social justice; it stresses the evils of working-class environment rather than the importance of working-class responsibility. The Tories are still the party of wealth, privilege, order, empire, refined experience, and are still committed to the general proposition that whatever is is right until it is demonstrated to be wrong; they stress personal responsibility for one's condition and the importance of restraint in tinkering with the social mechanism. Labor has no fears of big government; on the contrary it feels that individual freedom will be enlarged, not eroded, by extending the Welfare State. Conservatives are certain that big government will increasingly undermine personal liberty. The Labor Party draws the bulk of its financial support directly from or indirectly through the labor unions, while the Conservatives draw the bulk of their support from business, the professions, the farmers, and of course what is left of the upper classes.

But it is also true that in Britain, as in much of Europe, affluence and security have blurred the old political lines. The March 1966 election that returned the Labor Party to power with an increased majority suggested that the old cloth-cap unionism of the Laborites was being modified by the swollen middle class, many of whose members were deserting the Conservatives and the Liberals but were not much interested in old-fashioned Socialism. Also Labor's crusade has now lost some of its edge with the development of the Welfare State and the coming of full employment for the working classes, high wages, cars, new tellies and vacations on the Costa Brava. The slogans are still there but the fire is out. The only blood-stirring speeches you can hear on the old-time political religion of Labor are at Speakers' Corner in Hyde Park. Occasionally a member of the Labor Left Wing will deliver a kind of diluted jeremiad in the House of Commons or on the hustings, but fewer people listen these days, and even the British Communists give one the impression of merely observing the forms, at least on matters of economic policy if not on foreign policy. In short, a greater distribution of the good things of life has greatly narrowed the gap between the political parties. Even so, political alignment remains more socially homogeneous in Britain than in the United States, and this alignment separates many an educational issue into its political implications. Whether the argument is about examinations, streaming, grammar-school admission, the 11-plus, or getting to Oxford, the split between the haves and the have-nots, or perhaps the haves and the haves-plus, is related to political doctrine.

But the "political anatomy" of English education must encompass much more than party politics. Thus I use the term "political" in two different senses in this chapter. In the above comments I use it in its party and factional sense and will take the theme up again in this chapter in the section on the comprehensive school. In the selection below, however, I use it in its broader, nonpartisan sense to refer to the administration of education in England—that is, to the devolution of authority in education and to the apparatus that exists for the formation and enforcement of policy. I also mean the term to include the nongovernmental agencies that exert a major influence on English education.

## Authority and Influence in the Educational System

The ultimate authority in education is of course Parliament. But Parliament affects education only indirectly, through debates and through whatever general influence it can thereby have on the country and the government. Because the legislative and executive branches of government are merged in England, legislation is created simply by the elected government, or, more precisely, by the Prime Minister and his Cabinet acting on the recommendations of committees. Government by Cabinet is the British system. In theory, therefore, the elected party is free to make whatever laws it pleases in education. In practice, it is subject to the restraint of public opinion as well as of parliamentary debate with at least the possibility, however remote, of being brought down on a vote of confidence in the Commons if it enacts extreme measures. Thus Parliament, which incidentally includes, in sharp contrast to Congress, a large number of teachers and former teachers (mostly on the Labor side), exercises its authority in education mostly through discussion. Most national policies are made at the Ministry of Education, as it was called until a recent change.

In creating the Ministry in the 1944 Act, the government's intent was to introduce a considerable degree of centralized control in British education. Before that time, there was at the national level only the Board of Education, whose mandate was merely "to promote and encourage education" and which had very little authority over anything, and which in fact never met as a body. The Conservative R. A. Butler, as President of the Board of Education during the war, developed the 1944 Act and after its passage became the first Minister of Education. His term of office was brief, since Churchill and the Tories were thrown out of office in the summer of 1945. Because of the increasing importance of education in the postwar years and a steadily rising share of the national budget being allocated to it, the Ministry was changed in April 1964, again by a Tory government, to a "Department"; the Minister thus became a "Secretary" with a higher status than formerly. English education is now administered at the national level by a "Department of Education and Science," of which the politically appointed head is the "Secretary of State for Education and Science," who also sits in the Prime Minister's Cabinet. Hereafter I will call them simply the Department and the Secretary.

Operationally the Department might be compared to the Department of Education in one of the largest American states, perhaps New York or California. It has a staff of about 2,500 persons, of whom twenty percent form the Inspectorate of Schools. Apart from the Secretary and his Parliamentary Undersecretary, who are political appointees, the Department is run by that excellent breed of men and women, the British civil servants, whose education, training, and competence are widely and justly respected. Senior civil servants in the Department exert a considerable influence on national policy. They are supposed to be nonpartisan and to serve their political masters, whether Labor or Tory, with equal enthusiasm and impartiality. Their job is to advise the Secretary and his deputies on the feasibility of policies being proposed and to execute those policies already in effect. Being human and among the best-informed people in England on education, they have their opinions as well; and it seems to me a reasonable conclusion that their influence over policy often goes well beyond questions of feasibility.

The varied powers of the Secretary and the Department are chiefly concentrated in five areas: (a) The Secretary has the responsibility for setting national policy in education, though there is some uncertainty about what exactly this means; (b) he must approve general development plans and specific building plans submitted by the Local Education Authorities (the LEA's), meaning that in this regard alone he has a very great deal of power; (c) he seeks to ensure through the Inspectorate of Schools and other means that standards of instruction are adequate and that both state and independent schools throughout the country reach at least a minimum standard; (d) he appoints both permanent and *ad hoc* committees to advise him and the country on matters of educational importance; and (e) he "recognizes" (in effect, licenses) qualified teachers, and he plays a central role in establishing a nationwide scale of teachers' salaries by accepting or rejecting the recommendations of a national committee.

These powers add up to a considerable sum. However, the Secretary, by the long traditions of British government, uses compulsion as a last resort on local authorities; he seeks always to reach consensus and to proceed by persuasion. Very often the work of persuasion is done for him by the reports of national committees that he has appointed to look into particular problems. In recent years, for example, reports issued by the Advisory Councils for Education, bodies which he is required to appoint by the 1944 Act, have in themselves conditioned the LEA's and the general public to new national policies. In 1959 the Advisory Council for Education (England) produced the Crowther Reports on education in the upper secondary years; in 1963 it produced the Newsom Reports on the education of the average and below-average student; in 1967 it produced the Plowden Reports on primary education and the age of transfer to the secondary school. I will discuss these reports in later chapters; here I want only to point out the important function performed by government-appointed investigative and advisory groups in education, though such official bodies are not customary in the United States.

The Inspectorate is another means the Secretary has for encouraging and persuading, and if necessary of coercing, schools and local authorities. Most American educators probably associate the name of Matthew Arnold with the old and honorable institution of Her Majesty's Inspectorate of Schools, a closely knit band of about five hundred men and women who enjoy a special status in English education. They have a great deal of autonomy but very little authority; they are in, but not quite of, the central Department; they are independent of almost everybody except the Queen, but they work closely with the Department and are responsive to the wishes of the Secretary. They are probably unique. I know of no country in Europe that has an inspection system like the British. In the United States the closest we come to it is our various agencies of accreditation for schools and colleges, with which the Inspectorate offers some interesting comparisons.

Inspectors are almost all former teachers who have joined the Inspectorate after perhaps fifteen or twenty years of teaching. They are well paid and have considerable prestige. They are selected through an elaborate process that may begin with fifty or more applicants for every vacancy. But there are no prescribed qualifications such as one might find spelled out with great specificity in professional circles in the United States; the English still judge men individually without too many prior conditions. After an apprenticeship spent learning how an Inspector of Schools does his work, "a slow process of absorption," as one said to me, and a probationary period of perhaps two years, he is made a permanent "HMI."

The Inspectorate has its own hierarchy completely apart from that of the Department. It has its headquarters in the Department, though most of its members are scattered around the country. The typical inspector specializes in either primary or secondary education and is assigned perhaps 150 schools for which he is responsible. He operates with a great deal of freedom, often out of his own home, establishes his own schedule of work, and is expected to exhibit the necessary self-discipline implied in these conditions. "Inspection" is only one of his functions. Pastoral care is as much a part of his daily routine as policing. He is a missionary who, by reason of spending most of his time visiting schools and talking with teachers and headmasters, spreads the word about new ideas and good practices. He is both an advisor to teachers and an observer of them. Also, he is the eyes and ears of the Secretary, a guardian of tax monies, and a reporter from the field keeping the Department abreast of what is really happening on the local scene. He conducts "in-service" courses of instruction for teachers in new ideas and techniques. He often visits new teachers and discusses their problems. He helps gather material that goes into publications for teachers, bringing together in one place the combined experience of a number of inspectors. He tries to make at least a short visit to each of his schools each year but often does not manage it.

He no longer conducts as many full-scale inspections of schools as was once customary. Before World War II, schools were inspected every five years; after the war, with the great increase in schools and the great expansion of education, inspections decreased to one in perhaps ten years. Today many a school in England has not been formally inspected for fourteen or fifteen years. When an inspection does come, it is a thorough job, though quite different from the typical inspection of an American accrediting agency. The latter is likely to be done by persons for whom inspection is merely a hobby or an avocation and who are therefore tied to a set of standardized, quantified criteria. The HMI prefers a much less formal and predetermined approach. He puts more faith in seasoned judgment than in the slide rule. Typically, a full inspection of a school of six hundred students might involve a team of half a dozen HMI's representing a variety of specialties, for the better part of a week. The team produces a report for the Department, which usually "issues" it unchanged to the school. These reports are naturally considered confidential, though any school is free to make whatever use of its own that it wishes. If space permitted, I would reproduce a few representative reports in this book. I have read a large number of them and find that they contrast so sharply with the sort of job done by our own accrediting agencies that I would especially recommend them to anyone interested in ways of assessing schools; also they are perhaps the best way, short of actual visits to institutions, of acquainting oneself with the work of English schools. The customary HMI report would strike any American accrediting agency as hopelessly old-fashioned and subjective. But of course there is a good deal of subjectivism as well as ideological content in the reports of our national accrediting bodies, such as the National Council for Accreditation of Teacher Education, or in those of regional accrediting agencies, such as the North Central Association. I can only say that if I were running a school I would probably find an inspection from an HMI team, stressing consultation with teachers and observation of teaching, more valuable to me and my staff, and a lot less irritating, than an equally subjective inspection from one of our own accrediting organizations that parades as an objective evaluation.

The HMI is, I suppose, the least peremptory of school inspectors. He has no authority to tell anybody anything. He issues no orders, leaves no directives. Although he is a reporter to the Secretary, he is mostly an advisor to teachers. There was a period of the history of the Inspectorate when things were different. In the last half of the nineteenth century, a system of "payment by results" prevailed among the elementary schools of Britain. Pupils were examined by visiting HMI's who determined what number of them had reached each clearly defined educational grade; teachers were then paid according to these results. A powerful incentive to teachers, no doubt, and somehow symbolic of the Victorian mind; but full of abuses and injustice and hardly productive of good education. That system gave way so completely to the present system of friendly counsel that a national committee in 1943 suggested changing the name of the Inspectorate to "His Majesty's Educational Advisory Service." [1]

From my own travels in Britain, I would say that HMI's are far more welcomed in schools than are American accreditation teams. There are those who criticize HMI's for being conservative or for not being "research-oriented." At least one Chief Education Officer has suggested that the Inspectorate is obsolete.[2] And some teachers feel that teaching

has outgrown the need for external "inspection" and should be able to
police itself. Perhaps it should, but in fact it does not police itself in
either the United States or Britain. But most teachers and headmasters
welcome the advice of the inspector. Whatever its limitations—and most
of them are self-imposed—the Inspectorate is an essential part of the
English education scene and a major cog in the policy-making machine.

Of course, nobody knows in any measurable way how effective inspection is in Britain, or, for that matter, in the United States. There has never
been any sort of controlled experiment to find out, and probably there
could not be. Much is done on the basis of tradition and experience, and
very little on the basis of systematic analysis. Even so it seems to me that
Her Majesty's Inspectors of Schools, of whom I have met a large number,
fully deserve this tribute paid to them in 1965 in the House of Lords by
Lord Newton, formerly an Undersecretary of State in the Ministry of
Education:

> May I now for a moment . . . publicly proclaim my admiration for Her
> Majesty's Inspectors of Schools, an ancient corps, an elite corps of wonder-
> ful men and women, whose praises are very seldom sung. They work in
> and with the Department but they are responsible to Her Majesty the
> Queen and not to Ministers. They are all former teachers, erudite, experi-
> enced, unprejudiced, tactful and immensely wise—and there is no subject
> upon which one cannot find an expert inspector. . . . I think that very
> few members of the public realize how deeply the nation is indebted to
> Her Majesty's Inspectors.[3]

Having recorded that eulogy I should add that school inspections as
carried out by both the Inspectorate and our own accreditation agencies
are a most imperfect device. They are done much too seldom to prevent
abuses; it is easily possible for a school to drift a long way downhill
between inspections. Once a school has passed inspection, which in
American terms is tantamount to being "fully accredited," this recognition
is almost never withdrawn, just as our own schools are almost never
disaccredited. There are many accredited schools in both countries that
are poor institutions by any standard. HMI reports do afford school
administrators an important weapon with which to support demands for
more funds or equipment; and they can likewise be used by the Secretary
as pressure on LEA's for improvement. But it would be folly for anyone
to suppose that inspection of schools by external agencies in either
country is a safe guide to the quality of any particular institution.

The relations between the central government and the LEA's are a
useful illustration of balance of powers in education. The balance is delicate but has been maintained with great skill by successive Secretaries
since the 1944 Act, although in recent years there has developed for the

first time since 1944 a certain conflict between the authority of the central government and that of the LEA's, specifically over the issue of comprehensive schools. Since the Act, educational policy has been the product of an intricate give-and-take process that to an outsider looks very often like chaos but in fact is very effective in combining local freedom with national priorities. The process is not as efficient as that of a strongly centralized system like Sweden's, but efficiency is not perhaps the most important virtue in the government of education. As one educational spokesman puts it :

> The price we have to pay for shared direction is considerable. Decisions in education have always been reached by a process of discussion, dissension, confusion and compromise. It is as well that we recognize that sovereignty rests neither with the Department of Education, nor with the local authorities, nor with the professional teachers. We reach conclusions by what some people call "give and take" and others "conspicuous muddle." [4]

The process may in the end be productive of better education than direction from the center.

Local government in Britain exhibits the same virtues and vices as it does in the United States. The main units of local government are fifty-nine Counties and eighty-two County Boroughs, plus London and twenty Outer London Boroughs, each with a "Council" elected usually on party lines. There is a further devolution of authority down to very small units called "parish councils" (7,500 of them) and even smaller ones called "parish meetings" (3,300 of them) that have little power and less money, but sometimes have a lot of "parish-pump politics." The counties and county boroughs are also the bodies known as "Local Education Authorities"; they are, that is, the local authority in general matters of government, which include education. They have taxing power over real estate in their district and so have the thorny job of establishing local taxes, "rates." Rates are naturally an issue in local elections, and education, one of the main consumers of the rates, is therefore an issue also. Education, however, is rarely a major issue in national elections, being overshadowed by even more important domestic problems. Rates can be discriminatory for many reasons, and they vary greatly from one authority to another, depending on the amount of rateable property in the district and on other factors.

Each of the 162 LEA's in England and Wales is required to appoint an "Education Committee" to which it normally relinquishes all local control of educational matters except those having to do with rates and loans. Although an education committee has much in common with an American school board, there are also important differences that are more interesting than the similarities. The average education committee is larger in membership than the school board and serves a larger constituency. Most of its members are themselves elected members of the county or borough council, thereby ensuring that educational policy is married to political policy. By law each committee also appoints a number of "co-opted" members with extensive experience in local educational problems. Such members need not be professionally engaged in education, but often they are; thus it is very common for education committees to have university professors, classroom teachers, and other educational specialists among their co-opted members, as well as clergymen and others who for whatever reason have special knowledge of local education. This provision, which was incorporated into the 1944 Act, seems to me highly commendable. It makes expert knowledge available to the lay majority of the education committee while protecting their right to make the decisions, and may also be a counterbalance to the political interests of the committee. Many an American school board might be well advised to "co-opt" a few professors or classroom teachers, not to say an occasional clergyman.

A major problem to the English education committee now is that the caliber of people running for local government, who in turn are appointed to the committee, is falling, as has the prestige of local government since the war. The work load of the typical committee is exceedingly heavy, and the kinds of specialized knowledge needed to make intelligent decisions are constantly increasing. One result is that local government tends to attract people with spare time: retired persons and housewives with grown children, and not as many professional people, business executives, and others as would be desirable. It does attract union officials, since they are allowed to regard it as part of their work. Proposals have recently been made to consolidate local government into fewer units, which would also reduce the number of education committees. A Royal Commission on Local Government was appointed in 1966 and may well bring in a report in two or three years that will have a revolutionary effect on the present arrangements. At the least, the commission will probably recommend fundamental changes in the tax system and the reorganization of local government into some kind of regional units larger than the present ones.

One might suppose, given the political coloration of education committees, that policy would be at the mercy of whatever political party happened to be in control of local government. And sometimes this is true. In 1948, for example, the council for the county of Middlesex was controlled by the Labor Party; its education committee, despite some vociferous opposition within the county, decided to create a system of comprehensive schools and took a number of steps in that direction. The next year, however, the Tories were voted into power in Middlesex and promptly reversed the decision. But most of the time a kind of gentleman's agreement prevails that one party will not undo the work of another when taking over local government. There is a high degree of continuity in educational matters, both locally and nationally.

The administrative apparatus for education is everywhere much less grandiose in Britain than in the United States. Not only do schools themselves have much less in the way of administrative staff than American schools, but the county staffs are similarly smaller. I suppose the typical American administrator would contemplate with great unease the meager staff of even such a progressive and affluent city as Coventry: It has about 60,000 pupils spread over 150 schools with a central administrative staff of under twenty persons. Nor are these administrators nearly so "professionalized" as they are in the United States. Each LEA has its Chief Education Officer, for example, similar to the American superintendent of schools, but he rarely will be a "professional educator" in the American sense of the term. He will rarely have a postgraduate degree in "Education" (and never an undergraduate degree in it), much less one in Educational Administration, not to mention one in the Administration of the Secondary School or some other subspeciality common in the United States but not even offered in English and European universities. Instead he will have been a successsful teacher and will think of himself far more as an educator than as a businessman or an efficiency expert. Often he will have an academic postgraduate degree or perhaps a legal qualification. The British CEO by no means denigrates his function as an administrator, but no one who meets and talks with many such persons would ever confuse them with their American counterparts. Their education is different, their ways of thinking about education are different, and they are more apt to talk to visitors about the substance and meaning of what is going on in their schools than about administrative trivia. Heads of schools and Chief Education Officers pursue their duties with less technical training than ours, and less respect for organization for its own sake; but I think we could well ask ourselves if their priorities are not the right ones. Their tenure is much more secure than that of American administrators. One education committee member of long experience describes the typical relationship between the committee and its staff this way:

> Administrative officers, from the elected members' point of view, form a relatively homogeneous group. They are all professionals with academic qualifications. Promotion is, in the main, on merit and comes as a result of experience in the practical field of education as well as of administration. There is a clearly defined hierarchy and line of responsibility; there are powers of delegation, and, as the ladder of promotion is climbed, a supporting staff. The officer is paid, his job is his career, and unless he is grossly incompetent, negligent, or criminally inclined, he has almost complete security of tenure (in local government at any rate) of any post

to which he has been appointed. In contrast to the administrative civil servant the local government education officer, whose work is 90 per cent executive, is thought of as an educationist first and an administrator only second.[5]

Educational policy, then, is carried out in England through the co-ordinated efforts and joint financing of the central government and the 162 separate LEA's, with a fairly clear line of authority defined between them. The central Department has no voice whatever in what is taught in schools (except for mandatory religious instruction) or in how it is taught; no voice whatever in textbooks, methods, timetables, or in the hiring and firing of staff. It does have a strong voice in the overall provision made for education locally, in buildings, in teachers' salaries, and in the setting of somewhat vague national goals or priorities in education. Beyond that, the LEA's have the responsibility for education, acting through their CEO and his very modest staff, who in turn delegate a very great deal of authority to heads of schools and teachers. On the whole, this distribution of power, combining local freedom with national leadership, has worked extremely well.

## Professional and Lay Organizations

There is a third force of importance in the formation of educational policy: nongovernmental groups, which offer interesting comparisons with similar groups in the United States. The two most powerful non-governmental organizations in British education are the Association of Education Committees and the National Union of Teachers. The former is the counterpart of our National School Boards Association but with much greater power, and the latter the counterpart of our NEA but also with greater power. After the 1902 Act bringing education into county politics, a fear developed among boards of education that they might be submerged in county government. To protect their identity and more especially their budgets, they formed a national organization, the Association of Education Committees, to which all the education committees except London belong. London often acts separately in educational matters and is treated separately by the government because of its size and importance, although it in fact acts in unison on major questions with the Association. The Association is a highly influential body and is consulted by the Department on almost any substantive matter affecting educational administration. Although it is a voluntary, private organization, it has a great deal of political power, since its membership is made up of people who have been elected on party lines to local government. But it has political leverage also because of the role of the central government in English education: Since many policy decisions are made at the center, and not dispersed among fifty centers of power as in the United States, it is much easier than with us for national organizations like the Association to exert a national influence. For years it has also had a forceful chief administrator, Sir William Alexander, whose influence, given the vantage point from which he exercises it, over the course of English education should not be underestimated; it is very considerable.

Likewise, the National Union of Teachers, the NUT, although it has a smaller percentage of the total teaching force in membership than does the NEA, exerts a greater influence than the NEA because it can bring that influence to bear on the one center from which policy is made. It is the largest teachers organization in Britain and probably in Europe; but it is still far short of its goal of "unifying the profession" through universal membership, a goal sought also in the United States by the NEA. Teachers do not speak with a single voice anywhere in Europe. They are professionally divided everywhere because the school system itself is divided everywhere, with some types of schools and therefore teachers enjoying more prestige than others. In most countries the largest teachers organization is made up of elementary teachers, sometimes combined with teachers from nonselective, low-prestige secondary schools. These organizations are understandably found in support of various kinds of equalization measures, since equalization would for them be a raise in status: They favor equal pay for all teachers; they lobby in favor of uniform conditions of service for all teachers; they tend to favor comprehensive schools; and they tend to oppose efforts to reduce the teacher shortage through the use of electronic or human aides. Thus England's NUT is made up mostly of teachers in primary and secondary modern schools. It supports the equal-pay system that prevails in Britain (though not in Europe); it has a major voice in national settlements affecting salaries, retirement, tenure, and other conditions of educational employment; it lobbies quite vigorously, contributes to the political campaigns of a number of Members of Parliament, and has a fair number of MP's in active membership; it tends to favor comprehensive schools; and it stoutly resists any effort to reduce the teacher shortage by what it considers unprofessional measures. It is a powerful influence in English education.

The NUT has, however, two thorns in its side in the form of competing teachers organizations. One is made up of teachers and headmasters from selective secondary schools, both state and independent. It is really four organizations, one each for male and female teachers, and one each for male and female heads of schools—the Association of Head Masters, the Association of Assistant Masters, the Association of Head Mistresses, and the Association of Assistant Mistresses. The four associations present a united front on most questions through a body known as the Joint Four. The interests of the Joint Four are often in conflict with those of the

NUT. Thus it tends to oppose measures like those mentioned above that the NUT supports and to support those the NUT opposes. On occasion the two groups do get together about an issue of public concern and take common ground on it. The Joint Four enjoys more prestige than the NUT but a great deal less political power. The third organization is the NAS, the National Association of Schoolmasters, a peppery, outspoken group rather like our American Federation of Teachers. It has about one-sixth the membership of the NUT, which is not a bad showing in view of the fact that its membership is restricted to men. Its main object is, or was until recently, to restore single-sex classes in British schools in the belief that boys should have mostly male teachers and girls mostly female teachers; and it strongly promotes a return to separate salary negotiations for men and women teachers in the hope that men could insist on a higher scale. It does not really believe that separate salary scales for men and women are feasible in Britain, but it does hope to win a number of fringe benefits and extra payments of various kinds for men teachers.

This policy is obviously anathema to the NUT, where women are in the great majority; and so the two organizations spend a certain amount of their time in colorful combat that resembles the continuing tournament between the NEA and the AFT in the United States. (In Scotland, by the way, this academic battle of the sexes takes an odd turn: No man can be licensed to teach in that hard land unless he is a university graduate; and then if he intends to teach in the lower secondary grades he must also train for primary-school teaching. Both these requirements are probably unique in Europe, and costly: Scotland has few men teachers below the senior secondary schools, and has a severe shortage of teachers in general.) The influence of Britain's NAS is less than that of the Joint Four and much less than that of the NUT, but it is given representation on most of the appropriate national bodies in education and seems to be enjoying an increasing membership. Lastly, the National Association of Head Teachers should at least be mentioned. It is made up mostly of heads of primary and secondary modern schools and, although it has little power, it is represented on national committees and promises to increase its influence in the future.

Teachers organizations throughout Europe, as I have mentioned, reflect the structure of the school system and the status of different types of schools, and this greatly complicates the problem of achieving a "unified" profession. No nation has a teachers organization like the NEA, open to all people in education, both teachers and their bosses, and to which the majority of both groups belong; but no other nation has a school system as uniform as the American system. In almost all countries there is a fundamental split between teachers from selective and non-selective schools. In Germany, teachers in the selective school, the *Gymnasium,* have their own professional organization, Deutscher Philologenverband, which tends toward the conservative Christian Democratic Union (CDU) in politics and is regarded as reactionary in its educational policies by the other big professional organization, Arbeitsgemeinshaft Deutscher Lehrerverbände. The latter association is for elementary and some secondary teachers, is part of the trade-union movement and tends toward the Social Democrat Party (SPD) in politics, and wants to liberalize the educational system in various ways. The same thing is repeated in France, where a number of associations of secondary teachers seem to speak through a parent body, the Syndicat National de L'Enseignement Secondaire, and to take the usual conservative positions on educational issues, while the organization for elementary teachers, the Syndicat National des Instituteurs et Institutrices, is staunchly left-wing and includes a strong Communist element. In some countries, such as Italy, Belgium, and the Netherlands, a third major interest is involved in teachers organizations, the religious interest, but the types of schools from which teachers come remains the paramount consideration.

In Britain, the religious interest plays no part in professional associations, and the political alignment, although clear, is not so marked as in Europe. Yet there is, fortunately, no prospect in Britain of the amalgamation of existing associations into one. I say fortunately for the same reason that I would not want to see a single, monolithic organization in the United States: I would fear its power and I would fear its politics, especially if both were in the hands of educational administrators, as is the case with our NEA. I can easily sympathize with the desire of many teachers to have a united profession, but a united professional pressure group, which is what a single teachers organization would be, would seem to me far more a threat than a blessing unless it were organized and administered much differently from the existing agencies. One hears many pleas in both countries for professional solidarity, even from official bodies. Here is a typical one from an important national committee in Britain:

> All who are concerned in any way with the education service would wish to see divisions removed wherever their removal is possible. We believe that many of our findings—a universally trained profession, a common minimum length of education and training, the ultimate removal of the distinction between the graduate and the non-graduate teacher and the greater flexibility and adaptability that we have advocated in the education and training of all our teachers—all these should materially make it easier for every individual teacher to see himself as a member of a real profession.[6]

If these are the consequences of unity, unity is devoutly not to be wished. These are precisely the kinds of consequences to be avoided in the United States, at least until our knowledge of teaching and of the whole educational process is much greater than it now is. Meanwhile, the diversity of professional organizations that one finds in Europe, despite some disadvantages and even though it is a function of the selective secondary schools, has much to commend it. We could do with another association or two in the United States, if for no other reason than to leave teachers room for heterodoxy and dissent, to leave them free of the coercive power that in the present state of things can be exercised by the NEA; to preserve, in a word, alternatives. Whatever the arguments in favor of a single national teachers association, I believe there are far more, and far more compelling, arguments against it.

In addition to the NUT and the Association of Education Committees, which are the principal nongovernmental groups in education and which promote their views through their own journals and other publications, there are still other groups that have some influence on policy. One, for example, called the Confederation for the Advancement of State Education, is a middle-class pressure group similar to groups that spring up from time to time in the United States. It has affiliated chapters of varying enthusiasm and activity throughout Britain. As the name implies it plumps for more money for state schools; it supports the movement toward comprehensive schools and is therefore not very chummy with the independent sector of education; and it strives in general to enlarge the role of the layman in British schools.

Another interesting organization is the Advisory Centre for Education, an agency that aims its quarterly journal, called *Where,* and its other publications at the layman. It claims a dues-paying membership of about 20,000, a surprisingly large figure for this kind of organization in a country with a quarter the population of ours. It considers its main function to be the collection and dissemination to parents of information that they cannot easily get in any other way, and this is indeed a job that needs doing in British education. But it is also a propaganda group whose general line is the need to liberalize education and whose principal personalities are well-known spokesmen for the comprehensive school and other reform measures. It also has an ill-disguised hostility toward independent education, especially toward the Public Schools.[7] The influence either of these groups enjoys is difficult to measure, as is that of any pressure group. I would suppose that they do have some effect on the public discussion of educational issues in a small country like Britain, which is less subject than the United States to problems of regionalism and decentralization and sheer size. Still other groups are found on the fringes of the educational system, though they have little influence. Mostly they are religious groups or political groups, such as the Fabian Society on the left, publishing various pamphlets on educational reform to a small readership, or a left-of-center Tory organization called the Bow Group, publishing an occasional small volume on educational policy.

As to the forgotten man in education, the parent, his lot is often not a happy one in either Britain or the United States. He has even less influence, I am afraid, in England, singly or in concert, than with us, particularly in the state schools. The tenure of headmasters and other educational administrators is so secure in Britain that they do not have to yield much ground to local pressure groups, with the result that few such groups exist. They are obliged under the 1944 Act to heed the wishes of parents about the education of their children, but British parents rarely put this obligation to the test. Within the state system, most parents seem content to give over their children to the schools and to consider that an end to the matter; at any rate, they do not seem to take as active an interest in their children's education as is common in the United States. Parent-teacher organizations exist but are even less effective than ours. I suppose American parents would be shocked to find a sign outside their schools saying, "Parents Not Admitted Without an Appointment," but I found such signs on various occasions. Teachers and school heads in England take the position that they are the experts and are not answerable to the whims or criticisms of parents.

In practice the situation is not this black and white; parents do query and complain and schoolmen do listen and explain. But the whole tradition of the parent's relationship to the school in England is different from ours. One consequence of this fact is that British parents know even less than American parents about what is going on in their own schools specifically and in British education generally. The following comment from a well-known Tory and former junior minister who writes often on education strikes me as relating far more to what ought to be in Britain than to what is:

> One may claim on grounds of principle—and I should—that parents ought to be involved in the education of their children. But on grounds of efficiency alone, it is clear that they must be. If ever the idea was gaining currency that education is solely a matter for the expert and that the parents' proper role is simply to hand over their children to the school, recent research should have dispelled it. What the school can do for any child is necessarily limited or enlarged by the parent.[8]

When parents do show an interest, however, it seems to me that British schoolmen are less restrictive than ours are likely to be. It would rarely happen, for instance, that a school would try to restrain a parent from teaching his child to read on grounds that the child was not "ready" or the method was not the approved one. On the contrary, if the parent was interested, he would probably be given every encouragement by the school.

Parental attitudes in the independent sector of education are often different. Here many parents do indeed take an interest in the expensive education they have purchased for their children and educators do respond to parental wishes. I will discuss education in the independent schools in a later chapter; here I would only point to the significant, though controversial, influence that private schools have on educational policy in England (although not in Scotland, where private schools are rare). The most important constituent member of the Joint Four, mentioned earlier, is the Headmasters' Association. This professional organization is open to any male head of a nonprofit secondary school. Within this organization is another and more exclusive one known as the Headmasters' Conference, which antedates the association and is now a sort of club-within-a-club made up of the heads of Britain's leading two hundred "Public Schools" and "Direct Grant Schools." The Headmasters' Conference enjoys high prestige, though it is often thought of as archconservative. Independent education is thus a large and important segment of the British educational system, and the consumer has a large and important voice in it.

I think too that it is worth recording that private schools are established with great ease in England (as they are in some of our states), though they are now subject to more restraints than before the 1944 Act. There are about 4,000 private schools, many of them quite small, and only about 1,500 of them are "recognized as efficient" by the Department. The law says that anybody can establish a school, and that regular instruction given to any group of five or more children between the ages of five and fifteen *is* a school and must apply to the Department for "registration." Within a few months of such an application, the school is visited by an HMI, who makes a report to the Department as to whether the school meets a minimum standard for operation; if it does it becomes a "registered" school, the lowest qualification for remaining in business, and signifying only that the government is prepared to tolerate it. In practice almost all schools are granted registration, since the standard applied by the HMI is the minimum acceptable in the state system, and that can be pretty low. To illustrate: a total of ninety-five applications to register schools was received in the Department in the three years, 1961 to 1964; registration was granted immediately following the HMI's visit to fifty-seven, and the remaining thirty-eight were granted registration after the correction of some specific deficiency usually having to do with fire regulations. The law provides that the Secretary can lodge a "Complaint" against a school that continues to operate without correcting named deficiencies, but only two such instances have occurred since the 1944 Act.

After a school has been registered and in operation for several years, it can apply to the Department to be recognized as efficient, a status of some value to the school and to parents contemplating sending their children to the school. This application means a much more detailed HMI inspection and a higher standard all around before the application is granted. Most private schools covet the recognized-as-efficient label.

Beyond these controls, private schools are quite free. They are visited much less often by HMI's, since less tax money is involved and since the government is reluctant to interfere in the private sector. Nor do they have to meet state standards for teacher qualifications, salaries, and other conditions. In brief, private education in England is a large and diversified field, in which schools can be created with very few legal controls, but enough to ensure parents against outright fraud while leaving both school and parents as full a measure of freedom as possible.

There remains one group that should be mentioned as an important influence on education, the Schools Council for the Curriculum and Examinations. This is a new agency with a rather special status. It was created and is financed by the central Department but is not responsible to it. The Schools Council grew out of a 1964 report of a Working Party appointed by the Minister of Education, as he then was called, to consider ways of establishing "co-operative machinery in the fields of the school curriculum and examinations"; it grew out, that is, of a widespread feeling that, although control over educational administration might be effective enough in Britain, there was little coordination in the equally important areas of curriculum and examinations. The Working Party concluded:

> The present arrangements for determining the curriculum in schools and the related examinations are not working well: in particular, teachers have insufficient scope for making or recommending modifications in the curriculum and examinations.[9]

The British teacher is sensitive about his autonomy in the classroom and has an old habit of opposing anything that looks like direction from the center in matters of curriculum. Thus the predecessor of the Schools Council, a body appointed by Lord Eccles when he was Minister of Education, the Curriculum Study Group, met with hostility and suspicion from classroom teachers, who were not represented on it. Although the new group, the Schools Council, has much wider representation in which teachers predominate, criticism of it from the field is still considerable. To alleviate suspicion, the first Chairman of the Schools Council, Sir John Maud (Master of University College, Oxford), insisted that the organization be housed separately from the Department even though its money came from the government and that it be completely free, and seen to be free, of government control.

This was done so that now, in a typically British fashion, there is a national body, broadly representative of teachers, LEA's, and university institutes and departments of education, that has all its bills paid by the government but does not answer to it. "It means," as Sir John Maud commented, "that we at last have a Parliament of and for education with all interests represented." The Council decided that three problems were preeminent at the present time in British education: (a) the teaching of

English, which a good many people in Britain think is sadly deficient; (b) preparations for the raising of the school-leaving age, which is scheduled to go to sixteen in 1971, and for dealing with low-ability students when they all remain in school longer; and (c) reform of the curriculum and examinations for the sixth form of the secondary school. So far the most important work the Council has done in its brief existence is in the examinations field, and I will discuss it in Chapter IV.

The Schools Council is still a small agency as national groups go and is very new, but it has already had a considerable influence in British education. Ideologically the Council is on the side of those who are actively unhappy about English education and who want to reform and liberalize many aspects of it. Like the Inspectorate of Schools, the Council is charged with developing ideas and giving advice, not with twisting arms or giving orders. The HMI keeps the line between the two things clearly drawn; most people hope that the Council will continue this tradition and will resist the inevitable temptation to centralize control of the curriculum. It is the classic problem, of course—how to effect national reform in education without national direction. In the past England has met the problem by relying on compromise, consensus, and persuasion. Its future course, however, is not clear.

## Politics and the Comprehensive School

I mentioned at the beginning of this chapter that Britain seems now to be faced for the first time since the 1944 Act with a certain conflict over how much authority should be exercised in education by the central government. The Act gave a good deal of power to the central government, but in addition there has been a steady, unlegislated drift of power to the center since 1944. The whole question has been brought to a head in recent years by the debate over the comprehensive school and the forced conversion of the present system to one that is wholly comprehensive. This is the most pervasive and embittered controversy in English education. The strands of the argument are many and tortuous, and political doctrine overshadows the discussion.

What does the quarrel mean to the United States, where the comprehensive school is not even in issue? Nothing directly; several things indirectly. First, it is simply interesting in its own right, as a major development in the country closest to our own historically. Second, it is instructive, as a demonstration of what might be called the victimization of education by politics. Third, we have had little experience with control or influence from the central government in education, but that pattern may be changing now and we might well try to sensitize ourselves to the kind of conflicts that can develop between local and central authority.

I do not suggest that centralized control is always and everywhere a bad thing. One of the lasting impressions one gets from looking at education in Europe is the variety of successful practices in education that have evolved from a diversity of political and social traditions. Thus we might best look to Britain or Europe, not for the solution to problems, but for an illustration of how a common problem is met in a dozen different ways. Even a glance at European practices will reinforce the point. The degree of centralization in education varies in Europe from being more or less complete in a homogeneous country like Sweden to being a good deal less than prevails among our own fifty states in a multilanguage country like Switzerland. Sweden leaves very little indeed to local control. On the other hand, Switzerland's federal constitution imposes a few educational laws but leaves almost everything to the twenty-five autonomous cantons, not even providing a Minister or Ministry of Education. There is a Conference of Cantonal Chiefs of Public Instruction that achieves a degree of harmony in the system, but local autonomy is still the main characteristic of Switzerland's political arrangements.

France is often cited as the worst or the best example of centralized control, depending on one's bias. In fact there is a lot of freedom built into French education where it is most important—for the teacher in the classroom; but it is up to him to claim it. Nor is the customary picture of the dictatorial French Minister of Education valid. There is, among other things, an important national body, the Conseil Superieur de l'Education Nationale, with a membership of more than a hundred persons from seven national educational organizations, to which the Minister of Education submits any major question for advice. He does not have to take the advice, but usually he does. Nor does it follow, incidentally, that educational reform is necessarily easier in a strongly centralized system: If support from teachers themselves is lacking, as it has been in France for a number of reforms, progress takes place mostly on paper. In a decentralized system, reform can often go forward faster because local support is forthcoming voluntarily. In Belgium and the Netherlands, centralized control is diluted by the rival claims of religious groups—so much so in Holland that the Dutch apply the word *Zuilen* to much of their educational system to signify the three-way split in schools and control among the Catholics, the Protestants, and what I suppose would be called the Neutrals. The Dutch Ministry of Education in theory has a good deal of control but in practice finds it difficult to exercise it.

West Germany, of course, has eleven separate states, eleven constitutions, and eleven educational systems, a fragmentation that owes something to the memory of centralized control under the Nazis. The eleven *Laender* are themselves strongly centralized in education and guard their autonomy even more zealously than our states do, but they maintain a permanent conference of education ministers in Bonn, the Standige Konferenz der Kultusminister, that does a good deal more than its Swiss counterpart to unify and coordinate German education. Also, a national advisory council in education, the Bildungsrat, was established in 1965 to complement a similar body already in being for science and research; it will be a planning and study organization but without any real power.

One could devote a book to the variety of arrangements that have evolved in Europe for the government of education, but the point that concerns us is simply that the case for or against centralized control in education is meaningless until it is related to a lot of other things in a given country—traditions, institutions, religious pressures, social attitudes. In Britain the present system of secondary schools is based, as we saw in Chapter I, on the assumption that academic ability can be identified well enough at age eleven to justify separating children into different types of schools, the top quarter or so going to grammar schools and the rest going to "secondary modern," comprehensive, technical, or other institutions. Although the 1944 Act did not specify these types of schools, government circulars following the Act strongly suggested a "tripartite" system of grammar-modern-technical schools, and most of the LEA's in producing the "development plan" called for in the Act naturally came in with such a system. Grammar schools already existed throughout the country as well as some technical schools; so the obvious thing, if secondary education was to be universal, was to create another type of school for the mass of children not admissible to the established grammar schools. With what looks now like incredible naïveté, educational authorities seem seriously to have believed that what they called "parity of esteem" between types of schools was possible by declaring it to be so. Reports as far back as the Hadow Report in 1926 insisted on this quaint doctrine, as did the Spens Report in 1938 and the Norwood Report in 1943. Everyone was quite definite that the grammar school should not be regarded as superior to the new secondary modern school, only different. Everyone, that is, but parents and students and employers, who immediately, and one would have thought predictably, accorded quite different esteem to the two schools.

To many Britons today, this lack of parity or equality in schools bespeaks a lack of social equality as well. And this is the heart of the comprehensive controversy. Although many educational arguments are adumbrated to support or refute the policy of the Labor Party of "going" comprehensive, the quarrel is really an old one about equality. It may sound faded and anachronistic to Americans, at least to white Americans, but Britain still suffers, not so much from economic injustice, which has been lightened by the Welfare State, as from what Arthur Koestler once called "The psychological apartheid between the bourgeoisie and the proletariat." [10] The problem in contemporary Britain is nothing like it was when R. H. Tawney wrote scathingly about "the ravages of the disease of inequality," [11] but it is still real enough in English life. Working-class men no longer tip their caps and say "Good morning, sir" when they meet the squire in the village, but the psychological and educational distance between them is still great.

One of the contradictions of British society is that, having led the way for much of the world toward religious and political equality, England should have been so tardy in realizing the same goal in its social being. World War II, of course, brought a determination, especially on the part of servicemen, to change the old Britain after the war—which is the reason that Churchill and the Tories, much to the surprise of Americans, were not retained in power when the coalition government ended in 1945. Nothing expressed this determination better than the plans set forth in 1942 by the Beveridge Report, the revolutionary document that became the foundation of Britain's Welfare State. But a quarter of a century later the revolution is still less than complete. One now reads with a wry smile a passage like the following from one of Kingsley Amis' short stories about World War II; it is spoken by a British soldier to his fellow servicemen waiting to be demobilized:

> "We're going to build a decent Britain. Fair shares for all and free schools and doctoring and hospitals and no class distinction. The old school tie and the old-boy network aren't going to work any more. To make sure of that we're going to abolish the public schools and Oxford and Cambridge, or at any rate change them so that anybody who's got brains can go to them, and we're going to either abolish the House of Lords or make it a thing you vote on, just like the House of Commons. It's undemocratic any other way. Some of us want to abolish the Royal Family for the same reason, but we're not decided about that. Personally I think that if you scrap titles and the Honours List and all that carryon, then you can leave the King and Queen to stew in their own juice." [12]

I doubt that many British servicemen had mapped things out just this way, but many would have shared the general sentiment.

Today the remaining inequalities are much more subtle than formerly. To a visitor, British society now seems to be as equal and informal as any in the world, most of all at those hoary seats of class and privilege, Oxford and Cambridge, where one now finds, as an Oxford don comments, "an all pervading spirit of equalitarianism . . . [which] presents itself in many forms from a noble idealism to the cry of 'nobody better than me.' " [13] But at least one British educationist, a leading impresario of the comprehensive school, sees British society now to be as restrictive as ever:

> England in the 1960s is an aristocratic society, not a democratic one. That

is the main fact to be realized if its system of education is to be fully understood. The majority of its citizens still believe in aristocracy (government by the best people) rather than in democracy (government by all the people). . . . The Englishman of the 1960s does not believe in equality. What he wants is equal opportunity to be unequal.[14]

Whatever can be said for the speed of change within British society today, the educational system is seen by many to be the principal remaining barrier to equality, and the comprehensive school is seen as the principal means for surmounting that barrier.

One of the central arguments used by those who favor the comprehensive school is that the wide differences in grammar-school provision from one area of Britain to another is in itself a glaring inequality that can only be overcome by a unified school. The issue of unequal provision is a familiar one in the United States, where the differences in expenditure on education between one school system and another, one town and another, one state or region and another, can be much greater than they are in Britain or in most of Europe. In Britain there is far more equalization among the LEA's than among our own states, but the differences still remain great. As a national average, local property rates produce about forty percent of the money spent by local government for all services, including education; sixty percent comes from other local revenue and from the central government. But the difference in rateable property between, say, London and a village in Cornwall is far out of proportion to the numbers of children to be schooled in each place. London can therefore spend much more money on education relative to its needs than can the Cornish village, despite a weighting system applied by the Exchequer that reduces London's grant from the central government to perhaps half the percentage given the village. Across the land, substantial differences exist in, for example, school buildings and equipment, in the teacher-pupil ratio, and in the percentage of grammar-school vacancies available for children at the 11-plus separation.

But the whole question of differences of provision in English education is a good illustration of how unexamined statistics can distort educational discussion—a problem with which we have some experience in the United States. The fact of difference is not debatable. It is clear from the available statistics, just as it is with us. But a fact, as one of Pirandello's characters says somewhere, is like a sack: It will not stand up until you put something into it. Upon hearing the Secretary of State for Education and Science defending the government's comprehensive-school policy by stressing the fact that the grammar-school vacancies available for children at 11-plus vary from eight to forty percent in different British constituencies, one's first reaction might be to support the policy in order to remove such obvious injustice (though a comprehensive school would not necessarily do that). But one's second thought ought to be to ask why the differences exist and what they mean. Among other considerations, it seems to me, would be these:

*First*, grammar-school vacancies are naturally related to the supply-demand situation in a given area. They may not be wholly controlled by the number of parents or pupils wanting entry to grammar schools, but they will certainly bear some consistent relationship to demand, as does everything else in education. So if many more of the children in an affluent southeastern county go to grammar schools than in a rural county in the north, it must be at least partly attributable to demand. The senior secondary schools in Scotland have always taken a larger percentage of the age group than the English grammar schools. They have done so in response to the demands of Scottish parents, many of whom are from the lower and artisan classes but are educationally ambitious for their children. The same is true in Wales, which is a depressed area economically but has a high demand for grammar-school education and a high grammar-school provision.

*Second*, the reasons in turn for the differences in demand must be considered. What are the differences in background, attitude, and parental interest in education among people in different areas? Is it possible that differences in native ability are involved between people who migrate to the south, get executive jobs, and raise their children in affluent homogeneous suburban neighborhoods, and those who stay home even when home is in a relatively impoverished area? To illustrate: The percentage of grammar-school places is far higher in the well-off residential areas of the northern half of the West Riding (Yorkshire) than in the lower-class mining areas of the southern half. Unless one takes the position that intelligence is simply distributed at random across the population, then its unequal distribution might presumably bear some relationship to such things as income, education, and housing. This question has nothing to do with whether the nation's "pool of ability" is being sufficiently tapped by the educational system, which it is not.

*Third*, in many areas with low grammar-school provision, expanded provision is made for technical education, as well as for academic courses in the secondary modern schools, and for late transfer from modern to grammar schools. This is hardly the ideal answer to low grammar-school provision, but it is a balancing factor. Also, some areas with low grammar-school provision have large numbers of private schools, which take many of the children that, in all probability, would otherwise be going to state grammar schools.

*Fourth*, population shifts have something to do with the problem. In areas like Hertfordshire with a heavy influx of people, the Exchequer grant for buildings can be disproportionately large in order that school roofs can at least be put over children's heads, and thus a larger provision for grammar schools will be made than may prevail in areas with older buildings. Also, the administrative staff of the school system, especially the Chief Education Officer, can have a lot to do with how much money is got from the central government and how many buildings and grammar-school vacancies are created. It is perfectly possible for a county with a vigorous and persuasive Chief Education Officer backed by a lively education committee with well-drawn plans for buildings to get more money than it would be entitled to on a strict arithmetical division of funds.

*Fifth,* the LEA's themselves do not seem to feel that the differences in provision among them are a major problem. It is surely significant that the question of unequal provision is rarely commented upon, and even more rarely cited as a reason for going comprehensive, by the people who are closest to the problem of provision.

So the difference of provision, especially for grammar-school vacancies, among the various authorities in Britain may not in itself prove much. But it has become an issue now because of the larger controversy over the comprehensive school. One can easily collect perfervid denunciations of the injustice caused by differences in grammar-school provision, but one rarely gets a clear statement of the opposite, such as the following comment made to me by Sir William Alexander, Secretary of the Association of Education Committees: "There is no country in the world where educational opportunity is less dependent than in Britain on place of birth or on the economic and social status of parents." This probably puts the best light on the situation. My own feeling is that there is some injustice done able children in areas poorly provided with grammar-school vacancies—that is, that the same children who fail to find their way into a grammar school in a poor area might well have done so had they lived in a better area. But one might have had to change their parents as well as their neighborhoods, and that problem takes us into metaphysical questions beyond the scope of this book! Whether these same children would fare better in a comprehensive school in the same neighborhood is an unanswerable question.

Social inequality, then, great or small, real or imagined, turns the discussion over comprehensive schools into political channels. The Labor Party wants the present system of schools converted as rapidly as possible into one that is exclusively comprehensive; the Liberal Party, Britain's "third" party that occupies a middle ground on most issues and that attracts many academic and intellectual people, supports Labor's policy but lacks its militancy; the Conservative Party opposes a forced and exclusively comprehensive system and thinks there are more important things in education to worry about. The relevant political slogans might be "No sacrifice of the best" for the Tories and "No sacrifice of the rest" for the Laborites. Nobody puts the matter exactly this way, but the discussion is often carried on in this kind of emotive idiom. The President of the Headmasters' Association denounces "the omni-competent state" that seeks to create a "docile and malleable society" by imposing on it a particular brand of schools; or the Master of one of the constituent Colleges of the University of London attacks the "doctrinaire passions" of the Socialists and their policy of cramming good grammar schools "into the maw of this sacred crocodile," [15] the comprehensive school. Or an editorial in *The Sunday Times* speaks of the "prejudice and folly" of Labor's educational policy and reproves the Party for treating education "as a tool of Socialist egalitarianism." [16]

Labor supporters return the volley by accusing the Tories of wanting only to protect their privileges and accusing them of making small concessions that

> amount to no more than a series of clever maneuvers to preserve intact the position of a ruling group. Petty concessions and improvizations do not make a revolution, they show us instead a class set on self-preservation.[17]

Or a frank appeal to sentiment is made, as when a member of the education committee of the Labor-controlled government of London says that "We are trying to organize and develop the educational system so that in future no child will be a rejected child," [18] thereby suggesting that anyone opposing the comprehensive school wants to reject children. One professor of education, who is imaginative and forceful in the field of teacher training, even puts the issue of dividing children by ability on a religious plane: "Not only does selection divide families, it divides communities. As a Christian . . . selection just didn't make sense to me. . . . I still don't see how you can be a Christian and accept selection," [19] a view that would seem to call into question the schools and the Christianity of most of Europe.

The Tory rejoinder is likely to point out (a) that equality of opportunity is precisely what the selective system of secondary schools ensures, since selective schools can draw their students from a much wider area than a comprehensive school and since entry to them is on the basis of merit and not family background or neighborhood; (b) that in any case the equality provided by comprehensive schools is artificial and illusory; or (c) that Britain simply has too much to lose by converting good established schools into comprehensive schools. Sir Edward Boyle, formerly Minister of Education under the Tories and later shadow Secretary of State for Education and Science, likes to stress the Conservatives' belief that no particular form of school organization is necessarily superior to all others:

> Conservatives are opposed to legislation which would compel authorities to do away with all selective schools, and to adopt some form of the comprehensive principle, whether they are willing or not. We cannot accept

the proposal that every grammar school should be forced to lose its identity; nor do we concede—and this is just as important—that every boy or girl lower down in the ability range will be better off in a comprehensive school than in a modern school.[20]

And so the quarrel over the egalitarian society and whether it can be achieved by comprehensive schools continues today in Britain and no doubt will continue for many years.

In the meantime, however, the practical question of whether Britain will in fact convert to a comprehensive system would seem to be settled. In November 1964, a few weeks after Labor came to power following thirteen years of Tory rule, Michael Stewart, then Labor's Secretary of State for Education and Science, proclaimed in the House of Commons that a conversion to comprehensives was to be the national policy of England, and seems to have brought into vogue at the same time the evocative word "separatist" to define the existing system that was to be abolished.[21]

To counter the response from Tories about the folly of "abolishing" good grammar schools, Harold Wilson replied on numerous occasions that as a grammar-school boy himself he would allow them to be abolished only "over my dead body"; all Labor wanted to do was to abolish the 11-plus and "to make grammar-school education available to everyone." Stewart's successor, Anthony Crosland, took the next step some months later and issued a circular to all the LEA's in Britain requiring them to submit plans to him by the summer of 1966 for converting their secondary schools to comprehensive schools. For the first time since the 1944 Act, this brought a few cases of outright defiance on the part of LEA's that simply declined to prepare and submit such plans. In response to this unprecedented resistance, the Secretary in March 1966 issued another circular saying that he would henceforth not approve any building plans for schools "which would be incompatible with the introduction of a nonselective system of education." To the LEA's the message was clear: The central government, by whatever means were necessary, was going to compel local authorities to follow the national policy and go comprehensive. Thus the premonition of the Tories, voiced in the Commons by Quintin Hogg soon after the policy of going comprehensive was announced, was amply justified. Responding to the Secretary's announcement, he said then:

> If he means that it is his policy to coerce local authorities, to impose by means of compulsion on local authorities—whether they agree with him or not—a single unitary principle of reorganization all over the country, then I think he is undermining the whole philosophy of the Act of 1944 with which my right hon. Friend was associated. Indeed, he would be bringing back, I think, the bitterest political antagonism into the field of education.[22]

The issue, then, quite simply, is the degree of power that *should* be exercised over education by the central government. Although opponents of the comprehensive policy accuse the government of usurping power, the question does not seem to me as an onlooker to be one of whether the government has whatever authority it claims. In the British system of Cabinet government without a written constitution, the elected government presumably has whatever power it can lay claim to and can wield without being brought down. But tradition is extremely important in British politics. It is strongly against the coercion of local government and in favor of consensus. Whether the present policy is right or wrong, it does seem to violate, as Hogg pointed out, the spirit of the 1944 Act and of the development of English education since the Act. In a word, the question is a moral rather than a legal one. When the Secretary announced his intention of using the building budget to enforce his policy of going comprehensive, the Secretary of the Association of Education Committees, reflecting the views of many local authorities, said: "I can only express regret that the Secretary of State [for Education and Science] seems to be departing from the policy of persuasion to a policy of compulsion." [23]

The process of conversion to comprehensive schools is already well advanced, although it will be a number of years before it is complete and a great many more after that before its degree of success can be determined, if it can ever be. In all probability the present policy cannot now be set aside, even by a Tory government; but there remains at least the possibility of modifying it in important ways. I feel myself that the policy, considered on educational grounds and quite apart from political doctrine, is ill-conceived, and I will therefore return to this theme in Chapter VIII, which is addressed to British readers. I have tried to look at the issue in this chapter simply as another part of the political anatomy of English education, and as a demonstration of the tension that can develop between central and local authority in education when a clear consensus is lacking among the public at large.

The government of education in England throws some light on the present situation in the United States, where for the first time the federal government is taking a really large role in education. As we have seen, England stands somewhere between our kind of system and the centralized systems of France or Sweden, but it may well suggest the shape of things to come in the United States. Following the unprecedented legislation of recent years, the massive power of the federal government will presumably become, for good or ill, a permanent part of the American educational scene. Although this power is mostly expressed in grants of money, the government's influence over educational policy will necessarily become, and indeed now is, far greater than in the past. At the same time, there is a steady consolidation or nationalization of influence in education through national organizations: professional associations, foundations, accrediting bodies, testing agencies, and curriculum-reform groups.

The local school board has become a favorite target of reformers, who feel that we can no longer afford the political abuses, the intellectual limitations, or the financial inequities of local control. I myself share this feeling to some extent, but am less sanguine than many Americans about the blessings to be expected of centralized authority. Professional educators, politicians, or planners who operate from some center of power in education are not necessarily wiser, better, or more humane than amateurs, laymen, and local boards. A study of the mistakes inspired in the recent past by central educational authorities in other countries might be a salutary exercise for Americans who regard local control as one of the big remaining obstacles to reform. The balance of power between the federal government and the states, and between the states' and the local systems, is constantly shifting, usually toward the center, and apparently will continue to do so in the future. In England the system of educational control that has evolved since the 1944 Act has been highly effective, reposing important financial controls as well as responsibility for general policy in the hands of the central government but leaving local authorities and individual schools a large measure of freedom over most other matters. It is in the area of national policy, especially over the comprehensive school, that serious conflicts are now arising—just as they very easily might with us in the future. What the proper balance of powers should be in our own system is a matter of opinion, but we would be better off if our opinions were informed by an awareness of problems and practices in England and other countries.

## CHAPTER III

# English Schools

IN ACCORDANCE with the 1944 Act, English schools are divided into three types: primary, secondary, and establishments of "further education" that include all education after the end of full-time schooling. The term "state" schools is a little misleading, although in common use in England. The preferred term is "maintained" schools to identify all the institutions that are supported wholly or in large part by the LEA's or otherwise by taxes. In contrast to American practice, maintained schools therefore include large numbers of "voluntary" institutions, mostly related to religious bodies, that have elected to become part of the state system in one or another of the ways provided for in the Act. In addition to the maintained schools there are "direct-grant" schools standing half-

*Schools and Pupils in England and Wales* (January, 1964)

|  | SCHOOLS | PUPILS |
|---|---|---|
| Maintained primary schools (includes many church-related schools) | 22,941 | 4,203,949 |
| Maintained secondary schools | | |
| *secondary modern schools* | 3,906 | 1,640,549 |
| *grammar schools* | 1,298 | 726,075 |
| *comprehensive schools* | 195 | 199,245 |
| Direct-grant schools | 328 | 124,627 |
| Fully independent schools | | |
| *primary schools* | 2,054 | 169,196 |
| *secondary schools* | 528 | 95,445 |
| *primary and secondary combined* | 953 | 200,301 |
| All schools of all types | 34,123 *(over 80% are coed, mostly primary)* | 7,715,885 |

way between the state and independent school systems, and there are many wholly independent schools. A simplified table of the principal types of institutions and the numbers of students that attend them is on the opposite page.[1]

Our concern in this chapter will be with the main types of schools and what happens in them—that is, primary schools, nonselective secondary schools (chiefly the secondary modern schools), and selective secondary schools (grammar, direct-grant, and independent). I will also make some comparisons where appropriate with American schools.

## Primary Schools

At the moment, English primary education lasts for six years, from age five to age eleven. However, the age of transfer from primary to secondary school, and thus the length of primary schooling, will probably change in the near future, in some cases making for a shorter primary school but in most cases making for a longer primary school by one or two years. British children begin school between four and a half and five years of age and now move on to secondary school anywhere from ten and a half to nearly twelve. Many primary schools are divided between an "infants'" and a "junior" segment, and teacher-training programs for these age groups are slightly different. Pre-primary or "nursery" education is available in both maintained and private schools, but for only a small fraction of children; everybody recognizes the importance of nursery training, especially for children from poor families, but nursery schools are never given a very high priority in appropriations, and they remain numerically very small. Organizationally, the school year is divided into three terms, totaling about 195 working days a year in contrast to the average 180 days of the United States. The infants' division works a five-hour day in most schools, the junior division a five-and-a-half-hour day. The year runs from early September to nearly the end of July, an uncomfortably long calendar, no doubt, to many American schoolmen and parents.

Americans would also be disconcerted by the condition of many English primary schools. A visit to a primary building that was put up, say, about 1890 (not to say one that may go back to the 1840's), still with outdoor toilets and no piped hot water, congested, cold, badly equipped, with no room for the staff or perhaps even the headmaster—though it might be a happy and effective school—would be an unsettling experience for many Americans. Such schools are plentiful in Britain. The National Union of Teachers conducted in 1964 an extensive survey of the physical condition of English schools and brought in a very harsh report.[2] And official government information released in 1965 indicated among other things that forty percent of the children in the maintained schools were in establishments with outside toilets; thirty percent were in schools where the main building had been put up before 1902 (and before 1875, for thirteen percent).[3] While it is no bad thing in the independent schools, where age confers prestige, to be inhabiting antique buildings, it is a dubious pleasure in the state schools. Primary schools have been neglected relative to secondary schools for many years. Not only are the accommodations apt to be bad, but the number of oversize classes is apt to be high. The national teacher-pupil ratio in Britain is about the same as it is in the United States, but only because it includes a very large number of very small classes in rural schools and because at the other end of the system, the last two years of the secondary school, the classes are also small.

In theory, primary schools are under the immediate control of "Boards of Managers," usually made up of half a dozen persons of reputation in the community. In practice such persons are often figureheads, except in some of the church schools. The main decisions about the curriculum, standards, methods of instruction, and most other matters of moment are made by the headmaster in collaboration with his teachers. In sharp contrast with our own practice, the British headmaster is regarded by everyone, especially himself, as the "head teacher" and not as an efficiency expert or a professional administrator. However, the primary-school curriculum, in spite of the freedom of headmasters and teachers, is everywhere about the same in the maintained schools: English in all of its spoken and written forms is the most important subject; arithmetic and often mathematics are the next most important; geography is important and is treated as a separate subject, not lost in an effluvium of "social studies"; history is treated as a separate subject; there is sometimes a foreign language, even two, in the curriculum; science is done but not much emphasized; religious instruction is always required; and there is quite a lot of art and music, or painting and dancing. The primary curriculum, in short, is about as standardized in the subjects covered and in the progression involved as in the schools of a nation with completely centralized control. Experimentation seems to me less frequent in British primary schools than in ours, for better or worse, and England can point to few theoreticians and few innovations that have attracted much attention; Sir James Pitman's Initial Teaching Alphabet is about the only one of note in many years. An inspector of schools from France, that land of alleged educational rigidity, is reported to have said after visiting a number of English primary schools that in France everybody is supposed to be doing the same thing at the same time, and nobody is, whereas in Britain everybody is supposed to be going his own way, and nobody is.

Where the variety comes in English primary schools is in methods of instruction and in the general quality of schools. The range of teaching methods can be enormous between schools a few miles apart and even within the same school. Teachers can easily be found to prove anybody's horror stories about stultified, catechetical, textbook-tied teaching; others can be found in the advance guard of the craze for "creativity" or any other idea that comes along. Most teachers, of course, are somewhere between. In general I would hazard the guess that primary teaching in English schools, certainly for the upper thirty percent or so of the pupils, is more rigorous, systematic, and academic than in American schools, if for no other reason than the importance of preparing pupils for the 11-plus. Not that progressivism is without influence; far from it. The liberal pedagogical doctrines of nineteenth-century Europeans like Herbart and Froebel and twentieth-century Americans like Dewey have had plenty of effect on the teacher-training programs of British Colleges of Education and subsequently on schools. However, examples of what might be called pure and uninhibited progressivism are rarely found in English schools, apart from picturesque establishments like A. S. Neill's Summerhill. For one thing, the lack of a large body of accepted professional doctrine makes for variety in method in both the primary and nonselective secondary schools.

British educationists talk a lot about the "discovery" method, though the meaning of the term differs with different people; mostly it signifies a general conviction that education is better if students are actively involved in the learning process than if they are passive, that the curriculum should be flexible enough to exploit their developing interests, and that teaching methods should be equally flexible and adaptive. Beyond that, the discovery method, which is only another name for progressive education, means about what any individual teacher takes it to mean. It has been developing in British primary schools, more as an attitude than a codified methodology, since at least 1931, the date of the last major report on primary education before the Plowden Report of 1967. I would except Scotland from this picture. Scottish primary schools have always been more formal and academic than English schools (as well as a year longer, from age five to age twelve), and over the years have been noted for their achievement in basic subjects, even if the English themselves have never paid particular attention to Scottish education. It would be a rash man, however, who would forecast the survival of the Scottish tradition for many more years.

British primary schools depart in one important respect from those of other countries. Most of them are "streamed." Children, that is, are divided into various ability tracks, usually at the beginning of the junior school at age seven or eight. This practice may seem to many Americans as distasteful as the 11-plus, despite the fact that ability grouping is a very common practice in American elementary schools. Streaming has been widely criticized in England and is beginning to decline. It is still practiced, I would guess, in the majority of schools, although nobody can be quite sure about this. Little research has been done on streaming in primary schools, and what has been done in Sweden and elsewhere has not produced results on which one can put much reliance. One major investigation in England in 1964 concluded simply that "There is no clear evidence that children either benefit or suffer from being streamed." [4] But experienced teachers themselves do not seem to be in much doubt about it. Whenever they have been surveyed on the question, as another investigation found in 1964, they are found to be strongly in favor of streaming; [5] and certainly this is the impression I got in all of the primary schools I visited. Parents themselves do not seem to object to streaming, especially working-class parents, who tend to accept, "as an absolute judgment by the experts in the field," [6] the fact that their children are the ones most likely to be assigned to the lower streams. The issue seems to reduce itself in Britain to a political and social argument; educational considerations are really peripheral. Some kind of grouping by ability goes on in most countries in the primary grades, though there is probably no country that divides children into self-contained tracks as early as England does. Whether the British-type streaming is a good or bad thing, socially or educationally, is a question on which no one can offer much more than his own bias; and for American education, the question is presumably not very important, since streaming in the primary grades would be opposed by most parents.

### THE 11-PLUS

I discussed the development of the tripartite, or more accurately the bipartite, system of British secondary schools in Chapter II. With the creation after World War II of large numbers of secondary modern schools, it became necessary to develop some means for deciding how to separate the minority of children who were to go on to grammar schools from the majority who were to go on to the modern schools, a separation that takes place after the six primary years when children are aged between 10-plus and 11-plus. Various means were established by the LEA's, acting usually on their past experience with fewer children. The chief means is an examination at the end of the primary school for which the school prepares as many children as possible. It usually consists of an IQ test, objective tests in English and arithmetic, and perhaps an essay. Other means are often used along with this examination, such as school records and teacher recommendations. The 11-plus is often not a single, one-shot examination, as it is often accused of being even by Britons themselves, but a selection procedure. And because the selection involves the rejection, or at least the "nonselection," of children at a tender age, and affects their prospects in various ways, the 11-plus has always scandalized foreigners. It has been bitterly criticized in England as well, and is now disappearing as secondary schools become comprehensive. People say it is disappearing, but in fact it has only been transferred to the secondary school, where streaming prevails and where the school makes up its streams on about the same kind of basis as before: Either it uses the results of the customary exams and reports from the primary school, or it gives its own exams. What is disappearing is not selection or the 11-plus, but simply the two-level system of secondary schools.

Opposition to the 11-plus takes a great many forms, and it is not easy to distinguish the noneducational content of the argument from that which has truly to do with schools. As one of Britain's leading educational psychologists puts the matter: "It is largely because class-feeling and political bias are so involved that it is so difficult to view the problems of secondary school selection impartially, or to devise any acceptable solution." [7] Perhaps the greatest opposition to the 11-plus comes, quite simply, from middle-class parents whose children fail it, but it also comes from educationists and many others. Although the issue, like that of the comprehensive school, tends to become polarized around the political parties, with the Laborites attacking the 11-plus and the Tories defending it, one finds even Tories citing the psychological effects of failure at 11-plus. From a new Tory pressure group, for example, comes this lament:

> The sense of personal shortcoming and frustration produced in many children and their parents (and indeed their teachers) by this examination is a direct result of the final segregation of children into two types of secondary school, and thus to all intents and purposes, into two types of occupation. . . . the majority of our children are unavoidably branded as educational failures for the rest of their lives, before they have even had a chance to prove themselves. [8]

This seems to me a considerable overstatement of the situation, but it is characteristic of those who oppose the 11-plus. None of the research that has been done would give much support to the idea that failure at the 11-plus induces traumatic effects in parents or children, but the claim is passionately made that it does. Others cite the vast difference in grammar-school provision among the LEA's, which we discussed earlier, as a basic injustice in which the 11-plus plays the key role. One educationist reported in the 1950's that he found the difference to vary from a county that sent 62.3 percent of its children successfully through the 11-plus and on to grammar schools, down to one that sent only 8.7 percent. [9] Others say that streaming in the primary school is a "self-fulfilling prophecy," that those in the upper streams pass the 11-plus and those in the lower streams fail, thus in effect determining the child's future at the time he is first streamed, at seven or eight. Still others say that the tests cannot measure determination or motivation and that they put too much emphasis on a one-shot, do-or-die performance that may come on a day when the child is feeling sick or is otherwise prevented from showing his true ability. And still others say that it has a deadening effect on the primary-school curriculum, though again the available evidence is not very convincing. A survey in 1964 of 105 of Her Majesty's Inspectors of Schools concerned with primary schools on how they thought the schools within their constituencies were affected by the 11-plus showed that seventeen Inspectors thought it had a "marked" effect, fifty-nine that it had "some" effect, and thirty-nine that it had "no" effect. This of course leaves aside the whole question of whether such an examination *should* have a noticeable effect on the schools—one could surely make a case that it should.

Perhaps the most important argument against the 11-plus is the old one about heredity and environment. At one time the 11-plus was regarded as an instrument of social justice. It was a principal means for moving up in the world. It was an equalizer of educational opportunity in which wealth and position gave one no advantage. Now it is regarded by many Britons, particularly liberal sociologists and educationists, as precisely the opposite, as a selection device strongly biased in favor of children from the middle classes and against those from the lower classes. The complete environmentalists hold that intelligence or innate ability is not reflected in social classes at all, but only develops better in the middle and upper classes because the environment is better. "No one," say two authors unhappy about the intelligence testing at 11-plus, "is in a position to state that middle-class children are *inherently* more intelligent than working-class." [10] But most educational psychologists take a more conservative view. One of Britain's best-known psychologists, for example, Cyril Burt, writing in the *Times Educational Supplement* (Sept. 17, 1965), thinks the suspicions of sociologists and others about intelligence tests are unfounded: "The whole area of intelligence testing is said to be a moot point. It may be, but to whom is it moot? Certainly not to any large proportion of psychologists—the general validity of intelligence testing is hardly questioned by those who have really studied it." Another psychologist, after reviewing the whole nature-nurture controversy in some detail, thought that the evidence was

> inescapable that the intelligence test, however imperfect it may be in comparison with the psychologist's concept of the idea, is a good deal *less* affected by cultural and background influences than are tests of attainment. As such, it is an invaluable tool for research purposes, giving a nearer approximation to the level of innate ability than any other measure. The abolition of intelligence tests in educational selection, at any level, will result in a fuller and freer play of environmental factors and thus produce a less socially just result. [11]

I suppose no significant number of people anywhere still accept the rather grim view of human abilities set forth in Plato's *Republic,* though this view for a long time supported the split-secondary-school systems of Europe. The reader may remember that Plato in discussing how life was to be organized in his utopia, has Socrates say to Glaucon:

> "We shall," I said, "address our citizens as follows, 'You are, all of you in this land, brothers. But when God fashioned you, he added gold in the composition of those of you who are qualified to be Rulers (which is why their prestige is greatest); he put silver in the Auxiliaries, and iron and bronze in the farmers and the rest.' "

Few Britons today would want to be so dogmatic as to hold that the 11-plus separates the gold and silver from baser metals, but psychologists as a group continue to give greater weight to genetic endowment than educationists and sociologists, who tend to stress the influence of environment. Most psychologists now seem to agree that, as common observation has undoubtedly suggested to many people, human ability is a product of hereditary factors interacting with environmental factors in some still unknown and possibly changing manner. One of the principal attempts of recent years in Britain to review how much is known about selecting children for secondary schools found:

> The facts seem to be that individual differences in ability between children do exist and although in part they are related to differences in environmental opportunity, they are for the largest part ascribable to genetic factors or to influences so early in life and so deeply implanted as to be not easily modifiable under ordinary circumstances by the time school age is reached. . . . Tests of ability and all forms of educational assessment show that a greater proportion (but not a greater number) of more able children are in middle and upper class social groups than in other social strata. This may be due to a genuine correlation between social class and innate intelligence (intensified certainly by cultural opportunity or the lack of it) brought about by the processes of social promotion through ability and education and by selective mating. There is considerable (though not unchallenged) evidence from studies of twins and siblings brought up in different circumstances that this is so. There is however accumulating evidence that the cultural environment of the home, its value systems and modes of child-rearing play a very substantial part in determining the level of learning ability and capacity to adapt to the school's demands. As the child progresses through school, it also seems that initial differences related to differences in early and continuing cultural opportunity tend to be reinforced.[12]

Still another investigation, one of the largest of its kind to be done anywhere since the Second World War, reaches the same sort of conclusion. It is part of a "longitudinal" study of over 5,000 individuals who have been under observation in one way or another since their birth over twenty years ago. Several volumes have been published on the experiences of this group of 5,000 who are said to be representative of all children of their generation in England and Wales. One volume in 1964 was concerned with their attainments in primary school: It attempted to analyze "the test performance of children coming from different home backgrounds and to relate these to the results of the secondary selection examinations." Looking in particular at the junior years of the primary school, the report said:

> There was a strong association between measured intelligence, school performance and success at the "11+" examination. But the study has shown how, even within the narrow span of years between 8 and 11, measured intelligence responds to environmental factors (including the family environment) and also how, especially in the border zone of 110–120 I.Q., environmental factors affect the allocation of children to grammar and secondary modern schools. . . . Schools with a very good academic record show a continued high success rate even if children receive little parental encouragement; while when there is a poor record, even the children who receive much parental encouragement still do badly. But in the entry to primary schools, a much larger proportion of middle class than working class children attended schools with good records, while at the same time a larger proportion of middle class parents gave strong encouragement to their children. For middle class children, therefore, school and family environment tended to reinforce each other positively, for working class children negatively.[13]

One would have thought that if the environmental factors are of such importance, more consideration would be called for than has been given to what kind of school environment is the most promising for various ability groups; it may well be, for example, that the present system of separate schools affords a better environment for the average and below-average student than the comprehensive school. And surely it is equally possible that the grammar-school environment is better for able students than the comprehensive school.

As to the actual tests that make up the 11-plus, most of the LEA's use nationally standardized intelligence and achievement tests, though some authorities have developed their own. The intelligence tests commonly used attempt to measure the pupil's ability to see relationships in ideas, words, and objects; they ask him to make comparisons, draw analogies, and discriminate among answers not very far apart. He might be asked, for example, to deal with this kind of relationship: "*Water* is to *fish* as *air* is to (rock, bird, earth, wall)"; or he might be asked to underline among several choices the meaning of a word like "dawdle" or to make several different words out of a word like "patronage." I must say that in looking at a number of such 11-plus tests, I was reminded of the criticisms of our own IQ and achievement tests—that they seem to favor the unimaginative response and to penalize the really bright student. To ask a British child to name, for example, two things that a *farm* "always has" and then give him a choice among *animals, buildings, machinery, fields,* and *fences,* is to handicap the bright pupil who can conceive of farms without at least four of the items if he thinks of things like ant farms or worm farms or tree farms. The achievement tests used in the subject of English are sometimes indistinguishable from the IQ tests, again a little like some American tests. There is usually a reading-comprehension section, after which the pupil may be asked to rearrange sentences in which key words have been switched, or to finish sentences with the word that logically fits (again, one suspects that the bright pupils might easily think of several words that fit better than the one the tester had in mind). The arithmetic tests tend to be simply computational, no doubt because of the difficulty of mass scoring of conceptual problems. And there is often a writing test in which the pupil is asked to compose an essay on a theme, with some choice, supplied by the test makers.

How good is the 11-plus? It now seems to be generally accepted in England that the margin of error in the 11-plus is about ten per cent. That is, that as a national average, one child in ten is wrongly sent either to a grammar school or a secondary modern school.[14] It is this minority group that has caused a good deal of the controversy. Perhaps most people regard a ten-per-cent error on a mass test as relatively low, and thus are disposed to quarrel not with the exams themselves used at 11-plus, but with the uses to which the results are put. Even the Fabians are likely to admit that "if children are to be segregated into separate schools, the 11-plus is probably the fairest method of doing so that human wit could devise." [15] I should think the margin of error might turn out to be greater than ten percent if British schools really attempted to do more academically for the 11-plus failures. Whether or not the tests are as reliable as psychologists say they are, the fact of error does exist and English schools in the past have not made adequate provision for correcting it. Over the last ten years there has been great improvement in many modern schools. In some cases their curriculum overlaps that of the grammar school to a degree that weakens the case for comprehensive schools; but it is still true in many other instances that not enough provision is made for children who develop after the 11-plus to do college-preparatory work. Because of this lack of effort to rescue the 11-plus failures, the reputation of the modern schools has suffered. "The belief," as one senior research officer put it as early as 1953, "that the grammar school provides the only avenue to a satisfying career and the only environment in which a child can develop his intellectual powers to the full, needs not only to be attacked by argument but also to be disproved by demonstration." [16] But since 1953 the belief has not been attacked by argument, though it has to a small extent been disproved by demonstration in some schools, especially the private schools. The main answer to the 11-plus problem has been to move toward the abolition of the system of separate secondary schools on the theory that, as one headmaster of a comprehensive school confidently puts it:

> the comprehensive school exists, in my view, to provide equality of oppor-
> tunity for all children, an equality denied them under the tripartite system
> which determines their future—almost irrevocably—on the result of one
> (admittedly fallible) test taken before the eleventh birthday.[17]

Faith abounds in England that the comprehensive school can do these things and more. But the same problems of selection will appear in the first year of the British comprehensive schools and will probably be decided on the usual basis of examinations, school reports, and similar criteria. Selection will still exist, only it will be done under one roof, or perhaps under several roofs that together are called a comprehensive school. It is too early to tell whether the other criticisms associated with the 11-plus—the deep psychological effects of failing it, the lack of educational equality, etc.—will be cured in the comprehensive school, but it is difficult to see how such an administrative rearrangement in itself will meet the problems now encountered in separate secondary schools.

What is abundantly evident under the present system is that England is not schooling a great many of her young people as well or as long as she might. The "pool of ability" is not being tapped as deeply as it should be at any point in the system—primary, secondary, or higher—for a nation in Britain's position. It is the waste of talent rather than the 11-plus or the system of separate schools, it seems to me, that is the problem. That this is so is suggested from the work of the "preparatory schools," the independent primary schools in Britain, if from no other source. It has been known for a long time that the prep schools take in boys from the state schools who have flunked the 11-plus and whose parents withdraw them from the state schools rather than see them go to a secondary modern school. The prep schools then bring them along so that they pass successfully into the private secondary schools and often go on to higher education. I will refer again to this matter in a later section. Here I want only to point to the important role that independent schools play in English primary education, for parents who can afford the fees, and to their record in rescuing 11-plus failures from the state schools. Among the various types of prep schools, almost all of them for boys, the most important group is the 505 schools that make up the Independent Association of Preparatory Schools. Unlike the state schools, the prep schools take boys from age eight to age thirteen, currently about 60,000 of them, and prepare them for entry to the "Public Schools" and other independent secondary institutions. Like our own private schools, they now take in a number of first-generation prep-school boys, many of whom are transfers from the state system. They are generally well staffed but unendowed and wholly dependent upon fees. This means, among other things, that the consumer has a voice and must be satisfied with the product or he leaves; it also means that such schools take pupils over a wide range of ability. On the basis of a recent and comprehensive survey, one prep-school head-master says of the schools in the Independent Association of Preparatory Schools:

> They do not cater only for clever boys; few prep schools have a selective entry. How can they when demand for places is so heavy that vacancies have to be promised for boys still in their cradles? Less than half the IAPS schools have an entrance examination of any kind, and most of those who have one use it not to exclude boys but only to enable them to be placed in the correct forms when they start. It is consequently true that the intelligence range of their boys is very wide and goes surprisingly low. The eventual achievements of over 1,000 of such duller boys was measured in an earlier survey, and this proved beyond question that the prep schools have made the best even of the least promising material.[18]

Recognizing that most of the "least promising material" of the prep schools comes from a different home background from that of pupils in the state primary schools, one still cannot avoid feeling that the record of the prep schools indicates a substantial waste of talent in the state schools.

I discussed the work of the Inspectorate of Schools in Chapter II. The name is not entirely descriptive, since the functions of inspectors are now much broader than the inspecting of schools; but inspection remains important, and the reports that are prepared after an inspection of a school are one of the best means—and one of the most neglected by visitors—of acquainting oneself with the work of English schools. For a further insight into how the Inspectorate itself regards English primary schools, one might turn to a report prepared in 1965 for the Plowden Committee. Early in its deliberations on the state of primary education, the Committee became conscious of the wide range in quality among British primary schools, and wanted some further idea of how they were distributed qualitatively across England. One of the best sources, probably the only source, of such information was the Inspectorate, which undertook to survey the views of its own members concerned with primary schools. It asked them all to evaluate the schools in their own jurisdiction and to put each of them in one of nine categories, number one being the highest and nine the lowest. Over 20,000 state primary schools, practically all there are in England and Wales, were evaluated in this way. In the interests of simplicity, let me reduce the nine categories to four broad ones, recognizing that assessments of this kind can be no more than suggestive:

*First group:* Schools that were among the best in the inspectors' experience—both schools that were outstanding in general and those that were good schools with some outstanding features. The inspectors thought that about ten percent of British primary schools could be so categorized.

*Second group:* Schools in a wide middle band of quality—average institutions doing a reasonable job but without much to distinguish them. About forty percent were put into this category.

*Third group:* Schools somewhat below average but a heterogeneous group: some of fair quality, many with "the seeds of growth in them," some with good and bad features. The inspectors put another forty percent of the schools in this category.

*Fourth group:* Schools definitely poor, out of touch, and in need of reform. About five percent were put in this category.

A few schools were not classifiable for one reason or another. This evaluation of British primary schools in 1965 will seem pretty conservative to the admirers of these schools, and their name is legion; but it is surely as authoritative and knowledgeable a survey as any country could make, much more so than would be possible in the United States. What the survey seems to say is that in the opinion of highly experienced people whose careers have been in teaching in and visiting primary schools in Britain, something between eighty-five and ninety percent of such schools are without any particular distinction (in one sense, of course, "distinguished" work by ten percent of any kind of school is a good showing), and that perhaps a third of the rest of them are more or less unsatisfactory. In the original categories, almost a quarter of the schools were put into a rank for "good schools in most respects but without any special distinction"; and another quarter or more were put into a rank for "decent schools" without enough merit to be called good. This interesting evaluation of British primary schools, bringing together the matured judgment of a great many specialists in the field, is not any sort of comparative measurement but it deserves to be seriously considered by anyone interested in British and American education.

### THE PLOWDEN REPORT

This important report from the Central Advisory Council for Education was originally scheduled for publication in the summer of 1966, but was delayed for various reasons and did not appear until early 1967, too late for summary and discussion in these pages. However, its main findings and conclusions are pretty well known to informed people in England. It appears that the Plowden Report will recommend that transfer to the secondary school be made at age twelve instead of eleven, thus extending the "junior" or "middle" portion of primary education by one year. The transfer age was one of the most important of the problems with which the Plowden Committee was to deal, for the LEA's had been put into the absurd position by the Labor government of having to draw up plans for going comprehensive before the government's own Central Advisory Council had dealt with the age of transfer. Presumably those LEA's that made plans for continuing the transfer at eleven, or delaying it to thirteen, will be allowed to proceed in spite of the Plowden recommendation, which is not to be an arbitrary recommendation but a general one within which a good deal of flexibility will necessarily be allowed.

On streaming in the primary school, it appears that the report will take a middle ground. Those on the Plowden Committee who disliked streaming argued passionately against it on social grounds, but the available research, as we have noted, does not allow a clearcut answer to the question of whether streaming is a successful device in primary schools or not. Still, my guess is that streaming will slowly evolve in British schools into something like the ability grouping practiced in American schools. The report apparently will be something of a vote of confidence in the general quality of primary education in England: The Committee itself was mildly progressive in outlook, fond of the "discovery" method, like the "new math" and other recent developments in the curriculum such as a second foreign language; but felt strongly that the teaching of English, particularly oral English, left a good deal to be desired.

But all this is speculation, though I hope informed speculation. This report will complement others from the same body, and taken together they now cover the full range of the state schools in England.

## A RECENT STUDY OF AMERICAN AND
## ENGLISH PRIMARY-SCHOOL PUPILS

As a final part of our discussion of English primary education, we should take note of a recent comparative study, sharply limited but still more extensive than any that has been done before, of the academic achievements of elementary-school children in the United States and the United Kingdom. The study was done between 1963 and 1965 by the Research Foundation of the University of Toledo under a grant from the United States Office of Education.[19] Using a number of matched communities in both countries, the investigators tested a total of 2,659 American children of average and high ability in grades one through six, in both public and private institutions, and 1,562 British children of average and high ability in the same grades. Children of low ability were not tested except in grades one and two. Two series of tests were administered at different points during the school year; both were American, standardized, machine-scored tests covering general intelligence and achievement in basic subjects. Let me summarize the findings as they are given in the report:

1. *Reading vocabulary:* The British children had higher vocabulary test scores for most of the six grades, but by the end of the sixth year were not significantly ahead of American children.

2. *Reading comprehension:* British children began better but were overtaken by American children, who stayed even with them through grade five, then began to pass them slightly. In the private schools, British high-ability pupils were better than American, while American pupils of average ability were slightly better than British.

3. *Arithmetic reasoning:* No significant difference beween the two countries by the end of the testing period, the sixth grade.

4. *Arithmetic fundamentals:* British pupils began better than American and retained their lead throughout the tests.

5. *Mechanics of English:* American public-school pupils were "noticeably" better by the end than British. In the private schools, the British pupils of high ability did better than their American counterparts.

6. *Spelling:* The British began much better, but their lead gradually decreased and they ended up only slightly ahead of Americans.

From their data, the investigators concluded that:

1. British pupils did better in almost all subjects for the first four grades, suggesting to the researchers that "Pupils can learn at an earlier age than presently provided for in most United States educational systems." I don't suppose this will be news to most parents and a lot of teachers, but it might be to the remaining adherents of the old time "readiness" faith; whether it will affect their devotion to the idea is more doubtful.

2. American children were doing about the same level of work as British in grades five and six, suggesting a relative decline in the British schools.

3. Overall, British children were best in arithmetic fundamentals and American in English usage, suggesting the different emphases of the schools. It might also suggest a need to look at what the American testers thought British children should know about "English usage."

4. American children scored relatively higher on American tests, and British on British tests. However, this unsurprising conclusion did not prevent the testers from sticking with American tests for the major part of the project for both groups of children; British tests were used only as a check.

I find this project extremely difficult to evaluate. Judging only by my own observation, I find some of the conclusions surprising—I would, for example, have expected high-ability children in British schools to have done consistently better than high-ability groups in American schools. Other conclusions are not very surprising. But I would hope that American readers would regard the whole project with caution and that those sufficiently interested would read the official report with great care. The sample of pupils is very small indeed upon which to base such confident conclusions about many millions of children in both countries. I suppose one always wishes a project like this had taken other things into account.

I wish this one could have encompassed more of what the professionals call "variables" so that at least some plausible reasons for the findings could have been suggested. I wish, for instance, that they had factored into their research the scores of the various British groups that were in streamed classes. I wish they had included data on the training and backgrounds of the teachers involved. I wish they had matched their communities more closely than they did and in a greater number of important matters like comparative income. They might have included some comparative occupational data on the parents involved, especially since both British and American educationists are fond of collecting such information. I wish they had included in their analysis the amount of money spent per head in the schools involved in the investigation.

And of course I particularly wish they had not based their conclusions on American standardized and machine-scored tests given to British children. Although the report does not make the matter as clear as it might, the fact is that on the British tests, British children did better than their American counterparts in 114 comparisons; the American children did better in eight comparisons and tied the British in two. Yet this situation did not seem to suggest to the investigators the need for modifying the design of the project. The substantial differences between the results recorded with American tests, which the study used for its conclusions, and the results recorded with British tests would seem to call into question the conclusions of the whole study. But even if these conclusions are valid, the investigators might well have asked themselves why American children did not do a great deal better than English children; as it is, they seem reassured and comforted by the thought that American children—the best housed, clothed, fed, and looked after in the world, with far more money spent on their education than anywhere else on earth—held their own with British children on American standardized tests! The plague of educational research of this kind is the failure to take into account enough variables to illuminate the reasons for the findings. This project, although it is the most ambitious comparison we have of elementary pupils in the two countries, only suggests the need for a better one. There is presently going forward another large-scale comparative study, this time of the achievements in basic subjects of British and American high-school students. One hopes that this study is better conceived and will be better executed than the one of elementary school pupils.

## Nonselective Secondary Schools

About two-thirds of the children in British secondary schools are in what might best be called nonselective institutions. And two-thirds or more of this group are in secondary modern schools, the rest being in comprehensive, technical, or special institutions. This pattern of distribution will steadily change as Britain goes comprehensive, so that in another ten or fifteen years most students will probably be in comprehensive schools. But the general pattern of study will presumably be little affected by the change. Most students, that is, will be doing about the same thing in school as they now do, with about the same kind of staff, although there will be a further movement toward vocational and life-adjustment education as the school-leaving age goes up. Hence, a description of the main elements of the nonselective schools will remain applicable, I should guess, to the range of students involved no matter how schools are reorganized.

Perhaps the first fact that should be noted quite frankly about the secondary modern schools is that many of them are indifferent educational establishments, both because they are nonselective schools and because they have been inadequately supported (there is often a casual relationship between the two facts). If we were to distribute Britain's nearly 4,000 modern schools along a qualitative curve, the curve would be skewed toward the low side on most criteria of educational quality. But one needs to keep the condition of the modern schools in perspective. They are still a new type of school as schools go, much newer than the American comprehensive school. Many did not begin in new surroundings, but instead started life in broken-down "three-deckers," old elementary schools that sometimes go back to the nineteenth century when a three-way division of children by age and sex was reflected in three-story structures. And many of the modern schools are still staffed heavily with people from the old senior elementary departments of three-decker schools. Combine these conditions with, say, a minimum budget and a student body made up of whatever students did not pass the 11-plus and go to selective schools, and any school might have a pretty grim start. These limitations have now been overcome or mitigated in a great many places; and not all the modern schools by any means started this way. Some modern schools are splendidly housed, far better than a great many grammar schools, and have experienced headmasters and loyal staffs and students. One should also remember that poor facilities and low budgets are not restricted to modern schools. Probably all British schools suffer from the same basic problem of insufficient money. But the main fact is that the modern schools as a group, the largest group in the secondary-school system, are at the bottom in most things, not least in public esteem. They therefore go about their work and they struggle for improvement under a certain psychological handicap.

The second fact about the modern schools is that they represent a tremendous variety of programs and practices. It is not possible to delineate the education offered in the modern schools in the way one can for primary or grammar schools; one cannot describe the "standard program" in the way that many European countries with a centrally stipulated curriculum can. The modern schools were meant to have much greater freedom in what they did and how they did it than the selective schools. Basic policy about curriculum and other matters was made by the headmaster of the school together with the school's governing body. Secondary schools in Britain generally have a body of "governors" similar to the "managers" of primary schools; they often take part in the hiring of staff and take a varying role in the establishment of policy, some of them being figureheads and some being active partners with the headmaster. The modern schools were not supposed to worry about external examinations, while the selective schools had to keep them constantly in the foreground. In the early days of the modern schools nobody was quite sure what their proper role was, beyond their vague assignment to create an educational program appropriate to the kind of children who in the past had not stayed in school so long. The modern schools therefore tended to develop according to the talents of their staffs. They emphasized certain subjects or activities for which teachers were at hand, and ignored others. Even today, one finds some modern schools offering no work, for instance, in physics or chemistry, though they may have developed general science courses to fit their staff and students. Some will offer no work in foreign languages but may have developed other academic or non-academic activities that have come to mean a lot in those schools. In spite of this initial freedom to experiment and to exploit local advantages, the modern schools soon began to feel pressures for establishing programs leading to the external examinations. Such programs have had a stabilizing, though many people would say a deleterious, effect on the general curriculum of these schools.

The main concern of the modern schools has been with the education of average and below-average children for the four years between the 11-plus separation and the leaving age of fifteen. Beyond this they have now developed a fair range of work for five-year, "fifth-form" students who want to prepare for the lower-level exams of the General Certificate of Education, and some have developed sixth-form work beyond that. The modern-school curriculum for the first three years usually involves work in academic subjects for about two-thirds of the students' time and work in nonacademic subjects for the rest. More subjects are studied by all students than in American schools, but electives are much less in evidence. Even more important, courses are planned on a sequential, multiyear basis. Division of students by ability into tracks is standard practice, the number of tracks depending on the size of the school but usually being at least three. Here is a weekly timetable of periods (not hours) for the third year of work in a modern school; the school has three tracks, and this timetable, which varies little from the others, is for the middle track:

| SUBJECT | PERIODS PER WEEK |
|---|---|
| English | 5 |
| Library | 1 |
| French | 5 |
| History | 2 |
| Geography | 2 |
| Mathematics | 5 |
| General Science | 2 |
| Biology | 2 |
| Woodwork | 2 |
| Metalwork | 2 |
| Technical Drawing | 2 |
| Religious Instruction | 1 |
| Music | 2 |
| Art | 2 |
| Craft | 2 |
| Physical Education | 1 |
| Games | 2 |
| | 40 |

Most modern schools list sixteen or seventeen such subjects, but the subjects are by no means all taught by different or by specialist teachers. Nor are they all necessarily studied because they are in the timetable. Departures from the published timetable, and adaptations of it to the abilities of the staff or to the exigencies of local conditions, are very frequent. But students will study at least ten or eleven subjects during an average week, several of them with the same teachers. In the fourth year, the number of subjects declines a little and some elective work is introduced; but two-thirds of the time will continue to be in English, mathematics, history, geography, science, and possibly a foreign language. Before the start of the fifth year in a modern school, something between fifty and ninety percent of the students, depending on a great many factors, will leave. Those that remain will begin to study for one or another of the national examinations, thus using established examination syllabuses. The number of subjects will therefore be reduced again, but will still be broader than the typical American curriculum. A minority of the modern schools now go beyond the fifth year and have introduced a few sixth-form studies leading to the advanced-level exams of the General Certificate of Education; but such studies, requiring highly trained teachers, are a small and difficult operation in modern schools. Naturally, the examination results of the modern schools do not compare with those of the selective schools, but they have been rising steadily in recent years.

Students leaving the modern schools often obtain some national qualification other than the GCE, chiefly secretarial or vocational, and many others go into apprenticeships. There is very little psychology-based "guidance" in the British nonselective schools such as one finds in American schools, and practically no American-type "guidance counselors." But a great deal of guiding is done by teachers as well as by "careers" specialists in the schools. There is also a Youth Employment Service financed mostly by the Ministry of Labor and operated in all of the counties and boroughs by the Ministry or by local government. London, for example, operates about twenty Youth Employment Service bureaus, in each of which three or four professional staff people spend most of their time visiting schools and talking with students about jobs and career possibilities. If a student leaves school before eighteen, he may but is not compelled to use the Youth Employment Service to help in getting a job or a replacement for a job he has left. In general, neither career nor personal guidance is nearly as well developed in the nonselective schools of Britain as in the United States, but the inevitable influence of American practices is being felt and postgraduate study is now available in some British Institutes and Departments of Education in guidance work. I for one am not at all sure, looking at our own training programs for "guidance counselors," that this movement in England will turn out to be an unalloyed benefit.

What standards of work are maintained in the modern schools? Of course, one can reach no conclusions from a mere listing of subject titles and periods of study, any more than one can with American schools—as our own experience amply suggests, almost anything can pass under the name of "English" or "History" or "General Science" and assuredly under "Arts and Crafts." What is important is the substance of the course and the effectiveness with which it is taught. On both counts, I think it true to say that the doctrines of American progressivism have had a natural appeal for the modern schools. One British educationist, chronicling the development of the modern school, refers to the influence on them of Rousseau, Dewey and Montessori, and adds:

> The importance of the progressive movement on the curriculum of the Modern school must not be underestimated. Untrammelled by the requirements of external examinations; officially encouraged to experiment and find its own way; the Modern school was particularly open to the influence of progressive ideas. These had so many manifestations, were represented by so many different associations, and sometimes appeared to be united only by their own unorthodoxy, that it is difficult to categorize in simple terms their most prominent concepts. Without doing an injustice to the range of notions represented, it is fair to say that most of the "progressives" were of a radical social and political persuasion, and saw the future of education and society as requiring much less competition and more co-operation, attempting to place the child, instead of the curriculum or the subject, in the center of the educational stage and critical of "tradition." Ideas such as these were embodied or implied in much of the writing of

educational thinkers, and obtained a firm hold on many of those concerned with the training of teachers in colleges and universities.[20]

How extensive the effects of progressivism and its first cousin, life-adjustment education, have been on the standards of the modern schools is impossible to say, but one suspects they have been considerable. Since most modern-school students do not yet take a national examination before leaving school, one has no systematic or external means by which to judge these schools. One can gather any number of pro and con assessments of their overall quality from people who have taught in them for many years, though the negative comments would be the more frequent. Here is a rather embittered comment, from a modern-school teacher commenting on his own institution:

> The crucial aspect of this Secondary Modern School is the fact that the standard of elementary literacy is so low, that so many of the boys show little interest in their work, and that consequently few of them make significant progress whilst they are here, whether they can actually read and write or not. Surely, in a school less than five years old, beautifully designed, and elaborately equipped and furnished, this is a highly unsatisfactory state of affairs.[21]

If one were to judge by the paper qualifications of the typical modern-school staff, one's assessment would not be high. A small minority of staff members, perhaps ten percent, have a university degree. The rest are people with one, two, or three years of training in a teachers college, a few with a fourth year taken later in their teaching careers. As I will discuss in Chapter V, subject-matter training in the Colleges of Education may represent about half of the present three-year course. Thus those staff members of the modern schools who have been trained since 1960, the start of the three-year course, will probably have studied one or two academic subjects for one or two years in the sixth form of their own secondary school and will then have spent another year, or a year and a half, in one of the same subjects, though possibly in a different one, at a College of Education. In short, most members of a modern-school staff will have formal training in the subjects they teach that may be qualitatively somewhat below, and quantitatively is well below, that of their American counterparts.

"Misassignment" is not a problem the English seem to worry much about in the modern schools. At least they take a much more liberal view of what qualifies a teacher to teach a given subject than we do. The assignment of teachers in American schools to subjects for which they have no visible qualifications is a very old problem, from which our rigid state certification laws have not saved us. Certification standards are apt to be thick on the pedagogical side and thin on the academic side, and the requirements of individual institutions are frequently even more lopsided, but even within the relatively low standards that prevail for the teaching of academic subjects, misassignment is common.

In Britain misassignment is not a term in ordinary use. The certificate a teacher gets from an Institute of Education on the completion of training in one of the Institute's constituent Colleges carries very little information, if any, about the teacher's course of study. Headmasters, whether they have such information or not, are not bound by any regulations to assign teachers to subjects in which they have done formal study. A teacher's license in England is a sort of general qualification so far as the government is concerned. England differs sharply in this important matter from both Scotland and Northern Ireland, where the status of "qualified teacher" means, for secondary teachers, qualification in one or two stipulated subjects. Modern-school teachers in England normally teach at least two subjects, and many teach more. As usual, almost any member of the staff may find himself teaching the universal subjects like English, History, or Religious Knowledge, if timetable considerations make it necessary. In 1962 the Institute of Education at the University of Birmingham sent a questionnaire to its probationary teachers; that is, to the people graduated from its constituent Colleges the year before and who were then in their first year of teaching. Of those that responded, one-third of the modern-school teachers indicated that they were teaching subjects for which they were not qualified. Not only that, but half of the same teachers said that syllabuses for the courses they were to teach were not even available to them before the start of classes.[22] I would hazard the guess that this unfortunate state of things could be duplicated in a great many of the modern schools.

In defense of "misassignment," some headmasters would probably say that modern-school teachers need more humanity than knowledge; and others would say that formal training is not the only or perhaps even the best way to qualify for teaching a subject in the modern schools. Without commenting on the first of these positions, I should think in regard to the second that the criterion of formal preparation would be the only one available for young teachers fresh from the Colleges. For older teachers, some of whom might well be qualified by private study to teach certain subjects for which they are not trained, one can only rely in England on the judgment of the headmaster, who might be influenced by a number of extraneous considerations. In a word, misassignment in the American sense of the term is very frequent in the secondary modern schools and, I should think, could not help but have the effect of lowering the standards of these schools. Standards do not exist in a vacuum and are not handed down from the heavens on tablets of stone; they exist in relation to something else, in relation to the standards of some other school or type of school, or perhaps merely in relation to one's expectations arrived at after taking into consideration the conditions under which a given school operates. The modern schools are exceedingly difficult to compare to American high schools. Perhaps such unlike institutions should not be compared. Perhaps we should simply regard the modern schools as a major type of institution some aspects of which offer interesting contrasts to American practices.

"Nonselective" schools are not limited to the secondary moderns. They include both comprehensive schools, which represent the shape of things to come in Britain, and technical schools, which are a disappearing species. As yet there are very few genuine comprehensive schools in Britain, and there cannot be many as long as the upper range of students are sent to the selective schools. With the possible exception of Anglesey, an island off North Wales, no area of Britain is served with an American-type neighborhood secondary school that takes practically all students from that neighborhood. A few places such as Coventry, Leicestershire, the West Riding of Yorkshire, and London have had modified comprehensive schools for many years, and it is on the basis of their experience that many other local authorities are developing their own plans. London was a pioneer among the LEA's in creating comprehensives after World War II. Its Labor-controlled education committee pressed for them as a measure of social justice, has spent a great deal of money on them, and hypersensitively rebuffs any suggestion from Britons that these schools might be less than outstanding successes.

The variation among even the relatively few comprehensive schools that now exist is such that one cannot really speak of a typical British comprehensive school. As in the modern schools, students in the comprehensives are divided into ability tracks, and the subjects studied for the first three years are roughly the same for all tracks. There are very few electives. The bulk of the work is in five or six academic subjects and the rest in three or four subjects like needlework, crafts, art, and music. A foreign language, usually French, may be mandatory for all students but in any case will be taken by at least half. Special efforts are made to overcome the problems of the very large school by adoption of one or another kind of "house" system, similar to but much more organized and important than our "home-room" system. Conversely, size allows some of the comprehensives to offer a wider range of work than either secondary modern or grammar schools can offer; a big London comprehensive, for example, might carry enough students into its fifth form to permit study for thirty different subjects at the lower level of the GCE, though it cannot offer as wide a variety for its sixth form as can a grammar school. Teachers in the comprehensives tend to be better qualified than those in the modern schools; indeed they must be if the fifth and sixth forms are to be successful. Again, the question of what standards are achieved in the comprehensive schools is not answerable in any exact way until one specifies what the schools are being measured against. These schools are not yet comparable to American schools because they do not get an adequate representation of high-ability students. Under the Labor government's circular to the LEA's in 1965, local authorities can organize their comprehensive schools in at least six different ways, according to local conditions and desires; the one stipulation that must be met is that they reorganize their secondary schools to make them nonselective. Thus the future of the British comprehensive school promises to continue to be one of great variety.

Of the third arm of Britain's "tripartite" system of secondary schools, the technical schools, there is not much to be said. Full-time technical schools at the secondary level did not develop in the way hoped for after the 1944 Act. Too many LEA's could not afford to establish separate technical schools, and so a certain amount of craft work was taken up by the grammar schools and a good deal of it by the modern schools. Today only about three percent of secondary students are in technical schools. Hence it is really a fiction to speak of a "tripartite" system, for the basic division of British schools into grammar and modern schools makes it a bipartite system. Such technical schools as there are offer a combination of academic and pre-industrial study. The emphasis, that is, is less on vocational training narrowly conceived than on basic academic work together with a concentration on the technical and scientific principles of woodwork and metalwork and other skills. These schools, of course, will become part of comprehensive schools in the future, as will the modern schools.

Beyond the secondary schools, however, technical education is an extremely broad and complex field in Britain. Almost every English town of any size has some kind of establishment for "further education," an institution for full- or part-time post-secondary study, mostly in technical subjects. This bewildering multiplicity of schools below the university level includes National Colleges, Regional Colleges, Area Colleges, Local Colleges, Art Establishments, Agricultural Colleges, and Farm Institutes, altogether enrolling upward of 800,000 persons in full- or part-time study, most of them working toward one or another of a large number of industrially recognized diplomas or certificates. It is a vast field that goes some distance to compensate for the early departure from school of many English students. Qualitatively a good deal of further education would be comparable, at least to British educationists, to much of American higher education. Although some commentators claim that technical education has been neglected, and some even blame the classical tradition and the public schools for this neglect,[23] most people would find it an extremely well developed, if somewhat uncoordinated, field. A national committee reviewing the whole field in 1959 said that to our sorrow, there is hardly a single generalization that can be made about further education in England that does not require an array of reservations and exceptions before it is accurate. In part, this is because of the inevitable variety in the needs that have to be met. In the main, however, it is due to the fact that further education has grown up empirically, in response to one special need or demand after another. . . .

But the committee found much to praise in the existing system, not least its function of rescuing students who dropped out of school too early:

. . . one of the strongest points of the further education system in England—and one that has frequently been admired by visitors from other countries—is that it never closes the door or refuses a second chance to anyone who has the persistence to continue and the ability to succeed.[24]

In the field of adult education, incidentally, England's LEA's also support no fewer than 8,000 "Evening Institutes," enrolling well over a million persons in a wide range of courses that include both academic and avocational subjects.

The system of industrial and craft apprenticeships is much broader in Britain than in the United States and has much to do with the nature of technical education. In the United States the apprenticeship system is fast disappearing except in the construction industry and has little influence on schools. In Britain nearly forty percent of the boys that leave school at the legal age of fifteen go into apprenticeships, where many of them are given "day release" by their employers to attend a technical college for a day a week.[25] Here they get some further general education to follow up on their secondary-school study and technical training that often reaches a level comparable with that of a good many American junior colleges whose students are several years older. But the apprenticeship system has failed badly to keep abreast of the needs of a modern nation, either in industry or education. Most English apprenticeships are of four or five years' duration and must be completed by the age of twenty-one, meaning that they must be started between fifteen and seventeen. The system thereby forces, so to speak, many students to leave school earlier than otherwise might be the case and closes the door to apprentice training for students that remain in school into the fifth and sixth forms. Britain, I think, is alone in maintaining this medieval and self-defeating tradition.

To try to modernize the apprenticeship system and get many more people into British industry who are both more skilled and more educated, Parliament passed an Industrial Training Act that came into force in 1964. Briefly, it is aimed at compelling an entire industry to contribute to the training of people for that industry. Large companies can meet their obligation under this Act by carrying a certain number of apprentices in an organized program of training including day release; and small companies (eighty percent of British companies employ fewer than two hundred persons) that cannot afford apprentices contribute to a financial pool in relation to the number of their employees. This attempt to "rationalize" the further training of students who leave school at the legal age reflects the British feeling that such training has become the business of the whole community and can no longer be left to the uncertain arrangements of individual companies or industries. The same problem is seen in France, where apprenticeships and technical education are well-developed operations but cannot keep pace with the demands of modern industry. Even in Germany, which I suppose has the most complete system of technical training in Europe, so large that it really must be considered part of the educational system, the appetite of industry for skilled people cannot be met.

## VOCATIONAL AND LIFE-ADJUSTMENT EDUCATION IN BRITAIN

I have made a number of references in earlier pages to the chief problem that now seems to confront Britain and most of the European countries in secondary education: how to educate the average and below-average student; that is to say the mass of students, as the school-leaving age goes up. On the one hand the percentage of English boys that go into apprenticeships on leaving school is high at forty percent; on the other hand it only means that the majority, sixty per cent (for girls it is ninety-five percent) do not get apprenticeships and are not equipped for much of anything but unskilled labor. On the one hand it is true that modern industry needs many more well-trained and well-educated people than ever before; on the other hand it is also true that a very great many jobs in modern industry do not require a high level of training or intelligence and can be learned in a few weeks. On the one hand it is true that Britain has virtually full employment, taking the nation as a whole before the economic squeeze of 1966–67, and a great unmet demand for labor; on the other hand it is true that unemployment is a serious problem in some areas of Britain, especially among those leaving school at fifteen but substantial also among adult men with outmoded skills. On the one hand there is a very large body of opinion in Britain in support of vocational and life-adjustment training for the majority of secondary students; on the other hand there is at least a small body of opinion in favor of using the additional school time that will follow the raising of the leaving age to extend the academic education of all students.

The one thing that is perfectly clear in Britain and Europe is that most of the advanced nations are now facing the same stubborn problem we faced in American education when we universalized upper secondary education; and they are about as ready to meet the problem as we were. They are, in fact, even less ready in that both schoolmen and educational planners, as well as politicians and the general public, are conditioned in their approach to the problem by the traditions of the selective secondary schools. They seem to accept without much question the idea that only a minority of children are capable of sustaining academic study through the secondary school. There is, I am sorry to report, very little sentiment indeed in Britain or Europe for extending the basic academic education of all or most children through the upper secondary grades; the assumption everywhere seems to be that a nonacademic education, or rather some unspecified blend of academic-vocational-adjustment study, is the only feasible one after age fourteen or fifteen for students below the top thirty percent or so of the age group. But a fundamental conflict is thus created because nobody has yet figured out what this nonacademic education could or should be. There is only the assertion that academic work is too theoretical or abstract or uninteresting or useless for such students and that their schooling therefore should be brought closer to "life." The head of the Institute of Education at the University of London, writing in 1965 about the need for relating the curriculum to the society that such students see around them, said:

> This is the world into which they are going. Here we are failing almost entirely to develop any kind of critical thinking that will stand these young people in good stead. There are experiments in some schools, often showing enterprise and imagination. But by and large we have not thought this problem out, and we have not deliberately trained teachers to do it. If the higher school-leaving age comes into effect before we have done so the result will be not merely wasteful, but disastrous.[26]

The Schools Council, which has decided to give a high priority to the question of how to educate the mass of English children when the leaving age goes up, said in its final annual report that

> one of the most pressing needs [is] a reappraisal of what is offered the young school leaver under the general heading of the humanities (traditionally, English literature, history, geography, and religious instruction, but also topics from the newer fields of economics, psychology, sociology and anthropology). There is wide agreement that the study of Man and of human society is of the first importance in the education of the older secondary school pupils. There is equally considerable uncertainty both about content and treatment.[27]

In brief, England is in the position of having decided to raise the school leaving age to sixteen in 1971 without knowing to what purposes to turn the additional time.

Most British educationists and sociologists begin their discussion of the problem by referring to "the 75 per cent of adolescents for whom a grammar school curriculum is not suitable";[28] or with the assumption that "whatever sort of secondary schools we have, they will be forced to offer a greater variety of courses, particularly technical courses, for children who cannot or will not follow the traditional academic curriculum"; [29] or with an admonition like this one from a secondary-modern-school teacher, whose blinkered view of the purposes of education seems indistinguishable from that of the typical old-line progressive in the United States:

> There seems to be so little relationship between what is taught here [a secondary modern school] and between the work the boys will eventually do and their individual cultural backgrounds . . . there is little taught them that has any bearing on the world they know, of "pop" mass-produced culture, of "bingo" and the football pools and betting shops, of tobacco and alcohol, of sex and "X" certificate films, and of the "hidden persauders." This is often the world they live in.[30]

To this kind of approach there is a very occasional counter in England, such as this one from another secondary modern teacher:

> Why should the future shopgirl or hairdresser not know some French or biology? Why should the future boilermaker or dustman be incapable of any sort of appreciation of good literature? This kind of cultural apartheid, which seems still to underlie the English attitude to education, amazes me, living as I do in Wales, where a quarryman will quite happily converse with a university professor about almost any subject under the sun, usually with benefit to both. I am convinced that for too long we have underestimated these children (and thus encouraged them to underestimate themselves), and in underestimating them we have undereducated them. One is left with an appalling sense of waste.[31]

The unfortunate consensus seems to be that, while no one is sure of what can be done with the average and below-average student, everyone is sure of what cannot be done, and that is to give them an academic education.

The principal statement of this familiar idea in recent years has been in the form of a volume with the provocative title *Half Our Future*, otherwise known as the Newsom Report.[32] It makes enlightening, sometimes moving, but on the whole unhappy reading to anyone who remembers with regret the progressive and life-adjustment movements in American education. The report was produced by the Central Advisory Council for Education, whose chairman, Sir John Newsom, was formerly the chief educational administrator in one of England's liveliest education authorities, Hertfordshire. This document merits some attention because of its influence on educational thought in Britain. The Newsom Committee was charged in 1961 by a Tory Minister of Education to investigate and report on "the education of pupils aged 13 to 16 of average and less than average ability"; with, that is, the education of most of the children in the secondary modern schools—hence the name "Half Our Future."

Since the publication of the report, the "Newsom children" has become a common term and refers to rather more than half of the secondary-school population. The Newsom children are going to present the main problem when the school-leaving age goes up; indeed they are the reason for the decision to raise it.

It would probably be an unfortunate beginning for any report to divide English children arbitrarily into a lower and an upper half and then address itself to the education of the lower half on the *a priori* proposition that such education should be fundamentally different. Yet this is the beginning of the Newsom Report. The main thesis quickly becomes clear: that for the lower half of the school population, educational programs in British schools should be developed that are different not only in degree but in kind from those considered appropriate for the upper half. Because of the presumed natural limitations of the Newsom children, they cannot be expected to deal with abstractions or to respond very well to a study of the best that has been thought and said in man's long struggle for knowledge and understanding. These children must have, the report makes clear, a good deal of vocational training and beyond that must turn their attention to what, for lack of a better name, might be called aspects of modern living. Above all, their schooling must be brought close to the everyday life they see around them.

The Newsom Report develops across three hundred pages this highly determinist-environmentalist-behaviorist view of education for the children that represent half of Britain's future. It rejects out of hand the idea that an education concentrated in the basic subjects can be made to mean anything for the lower half:

> One point cannot be made too soon or too strongly. An exclusive diet of the "Three R's" just does not work. Boys and girls brought up in this way disappoint their teachers by failing at the end to have acquired the equivalent of even one R.

The report speaks, sometimes in the language of American Educanto, about "providing experiences" of a different nature for these children, about meeting their "felt personal needs," about beginning "where our boys and girls are," and about the "personal development and social competence of the pupil." The report suggests that four criteria be applied to the instructional program for the lower half: It should be practical, realistic, and vocational, and should have a large element of free choice. The committee apparently did not ask itself if, according to these criteria, there were any activities in which human beings engage, including the world's oldest profession, that could be excluded from schools. By way of commendatory examples, the report cites courses in "Housecraft," "Retail Studies," "Photography," "Rural Studies," and "Film-Making" as subjects offering "creative and civilising experiences." We are told that "rewarding courses may be built around" subjects like "gardening or dressmaking or model building and sailing . . . [or] the wider aspects of home making and marriage." We are told that there "is much scope for valuable work which schools can undertake with their older pupils, both in consumer studies and in examining the influences extended by newspapers, magazines, comics, advertisement hoardings, films, and television." We are told that "one line of advance lies in courses built round broad themes of home making, to include not only material and practical provision but the whole field of personal relations in courtship, in marriage, and within the family—boy and girl friend, husband and wife, parents and children, young and old." The report goes on to say that

> partnership in marriage, whether in household chores or in bringing up the children, is an important concept for our society. We note with interest the ingenuity of one boys' school which, lacking the focus a housecraft department might provide for studies of the family, has introduced, for pupils in their final year, a series of discussions on personal relations; many of these topics relate to family life, and are largely treated from the standpoint of the boy, thirty years on, married and with a son much resembling himself as he now is [something the student might find, after all, a pretty grim prospect]. Many of the adolescent difficulties of the boys themselves are illuminated by discussion of the problems of these hypothetical families—the responsibilities of parents to children; pocket money; staying out late; undesirable friendships; social loyalties.

One could go on at great length reviewing the kinds of study or activity the Newsom Report recommends for the lower half of the school population. But this perhaps suffices to indicate the wholly pragmatic means by which the wholly utilitarian ends of the report are to be realized. What the ideology of the report ultimately comes to is simply this: Any kind of activity that a school can discover or invent that will engage the interests of the Newsom children is what the Newsom children in that school should have. The object in view is not to develop whatever intellectual capacity students have through systematic education in basic subjects, in the hope of equipping them with the inner resources with which to come to terms with life and perhaps to improve both themselves and their environment. Instead, as in similar reports in past years in the United States, the object is to satisfy as many of their passing interests as possible in whatever ways are possible, in the hope of adjusting them to society as it is, their condition as it is, and the labor market as it temporarily is.

The report does not suggest the abandonment of work in the fundamental subjects. In fact it supports the idea of some work in these subjects for everybody, though without much discussion of what the real substance of such work might be. But beyond what the report calls "the minimum essentials," there should be no attempt to standardize a curriculum. "A universal fixed curriculum," says the committee, "ought to be ruled out if only because of the wide range both of capacity and of tastes among the pupils with whom we are concerned."

I found this report disquieting enough in itself but was even more disquieted by the uncritical reception accorded it in Britain. It seems to have stimulated a kind of national consensus about the education of the lower half of secondary-school students. Partly this general endorsement of the report may be due to the fact that Sir John Newsom himself is a charming and persuasive man with whom one would like very much to agree; partly it may be due to the emotional and humanitarian appeals made in the report and to the obvious necessity of doing something in Britain to improve the education of the Newsom children; but mostly I would think it due to the belief so easily arrived at because it has so much surface plausibility: that average and below-average students are more interested in things of the flesh than the mind, that impoverished home backgrounds put a lid on what the school can hope to do for them intellectually, that the only hope of keeping them in school longer is to bring school closer to the humdrum life outside school, particularly to jobs. Most people in Britain seem now to regard these ideas as self-evident. Few indeed seem inclined to question the strongly deterministic and utilitarian bases upon which the Newsom Report is built. My purpose here is not to refute the report, though I will return to it in Chapter VIII in order to try to sound a warning to English readers. I mean only to indicate its mood and content and its clear relationship to older American theories about the education of the lower half of the school population.

Interestingly enough, Scotland has produced a report of its own, the Brunton Report, on almost the same subject as the Newsom Report; and it bears a strong resemblance to the Newsom Report, though its concern is somewhat broader and includes post-secondary technical training. If anything, the Brunton Committee recommends an even greater stress than Newsom on practicality and vocationalism. It is also addressed to a larger group of children: the sixty-five percent of Scottish secondary students who do not take the school-leaving certificate, the Scottish Certificate of Education. The Brunton Committee found the basic problem in Scotland to be the same as the Newsom Committee found in England. The problem began at the time

> when it became obligatory for all pupils to receive a secondary education.
> The academic type of education which was traditional, and not unsuitable,
> for the relatively small and able minority of pupils who entered secondary
> schools in earlier days was not appropriate to large numbers of the boys
> and girls who entered these schools after 1947, and teachers found them-
> selves faced with the problem of devising new types of education. . . .
> The relative lack of success achieved at present by many schools in the
> education of ordinary boys and girls at the secondary stage must surely

point to some weakness in the schools themselves. In too many of our schools children are still being forced into a pattern of existing courses with established goals and those who do not fit the existing pattern are regarded as failures.

Speaking of the majority of the secondary-school population in Scotland, the report says bluntly:

> As a general rule, they are not interested in academic learning and prefer physical activity to thinking; their mental activity is stimulated by real things and happenings in the physical world rather than by ideas and concepts. Though generalizations appeal less readily to them than to their abler fellows, they have nevertheless some ability to generalize from particular illustrations. The less their ability, the less well do they meet demands for sustained effort; they respond best to tasks which yield quick results, and most of them do not look far ahead.[33]

Rather a patronizing attitude, even for a Scot, toward sixty-five percent of the future adult population of Scotland, a land that used to be known for its tradition of opening educational doors to the working-class "lad o' pairts." One finds very often the same kind of quite unintentional condescension in England in regard to the nonselective schools and their curriculum. Here, for instance, is Quintin Hogg, a Tory front-bencher, defending the secondary modern schools in Commons and betraying an attitude toward them that, unhappily, is shared alike by people who want to abolish the modern schools and those who want to keep them:

> I can assure hon. Members opposite that if they would go to study what is now being done in good secondary modern schools, they would not find a lot of pupils biting their nails in frustration because they had failed the 11-plus. The pleasant noise of banging metal and sawing wood would greet their ears and a smell of cooking with rather expensive equipment would come out of the front door to greet them. They would find that these boys and girls were getting an education tailor-made to their desires, their bents and their requirements.[34]

This sort of modernized Platonism that divides people neatly by their natural abilities or inabilities should not surprise Americans who can remember the recent past in our own schools. The Newsom and Brunton reports have much in common, for example, with our own Conant Report of 1959, *The American High School Today*. Indeed, all three reports start from precisely the same set of assumptions. They all share the same view of the limited possibilities and the practical educational needs of the majority of secondary-school students. The fact that this majority is educated in separate, nonselective schools in England and Scotland and in comprehensive schools in the United States seems to have no effect whatever on the kind of education they are to receive. Conant's preoccupation with what he calls "marketable skills" is matched by Newsom's preoccupation with "outgoing school activities" and by Brunton's preoccupation with the "vocational motive." Moreover, it is only too clear in all three reports that the vocational curriculum they espouse is not to be restricted to what used to be thought of as vocational education—training in the specific skills of working in wood or metal or cloth or food. It is to include life-adjustment and personal-problem courses of all kinds. Apparently the step is always a short one from training in certain useful skills, for which one might make a case, to organizing instruction around what might be called purposeful activity among amorphous and probably unteachable subjects. In both the secondary modern and the comprehensive schools in Britain one now finds being created many of the same nonacademic and even nonvocational courses that have been so long a part of the comprehensive school in the United States. The Schools Council speaks approvingly in one of its publications of the efforts being made in some of the nonselective schools to help students make

> some sense of the whole business of living in both its private and its public aspects. Corresponding to these two aspects there have been many experiments with the curriculum—especially, though not entirely, in the last year of compulsory schooling. There have been "personal grooming" courses, "world of work studies," "design for living projects" and the like, which have dealt more particularly (though not exclusively) with the personal aspect of human understanding.[35]

"The personal aspect of human understanding" is also reflected in the curricular innovations increasingly found in London's comprehensive schools. A course in one called "poise, dress and personality" sounds like yesterday's innovations in our own comprehensive schools. In 1964 London's local school inspectors made a survey of eighty-four secondary schools in the London area, looking for curricular developments growing out of one of the Newsom Report's principal recommendations, which said that "The school program in the final year ought to be deliberately outgoing— an initiation into the adult world of work and of leisure." The inspectors' report found the headmasters of London's secondary schools "following this recommendation with enthusiasm and discrimination." One school, for example, organized its outgoing activities around visits to such interesting institutions as the Silk Center, Celanese House, United Dairies, British Museum, Gas Works, Power Station, London Planetarium, Royal Dairy Show, London Zoo, Covent Garden Market, Billingsgate Market, and the Tower of London. Another school organized a social-studies course around the building of a model town, "Newtown," and actually constructed it in miniature on the school roof. Another one created a two-year course in "Social Education" for girls of average and below-average ability and organized it around such themes as "Myself" (how to speak, spend money, get a job, take care of skin, hair, hands, teeth, etc.), and "Our

Homes and the Place Where We Live" (home decoration, visits to parks and museums and outlying villages). The report abounds with descriptions of projects in "mothercraft," "housecraft," retail distribution, boat-building, horseback riding, home designing, shopping in central London, and instruction in "how to behave in restaurants and cafes." At one point the report observes that "In recent years, as informal approaches to education have been better understood and more widely practiced, the line between the curricular and the extra-curricular has become more difficult to draw" [36]—an incontestable assertion.

The reader has probably found it more than evident by now that Britain, faced with the same problem that has bedeviled American education for half a century—how to educate the mass of students who fall below the top quarter or third of ability—is going to take the same road we took and presumably make the same mistakes. In the United States I believe we are at last beginning to move away from at least the more ritualistic kind of progressivism and surely away from the debacle of life-adjustment education. But Britain and much of Europe seem to be only at the beginning of the cycle. If this is to be the nature of the education offered in nonselective secondary schools, one can hardly be surprised at the low esteem in which such schools are usually held. If the same kind of education is to be transferred to comprehensive schools in Britain, one should not be surprised if these schools fail to build reputations for excellence.

## Grammar Schools and Public Schools

"The grammar-school tradition" is spoken of with devotion or at least respect by most Britons. A few revolutionaries regard it with hostility as a manifestation of class and privilege and would be delighted to see it disappear in the new comprehensive schools. To most people, including many of those on the Labor Left who breathe so hotly down the neck of the Public Schools, the grammar-school tradition is one of the great characteristics of English education. But the tradition means different things to different people. If it means education, no matter how excellent, in separate, selective establishments for high-ability students, it is probably a dying tradition not to be mourned by many; if it means dedication to the rigorous training and furnishing of the minds of high-ability students, and an intellectual intensity among staff and students who are selected by merit, then most people hope the tradition will survive and grow in whatever kinds of secondary schools come into being.

A kind of grammar-school tradition exists, of course, all over Europe. The French *lycée*, the Italian *liceo*, the German or Swiss or Swedish or Dutch *Gymnasium* are all roughly comparable to the English grammar school: They all take in the top twenty to thirty percent of the age group, divide them along the way by ability and usually by specialization, and in their academic demands do not worry very much about sparing the student; he is expected to work to his capacity and to extend himself, for the school aims to put as many students as possible through national examinations at the end. The English tradition does depart, as we will see, in one important way from others, in the work of the last two or three years of the selective school.

## STATE GRAMMAR SCHOOLS

There are about 1,300 state grammar schools in England and Wales, enrolling three-quarters of a million students between ages of eleven and eighteen, which is about twenty-five percent of all the children in state secondary schools. In addition there are at least as many private grammar schools of various kinds, though many are small and enroll far fewer students than the state grammar schools. Commonly students in the state schools are tracked on the basis of ability from the first year, the number of tracks depending on the size of the entering class. In addition to, or occasionally in place of, the tracks, students may be divided by ability into "sets" in certain subjects such as English and mathematics. In almost all schools, finer distinctions in ability will be made, whether in tracks or sets or other ways, than in American high schools. As in the nonselective secondary schools, a stipulated curriculum usually prevails for all students for at least the first three years. Some choice or specialization begins in the fourth and fifth years, though the bulk of the curriculum remains the same for all students. Below is a kind of composite timetable that I have made from the separate schedules of a number of schools. The figures are for periods per week, each of forty minutes. In the fifth and sixth years, they indicate offerings, not requirements; individual students will have some choice and will take thirty-five to forty periods a week. Sixth-year students will choose three major subjects, though a few will take either two or four, plus a minority of time in other subjects. Small differences and departures from this timetable would be found in all schools, but a typical grammar school program would be pretty close to the table on p. 85.

The content of these courses is controlled in the first three or four years internally by the headmaster and his staff. In the fifth year and often in the fourth, the influence of external examinations becomes important and course content is strongly dependent on the published syllabuses of the national examining boards. British teachers and headmasters in all types of schools make a great deal of their freedom to decide what they teach and how they teach it, as they also do in many parts of Europe. Technically they are completely free in Britain in regard to curriculum and

| Subject | First 3 years | Fifth year | Sixth year | |
|---|---|---|---|---|
| | | | SCIENCE SIDE | ARTS SIDE |
| Latin | 4 | 5 | – | 6 |
| English | 5 | 5 | – | 6 |
| French | 4 | 4 | – | 7 |
| Mathematics | 5 | 5 | 10 | – |
| History | 3 | 4 | – | 7 |
| Geography | 2 | 4 | – | 7 |
| Physics | 2 | 5 | 7 | – |
| Chemistry | 2 | 5 | 7 | – |
| Biology | 2 | 5 | 7 | – |
| Art | 2 | – | – | 7 |
| Music | 2 | 3 | – | – |
| Physical Education | 3 | 3 | 3 | 3 |
| Religious Knowledge | 1 | 1 | 1 | 1 |
| Domestic Science/Handicrafts | 2 | – | – | – |
| German | – | 4 | – | 7 |
| Spanish | – | 4 | – | – |
| History of Art | – | 2 | 2 | – |
| Use of English | – | – | 2 | 2 |

methods, and this freedom does mean something, especially as we have seen in the nonselective schools. But the fact that I can put together the kind of grammar-school timetable above and let it stand as typical suggests in itself that the British teacher's freedom may be somewhat illusory. The pressure of the external exam system is such that no school could depart very far from the accustomed pattern. Even if it could, I suspect that only the rare school would have any desire to depart very far from the present pattern. The simple fact is that both headmasters and staff members are themselves educated in a highly homogeneous way in British universities, having before that been through equally homogeneous grammar schools. They are therefore apt to share a common view of educational purpose and give about the same priority to particular subjects. If the external exam system were abolished, I would be surprised if the grammar-school curriculum would be radically altered except possibly for a broadening of the sixth form. I do not suggest that this homogeneity is a weakness; on the contrary it seems to me an important source of strength. One noticeable effect of national, essay-type examinations like the GCE is that the schools put great emphasis on essay writing. I would guess that English grammar-school students do two or three times as much writing as good students in American high schools, and it is supervised writing. In part this is made possible by the small student-staff ratio in the English sixth forms, but the essay-type exam system is also a strong influence.

How good an education in general is offered in the grammar school? Is it all that it is reputed to be? I will say something about standards in Chapter IV, but here would record the fact that very few full-length studies have been done of the English grammar school. Only one has been done since World War II, the Crowther Report, which is the most detailed study available of the upper-secondary system of education. It is another of the notable investigations of the Central Advisory Council for Education. The Crowther Committee was appointed by the Minister of Education in 1956 and reported three years later on the whole subject of British education for the four years from the legal leaving age of 15 to the end of the 18th year. It is a detailed discussion of the fifth and sixth forms of English schools, as well as of the multifarious system of "further" and technical education in Britain.[37] Its many findings and recommendations might be summarized in the following way:

1. After an exhaustive exposition of the social, economic, and personal reasons why the leaving age should be raised, the report recommended that it go up to sixteen by 1969 at the latest, following a careful program of preparation (it is now scheduled for 1971).

2. On the subject of examinations, the committee recommended that no external exam be imposed, as had been suggested, on the lower half of the school population, but that an experimental system of regional exams might be created for the second quarter of students that fall between the lower half and the group that now take the GCE.

3. The report cited the fact that the 1944 Act "did not envisage anybody's education as stopping at 15 or even at 16," and strongly recommended that the provisions of the Act calling for the creation of a system of "county colleges" for the compulsory part-time education of all persons aged sixteen or seventeen not in full-time education be put into effect as quickly as possible, such education to be a combination of academic, vocational, and aesthetic study.

4. The report deplored the tendency in grammar schools for the specialized work of the sixth form to influence the curriculum of the fifth and lower forms, congesting the timetable, and recommended the postponement of a decision about sixth-form subjects until students actually reached that form. Nothing much has been done about this recommendation, and early specialization is a continuing problem.

5. The report endorsed the specialized study characteristic of the sixth form, but recommended that certain steps be taken to broaden the curriculum and to make better use of "minority time."

6. The report recommended that external examinations at the end of the sixth form be "backward-looking," designed to "record achievement," and not be the main selection device of the universities. Nothing was done about this recommendation either, and the GCE remains the principal means of gaining admission to all forms of higher education.

7. The report thought that the "neglected educational territory" of the

system of "further education" in technical and vocational fields should be exploited, greatly expanded, and integrated with the schools.

8. The report recognized the central importance to all its other recommendations of an adequate supply of well-trained teachers, from both the Colleges of Education and the universities, and made a variety of suggestions about how it might be ensured.

The report also said, in recognition of what is called its "formidable" recommendations:

> We do not believe that there is any hope of carrying out the measures we have outlined—or any other list of proposals adequate to the needs— unless they are worked out and adopted as a coherent, properly phased development program, extending by timed and calculated steps a long way into the future.

This was not done. A great many of the report's recommendations were not adopted for the usual reason, lack of funds. But the Crowther Report remains the most detailed study of upper-secondary education in Britian that is likely to be produced for some time.

The report rightly stressed the matter of staff in its analysis, always the center to which one returns in education. Practically all grammar-school teachers in England are university graduates. Their preparation in the subject they teach has thus included at least five years of concentrated work in that subject: two years in the sixth form and three more in the university. Increasingly they will also have done a postgraduate year of work for the Diploma in Education. This comes to a very substantial kind of preparation, and I would have no hesitation in saying that the typical grammar-school master in England has a deeper grasp of his subject than people teaching the upper range of students in our own high schools. Nevertheless, complaints are frequent about the decline in the quality of grammar-school teachers in England. Headmasters will point out that the group of men and women who entered teaching in the Depression years when competition for any vacancy was fierce were often among the top university graduates, a great many of them with first-class honors degrees. These people raised grammar-school teaching to a very high level, but they are now retiring and are not being replaced by persons equally good. Now the competition from industry and other quarters, including the Colleges of Education and the universities, is such that the average grammar-school staff will include very few people indeed with first-class degrees. One headmaster, responding to a questionnaire from the National Union of Teachers, said: "It may, of course, be my age, but it appears to me that the quality of applicants for vacancies is slowly going down, both in personal quality and in background"; while another observed that "We can always fill vacancies, but too often with graduates whose degree is not of a standard to secure their desired profession. These seldom stay. The curriculum has to be dictated by the abilities of the staff not by the needs of the children." [38] Staff turnover is also high, though not nearly as high as in the nonselective schools. The staff-student ratio is about 1/18 in the grammar schools, the average being brought down by the small classes customary in the sixth and seventh years. Teachers will usually teach between thirty and thirty-five periods a week, rather more than highly qualified teachers in Europe and a great deal more than, say, the French *professeur agrégé*, who may teach only fifteen hours a week. They will also mark more papers and take on more extra-curricular activities than their counterparts anywhere on the Continent. A great many new teachers these days, probably most, are the first generation of their families to get a university education; and most of them in the state schools will no longer come from Oxford or Cambridge. Until recently, the grammar schools were, as the Crowther Report put it, "living on their capital" in the matter of staff; now they must somehow find the means of attracting better people.

The most interesting aspect of the grammar school to many visitors is the sixth form, though it is now a strongly criticized aspect of secondary education. The sixth form normally extends through the last two years of the grammar school, the sixth and seventh. As can be seen from the timetable printed earlier, the lower sixth is the point at which students at age sixteen make a fundamental choice of specialization. They choose either the "arts side" or the "science side" and will usually choose further within these divisions a combination of three related subjects upon which they propose to concentrate for two years and which they will take to the advanced level of the GCE examination. If they are aiming at Oxford or Cambridge, they will remain in the sixth form for part of a third year preparing for the special examinations given by the constituent colleges of these institutions. For many students the split between science and arts comes even earlier, at fifteen and very often now at fourteen when some subjects are dropped and others added, and when specific study begins for the lower level of the GCE. By the time a student reaches the sixth form it will be almost impossible for him to study, for example, both physics and French, or classics and mathematics, or history and chemistry.

Britain is probably unique in the degree of forced specialization in the upper secondary school. Most of the European countries require study on a much broader front than Britain—or the United States—through the secondary school. In some countries, such as Germany, the number of required subjects of study has been so large, thirteen or fourteen, that recent reforms have been instituted to reduce them to eight or nine. Scottish students, although allowed to specialize if they wish, ordinarily take four or five subjects, much like their American counterparts, in the upper secondary years. In England, early specialization began in the nineteenth century for economic reasons and because advancements in many fields of knowledge required more concentrated study than before. Specialization is strong in England also because admission to the universities is controlled by the universities and often by the separate departments within them, which tend to set high specialist qualifications, and not as in Europe by the state through the school-leaving examination. Now, ironically, one of the problems that specialization was designed to solve, the lack of adequate knowledge in science and technology of students beginning university work, has become worse in that a disproportionate number of sixth-form students, faced with the necessity to choose in the secondary school, have been choosing the arts side of the curriculum. Thus in the universities, the arts subjects are crowded while a sizable number of science vacancies go unfilled each year at a time when Britain desperately needs more scientists.[39] American readers will recognize the connection between the matter of sixth-form specialization in England and the hypothesis of C. P. Snow (now Lord Snow) about the "two cultures" that was so much discussed some years ago in the United States.

The whole specialization issue—and it has become an important issue in England—is complicated by the tremendous growth in sixth-form enrollments over the last ten years. In the average grammar school of a decade ago, no more than thirty percent of the students that finished the fifth form proceeded to the sixth; the rest left school with some pass grades from the lower level of the GCE and went to work or perhaps to a teacher-training college. Today the number remaining is more like sixty percent. One result is that sixth forms are now filled with first-generation grammar school students who lack the home background that would help to balance the effects of early specialization, particularly in science. Moreover, many of the sixth-formers today are not the genuine "high fliers" to which the sixth forms used to be limited and who, as one Cambridge don puts it,

> took examinations in their stride. Since the war the increase in the size of these forms has brought into them many young people of a narrower range of ability, with some interest and flair perhaps, but for one or two subjects only. . . . These pupils have to work hard to pass examinations and they have less time therefore for the general education which they badly need.[40]

The fact that many sixth-formers now come up through the lower-ability tracks of the fifth form may also account for the bulge on the arts side of the curriculum, the softer side.

Even so, the Crowther Report, after a detailed consideration of the problem of the "monocular vision which our present system too often produces," supported the traditional sixth-form specialization, which it preferred to call "intensive study." In no other way, the committee seemed to feel, could the peculiar excellence of English sixth-form study be retained. That excellence was achieved in the committee's view through five characteristics that might be contrasted to the American situation: (1) a close link between the sixth forms and the universities; (2) a preoccupation with "subject-mindedness" on the part of both staff members and students; (3) a great deal of independent work made possible by the student's background in the subject; (4) a close relationship between students and teachers probing into the subject together over an extended period of time and often producing an "intellectual discipleship" on the student's part; and (5) a developing sense of social responsibility. At least two of the five are directly linked to specialized study. The committee wanted better use made of "minority time," which usually makes up about a quarter of the sixth-form program in study from the opposite side of the curriculum from the student's specialization. The committee found such time to be frivolously or ineffectively used in a great many schools. But it also found that "able boys and girls are ready and eager by the time they are 16—the ablest by 15— to get down to the serious study of some one aspect of human knowledge." So far as Britain's being alone among the advanced nations in its concept of sixth-form work, the committee thought the United States might be even more removed in its own way from the generality of nations:

> . . . if American and continental practices are united against the English in being non-specialist, there is one important respect in which England and the continent take the same side against America. In Western Europe, as in England, the secondary school is traditionally concerned with educating an élite, an intellectual aristocracy on whom the most stringent academic demands can be made and in whom there can be awakened a real love of learning. It treats them as adults capable of a reverence for knowledge, beginners in a lifelong quest for truth, which they can share with those who teach them. This outlook is shared equally by the *professeur* in a French *lycée* and the English Sixth Form master, widely though they differ in their actual methods of teaching. The intellectual task of an American Senior High School differs entirely from that of an English Sixth Form, because it is not dealing with, and would not wish to deal with, a segregated few. Not only is the climate of public opinion strongly against the segregation of the abler pupils into selective schools (though there are some recent signs of a willingness to consider this), but the standard pattern of an American High School does not even allow for the segregation of pupils inside the school into faster and slower streams. All are educated together, and there is an emphasis on problems of individual adjustment to a mass society which we would regard as more appropriate to the modern school than to the grammar school, whose pupils' characteristics (so rightly or wrongly, the English tradition insists), can be

trained simultaneously with their minds by the "full rigor of the academic game" and the freedom of out-of-school activities. Thus while the English grammar school differs from the American High School both in its methods and in its objectives, our difference from the Europeans is chiefly one of method.[41]

In spite of the Crowther Committee's findings that affirmed the wisdom of specialization, I think it fair to say that the sixth forms will be changed in this regard in the future. Exactly in what way is still unclear. One of the GCE examining boards has been experimenting for over ten years with a "General Studies paper" in an effort to give teachers one means of mitigating the effects of specialization, though I must say that both the syllabus for this exam and the exam itself seem remarkably loose and unpromising, a little like work often done in "general studies" in the United States. Of this examination, the board's own examiners said, in reporting on the 1965 results of the General Studies paper:

> The majority of [student] scripts were mediocre and unimaginative, and did not reach the level of discussion implied by the standard of the questions. There was a marked lack of knowledge of a kind which could reasonably be expected from sixth-formers with some intellectual curiosity and access to newspapers, journals and radio. Factual errors on subjects such as the Commonwealth, possession of nuclear weapons and British electoral procedure were common. There was also a prevailing lack of judgment and perspective on social and political questions, leading to overstated, assertive or emotional answers. The main fault which the majority of scripts displayed, however, was lack of care in planning answers to questions which, as should have been recognized, had been carefully constructed.[42]

It is possible that weaker students tend to take the general-studies course in the first place, and thus perform badly on the exam. Student opinion on the specialization question is, I think, extremely mixed. Nobody has done a sufficiently large and reliable survey of the subject to be able to say whether there is a consensus among students themselves for or against sixth-form specialization. The Gulbenkian Foundation sponsored one survey in 1960 in which seventy percent of a small sample of sixth-form students said they would prefer a mixture of arts and science study;[43] and a survey of students at Keele University, done by the students themselves in 1965, indicated that many had changed their specialization after being at the university, though Keele students may not be very representative of British students.[44] The journal of the Advisory Centre for Education printed a survey in 1966 of the opinions of its own members, which were strongly negative about specialization, though again ACE's membership is not very representative of British parents.[45] My own opinion, formed from simply talking with grammar-school students and staff members in many parts of Britain, is that student views are so split as not to indicate any particular consensus; there are plenty who are content with their subjects, who are doing what they want to do, and plenty who would like greater flexibility and variety.

Whatever the opinions of the students, a great many of their elders are not in any doubt about what should be done. There is a movement among grammar-school teachers themselves to introduce some kind of general studies into the sixth forms; and 2,000 teachers belong to an organization called the General Studies Association, whose *Bulletin* reflects a marked confusion of aims and methods among the members but a common devotion to the idea of broadening sixth-form study. The Schools Council, too, which will be giving a lot of attention to the sixth form in the next few years, said in its first annual report that

> it cannot be right to prolong indefinitely a situation in which, for many pupils, education after the age of 15 or 16 is excessively concentrated upon one branch of knowledge or a limited area of human experience. There are many opinions about what should be done and, in the Council's view, the main immediate need is to create greater flexibility for the schools in the construction of curricula, so that a variety of reasonable alternatives can be explored and evaluated.[46]

British educationists, for their part, are quite unhappy about the control of sixth-form curriculums by, in effect, university departments that demand specialized knowledge for admission. "What we need," as one Institute head puts it, "in this sector of education is a Tudor monarch to rescue us from the anarchy of the medieval barons." [47]

Looking at the matter in the light of American practice, I would say, first, that sixth-form specialization as it is typically done is unfortunate in closing the doors at too early an age on one side or the other of the curriculum; but, second, that American schools have no reason whatever for complacency on the point. I am quite sure that if a breakdown were made of the total educational exposure, so to speak, of an average sixth-former at the end of his secondary school with that of his American counterpart, the Briton would be well ahead in *all* subjects. To begin with, he studies ten or eleven subjects, often more, for at least three years, from ages eleven to fourteen, while his American counterpart may be studying six or seven, or fewer. He then studies seven or eight or more subjects for two years, from ages fourteen to sixteen, while his American counterpart may be studying five or six. And he then studies three subjects for two years, from ages sixteen to eighteen, plus a few minor ones, while his American counterpart may be studying five. If one factors into the equation the longer school day and school year in Britain and the greater amount of homework, plus the fact that the English student will have done thirteen years instead of the American twelve, and relate the quantity of time to the subjects studied, American students would be even more specialized than English students. American students, however, do have an advantage in being able to postpone the decision about their specialty or profession until they reach college or university, and even then can continue to postpone it for a year or two provided they do not fall behind in basic science and mathematics study; if they do fall behind, the decision has been made for them. Having said that, I should also add that the Crowther Committee's comment about sixth-formers being ready and able and wanting to specialize is clearly true of some able students, who after fully five years of broad, general study at the secondary level are not in any doubt about their interests and professional plans. It seems both wise and humane to allow them a degree of specialization of the kind the Crowther Report endorses. What the whole matter comes to perhaps is that greater flexibility in sixth-form programs is badly needed so as to preserve alternatives while also preserving the traditional virtues of the English sixth form.

## INDEPENDENT SECONDARY SCHOOLS

The English "Public Schools" are what most Americans would think of as the principal independent secondary schools of Britain, but some clarification is needed on the point. The most widely accepted criterion of a Public School is membership in the Headmasters' Conference, but this inner group of the Incorporated Association of Head Masters consists of only 200 members representing only a small minority of the more than 1,500 members that make up the Headmasters' Association and a minority of independent schools. Even within the Headmasters' Conference there are a great many "direct-grant" schools that are not fully independent institutions. So there are at least four major categories of secondary schools outside the state system: direct-grant schools, independent schools represented on the Headmasters' Conference, other independent schools that are members of the Headmasters' Association, and still other independent schools outside all these categories. Our purposes will be served adequately by distinguishing only between the direct-grant schools, many of which are also considered Public Schools, and other schools that are fully independent and that include Public Schools.

Standing halfway between the state grammar schools and the wholly independent schools are a group of 179 institutions probably unique to England, the direct-grant secondary schools. They were all fully independent at one time, and thirty percent of them are still represented in the Headmasters' Conference. Although they are still frequently lumped together with the independent schools, their distinguishing feature is that they are partly supported by local and national tax monies in exchange for admitting a substantial number of students from state primary schools and submitting to a certain degree of government control. Specifically, they maintain at least a quarter of the vacancies in their entering classes as "free places," which in effect are scholarships for able children coming from the state schools and paid for by the LEA's involved. And they agree to make another quarter available as "reserved places" if LEA's wish to take and pay for them. The rest of the entering class is made up of "fee-payers" whose parents pay according to a means test. But in any of these categories of entry, the inability of parents to pay is not a bar, for admission in all categories is on the basis of demonstrated ability. This means that the direct-grant schools are the most selective class of secondary schools in England: State grammar schools admit children from a wider range of ability than these schools, and fully independent schools, relying on parental fees, often take in a very wide range indeed. Thus the direct-grant schools include many of the best schools in England, such as the Manchester Grammar School, the Bristol Grammar School, Haberdashers' Aske's School, and King Edward's School (Birmingham). It also means that they are far more mixed socially than independent schools. The same standard of admission is applied to all comers, and the direct-grant schools, since the inception of the arrangement in 1926 and its refinement in 1944, have been one of the chief means by which bright children from working-class families have made their way to Oxford and Cambridge and beyond. These schools are an invaluable link between the state and private sectors of British education, operating as they do through a typically British balance of powers between state and private authority.

The curriculum of the direct-grant schools is very much like that of the state grammar schools. They offer, that is, about the same sixteen or seventeen subjects in a sequential program over a period of seven or eight years: Latin, English, History, Geography, two or three Modern Languages, perhaps Greek, Biology, Physics, Chemistry, Mathematics, Art, Music, Religious Knowledge, plus Physical Education, and Crafts and Needlework. However, their sixth forms retain a very much larger percentage of their entering classes than in the state grammar schools, and they therefore have particularly well-developed work in the last few years of the program. Many of them offer a considerable amount of third-year sixth-form study for their best students who want to prepare for the Oxford and Cambridge entrance exams. Their records in placing their graduates are, of course, better than those of the state schools.

A brief look at what is perhaps the best of the direct-grant schools, the Manchester Grammar School, may suffice to indicate their particular characteristics. Manchester Grammar is an ancient establishment, tracing its lineage back to 1515, when the Bishop of Exeter, the son of a Manchester accountant, spent five pounds to buy a site in Manchester for a "scole house" where boys from all backgrounds could be prepared for the university by training in Latin and Greek. Unlike many ancient schools in Britain, it no longer occupies any of the original buildings or the original site. Instead it is housed in a massive, ugly, dim, drafty, red-brick edifice south of the city center and near the "Redbrick" University of Manchester. Let me note in passing, for those who think that selective schools are always better treated than nonselective, that the opposite is nowadays very often the case in England, at least in buildings and equipment. Next door to Manchester Grammar is a new and resplendent glass-and-concrete establishment run by the Manchester LEA for training school dropouts in baking, catering, hairdressing, laundry work, and nutrition. Many a secondary modern school, being new, is more attractive and better financed than Manchester Grammar or any of a great many other selective schools.

Manchester Grammar with about 1,500 boys is extremely large by English standards. It is also, I suppose, the most highly selective school in England. Boys enter at about eleven from both state and independent schools. For an entering class of just over 200, the school will receive about 1,000 applications from boys who are themselves selected to some degree. The school gives its own entrance examinations, which are a good deal more discriminating and sophisticated than the ordinary 11-plus. Although a day school, not a boarding institution like many of England's prestige schools, it draws its students from an extremely wide area, many of them traveling very considerable distances to attend. Because of the commuting time required for many students, Manchester Grammar operates a shorter school day than most schools and a shorter school year—but it gets better examination results than any other school in Britain. It sends ninety percent of its graduates on to higher education and professional training, seventy-five percent to British universities, and it regularly tops the list for the numbers of students it sends to Oxford and Cambridge, about forty percent of its graduates. Nearly three-quarters of its graduates pass three or more subjects at the advanced level of the GCE, a record that probably cannot be matched by any other school large or small. As one would expect, the school attracts an outstanding staff, though it has trouble keeping people now, since it cannot compete with various institutions of higher education that regularly raid the staff.

The school has its critics. Some say that it is nothing but a cram school, an efficient forcing house to get able boys through examinations. And others say that by being so selective, it is "meritocratic" and divisive. Both criticisms are, in my opinion, unwarranted. It is not nearly so much a cram school as many an ordinary grammar school, where less able boys need to worry far more about getting through the GCE. Also, it attracts the kind of teacher who is not likely to be interested in cram teaching. Nobody who visits this school, I believe, could come away with the impression that it is a forcing house; on the contrary, he would most probably come away as he might from a visit, say, to the Bronx High School of Science, with an impression of unusual intellectual vitality and variety, as well as an awareness of extracurricular activities of great scope; the school has a couple of orchestras, a large choral society, an active dramatic society, and something over forty clubs of different kinds. It competes in soccer, rugby, cricket, lacrosse, tennis, track, swimming, squash, basketball, and other sports. And it is very active in a favorite English schoolboy activity: trekking and camping both in Britain and the Continent.

As for its being divisive, Manchester Grammar has a body of students far more heterogeneous than that of many state grammar schools serving homogeneous suburban areas and fully as heterogeneous as any number of our own comprehensive schools. As for its being "meritocratic," it certainly is but again is surely not as divisive socially as many schools serving exclusive areas in both Britain and the United States. "There can be few schools in the western world," as one headmaster put the case for the direct-grant schools, "where the sons of a Bishop, an MP and a [university] Vice-Chancellor can mix on terms of complete equality with the sons of a fitter, a cotton operative and an invalid widow on public assistance." [48] Lord James, the former High Master of Manchester Grammar, now Vice-Chancellor of the University of York, seems to me to overcome his natural bias in favor of Manchester Grammar in offering this assessment of the school during a debate on comprehensive schools in the House of Lords:

> I know that if the school I worked in for sixteen years became a neighborhood school the social range of its pupils would be far less than it is to-day. Its greatest glory, in my eyes, was not its academic excellence. Its greatest glory was that it gave a boy from any home background the opportunity to share in that excellence. It was able to do so because it drew from a wide area, and because the only criterion for admission was ability. Of course the poor were under-represented compared with the middle class. Of course this is true of most grammar schools, and of all universities, for inevitably the child from the home which is poor culturally and socially is denied from his birth many of the opportunities that are given to the more fortunate.
>
> But no system of education . . . can of itself change completely an inequality that arises from such deep social forces. It may, and should, alleviate it by providing opportunities that the home cannot give. But it may also accentuate it by driving more pupils and more staff into the private sector. It may do so still more by limiting by the accident of neighborhood the opportunities of those who, by ability and character, manage to transcend the limitations of background and environment. For every school there must be selection. . . . As soon as you have a school, you have to decide who is going to it. There must in fact be selection. We delude ourselves—or, rather, we do not probably delude ourselves; we

delude other people—when we talk about abolishing selection. What we have to decide, quite simply, is whether that selection shall be by birth or wealth, by ability and aptitude, or by neighborhood, which is so often the same as wealth.[49]

Not all the direct-grant schools are distinguished institutions. They represent a spread of quality that one would expect to find in any large group of schools. But most of them bring together a first-rate staff with a first-rate body of students; together they address themselves over an extended period of years to academic study that is both broad and deep, and that is balanced by extensive extracurricular activities. In a word, they are impressive establishments of which any nation could be proud.

Fully independent secondary schools are a much more varied group, ranging from such famous Public Schools as Eton, Rugby, Winchester, and Harrow to dreary and impoverished institutions that cannot be "recognized as efficient" by the Department or by anybody else. It is the top of the line that people have in mind when they speak of the Public Schools. Many people would narrow the field to perhaps the twenty or twenty-five leading schools of the Headmaster's Conference. But one can seldom be certain of precisely what group of schools is meant in most references to the Public Schools. Members of the Headmasters' Conference themselves seem unsure about it and increasingly prefer to use the term "independent schools," not least because of the criticism being directed these days against the Public Schools. If one includes within the term all of the schools of the Headmasters' Conference that are not direct-grant schools, Public Schools might then be defined as independent, fee-paying, mostly boarding schools of high academic standard, high social prestige, and a special ethos of their own. There is an old saw about the English Public Schools that says the term is all wrong: They do not teach English but Latin; they are not public but quite private; and they are not schools but sports plazas. It has a measure of truth but a diminishing one.

Many of the Public Schools would be incredibly old in American eyes. The King's School at Canterbury claims to be the oldest, having been founded in the year 600 (it was reconstituted, however, in 1541 by Henry VIII); but its claim is disputed by St. Peter's School at York, a city with which Canterbury has disputed a number of matters in the past. The most renowned of the Public Schools were monastic institutions established in order to give a religious and general education to boys without regard to their social background. Eton was so established in 1440, Winchester in 1382, Rugby in 1567, Shrewsbury in 1571, Westminster in 1339, Harrow in 1571, and Charterhouse in 1609. They were then "public" schools in that they took many boys from poor families; the name persists if the function does not. But a great many other Public Schools are Victorian establishments, founded to put middle-class sons through a rigorous intellectual, spiritual, and physical training, and to get them ready for political, military, and industrial leadership in the Empire—schools like Monkton Combe (1868), Clifton (1862), The Leys (1875), Marlborough (1843), and Cranleigh (1863). Together the Public Schools, ancient and Victorian, have exercised a great and unbroken influence over secondary education in England. They have been the models, admirably summed up in Thomas Arnold's famous regime at Rugby from 1827 to 1842, upon which innumerable state grammar schools have been conducted. Their role has been incomparably greater than that of our own independent boarding schools or of private schools anywhere in Europe; they are a distinctly English creation.

Most Public Schools today take in students from a much wider range of ability than do either the direct-grant schools or the state grammar schools. Hence they are, as some diffidently claim to be these days, comprehensive schools in that they accept a considerable cross-section of academic ability. They are not comprehensive socially, of course, since attendance at them depends on the ability of parents to pay. Most of their students are from middle-class families. Take, for example, Marlborough, one of the leading Public Schools. The occupations of the fathers of Marlborough boys break down something like this: 43% are in managerial positions in business and industry; 11% are doctors or dentists; 7.5% are clergymen; 7% are farmers, gentlemanly or otherwise; and there are a few journalists, musicians, artists, and sportsmen. This social homogeneity is reinforced by the staff, most members of which are graduates of Oxford or Cambridge; and Marlborough in turn sends a large proportion of its graduates on to these two universities.

The curriculums of the Public Schools are very much the same as those of the other selective secondary schools, though their timetables call for less work. They are, I suppose, the original "whole-child" schools. Public School traditions put great stress on balanced activities and all-round development. These schools still pursue the Victorian virtues in which they trained so many of the rulers and administrators of the defunct Empire. They put great emphasis on character development, on religious observance, on leadership training and chin-up stamina in the face of adversity, and on all kinds of sports and games, especially rugby and cricket, and on clubs and societies. They tend to make a virtue of the spartan conditions in which their pupils commonly live. The food is often bad, even for England. The buildings and plumbing are often ancient and in bad repair. And any American who is exposed to the cramped, unlovely, bone-chilling dormitories characteristic of the Public Schools might wonder just how "privileged" the boys are that live and sleep and have their being in such places. Boarding-school life is also spiced with "fagging," a tradition that makes junior boys servants to senior ones, and "caning," a tradition of physical punishment, often inflicted by the boys themselves but usually by the masters, for infringements of the multitudinous rules under which these self-contained societies are run. The regimen they impose and the way of life they foster make a permanent impression on their students. Their alumni, their "old boys," are among their greatest supporters and sometimes have to put their sons practically at birth on the old school's rolls to be assured of a place for them thirteen years later.

The Public Schools are of recognized excellence academically and a few of them, such as Winchester and Rugby, are probably among the best secondary schools in the world. Boys usually enter the schools at age thirteen from independent preparatory schools. For admission they take the Common Entrance Examination, which each school grades according to its own standards. Since the schools are dependent on fees, their entrance standards react to the laws of supply and demand. On admissions, one experienced Public School man comments:

> The Common Entrance Examination tests whether a boy has been well taught and is conscientious, rather than whether he is intelligent: so that even those schools which demand a high level of attainment in the Common Entrance papers cannot be certain of receiving a uniformly intelligent clientele. In any case, a considerable proportion of boys are admitted for other reasons: their parents are wealthy, or titled, or old boys of the school, and so forth. One is not surprised, therefore, to find an I.Q. range of 90—sometimes even of 80—to the maximum: an interesting comparison with the minimum I.Q. for entry to a grammar school, which may be as high as 130. This means that a great many boys of low I.Q. are ingested into a curriculum which, like the grammar-school curriculum, is highly academic.[50]

Estimates vary about how many Public School pupils could not be admitted to state grammar schools. One investigator of the subject in 1966 thought that something between twenty-five and thirty-five percent of the entering students in the Public Schools "were of only moderate ability and would, had they been in the maintained schools, have gone to secondary modern schools."[51] Yet large numbers of Public School pupils who actually took and failed an 11-plus, and others who would have failed it had they taken it, do work in Public Schools not only at the Ordinary level of the GCE but at the Advanced level as well, and despite the shorter academic timetable.

An illuminating study was published in 1963 by two Public School teachers in which they traced the record of a number of 11-plus failures. They began by surveying seventy-seven prep schools that had taken in 1,000 boys from fifty-eight different LEA's after they had flunked the 11-plus in the state schools. The prep schools then prepared them successfully for the Common Entrance Examination after which they were admitted to 108 Public Schools of the Headmasters' Conference. At the end of their Public School careers, seventy percent of these 11-plus failures had passed five or more subjects at the Ordinary level of the General Certificate of Education, and many had done so at the age of fifteen instead of the normal sixteen; over twenty-five percent passed two or more subjects at the Advanced level, half of them in the sciences; and between twenty and twenty-five percent of them went on to a university, while another thirty percent went on to some other kind of further education.[52] An impressive job of what might be called educational retrieval.

In 1963 John Dancy, the Master of Marlborough and one of the leading voices for Public School reform, estimated that "about 20 percent of the successful 'A' level candidates in a public school fall into this category [of 11-plus failures]."[53] Even allowing for the middle-class backgrounds of such boys and the educational advantages of boarding school, the message is clear: The pool of talent is much deeper than has been assumed by a good many people in British education, and a good deal more provision is needed for correcting the errors inevitably made at the 11-plus separation. I dwell on the point because of its relevance to an old problem in American education: the assumption by so many educational administrators and of national figures like James Bryant Conant that sustained academic work is simply beyond the reach of, say, the lower half or two-thirds of the student body. The record of the English Public Schools is strong in taking boys of average and below-average ability who would not have made their way to a grammar school in the state system and then putting them through one or both levels of the GCE. The most probable explanation, which should be no surprise to experienced schoolmen, is that intelligence is not a stable quality, but interacts, as we noted earlier, with environment, which can drive it up or down. The Public School environment is, so to speak, total: Pupils live where they work and play, in a carefully supervised society, with constant contact with teachers, and where they are expected to perform. The Public School environment is, as the psychologists say, "self-fulfilling" in regard to examination success. The moral for English education is not necessarily to abolish the 11-plus, as is being done, but to assume and to act on the assumption that an unknown but very large number of pupils who do not succeed at the 11-plus will succeed later if the appropriate program of study is available to them in the schools to which they are sent. The moral for American education is to abandon the assumption that the intellectual limitations of average and below-average children are inherent and not to be changed by the school, thus dictating a lot of non-academic, vocational, and life-adjustment courses.

THE PUBLIC SCHOOLS UNDER ATTACK

The movement toward social and educational equality in Britain has made a special target of the Public Schools. The Labor Party and its supporters denounce them in flamboyant terms: "A world of utter fantasy"—"nurseries of privilege"—"cocooned upbringing"—"hothouses of snobbery"—and promise to "integrate them into the state system." They are accused of many sins, mostly social. "All independent schools," say the Young Fabians without qualification, "foster class division." [54] A well-known clergyman says that the Public Schools create "another world than that to which the rest of the school system of the country belongs. . . ." [55] They foster, many say, an attitude of aloofness marked by special manners and a special accent. They are even said to create recognizable types: An Old Etonian is supposed to be readily identifiable among the *cognoscenti;* there is a Stowe type, they say, and certainly a Harrovian and a Wykehamist (the latter being a Winchester man, so named after the school's founder, William of Wykeham). Labor's Left Wing would like simply to abolish the Public Schools. The mere thought of Eton's tails (which *are* absurd) or Harrow's boaters is enough to make many a Laborite yearn to nationalize these and all other independent schools so that all children would be forced to attend state institutions. "It is surely untenable in a democracy," says one Labor politician, echoing a good many others, "that we should have a dual system of education. . . . Only when everyone from dukes to dustmen have to send their offspring to *real public* schools will every child have a real chance of a good education as a right." [56] Presumably this principle puts every democratic nation in the world, including the United States, in an untenable position, since they all have dual systems of public and private schools. Lady Gaitskell, in contrast to the more moderate views of her late husband, assures the House of Lords:

> We are not going to win the present battle of Britain by maintaining the public schools as bastions of privilege. We suffer from the kind of image that they helped to create. I have noticed that many of the titles inherited or bestowed on us in this House—the labels that we bear—have in countries like America passed into the language of Christian names, such as Duke Ellington, Marquis Childs and Earl Gardiner [*sic*—Erle Stanley Gardner]. I look forward to the time when great names like Eton and Winchester will survive with the label "comprehensive" attached to them.[57]

One of the favorite pastimes of those who criticize the Public Schools is counting up the numbers of their alumni who wind up in important jobs. Anthony Sampson's *Anatomy of Britain* is one of the most exhaustive efforts; Sampson himself is an old boy of one of the best Public Schools, Westminster.[58] Laborites took delight in pointing out the closed-club backgrounds of Sir Alec Douglas-Home's cabinet (ten from Eton, two from Harrow, two from Marlborough, etc.). To R. H. Tawney's favorite taunt about whether Englishmen really preferred to be ruled by

Old Etonians, the answer would seem to be yes, at least until recently. It must be said that the number of Public School old boys inhabiting the corridors of power in Britain is disproportionately large, even with the Labor Party in office; they still dominate the Foreign Office, the Senior Civil Service, the Church of England, and the big jobs in business and industry.

Public Schools are also criticized for conspiring with the ancient universities to fill more of the available places than they deserve. It is certainly true that the schools fill a seemingly disproportionate share of such places,[59] but the reasons for it do not suggest so much a conspiracy as a natural course of events. Public Schools are staffed mostly by graduates of Oxford and Cambridge, who have established relationships of long standing with most of the colleges of these universities. Also, Public Schools are better equipped than state grammar schools to prepare students for the special examinations, involving a third year in the sixth form, that are usually taken by applicants to these universities. And many state schools simply do not choose to compete for the Oxford and Cambridge vacancies. One gets the impression that these universities, conscious of the criticism, now bend over backward to give applicants from the state schools their chance, but the fact remains that they get more and better applicants from the Public Schools and the direct-grant schools.

A questionnaire distributed to a sample of Members of Parliament after the October 1964 election that brought Labor to power indicated, among other things, that forty-seven percent of the Labor MP's responding were in favor of simply abolishing the Public Schools, but none of the responding Tory MP's felt that way; forty-four percent of the Labor group had attended the state schools themselves, while only twelve percent of the Tories had; sixty-one percent of the Labor group were sending their own children to state schools, while only two percent of the Tories were.[60] Public School critics, however, find themselves in a kind of Tolstoyan struggle between their beliefs and their practices. Like Tolstoy, who suffered half a long lifetime because of the gap between his equalitarian social convictions and his patrician way of life, many people who support a more equalitarian educational system in England find themselves nonetheless sending their own children to the Public Schools. The issue breaks out frequently in Parliament, where a visitor to the public galleries can expect any educational debate to produce challenges from the Labor bench about how many Tories refuse to send their children to the state schools at the same time that they praise the state schools; and where occasionally a Tory will manage to embarrass a Laborite on the same issue. Here, for example, is a passage at arms in the House of Lords between Viscount Eccles, a former Minister of Education under the Tories, and Lord Snow, then a Labor spokesman in the

Lords on education and science who for many years had been scolding the English about their snobbery and class consciousness:

> *Viscount Eccles:* If all the schools are comprehensive, more children will go to a school where there is a tension between the home background and the school. . . . Noble Lords opposite realize this danger very well when they are deciding on the schools for their own children. I think I am right—and anyhow, I applaud him, if I am—in saying that the noble Lord, Lord Snow, is sending his young son to a comprehensive school? No? To a secondary modern? No? To a grammar school (where he went himself)? No? But to Eton. The decision to send the boy to Eton is, in my humble opinion, right, because there the tension between the noble Lord's home background and the school will not exist, and the chance of the boy's emerging with what they call an "integrated personality" is greater.
>
> *Lord Snow:* My Lords, may I reply to the noble Viscount's somewhat personal remarks? It is perfectly simple. It seems to me that if you are living in a fairly prosperous home it is a mistake to educate your child differently from most of the people he knows socially. I should not think it right to impose whatever ideologies I have upon someone who may not have those ideologies.[61]

It would not be easy to find a clearer illustration than Lord Snow's comment of the conflict of purpose and confusion of thought in the ranks of those who want to "do something about" the Public Schools. The Labor Party now sounds less strident on the issue than it did before coming to power in 1964, when it was promising to appoint a Public Schools "Trust" to force some fundamental but unspecified reform on them, perhaps even nationalization. At the end of 1965, the Laborites finally appointed a Public Schools "Commission" under the chairmanship of Sir John Newsom, a quite reasonable, unfanatical man whose 1963 report, *Half Our Future,* we looked at earlier in this chapter. The commission is charged with developing a way of "integrating the Public Schools into the state system," and its membership of fourteen is heavily weighted on the side of reform. Fortunately the commission will have available to it the results of a factual and statistical survey published in the fall of 1966 that for the first time brings together extensive and reliable data on the Public Schools —data that do little to support the unfavorable picture of these schools often painted by their political opponents and that do much to support their claims to academic excellence.[62]

The Newsom Commission's inquiry will not by any means be the first time that the Public Schools have been scrutinized by a reform-minded Royal Commission. Such bodies go back at least as far as 1861, when the "Clarendon Commission" was appointed in the twenty-fifth year of Victoria's reign to "Inquire into the Revenues and Management of Certain Colleges and Schools, and the Studies Pursued and Instruction Given Therein." It was composed of seven members, headed by the Earl of

Clarendon, who apparently thought various of his colleagues on the Commission "weak," "pedantic," "idle," "quirky," or "mad." [63] Nine schools were stipulated for inclusion in the investigation: Rugby, Shrewsbury, Winchester, Harrow, Charterhouse, Westminster, Merchant Taylors', St. Paul's, and Eton. The Clarendon Report of 1864, four fat volumes of it, is an amusing and even fascinating document, covering every aspect of the operations of these nine old schools whose combined enrollment at the time was 2,696 boys between ages eight and nineteen. The masters were mostly classical scholars, and the curriculum was built around classical languages and literatures, arithmetic and mathematics, French or German, and a little science. Like many a modern educational investigation, the Clarendon Commission reported that it had "found no difficulty in ascertaining what is taught in these schools [but] to discover what and how much is learnt in them is difficult, and is only roughly practicable." In an effort to discover how much was learned as well as taught, the commission proposed to the nine schools that an examination be given to all of their pupils; but, the commission complained, it could get the cooperation of only two, Rugby and Shrewsbury.

The Clarendon Report's findings and recommendations did not at all spare the schools. Fundamental reform was called for, especially in the way in which the schools were governed. The report led to a Public Schools Act in 1868 as well as to still another commission, the Taunton Commission, to investigate the hundreds of grammar schools not covered by the Clarendon inquiry. Interestingly enough, it was at this same time that the Headmasters' Conference was formed as a watchdog group to protect the Public Schools from too much government interference.

Eighty years later, that educational catalyst World War II caused the appointment of another national investigatory group, the "Fleming Committee," whose charge from the government was "to consider means whereby the association between the Public Schools . . . and the general educational system of the country could be developed and extended . . ." The committee's report in 1944 strongly recommended the systematic infusion into the Public Schools of pupils from the state schools, whose attendance would be financed by their Local Educational Authorities. What the committee had in mind was not radical transformation but a kind of gradual assimilation and integration, making the special advantages of "boarding education" available to a wider group of pupils. "We are led," said the Fleming Committee in its report,

> to the conclusion that the education given by the Public Schools includes elements of very high educational value, especially but not entirely on the boarding side. It would, therefore, be wrong to destroy them, as the more extreme of their critics desire (by the appropriation of their endowments and the diversion of their buildings to other purposes) or to refuse to associate them in any way with the general system of education, pro-

vided that the number of boys admitted to them from Primary Schools is sufficient to avoid the dangers which have been discussed. The problem of providing boarding education for all who can benefit will only be partly solved by this means, but the contribution of the Public Schools, though relatively small in numbers, would be very far from negligible in other respects. The Public Schools have been giving a boarding education for generations, and some for centuries, and thus they have experience in a matter where experience is of the highest importance, and they have also in most cases, sufficient and suitable accommodation and equipment to make a sound start. Above all, they are willing and anxious to play their part and they can begin without delay. We see the risks and difficulties, but these are not sufficient to persuade us that proposals cannot be framed which will be to the immediate educational advantage of thousands of children and will be a first step towards a much greater measure of social and educational unity in the nation.[64]

After twenty more years, the British government was supporting another inquiry into boarding education and how to make it available to more children, for, unfortunately, the recommendations of the Fleming Report, though widely applauded, were not adopted. Few LEA's, that is, were willing to put up the money necessary for pupils from state schools to attend Public Schools; and in 1965 the investigator found the LEA's "spending annually six times as much money on transporting pupils as they are on help with boarding fees." [65]

So now the Public Schools are faced with still another commission whose "main function," as the Secretary said in announcing the commission in the House of Commons,

will be to advise on the best way of integrating the public schools with the State system of education. The Government are determined that the public schools should make the maximum contribution to meeting the education needs of the country, and that this should be done in such a way as to reduce the socially divisive effect which they now exert. This implies that the schools should, like other parts of the education system, become progressively open to boys and girls irrespective of the income of their parents; that the schools should move toward a wider range of academic attainment, so that the public sector may increasingly play its own part in the national movement towards comprehensive education. . . .[66]

It may be that many people who have welcomed this new commission and who would welcome a broadening of the social spectrum of the Public Schools misunderstand the government's intention. The Secretary's purpose seems to go a good deal beyond the Fleming recommendations. Now "integration into the state system" apparently means not a way of making a Public School education available to able children from poor families, but a way of making the Public Schools something like state comprehensive schools. If these schools, as the Secretary's announcement indicates, are to accept "a wider range of academic attainment" than they already accept, which as we have seen is much wider than state grammar schools, and if they are to take in state-financed pupils at the same time, it can only add up to conversion of the Public Schools to some sort of commonplace comprehensive institutions.

It may yet be that the English Public Schools, like Louis XVI, will have to be guillotined not for what they have done but for what they are. No Reign of Terror will follow their execution, but the educational loss to Britain will be great. Of course, things may not turn out this way. In the past the Public Schools have shown great staying power under attack because they have in turn enjoyed the tenacious support of a large segment of English society; and they may yet be able to retain something of their peculiar identity within whatever recommendations the Newsom Commission produces. One can only hope that moderation prevails and that these schools, so widely and justly admired in other countries, can be liberalized without being destroyed.

This controversy about the Public Schools is similar to the quarrel that occasionally comes to the surface in the United States. We had a flurry of comment about our own independent schools and whether or not they were socially divisive in 1952, when James Bryant Conant made news at the annual conference of the American Association of School Administrators by seeming to attack private schools as an evil. He later clarified his position by voicing his fears that "a dual system of secondary education may in some states, at least, come to threaten the democratic unity provided by our public schools." [67] Private education has continued to prosper, however, in the United States, at least in part because of parental dissatisfaction with state schools, and today independent schools are flourishing as never before. I for one doubt very much that they offer any threat to democracy; and educationally, they have a very healthful effect on state schools by giving them some badly needed competition. In 1966 there was an Independent Schools Talent Search Program established in the United States to try to bring more pupils from poor families into the leading independent schools, thus echoing in a minor key the dominant theme of the present quarrel in Britain.

As this chapter has indicated, there is much that we in the United States could learn from English schools. We could learn that children are capable of working effectively in language and numbers earlier than they do in American schools; that they are capable in the elementary school of more systematic and sustained study in basic subjects than they generally get in American schools; that the true abilities of many children are often buried by low scores on standardized tests or by poor home conditions or by low expectations on the part of teachers; that children do not suffer from a longer school day and year than is standard in America.

Even more important, we could learn that a limited, though by no means a rigid, curriculum for students at every ability level is important; that schools cannot try to do everything and anything and still be schools; that they must establish some priorities thought by adults, not children, to be important; that secondary-school students of modest ability can be brought further in basic subjects, including mathematics and foreign languages, than they commonly are in American schools; that students of high ability can be brought a great deal further in basic subjects than they commonly are in American schools. And we could learn that the elaborate administrative machinery that characterizes our schools and school systems, with their plenitude of nonteaching supervisory personnel, is not visibly superior to the looser and much less grandiose system of the English (and European) schools, where the emphasis in administration is on classroom freedom, not restriction, and on the selection of part-time administrators who are respected for their ability as teachers. All this and more we could learn from English schools, while at the same time recognizing and eschewing their weaknesses. But first there must be a willingness to look abroad for ideas on the part of those in charge of American schools.

## CHAPTER IV

# Public Examinations and National Standards

"THE DESIRE TO SUBMIT TO PUBLIC EXAMINATION," says one lifelong observer of the examinations scene in Britain, "is endemic to English education." [1] Many educationists in England would agree, feeling that their school system is the most "exam-ridden" in the world. And indeed it must seem so to a twenty-one-year-old student at the end of his university career as he accepts his classified degree; for by that time he will have been through at least four major public competitive examinations, at ages eleven, sixteen, eighteen, and twenty-one. His American counterpart may have been through one more or less public examination in the form of the College Boards, or other standardized test series, but many will have been through none at all.

The British system of examinations is in the European tradition, but like so much else in English education, it makes a greater number of distinctions among students than most of the European systems. Beyond the 11-plus, one never merely passes an examination; one passes at a particular level, of which there are quite a few. Although the selection procedure at 11-plus is disappearing, or rather the system of separate secondary schools is disappearing, other exams are by no means diminishing in importance. On the contrary, more students than ever are taking examinations for the General Certificate of Education (the GCE), and it continues to play a decisive role in the lives and fortunes of Englishmen. Moreover, another national examination, the Certificate of Secondary Education, is now being developed as a complement to the GCE and will be taken by an even greater number of students. A devotion to public examinations may not be peculiar to England, as any French or German student working toward his *Baccalauréat* or his *Abitur* would testify, but the English have more of them. And not without controversy.

In this chapter I will treat the subject of public examinations in considerable detail. We are now engaged in the United States in a discussion about national scholastic standards or the lack of them, about a national curriculum or the lack of it, and about a national "assessment" that is currently going forward. After several years of preparation, a "program of national assessment" wholly financed by nongovernmental means has now been established in the United States. It will be conducted over a number of years beginning with tests in 1967 in the basic subjects, the fine arts, and vocational education, given to a large sample of children throughout the country. The tests have been so constructed that no individual or school or school system or state can be identified or compared with any other. It is to be a national assessment, an attempt to do something we have never yet been able to do in American education: find out how well we are doing as a country in education. The project has predictably outraged a lot of our educational administrators, who gave it a roughing up at the 1965 White House Conference on Education, and also at the 1966 annual conference of the American Association of School Administrators—a body of gentlemen who are wont to breathe fire at the smallest suggestion of any sort of centralized or comparative testing in American education, but who see nothing wrong with the centralized authority exercised over American education by their own professional association. "A handful of starry-eyed though well-intentioned idealists," cried the Superintendent of Schools from St. Paul,

> from their ivory towers dreamed up "national assessment" to identify the many vague and undiagnosed illnesses they honestly assumed were hampering the educational body. Though advised that the proposed "purging" and "blood-letting" had been tried before with little success in various states, they persist in their allegiance to their original commitment.[2]

I have a feeling that he may have been reflecting the views of a good many school administrators about the whole idea of national examinations or "assessments." The stormy passage that this project has already had on the administrative seas suggests to me, even more strongly than my instincts, that the chances of our even experimenting with a national system of exams are exceedingly thin. Yet I want to make that proposal in this chapter, improbable though it may be of realization. We badly need the kind of *ad hoc* educational assessment now being conducted, which in fact may become a permanent part of the education scene; but I believe we need more than this. We need a means of regular and *comparative* assessment that will tell individual students and their parents and their teachers and their schools where they are in educational accomplishment. It is precisely this kind of comparative measurement that the present assessment project is carefully avoiding, since it would otherwise be even more controversial than the present program.

One way of creating such a comparative measurement is a publicly recognized "school-leaving certificate," not necessarily controlled centrally but of a known standard. The British and European national examinations have plenty of imperfections, and I would not want to see us attempt to import any of them. But since we have nothing like the "external" exams and school-leaving certificates (with the possible exception of the Regents exams in New York State) that prevail in England and Europe, we might, by looking at them, at least illuminate the problems and possibilities of an experiment of our own. We are alone among the advanced nations of the world in having no national system of regular educational evaluation.

I will devote the first part of this chapter to a factual discussion of how the GCE works in England, not to encourage our adopting the GCE or any other existing exam system, but simply to give interested readers a detailed look at how one system operates. I will include a sampling of typical syllabuses used in connection with the GCE exams, and a sampling of questions from recent exams themselves. I will also include excerpts from two representative students' papers written for a recent exam of one of the major GCE boards. I believe this is the first time that publication of actual student papers from GCE exams has been allowed, and I would like here to express my appreciation to the English authorities for their help and permission; I only regret that space limitations prevent my reproducing a number of other student papers in the appendices.

After describing the operations of a GCE board, I will turn to a critical discussion of the whole system, then will discuss briefly the new national examination being created in England alongside the GCE, and finally will discuss the place that an external examination system might play in the United States. Some readers may find that this chapter, like books on penguins or water buffaloes that tell them far more than they care to know about such esoteric subjects, tells them more than they want to know about examinations; but some others, I hope, will find the extended discussion useful.

## How the GCE Works

Public examinations in England are about a century old, but the GCE, the most important of them, dates in its present form only from 1951. It is now taken by upwards of three-quarters of a million students a year, most of them between the ages of sixteen and eighteen from selective secondary schools. Briefly defined, it is a voluntary, two-level, public, written examination of the essay type, prepared and graded "externally"—that is, by agencies external to the individual school—and acts as both a "leaving" and a "matriculation" exam. It is usually taken at its lower level, the Ordinary or "O" Level, at the end of the fifth form of the secondary school, at age sixteen. It is taken at its upper level, the Advanced or "A" Level, at the end of the "upper sixth form," at age eighteen. Unlike the usual European leaving examination, with its compulsory groups of subjects, the GCE is a separate-subject exam in which the candidate chooses the subjects he will attempt and the number of them he will attempt. Thus a student does not "pass" or "fail" the GCE. He passes or fails in whatever individual subjects he has elected. Scotland has followed England's lead in this regard: Traditionally the Scottish Certificate of Education was awarded only to students who had passed in at least five subjects, two of which had to be at the Higher Grade; now it is a separate-subject exam like the GCE, although taken successfully in either its Ordinary or Higher grade by a considerably higher percentage of the age group (thirty-five percent) than is true of the GCE.

In addition to the pass-fail verdict, a student's performance in each subject of the GCE is graded. At O Level there are no fewer than nine possible grades, 1–6 being pass grades and 7–9 fail. One can pass triumphantly, that is, and get a 1, or barely and get a 6. One can barely fail the subject and get a 7 or fail resoundingly and get a 9. Grades at O Level are "unofficial" and are not entered on the certificate that is awarded to successful candidates by the examining bodies. They are, however, sent back to the school, where the headmaster may and usually does make them known to the student. At A Level, there are five pass grades, one fail grade, and one special category known as "Allowed Ordinary," a grade given students who do not quite reach the lowest pass mark for A Level but whose paper is judged to have reached the standard of O Level. Grades at A Level go on the certificate given the student and are also sent by the examining bodies to all British universities for use in admissions.

The GCE is run by means of a typically complex piece of English educational machinery. Each of eight separate boards, "approved examining bodies," scattered around the country, operates its own GCE examination, meaning that there are eight GCE's, not one. Seven of the boards are associated in a loose fashion with one or more universities that may or may not exercise a measure of control over them. Each has been approved by the central Department and is subject to a certain amount of supervision, in practice very little, by the Department. Each issues its own certificates to successful candidates. These documents carry the signatures of the chief administrator of the board and of the Secretary of State for Education and Science, signifying thereby the not always happy marriage of the central government and the separate boards in carrying out a national educational evaluation.

Although the eight boards are to some extent regional in their clientele, each school and each head is free to use any one or any number of boards. Often the choice is made on simple geographical grounds, but often also on grounds of hard experience, reflecting the record a school has made with a given board in the past. Often it is also made on frivolous, uninformed, and sometimes snobbish grounds. Most boards have by now acquired reputations among school heads. The board in Wales, known as the Welsh Joint Education Committee, and one of the London boards, known as the Associated Examining Board, are regarded as easy boards, while the Oxford and Cambridge Schools Examination Board is thought to be the toughest and most desirable. Among the Public Schools the customary thing is to use the Oxford and Cambridge board. Some schools will pick the Cambridge Local Examinations Syndicate on the strength of its antiquity. And some heads will pick a board for no better reason than that they happen to have gone to the university with which it is associated. Some boards do a good deal of overseas examining, especially in Commonwealth countries, and some develop particular lines of specialization. Some are rich and some have trouble surviving; one went out of business in 1964 for lack of sufficient candidates.

But the diversity of the boards can easily be overstated. The two largest boards, the Joint Matriculation Board (in Manchester) and the University of London School Examinations Council, together examine about two-thirds of all GCE candidates. There are far more similarities than not in the operations of the eight GCE boards. Whether the differences among them, especially the possible differences in standards, are substantial is a vexed question to which I will return later in this chapter.

Although the GCE is still a very young examination, it is an integral part of a system of examining that goes back to the middle of the nineteenth century. Public examinations in England, as in other countries, grew out of political and social reform movements, as a way of equalizing opportunity among all classes of society and of diminishing the effects of patronage. They continue even today to fill that vital function all over Europe. Until World War I such examinations in England were dominated for matriculation purposes by the separate universities and by a number of professional bodies. But the multiplicity of exams and the variation in standards among them were such that the schools were put into an untenable position in trying to prepare students for university admission and professional qualification. In 1917 the Board of Education, as the national education authority was then called, designed a more or less unified national system of exams that was to be conducted by the several examining bodies already in operation. There was to be a "School Certificate" examination for students at sixteen, and a "Higher School Certificate" examination at about eighteen. Both were examinations in which the candidates had to earn passes in a number of subjects simultaneously in order to pass in the exam itself. The School Certificate required a pass in English Language and five other subjects, including a science, a foreign language, and mathematics. It was graded simply "Very good" for an average and above performance, or "Pass" for a lower performance. Looking at the old syllabuses and examination questions, I would suppose that the pass standard was not very high, but it had to be achieved in six subjects. Thus England got its first state examinations, which became in effect national leaving certificates representing, it was hoped, something like a national standard.

As often happens in national examinations, this system became controversial as the uses to which its certificates were put went beyond the original intentions, and as the schools themselves changed, particularly in the size of their enrollments. In 1941 the Secondary School Examinations Council, an overseeing body created at the same time as the School Certificate system, conscious of a growing body of criticism about the examinations, appointed a committee to "consider suggested changes in the Secondary School curriculum and the question of School Examinations in relation thereto." The committee produced in 1943 the Norwood Report,[3] named after Sir Cyril Norwood, its chairman (then President of St. John's College, Oxford). I would recommend this report to American readers interested in comparing the twentieth-century development of English and American education. The report is strongly progressive in ideology, but contains excellent summaries of the arguments, pro and con, about the basic problems of mass education. I will refer later to its discussion of the examination system; here let it suffice to say that the report found much to quarrel with in the School Certificate system and recommended a number of major changes, including the eventual adoption of an internal exam run by classroom teachers in place of the external exam at age sixteen. Because of the war and the coming of the 1944 Act, most of the Norwood recommendations were not put into effect, but they prepared the way for important changes that have come about recently.

A few years later when the LEA's were in the midst of reconstructing their schools in accordance with the Act of 1944, the Secondary School Examinations Council produced a report upon which the present GCE system is based. The "general" in the name General Certificate of Education signified the council's hope that the new exams would be taken by mature persons at various stages of their careers as well as by students. The council also wished to liberalize the existing system by removing the group requirement of the School Certificate and by other measures. The new system came into effect in 1951 and quickly demonstrated once again how difficult it is to restrict national examinations to limited purposes. The intention of the Secondary School Examinations Council was to create chiefly a qualifying exam (not a leaving or even a competitive exam), to be used by persons wanting to demonstrate their qualifications for some kind of further education. But the GCE soon took on all of the coloration of the old School Certificate and Higher School Certificate. It was regarded universally, as it is today, as a competitive device serving at once the functions of a leaving, a matriculation, and a qualifying examination. Now it is sedulously pursued by many secondary modern schools, by all streams of the grammar schools, and by all streams of the swollen sixth forms in any kind of school. It is the principal criterion for admission to almost all forms of post-secondary education and to most of the desirable jobs in business, the civil service, and other fields.

Admission requirements in higher education are commonly stated in GCE terms: Five O Levels are the minimum for entering Colleges of Education (although, as we will see in Chapter V, most entrants now do better than this), and two A Levels for the universities; the range of ability so encompassed can be very wide. Banks and other prestige employers often state that their preference is "strongly for the A Level man." Over seventy professional associations in England use the GCE as evidence of preliminary education and as a qualification for admission to their own specialized exams. The British army advertises for potential officers with a photograph of a dozen new officers in a clubby atmosphere, with a caption that asks: "Does it matter what school you went to?" The text of the ad indicates that, whereas the officer ranks were once the domain of the Public School boy, nowadays it is strictly a matter of the GCE. Perhaps the army is only the most recent example of the traditional equalizing function of public examinations.

As the principal door to status and advancement, the GCE is necessarily a minority examination. The numbers of students taking it have increased dramatically in recent years, but it remains an exam that nearly two-thirds of the children in English schools do not even attempt. Of those that do attempt O Level, perhaps half, 17.9% of the age group, will get passes in five or more subjects—the standard that has come to be regarded as about minimal for proceeding to A Level and beyond, though it does not in itself mean very much unless one knows in what subjects the five passes were secured and the grade of pass achieved. At A Level 8.2% of the age group will get passes in two or more subjects, thus reaching minimum qualifications for entrance to a university, and 5.1% will now gain three passes. The best students commonly take and pass a wide range of basic subjects at O Level, often seven or eight—for example, History, English, perhaps two languages, Biology, Chemistry, and Physics. Two years later they will pass three subjects at A Level. Some of them will also do one or more "Special" papers at the same time that they do their A Levels, which if successful are graded either "Distinction" or "Merit" and which increase their chances of a good university place.

The logistics of running the GCE system are formidable, involving the coordinated services of many hundreds of examiners and the reading and grading of millions of individual student papers a year. Most of the important aspects of the work cannot be handled by computers or data-processing equipment, as can American standardized tests. A closer look at one of the eight GCE boards will perhaps suggest the main virtues and vices of this kind of examination system. I will take one of the larger and better-known boards as an example, the Joint Matriculation Board (the JMB), whose operations are typical in most respects of the other seven boards, although this board is probably more efficient and has done more research on its own operations than the other boards.

The JMB was set up in 1903 in fulfillment of the provision in the charters of the universities of Manchester, Liverpool, and Leeds that a joint authority should be formed to conduct matriculation exams for these institutions. Two more universities, Sheffield and Birmingham, were later admitted to the JMB, which today still does the bulk of GCE examining for students applying to these five universities, though, like the other GCE boards, it also draws clients from all parts of Britain.

The first job of the JMB is to print syllabuses for the subjects at each level that it proposes, two years hence, to examine. Thus if it intends to conduct examinations at O Level in half a hundred subjects in 1970, it must have syllabuses for all these subjects in print in 1968 for distribution to the schools and individuals that wish to prepare for these examinations. For this purpose the board appoints a preparatory committee for each subject at each level. With a GCE board that has been in operation a long time and whose syllabuses have been refined over many years, these preparatory committees become in effect bodies that review and revise the existing syllabuses more often than they create wholly new ones. The committees vary in size and complexion with the subject, but in most cases will include both classroom teachers and university faculty members. They are informed through the JMB itself and through other channels about the current experience of the schools with their subject and syllabus. When any change in an existing syllabus is made, it is submitted for approval to the Schools Council, the central agency in London now charged by the Department with supervision of the GCE boards. In future, however, this practice, which has been a source of friction between the boards and the Council, will be discontinued.

With the necessary approvals in hand, the JMB prints in one volume all the syllabuses for a given year. For 1967 its volume of *Regulations and Syllabuses* is a 132-page document that gives the syllabuses for forty-six subjects at O Level stretching from subjects like English and Mathematics that will be taken by many thousands of students to Greek and Textiles that may be taken by a few hundred or even dozens. It also contains the syllabuses for thirty-five subjects at A Level, in twenty-five of which Special papers will also be offered in the examination. Some subjects will also carry a number of alternative syllabuses. O-Level His-

tory, for example, offers the possibility of ten historical periods and therefore of ten syllabuses to the teacher or school. The JMB is thus involved
in keeping a very large number of syllabuses under review.

The next and more complicated job is the annual preparation of the
examinations themselves.[4] Unlike our own mass-testing organizations,
which make almost a fetish of secrecy, the JMB and most of the GCE
boards indulge in full disclosure of their examinations, as do most of
the national exam systems in Europe. Each year the JMB publishes the
previous year's exams in full. This means of course that a new exam
must be prepared for each syllabus each year, or rather two sets of
examinations, since the GCE is given twice a year, in the summer and
the fall. These papers are prepared by the chairman and chief examiner
of a panel of examiners that will also read and grade the student papers.
One of these posts usually goes to a university teacher and one to a school-
teacher, both of whom will have had experience in marking papers and
perhaps in other aspects of examination work. Together they draft both
of the year's examinations in the subject, and the draft is then submitted
to a reviser, who is always a practicing teacher and who has veto authority over the drafts. Copies of the drafts are also sent to the preparatory committee responsible for the syllabus of the subject. Comments
from these persons go back to the chairman and chief examiner, and
then all meet to discuss a revision. The revised drafts go back again to
the reviser for more comment and in particular for comparison with the
examinations of previous years. If satisfied he accepts the papers and
they become that year's examinations. There is no attempt at "pre-
testing" the exams, as is customary with American standardized tests.

Next comes the intricate and formidable job of reading and grading
the papers. The panel of examiners in a basic subject can be very large.
In addition to the chairman and chief examiner, who have responsibility
for the questions, there may be several assistant chief examiners and any
number of marking examiners, perhaps fifty or sixty in a popular subject.
If the JMB has 80,000 students taking its O-Level English exams, as it
often does, a panel of well over a hundred people will be necessary.
Altogether the JMB may appoint between 1,500 and 2,000 examiners to
its panels in any given year. They are paid three or four hundred dollars
for reading four or five hundred papers in the space of three or four
weeks following an examination. A-Level examiners are appointed by
invitation of the JMB, mostly from the ranks of O-Level examiners but
as often as possible from university faculty ranks.

A central problem with a large panel, especially in subjects that do not
lend themselves to precise grading, is that of securing adequate standardization in the marking. Some months before an exam is given, the
chairman and chief examiner of each panel will develop a marking guide
that allots a certain number of points to each major part of each ques-

tion. This guide will also discuss the variety of possible answers, point out special items to be looked for, and will give general directions for the grading. The guide is then sent as a draft to each member of the panel for comment and revision.

When the exam has been given, the student papers are mailed to the examiners, who are expected within one or two days to read, with the help of the marking guide, a random sample of twenty-five papers. Immediately thereafter all members of the panel assemble for a standardizing meeting. Examiners' experience with their own samples is discussed and photographic copies of other samples are circulated and marked during the meeting. The marking guide is then given a final revision, if necessary, after which examiners go home to wrestle with their conscience and their papers. After the marked papers are returned to the JMB there is a final meeting of the senior examiners of the panel to review individual reports from the panel as well as statistical data comparing this year's scores with those of previous years. It is at this meeting that the minimum pass mark is decided upon for that subject that year. Once this pass mark has been established, everything else follows mathematically so that the various grades of pass and fail describe the bell-shaped curve of normal distribution of ability. A number of other checks against errors or injustice have been developed over the years at the JMB to ensure that every student's paper gets as fair an assessment as is possible under the unavoidably limiting conditions of a mass written examination. Finally, the JMB receives each year reports on the student papers. These reports are the final and considered comments from its senior examiners about the way in which students responded to the questions on the examination. Each year they make a small volume of enlightening and amusing reading.

Thus it is that anyone sufficiently interested in the GCE, and this obviously includes great numbers of British teachers and students, has access to a pretty full record: syllabuses, the examinations themselves, the examiners' reports, and sundry other documents. How much help this kind of disclosure gives candidates is an open question. The JMB pass rates remain about the same from year to year: 55% of O Level papers are passed, and 75% of A Level (the national average is 57.6% and 67.9%).

## A SAMPLING OF ITEMS FROM
## GCE SYLLABUSES AND EXAMINATIONS

Although each of the eight GCE's has its own syllabuses, examinations, and grading procedures, they have, as I indicated earlier, far more in common than not. Hence, the general reader can get a fair picture of the content and standards of the GCE by some judicious sampling. Readers are likely to be more familiar with English literature than with other subjects. Looking, therefore, at recent O-Level syllabuses in this subject, we find that they tend to be quite brief, often only a list of readings with very few if any directions to the teacher. The JMB gives the school a choice of two syllabuses in this subject, each of which has three parts: drama, poetry, and prose. The first syllabus gives the teacher a further choice of one out of two Shakespeare plays, one out of three selections of poetry, and one out of the following three books: Dickens' *Great Expectations,* Hardy's *Far from the Madding Crowd,* or Sassoon's *Memoirs of a Fox-Hunting Man.* The alternative syllabus includes one play, a smaller selection of poetry, and two out of the following four books: Jane Austen's *Pride and Prejudice,* Hardy's *Under the Greenwood Tree,* Evelyn Waugh's *Scoop,* and Laurens van der Post's *Venture to the Interior.*

The recent syllabus of the Associated Examining Board, widely thought of as a lenient board, prescribes a Shakespeare or a Shaw play, a selection of poetry, and one or more of these novels: Priestley's *The Good Companions,* Hardy's *Far from the Madding Crowd,* Monsarrat's *The Cruel Sea,* and "Miss Read's" *Village School.* There is other prose to choose from also. Directions to the teacher say simply: "There will be no context questions set on the prescribed books. The intention is to encourage wide reading and, where possible, to relate reading to modern life."

One of the Oxford boards, the Oxford Delegacy of Local Examinations, gives a choice of two syllabuses, one "Selected" and one "General" English literature. The Selected syllabus gives a choice of one out of three Shakespeare plays; Chaucer's "Nun's Priest's Tale" or one of three other poetry choices; and one book out of these four: Defoe's *Robinson Crusoe, Part I,* Jane Austen's *Pride and Prejudice,* Conrad's *The Rover,* or Orwell's *Animal Farm.*

In short, the typical O-Level exam in English Literature involves one play, one novel, and a quite modest selection of poetry. The JMB examination on the syllabus described above is divided into two sections and the student is asked to answer three questions from a variety of possibilities in each section. In the first and less important section, passages of a dozen or fifteen lines are reprinted from the prescribed plays and poetry and are followed by questions. For *Henry IV, Part I,* the question might be: "What impressions of the characters of Glendower and Hotspur do you gain from the above passage?" Or for *The Tempest,* a student might choose this problem: "Give a brief account of how Antonio, with Alonso's aid, had succeeded in supplanting Prospero as Duke of Milan." Similarly with the novels, passages of several hundred words are followed by such questions as: "What are the general effects the author wishes to produce in this description, and how does he achieve them?" or "What general characteristics of the rustic characters do you find illustrated in this passage?"

In the second section of the exam, upon which the student spends most of his two and a half hours, no passages are reprinted, but from the choices available a student might take these three:

1. There are those who find Prince Hal, in *Henry IV, Part I*, an unattractive person. By means of a full character sketch with close reference to the text state your views on his character as presented by Shakespeare.

2. From *English and Scottish Ballads* choose two poems which are interesting and impressive because of the strong feelings involved. Give the substance of each in such a way as to bring out their emotional quality.

3. Choose one incident in *Far from the Madding Crowd* which seems to you to be particularly exciting or dramatic, and one which seems particularly pathetic or sad. Give an account of each incident in such a way as to bring out the qualities for which you have chosen it.

At A Level, which is taken two years later by students who have usually concentrated during these two years on three subjects, the syllabus is much more extensive. A total of twenty-four works which seem to me worth listing here are prescribed in a recent JMB syllabus, although students are by no means expected to have a mastery of them all:

Shakespeare, *A Winter's Tale* and *Hamlet*
Chaucer, *Prologue to the Canterbury Tales* and *The Squieres Tale*
Spenser, *Faerie Queene, Book VI*
Jonson, *The Alchemist*
Milton, *Comus* and *Samson Agonistes*
Defoe, *Robinson Crusoe, Part I* and *Journal of the Plague Year*
Fielding, *Joseph Andrews*
Sheridan, *The Critic* and *The School for Scandal*
Wordsworth, *The Prelude, I and II* together with *Lines Composed above Tintern Abbey*
Jane Austen, *Persuasion*
Byron, *Childe Harold, Canto IV* together with T. L. Peacock, *Nightmare Abbey*
Emily Brontë, *Wuthering Heights*
Browning, *Men and Women*
Hardy, *The Mayor of Casterbridge*
Conrad, *Nostromo*
T. S. Eliot, *Murder in the Cathedral*
W. H. Auden, *A Selection*

The examination on this syllabus allows students to choose questions pertaining to only a few of these works. The A-Level exam takes five and a half hours, unless the student elects also to do the Special paper, which takes an additional three hours. Half the exam is again made up of questions arising out of reprinted passages from the Shakespeare plays and out of both prose and verse passages not seen before by the student. He may be asked to identify the speakers in the Shakespeare quotations and to discuss the dramatic significance of the quoted material. With the unseen passages, he is asked general questions; for example, to comment on the imagery and the verse form. The other half of the exam asks him to answer four questions out of nineteen, mostly on the prescribed books, and gives him two choices within each question. If the student picks Defoe, for example, he must answer:

*Either,* (a) What do you find in *Robinson Crusoe* to account for its sustained popularity?

*Or,*    (b) What does Defoe say about (i) the narrator's religious faith and (ii) that of the citizens in general, in their attitude toward the Plague? What contribution does this religious element make to the vividness of the narrative?

If the student picks the prescribed poetry of Wordsworth, he must write an essay on these problems:

*Either,* (a) Discuss the qualities of Wordsworth's poetic style, with illustrations from both *The Prelude, I and II* and *Lines Composed above Tintern Abbey.*

*Or,*    (b) What has Wordsworth to say in each of these poems about the Wisdom and Spirit of the universe?

If he elects to try the Special paper as well, as many do, he will not have a special syllabus to worry about but will simply have an opportunity to demonstrate his talents on prose and poetry that he has not seen before and on general literary questions. The questions might be so specific as to ask for the meaning of a particular phrase or so general as to ask the student whether he thinks the whole passage is "good English prose." Or he might choose this option:

"Emotion recollected in tranquillity." Explain what you understand by this statement of the content of poetry, and discuss, with relevant illustration, how far you think it applies to poetry and the conditions in which it is composed.

Or this one:

"The disintegration of the novel." Explain in what sense it has "disintegrated" and try to assess, with relevant illustration and reference from your reading what has been lost and gained in the process.

For the many other subjects in which the GCE is given, I cannot hope to do more than give the reader a sprinkling of examples to complete the review of English Literature above. Looking at the following typical GCE questions, one should remember that stipulated syllabuses have been followed in each case by the student in preparation for the exam, that O Level is usually taken at age sixteen in a number of subjects simultaneously, and that A Level is taken at eighteen in two or three subjects.

*O-Level Questions in History:* (1) Explain how Henry VII laid the foundation of the Tudor monarchy. (2) Give an account of Oliver Cromwell's conquests of Ireland and Scotland, and describe his treatment of the Irish and the Scots. (3) Describe the main changes in British farming in the eighteenth century, and give the results. (4) Examine the [provided] map of the Middle East after the First World War, then in your answer-book, name [a number of features identified by letters on the map]. . . . What problems faced Great Britain in the Middle East after the First World War?

*O-Level Questions in Biology:* (1) If a small mammal, such as a rabbit, accidentally presses a foot on a projecting thorn, what reaction would you expect the mammal to make? With the help of a large, fully-labelled diagram, explain how this reaction is brought about. (2) Make a large, labelled diagram of a winter twig of a named deciduous tree. What adverse conditions face the plants and animals of this country in winter? How is survival during the winter ensured by (i) deciduous trees; (ii) annual herbaceous plants; (iii) frogs; (iv) butterflies or moths?

*O-Level Questions in Physics:* (1) Write an account of the nature, properties and uses of infra-red radiation. (2) How would you find by experiment the frequency of vibration of a tuning fork? (3) Explain the statement "the refractive index of glass is 1.5." (4) Give three reasons why mercury is a suitable liquid for use in a therometer [and] state one way in which the design of a thermometer can be modified so as to increase its sensitivity. (5) With the aid of labelled diagrams explain the action of any two of the following: (a) an alternating current generator, (b) an induction coil, and (c) an electrophus.

*A-Level Questions in Geography:* (1) Give a reasoned account of the distribution in the British Isles of either dairy farming or the heavy chemical industry. (2) Describe and suggest reasons for the distribution of population in South Africa. (3) With reference to the U.S.S.R. either assess the importance relative to each other of the seas bordering her shores or discuss the growth of urban areas east of the Urals. (4) From the viewpoint of their agricultural geography compare either California south of the Golden Gate with Florida or Uruguay with Chile.

*A-Level Questions in British Government:* (1) "House of Commons Reform." What reforms, if any, would you suggest, and why? (2) Have recent critics of the civil service established a case for reform? (3) Discuss the special problems of local government in large conurbations outside London. (4) What are the different methods by which organized interests seek to influence government policy, and how effective are these methods?

*A-Level Questions in Botany:* (1) Briefly describe what is meant by alternation of generations. Illustrate, by means of a labelled diagram only, the structure of the gametophytes in a moss and a fern. Describe the process of fertilization in these plants. (2) Using a named example of each, give an illustrated account of leaves modified (a) for food storage, (b) for climbing, (c) as spines. (3) Briefly discuss the structure of three named carbohydrates and their importance to plants. If you were provided with a mixture which you suspected to contain starch and sucrose, what steps would you take to separate them and confirm their identity? (4) Give an account of the structure and life-history of *Fucos.*

The GCE is not wholly written or theoretical work. Where appropriate, practical application is also required. Exams in geography may involve interpreting a photograph; those in art may involve drawing from a live model or criticizing a painting supplied at the examination. Geometrical Drawing will use blueprints, Geology will need rocks, music students will play for the examiners, and language students will perform in an oral as well as a written test. The sciences will require laboratory work. Advanced Level Biology, in the words of one set of directions, may require for each candidate "a large female rat, not in an advanced stage of pregnancy, fresh or deep frozen . . . [which] should be thawed out for examination at room temperature, *not* in hot water." One year's General Certificates at the JMB may, in the words of its chief administrator, "require twenty thousand yards of ribbon . . . for one examination in Biology ten thousand blow-flies were bred, slaughtered and impaled each singly upon a cork-sheathed pin and, if sweet-peas are set as specimens by the examiners, market-gardens are swept bare of every bloom. Everything from logarithmic tables to dog-fish, must be at hand at the places, in sufficient quantities and at the times it is required." [5] By contrast with the essay-and-demonstration-type exam represented by the GCE, the American standardized tests are an administrator's dream; but they have their own limitations.

## The GCE Critically Considered

Because we lack experience with external essay-type examinations in the United States, I have thought it useful to review in the above fashion the mechanics of the GCE system. And because I believe we can profit from English experience with this system, I turn now to a critique of it. British opinion itself is becoming increasingly divided on the GCE. Within the education field, people who make the greatest use of the GCE, the heads and the staff of selective secondary schools, give it their support. Many of them complain about the way one or another subject is examined, and many grammar-school teachers are pressing for syllabus revisions, but there is no general dissatisfaction or hostility among them to the present system. Substantial support for the GCE is also found in the Department and in the Inspectorate of Schools. Other users of the exams, especially those in nonselective secondary schools, are more critical. They enter as many of their students as possible in the GCE exams, but out of necessity as much as admiration. The greatest opposition to it comes from educationists in the Colleges and Institutes of Education, and from an assortment of sociologists and psychologists. The Schools Council, the body that now has responsibility for supervising the GCE, is also critical of the system in many respects. Occasionally one also finds an experienced GCE man who has grown disillusioned. R. A. C. Oliver, for instance, says that the JMB, with which he has been associated for a great many years, "is an extremely efficient organization running an old fashioned examination with old fashioned procedures." Among the public, there is not much opposition to the system in spite of the fact that parents have children with unsuccessful experience in it; such parents perhaps accept it as they do much else in English education. Nor are employers disposed to protest against the GCE; on the contrary they use its ratings regularly as a yardstick of employment.

Opponents of the GCE are far more vocal than defenders and thus give the impression of greater general dissatisfaction than in fact exists. The Director of the Institute of Education of the University of Reading, for example, traces the whole idea of external examinations to the nature of capitalistic, competitive society, though he seems oblivious to the contrary picture in the United States, which has no external examination in the English sense but a highly competitive society. Indeed he regards external written examinations as

> the greatest obstacle to preparing young people to understand the world in which they are growing up, to be able to dominate their craft or professional skill, and to be able to contribute to the building of the harmonious co-operating world, longed for by every normal man and woman . . .[6]

The Director of another Institute of Education, a former grammar-school teacher himself, is particularly angry about the O Level of the GCE:

> I have then got to say that the grammar school's curriculum is largely dominated by these examinations, that they determine syllabuses, and that teachers find themselves teaching what is easy to examine instead of examiners looking at what the teachers have decided to teach because of its educational value. The emphasis is placed on the uniform rate of progress of a class instead of on the individual needs of a pupil, and teaching becomes a business of filling up pupils with information as if a

school were a petrol-station. I say roundly that G.C.E. O Level has becomes an incubus and an educational catastrophe, an obstacle in the way of revision of subject syllabuses and an encouragement of lazy and rank bad teaching.[7]

Administrators in the nonselective secondary schools often take a critical if less caustic view of the GCE system. Here is a typical comment:

The anomalous position exists whereby the academic output of the entire secondary school system is graded for a fee by independent bodies outside the complete and effective control of either the teachers or the Minister or the Local Education Authority. These bodies are unlikely to desire fundamental change of their own accord; and the system, like any other, has its own momentum which tends to resist change.[8]

The fact that the GCE is an "external" exam, prepared and graded by agencies outside the school, accounts for much of the controversy about it. While there is among a few educational sociologists a dislike of any public examination, external or not (indeed against exams of any kind— "examinations," as one of their more combative number says, "just aren't made for people"), most of the opposition to the present system is based on the "external" organization of the GCE. Let us again turn to the subject of English for illustration, since this subject is no doubt the most familiar to most readers. Exams in this subject at O Level are the most important of all GCE exams. They are taken by the greatest number of students, almost half of whom regularly fail them. Written English is perhaps the most difficult of all subjects in which to define a pass-fail standard, not to mention defining a variety of grades within each category. It demonstrates more clearly than most subjects the problems of external examining. With a large board like the London or the JMB, the English panel of examiners at O Level may well be 100 to 150 persons, and to standardize their judgments about a thing like written English is a highly uncertain business. The very attempt to write questions that lend themselves to standardized grading operates against good writing from the candidates. A look at the typical O and A Level questions in English that are reproduced earlier in this chapter will indicate their rather pedestrian nature.

In considering the effectiveness of the GCE, one might simply begin by asking whether half a century of external examining in English (beginning with the national School Certificate in 1917, the predecessor of the GCE) has produced adequate results. Or, to put it another way, does the GCE impose a higher standard in English language and literature than is achieved by students of comparable ability in the United States? Complaints from employers and university teachers about the inability of young people fresh from the schools to express themselves orally or in writing sound very much the same in Britain (or for that matter in most of Europe) as they do in the United States. The problem seems to be universal of bringing large numbers of young people up to an acceptable standard in their mother tongue by the end of their secondary education, no matter what examination system is involved, and is universally unachieved.

Nor does it seem to have been much better in years past when the number of candidates was much lower than at present. In 1938, for instance, the JMB examiners were saying, about the English Language exam for that year:

> . . . the general standard was disappointing. Too few candidates had achieved exactness in the use of words, and exactness in understanding words written by others. Of those who understood the difference between, say, wit and humour or between self-interest and honour, too many, in trying to convey this understanding, wrote as if they were younger. Successful work in the main comprehension test came from those who had used the study of English as an intellectual discipline and as an encouragement, in reading, to look below the surface. Not a few definitions of logical opposites failed to define, or ended in confusion; and not a few "summaries of the meaning" lacked a meaning.

In 1950 they said:

> Slovenliness and carelessness are undoubtedly at the root of the poor performance of many candidates. These faults were evident in spelling and punctuation. Examiners believe that children spell badly today because they read so little; but this would not account for confusion of *is* for *his*, or for writing *of* for *have* as in *could of been*, or for the mis-spelling of words printed on the question paper.[9]

In spite of such quite customary comments, I believe the GCE does impose a higher standard at both O and A Level than is generally achieved by students in the upper range of ability in the United States. It might be helpful to reproduce below two passages verbatim from GCE student papers in English, to illustrate the general standard. The first one is from an O-Level exam in English Language, done by a sixteen-year-old boy, who was awarded 41 points out of a possible 50 on this section of his exam. The essay represents about an hour of his two-and-one-half-hour exam. He is answering a question that asks him to consider the pros and cons of "school societies" and to write an essay on their value:

### The Value of School Societies

Many people at school shun societies, saying that they are unimportant and uninteresting. Others say that participating in the societies will not benefit them much in the long run. However, it is clear that these people have not examined closely the value of these societies.

For example, there are many types of school society, and all tastes are catered for. Thus if a person is interested in a topic he can help in the school society, make it interesting himself, and enjoy himself. This hardly points to "uninteresting" societies.

Some, however, would say that time out of school should be used on homework. This is quite incorrect: societies often meet during the lunch hour, and do not usually take up much time after school. However, there is a more important point: surely, in later life, the boy or girl will be entirely devoted to work! It seems a good thing that school children should have interests outside the classroom or games field, for indeed "all work and no play makes Jack a dull boy."

There are those, however, who complain of the work involved in school societies. This may be faulted on a number of counts: firstly, the energy needed is hardly excessive; secondly, it is important for people to give service outside the form room; and, thirdly, it should be reasonable to serve something from which you derive pleasure. Moreover, working in a society, particularly in a secretarial capacity, will develop a sense of self-confidence and, above all, initiative. This is not only useful at school: it is invaluable in later life.

Nevertheless, the parents of some children say that the societies are not educational. However, education is well catered for. There are societies for those not interested in science, art or poetry. The work done in these societies is extremely useful, particularly at advanced level.

On the other hand, the other societies play a valuable part. When a university candidate makes his application, he has a better chance if he has taken an interest in music or drama, or even philately. Some scholarships are even awarded for project work done outside standard school work. Thus one's education is greatly aided by attending these societies.

Of course, one should not ignore the inestimable good done in showing children how to work together. If, at an early age, young people can learn to live with one another, and to co-operate with one another, they should be able to live in a community with great concord. A person who goes it alone finds it difficult to fit in to society later on.

Now it has been said that these societies rest heavily on teachers' efforts, but this is not entirely true. Teachers are present in a purely conciliary position. They can give advice: but the final effort rests with the children. Their acting, their music, their displays, are the factors which determine the success or failure of the society. Later on in life the teacher will not be there, but the children will have learned something, and will then be able to manage themselves.

On the other hand, the presence of teachers does good in another respect. After all, the children work with their teachers for a good part of their youth, and their success depends on mutual understanding. The societies provide an excellent medium for this understanding.

Finally, one should not forget that getting used to societies will give one a basis for organizing societies later on in life. One who had been interested in the school architectural society would be able to help in town planning. Hence one can play a useful part in later activities.

In conclusion then, we have seen that there are enough types of society for everyone, if they are prepared to make an effort, and that they augment and aid, rather than hinder education. We have noted the benefits of initiative and self-confidence gained from the work and that societies can help chances of a university place. It has become clear that children can learn this way to live in a community; and that teachers do a valuable job, advising, and bringing about understanding; and that the society experience may be in later life used.

There is no doubt therefore, that each and every student should study these facts, so that he may realize the value of school societies.

This essay seems to me a pretty dull and artificial effort, perhaps because the student is not much interested in writing about school societies. But it also demonstrates, I submit, a grasp of the fundamentals of written English that would not be found very often among good sixteen-year-old students in the United States, especially if they were writing under the time limit and general pressures of a major competitive examination in which they might be attempting to pass five or six different subjects simultaneously. The GCE unfortunately does not require passes in a number of subjects, and in that regard is inferior to the old School Certificate that it displaced, even though the pass level of the School Certificate was lower. But the best students do pass in at least five and often in eight or nine subjects at the same O-Level exam. One excerpt from one examination paper does not prove much, but if fairly chosen, as this one was, it surely gives force to the hypothesis that the GCE O-Level exam in English Language produces a higher standard of literacy than is found in the American school system.

I think also that it is worth recording here the comment on this sample paper made by one of my friends of long acquaintance whose background gives him an unusual vantage point from which to compare the teaching of English in Britain and the United States. He is Professor Derek Colville of Harpur College (part of the State University of New York), an Englishman who, after earning an honors degree in English literature at a British university, came to the United States and earned a Ph.D. in the same subject while teaching at an American university. He now has seventeen years of teaching experience in a number of American universities and has a deep interest in and knowledge of the educational systems of the two countries. He happened to be in England for a time during the course of my own study, gathering material for a book of his own on English and American education. We visited a number of institutions together and also spent some time going over student papers from GCE examinations. I invited his comment on this paper and how it would compare with what he would expect from American students in the upper range of ability. His comment follows:

This essay suggests to me a fairly good entry for the University of California "Subject A" examination. Subject A is a test, imposed by the University on all its entrants, designed to show whether the undergraduate can express himself well enough in writing to proceed with his university career. As you know, the University of California draws most of its students from the upper 12½% of high school graduates. Between 40% and 50% of the entrants fail this test each year and must then take a non-credit course in the writing of English and must pass this remedial course before they can take regular freshman English. I was chairman of the Subject A committee on one California campus for two years, and came to know the examination and the sort of essays it produced quite well.

This essay, I should say, would pass fairly comfortably with a grade of about 7 (or possibly 8) out of ten, assuming 5 as the passing mark. The essay is a reasonable, sustained piece of thought, and the general handling of language and phrasing are adequate and correct, if somewhat on the trite side. There are two important flaws in expression which lower the grade, along with the general sense of triteness in phrase, and, behind that, in idea. (These latter would not matter as far as passing the examination is concerned, but would prevent a grade of 9 or 10.) But the unclear reference of "*This* is quite correct . . ." and lesserly of "*This* may be faulted . . ." are loosenesses of the sort which lower the whole grade, and so five of them would fail the paper. On the whole, though, this would be judged a rather good piece of writing from a California entering freshman.

That is to say, from an American student entering one of our best universities from the top section of his class and about two years older than the student who did this paper.

The second example I would like to reproduce is from an A-Level exam in English Literature, done by an eighteen-year-old boy. His exam as a whole received a high score, but this passage, representing about a quarter of his three-hour exam, was rated lower than average by the examiner. In the question involved, a dozen lines from the gravedigger scene in *Hamlet* beginning "Alas, poor Yorick!" are reproduced. The student is then asked these three questions:

(1) By whom and in what circumstances is the passage spoken? (use not more than 50 words); (2) What is the dramatic significance of the subject-matter of the passage; (3) What do you consider to be the interest and importance of the way in which this subject-matter is expressed?

The student's answer:

(1) This passage is spoken by Hamlet, ostensibly to Horatio, although in fact addressed to no one in particular. Hamlet had killed Polonius and revealed his Uncle's guilt by means of the "Mouse-trap". He had been sent to England by Claudius, but had escaped. In his absence Ophelia had died; here, unwittingly, he jokes with the clowns who are digging Ophelia's

grave. This leds to the fight with Laertes and the plot for the duel scene.

(2) In the passage one sees Hamlet in a more light-hearted mood. He is joking, and parodying the philosophers by his mock-serious philosophy about death. In this way the passage reveals another aspect of Hamlet's complex nature.

The speech and the scene from which it is taken, provides a telling comment upon the main action of the play, for it shows a completely different attitude to death. The pathos and seriousness of the previous scene, with the reported death of Ophelia, contrast with this more light-hearted view of death, and this passage reflects the truth that everyone meets death eventually. In this way the tone of the speech comments upon the futility of Hamlet's desire to kill Claudius.

It is ironic that Hamlet should make this light-hearted speech over the grave which, unknown to him, is being dug for Ophelia.

(3) The passage is spoken in prose, which adds to the great variety of style in the play. The prose is admirably suited to its purpose here, for Hamlet is parodying the philosophers, in a macabre way.

The passage is characterized by much rhetoric, which reflects Hamlet's introvert state of mind and suits his mock philosophy.

Though Hamlet appears to address himself to his friend: "I knew him, Horatio", this is in fact merely a token. The passage is merely Hamlet speaking his own thoughts, to no-one in particular.

Hamlet's macabre treatment of the subject is well represented by the phrases. He comments upon the inevitability of death by saying:

"Get you to my lady's chamber, and tell her, let her paint an inch thick, to this favor she must come; make her laugh at that."

The passage is constructed of several short phrases, many of them rhetorical.

Comparisons are not simple to make at the A Level of the GCE between English and American students. As we saw in the preceding chapter, the last two years of the British grammar school are more specialized than are the junior and senior years of American high schools, and a student at the end of them has completed thirteen years of schooling while his American counterpart has completed twelve. Nevertheless, the reader might be able to make some rough comparisons. On the whole, I find myself in agreement with this comment, made in a private memorandum a few years ago by an American professor of English after visiting Britain on an educational study:

> I have inspected with interest the General Certificate Examinations in English on the Advanced Level, of the University of Durham, of the Oxford and Cambridge Board, and of the University of Manchester . . . and I feel confident that they are, in the range of reading and the maturity of critical judgment they demand, beyond the powers of the majority of American college sophomores intending to major in English.

I also invited Professor Colville's comment on this A-Level paper, and how it compared with what he has seen in many places from American students in good universities. His comment was:

> Despite the exceeding of 50 words in Part (1), and a faulty verb agreement in the middle paragraph of (2), I think it would be a fairly exceptional college sophomore who could write this answer. The American level it suggests to me is that of a junior at a good institution. At that level, I should give the paper about a "B-minus."
>
> The placement of the passage (1) obviously is quite adequate. The comments on (2) and (3)—dramatic significance, interest and importance —are informed and intelligent, and quite above average. There are several sound, even enlightening, ideas: parodying the philosophers, the role of the passage in broadening the play's consideration of death, the comment on the futility of Hamlet's desire to kill Claudius, the irony of his not knowing that the grave is Ophelia's, and the macabre quality of the speech.
>
> All this suggests at least good "B" thought assuming "C" were an average passing grade for the exam. What holds it down is a certain failure to develop even briefly the ideas he has, though this failure may be due in part to the general way in which the questions about "interest" and "importance" are put. How does the *prose* medium work on the reader, as opposed to blank verse or rhyme? How is the passage macabre, and what does this do? How does the rhetoric *work* to give interest or importance? There are, in a word, good ideas, but the answer is slight in explaining them so as to penetrate the question of the passage's interest and importance. Room to do this could be made by avoiding the repetition in the last phrase of the answer and in the middle paragraph of (3).
>
> The answer is typical of a fairly good junior-level American undergraduate performance.

Whether or not the GCE system of examining imposes a higher national standard in English than we achieve in the United States, and I believe that it does, one must take cognizance of the dissatisfaction of many people in England with results. Criticism abounds, as I have said, among employers and among institutions of higher education about the low level of literacy of many students with pass grades at O and A Levels in English. Nor is the criticism recent. In 1943 a national committee looking into the whole question of examinations made this unflattering comment:

> From all quarters, Universities, Professional Bodies, firms and business houses, training colleges and many other interests and many individuals we have received strong evidence of the poor quality of the "English" of Secondary School pupils: this weakness has been stressed even by those who might have been expected to be concerned chiefly with other aspects of secondary education. The evidence is such as to leave no doubt in our minds that we are here confronted with a serious failure of the Secondary

Schools. The complaint briefly is that too many pupils show marked inability to present ideas clearly on paper or in speech; they read without sure grasp of what they read, and they are too often at a loss in communicating what they wish to communicate in clear and simple sentences and in expressive and audible tone.[10]

In the last few years Oxford and Cambridge as well as the five universities served by the JMB have grown so wary of the value of O-Level English Language grades that they now require all applicants to pass still another exam, a "Use of English" test, as part of the normal admissions procedure. Whether these new tests will improve the teaching of English in the grammar schools remains to be seen.

It also remains to be seen whether the additional test in English will itself be an improvement over the GCE O Level. An early investigation by the JMB into the reliability of the new exam in English was not very encouraging.[11] One of the interesting elements of the JMB test is that it is graded, not by teachers of, or experts in, the subject of English, but by people from many different fields, lay and academic. To some commentators this additional test in English is just more of the same old medicine that is blindly prescribed and accepted in Britain for any educational ill and that, as one commentator puts it, may even "appeal to some deep-seated insecurities in our society." [12] But to others, probably the vast majority of informed persons, the objectors have not offered any alternative.

The interesting point is the degree of consensus that does appear to exist about the unsatisfactory state of English teaching in Britain. In 1964 the Secondary School Examinations Council issued a report on the teaching and examining of English that can only be called an indictment. Like the earlier reports of this national body, this one took a strong line against current GCE standards and practices. It all but banished the O-Level exam in English Language in favor of "internal examinations with external moderation." The report named four reasons for the decline of standards in English: (1) Reading and writing are now less important than they were before British society became dominated by movies and television, so that young people now "prefer oral and pictorial means of communication to the written word"; (2) methods of teaching English are outmoded, being overly concerned with grammar and abstract theory; (3) sixth-form enrollments have grown so fast as to strain teaching staff and resources; and (4) competition for admission to universities has forced sixth-form students to abandon the study of English as soon as they have passed their O-Level exam in it, since this is the minimum requirement for matriculation.[13] At least three of these four criticisms would be familiar to any American who has kept abreast of educational developments in the United States.

So no one should suppose that the British are uniformly content with their present GCE examinations. But neither should anyone suppose that whatever weaknesses exist in the examining of English are necessarily true of other GCE subjects. Many people who criticize the exams in English support the system of external examining in principle but want to see it reformed in this subject. Also, one should note again that the bulk of general criticism of the GCE comes from English educationists, from national advisory groups that have a progressive educational persuasion in general, and from nonselective secondary schools. The fact remains that the institutions making the greatest use of the GCE, the grammar and other selective secondary schools and the universities, are reasonably happy with the system. And I repeat my own conviction that even in the troublesome subject of English, the GCE is a more effective means of achieving national standards than anything we now have in the United States.

Let me turn from a discussion of external examining in English and mention a number of other problems regarding the GCE that ought to engage our interest in the United States:

1. *Research:* Because of the unplanned and haphazard way in which the present examining boards developed in Britain, none of them has undertaken what might be called a systematic research program into their own operations or their own exams. Although I frequently find it difficult to accept the findings of "educational research," there are some matters on which it is possible to gather information that can lead to useful evaluation; and examinations are one such area. But remarkably little is known even today about the efficiency of the GCE exams or about technical questions of many kinds that the boards should be able to answer. To an American professional tester, the GCE would appear a hopelessly amateur affair, run by former grammar-school teachers and other interested parties on the basis of intuition and uncoordinated experience. In the past the boards have made little use of psychologists and psychometricians, though they are changing now. They still do not normally pre-test their exams, nor have they developed any particular techniques of item analysis or general validation. Amateurism, an old English tradition, plays a large part in the work of the GCE boards. Their supporters would say that despite this amateurism and what may look to an outsider like confusion and uncertainty in GCE procedures, the system works. And of course the system does work, but many people would like to know just how well it works and in relation to what other possible systems.

Only within the last year or two has serious attention been given to the need for research. The largest boards, the JMB and the London board, have now established research units. Both are quite modest in size and scope, and it will be a number of years before many results are in. Meanwhile, the lack of knowledge about technical aspects of the GCE must be kept in mind in any attempt to evaluate the system. The boards must be held accountable for this unfortunate state of things.

2. *Comparability among the GCE boards:* Typical of the important questions that remain unanswered for lack of research by the boards is that of how their standards compare with one another. Implicit in a national examination is the assumption that a national standard is maintained for all candidates alike. No one would argue that such a standard can be exact and unerring in essay-type exams, or perhaps in any other type, but one would rightly expect a reasonable equivalence to prevail throughout the system and that continuous effort be made by the authorities to ensure that it does. This has not been the case in England. For years the responsibility for ensuring a uniform standard among the GCE boards was technically that of the Secondary School Examinations Council, an advisory body appointed by the Minister of Education, but it was wholly ineffective in this regard, partly because of opposition from the boards themselves to what they regarded as interference in their affairs. Now the responsibility has passed to the new Schools Council, which will probably be more successful. The Council has at least made a start in the systematic analysis of GCE scores and in the comparing of boards, though it is not yet able to offer a judgment about comparability.[14] For years, too, the boards have had arrangements among themselves for comparing their grading standards and techniques, but the process has been, like most GCE matters, informal, nonstatistical, and intuitive. For all that, it too may have worked, but how does anybody know?

In the absence of data, we must judge the question of comparability as best we can. The experience of some heads and those who use the exams year after year suggests that they at least have doubts about comparability among the eight boards; for they sometimes put their classes in for two different boards as a measure of insurance, and they will often seek out for certain of their classes a board that is reputed to be easy in a particular subject. "Schools know there is a difference," as one experienced examiner says, speaking of exams in English, "when they shop around for the [exam] paper with the shortest précis, the easiest comprehension or the least grammar."[15] And students themselves may be persuaded that differences exist. At its annual meeting in spring of 1966, Britain's National Union of Students proposed that the GCE boards be consolidated into one to ensure a single standard. In 1965 the head of a grammar school in the West Riding of Yorkshire conducted an experiment in GCE comparability by entering a class of twenty-eight students for the O-Level English exam of two different boards, with dramatic results. In one board, twenty-seven students passed and one failed; in the other, three students passed and twenty-five failed. In one board the average grade for the group was four, which is a lower-middle pass grade, and in the other it was eight, which is a solid failure. The board passing the twenty-seven students was the Associated Examining Board in London, which has a reputation in the schools as an easy board; the other was the JMB. Before making too much of this incident, one would need to know, among other things, whether the syllabuses for both boards were given equal time in the classroom in preparation for the exams. But even viewing the matter with caution, one must admit that the experiment raises a serious question about comparability.

The reader will have noted by now that exams in English, the hardest of all subjects to examine, are the most frequently used examples of GCE shortcomings. Whether the above experiment could be duplicated in history or mathematics or French is more doubtful. Even so, my own feeling is that an unnecessary degree of difference does exist in the standards maintained by the eight boards, but is widest in English. Some of the boards probably have an insufficient number of candidates or serve too restricted a clientele for their grading curve to match that of the largest boards. Also the training of examiners and their methods for arriving at grading standards differ widely among the boards, though in some cases the same examiner may be employed by two or more boards. So there probably is a measure of injustice in the administration of the GCE due, not so much to the multiplicity of boards, which in itself is not a handicap and may have some advantages, as to their failure to coordinate their work and to meet the problems of comparability that follow wherever more than one examining authority exists in the same field.

3. *Standardization of grading within the boards:* In addition to the problem of comparability among the eight boards, there is also the problem in essay-type exams of standardizing the marking of papers within each board. No doubt this problem, and for that matter most others in examining, depend on the caliber of the examiners; and it should be said that the qualifications of GCE examiners have been going down in recent years as the numbers needed by the boards have gone up. Not many years ago, for example, almost all A-Level examiners were senior faculty members of the universities; now there are a great many grammar-school teachers also involved. Turnover is also greater at both the O and the A Level than in previous years; and other problems with examiners have crept in along with the expansion of the system.[16] Sad tales of bad or nonexistent standardization turn up now and then in the English press, written by former examiners.[17]

Once again, one must make a judgment on inadequate data. I outlined earlier the steps taken by the JMB to effect a common standard in each subject among its own examiners so that any paper, it is hoped, will receive the same mark no matter who reads it, and the same mark if the same examiner were to read it at two different times. Certain subjects are obviously much harder to standardize than others. Subjects like mathematics and foreign languages are relatively easy; English, history, and some others are more doubtful. After reading a variety of papers and the "grading guides" that go to the examiners, I would say the degree of standardization reached is fairly good, probably as high as can be achieved in a mass essay-type exam. Certainly it is higher than is achieved in the grades awarded regularly by the staff of any given department in a school or a university on a departmental exam.

Many investigations over the years, from a classic one in 1936, called *An Examination of Examinations*,[18] to informal, single-school experiments done every year, point to the fallibility of people who examine other people. Examiners often disagree with one another's assessment of a paper and sometimes disagree with themselves; their grading standard yesterday may have been related to what they did the night before, or to the candidate's handwriting, or to whether their mother-in-law has come for a visit. Change one or all of these things today and their grading may be different. In 1960 a committee of the Secondary School Examinations Council found "far from satisfactory" the arrangements for standardizing marking within the boards. It said:

> A scrutiny subject by subject of the examinations available to us revealed all too often that marking was decidedly uneven; detailed mark-schemes often appeared to be lacking, and moderating arrangements to be defective. Moreover the marking seemed to be unduly lenient: while there were notable exceptions, we too often had the impression that the standard implied by a question was denied by the leniency of the marking.[19]

Perhaps these observations had their effect on the boards, for it seems to me that internal marking now is reasonably standardized. Capriciousness and variable standards presumably affect all educational, if not all human, activities; but more provision is made to combat the problem within the GCE boards than their critics will admit—far more than is made within schools themselves, where, after all, serious injustice occurs much oftener in assessing students than would be possible in the GCE.

4. *Does the GCE stultify teaching?* Perhaps the strongest and most frequent criticism of the GCE is that it usurps the authority of teachers over the curriculum, forces them to conform to somebody else's ideas about what should be taught and how it should be taught, kills the initiative of both teachers and students, and encourages dull teaching and rote learning. Does it? The question, like so many others about external exams, cannot be answered with a simple yes or no. But when all the necessary qualifications are made, my answer is no. There is plenty of dull teaching in English schools and plenty of fact-grubbing in preparation for the GCE, but the responsibility for this rests with the teachers involved much more than with the examining bodies. There is enough latitude built into the GCE system, enough choice of syllabus and more than enough choice

of examination questions, that the rigidities of the GCE so often attacked by its critics seem to me mostly the rigidities and limitations of teachers. It is not clear to me how the problem of bad teaching would be resolved by abolishing the examination system or making it even more flexible than it is. On the contrary, bad teaching might only get worse. Teachers have always had it within their collective power to effect changes in the GCE, and indeed the exams have often changed in response to pressures from teachers. The main fact, however, is that most of the teachers using the GCE do not feel hamstrung by it or unhappy about it. Educationists tell them they should be, that they should rebel against so constricting a force, that they should make a break for freedom. But most teachers do not feel imprisoned or particularly constricted by the GCE. Even if they did, one would need to ask whether a certain degree of such control is not desirable, since one of the major functions of an external examination system is as a check on teachers and schools.

Teachers who do feel oppressed by the GCE are often those whose discussion of examinations is apt to be, as one teacher puts it, "a mixture of theoretical anarchism and passive obedience." [20] Teachers have always had an escape route open to them within the GCE but have rarely taken it. It has always been possible for any teacher dissatisfied with the required syllabus to submit his own individual syllabus to his GCE board for approval, and so free himself from the bonds of the standard syllabus and examinations. But only a handful of teachers have ever done so. Even the largest of the boards will have no more than ten or a dozen such syllabuses in effect in any given year. Granted that the process of approval is complicated, it is not so cumbersome as to deter any teacher who feels genuinely put upon by the GCE syllabus from undertaking his own. The fact that so few teachers take advantage of the provision for writing their own syllabus lends little support to the claim that they are being "dictated to" by an "external" agency.

In schools that I visited I often made it a point to ask teachers what they would do if there were no GCE to worry about. Most of them did not have in mind any radical new departures in curriculum or method. Most said they would probably continue in the same general way. A few talked vaguely of bringing the GCE under the control of teachers, but were not very clear about how this would change things; nor did they seem to realize the degree to which teachers already influence the GCE. For example, the JMB in its annual report for 1964–65 noted:

> Of the 1,438 men and women who constituted the Ordinary Level panels of examiners for the Board's 1965 summer examination [the main one each year] 65 per cent were practicing school teachers as compared with 9 per cent of university teachers and 11 per cent of teachers in Colleges of Education and Technical Colleges. In addition the greater part of the balance was made up of persons who recently retired from teaching in

schools. Of the 535 Advanced Level examiners 41 percent were practising school teachers as compared with 42 per cent of university teachers and 9 per cent of teachers in Colleges of Education and Technical Colleges. At both Ordinary and Advanced Levels teachers from schools which present candidates for the Board's examination were in a majority.[21]

On the whole, then, the restrictive effects of which the GCE is often accused are overstated. If some degree of restriction is not acceptable and desirable, the whole function of external exams is defeated, but the charge that the system robs teachers of their freedom or that it imposes an arbitrary power over the curriculum is without substance.

5. *Is the GCE a good "predictor"?* Professional testers speak of the "predictive" value of an exam, by which they mean the accuracy with which it is able to forecast the future performance in some job of people who take it. A student's performance on the GCE is the principal criterion for his admission to institutions of higher education in Britain, and so one is entitled to ask how well it forecasts his success when admitted. Again, the lack of research is surprising on such an important question, and what there is does not give a clear picture. One of the most detailed studies yet done of university entrance in Britain, called *The Chosen Few,* found the GCE to be the best single predictor of success though still falling short of what it might be.[22] Other investigations give less comfort to the GCE boards. R. A. C. Oliver, one of the most experienced men in Britain with the GCE, found the predictive power of the JMB exams at A Level disappointing and concluded that "selection of university students . . . is likely to remain a very chancy business—even the most efficient methods using the best techniques give a very imperfect prognosis of success." [23] But J. A. Petch, equally experienced, interprets JMB's record more optimistically and feels that the A Levels are as good a predictor as anyone could rightly expect of external exams.[24]

Hence one's judgment of the issue depends on one's expectations. How accurate can a national exam as a forecasting device be expected to be? Should it predict merely general success or failure in college, or should it be able to foresee grade point averages or, in Britain, the class of degree the individual will be awarded? Some people would agree with Petch when he says, "There is little theoretical justification for expecting any high degree of correlation between G.C.E. performance and performance in the subsequent university course," [25] but that only leaves the question of what is "high" to be settled. In a university system as selective as Britain's, I would suppose that if an examination is to play the main role in this selection it should be a better predictor than the GCE appears to be.

The GCE *is* a good predictor sometimes, in some subjects, at some institutions. The supply-demand situation in British higher education varies greatly by department. At a Redbrick university, the classics department may have so few candidates for admission that its GCE standards go well below those of, say, the science departments of the same institution. At a technological university, demand for admission to the biology course, reflecting the current excitement in this field, may be several times as heavy as to an engineering course, and entrance standards are adjusted, within limits, accordingly. What then does "prediction" mean? Also, the percentage of first- and second-class honors degrees varies by departments and by universities in Britain, and both vary from year to year, so that it is difficult to collect data that can rightly apply to more than one institution or even department at one point in time. Nevertheless, I feel after considering all the facts available that a student's scores on the GCE should have a closer relationship to his performance in the university than they do.[26] My feeling is reinforced by the fact that Oxford and most of the Cambridge Colleges, which have the lowest dropout rate in England if not in the world, are so skeptical of the predictive value of the GCE that they continue to give their own examinations to candidates for admission on top of the usual A Levels.

6. *Some final questions about the GCE:* So far I have tried to explore five important facets of this exam system, and to establish: (1) That more and better research is needed before many judgments about the GCE can be based on more than informed argument; (2) that what information is available suggests a lack of adequate comparability in the standards of the eight boards; (3) that standardization of grading within the boards is as good as can be expected in this type of exam; (4) that most of the rigidities of curriculum and method found in English schools are due more to the limitations of teachers than to external examinations; and (5) that the predictive value of the A Levels, so far as a student's university record is concerned, is not as high as one would expect of an exam upon which so much weight is put in admitting students. There are still a few other points, pro and con, that should be mentioned.

The existence of eight authorities for the GCE creates problems beyond the major one of comparability that we have discussed. It means that the various boards sometimes compete with one another for business, which is bad in a national exam seeking to maintain a national standard. It means duplication and waste of resources. In a small country it means that some are too small to operate efficiently or to sponsor the kind of research that needs to be done. And it means confusion and manipulation on the part of schools using the examination. These problems could conceivably be avoided, and the virtues of multiplicity preserved, by some kind of centralized policy-making body, but this has not been done in Britain.

The GCE supports a fair-sized industry outside the boards themselves. Publishers have a large stake in supplying textbooks to fit the hundreds of GCE syllabuses and are naturally disposed to encourage the expansion of the present system rather than the reform of it. The exams also give rise to a variety of cram publications. Volumes of "model answers" to old

GCE questions come out regularly as well as a variety of guides about how to beat the exams. This kind of commercial by-product will perhaps accompany any national examination system, as it does even with standardized tests like our own College Boards, and I am not suggesting it is necessarily bad. Some of the "Model Answers" I have seen might serve a purpose for some students if sensibly used,[27] though I am greatly troubled by the artificiality and even the pernicious effect of others. Consider, for example, a problem like the following, from a cram book called *Model English Test Papers*, in which the author is reviewing the subject of grammatical structure with his student readers. First, he reproduces this piece of Wordsworth's poetry:

> There was a time when meadow, grove and stream,
> The earth, and every common sight,
> > To me did seem
> Apparelled in celestial light,
> The glory and the freshness of a dream.
> It is not now as it hath been of yore;—
> > Turn wheresoe'er I may,
> > By night or day,
> The things which I have seen I now can see no more.

Following this lovely passage, what exercise does the author give his students?—"Divide [the passage] . . . into main and dependent clauses, stating the kind and function of each of the dependent clauses." [28] If that were really a "model" exercise for the GCE, one might condemn the system out of hand. Fortunately, it is not, but one needs to remind oneself that a national exam creates a service industry around itself that acts as a kind of lobby for the system. Further, there is another lobby within the boards themselves in the form of the thousands of examiners who each year are paid something between a few hundred and a thousand or more dollars for their services. Again, there is nothing reprehensible in this, any more than there is in our own wealthy testing organizations that support thousands of full- and part-time people as well as a number of peripheral light industries. It is simply advisable to take vested interests into account in any assessment of a national examination.

Finally, we need to ask whether the GCE examines the right things. Is it, as the professionals say, a "valid" exam? I think it is in most subjects. Any system that examines hundreds of thousands of students over a range of sixty or seventy subjects, in which any one subject will be taken as a matter of free choice by some students and an obligation by others, is going to be limited in the kinds of questions it can ask. The urge to quantify, simplify, and codify is strong in the GCE boards. Questions are often framed in such a way that the student's answer can be checked off against a guide and a quantitative value assigned to each part, a grading procedure that seems quite artificial for some subjects. Questions are likely to be rather "safe" and dull because of the uncertainties of standardizing the grading of questions that allow for an imaginative answer.

But these are limitations of any public examinations. No mass exam is going to give adequate consideration to a student's idiosyncrasies and private virtues, or to the nuances and subtleties of his response that his own teacher might recognize. Our own College Board exams are even worse in these matters. One should not look to a national exam to make fine distinctions but to maintain within rather broad limits a national scholastic standard. Much of the criticism of the GCE comes from people who assert that it fails to do things it does not claim to do,[29] and that probably cannot be done in any sort of national examination system. Any professor from an American college reading GCE exams in his specialty could probably think of better questions to put to an individual student or an individual class than he would find on the exam, but if he were faced with examining 40,000 students and coordinating the services of a hundred examiners in the subject, I doubt that he would make great improvements in a system that has already been refined over a period of a great many years. The reader can judge for himself from the questions reproduced earlier in this chapter, but I feel that, considering the conditions under which a large public examination must be given, the questions typically found in the GCE are adequate for the purposes of the exam.

The real question for the United States is whether an external examination of some kind is desirable or not; and to that delicate matter we now turn.

## The Place of an External Examination in the United States

I believe that we should undertake a serious experiment in external examining. I say "experiment" advisedly. After looking at some length at English and European experience, I find myself in an unaccustomed place, the middle. I don't know whether an external exam is workable and, if workable, desirable in the United States. I think it is, but the case is not so conclusive that one can say without hesitation that we should create such an exam. I know that we badly need a better means of national educational assessment than we have. We have in fact no particular means now. Certainly we have nothing approaching a method of regular national evaluation. Some people say this is a good thing, for as soon as we have national evaluation we have national control, and that is bad. But the dangers do not seem great. Some measure of control over the curriculum by "outside" forces is a necessary part of an external examination system, but we have a considerable degree of such control already and without the benefits of a national exam. The fact is, a British teacher has more freedom in his classroom, despite the GCE, than an American. Anyone who thinks American education is happily free of centralized influences might consider the coast-to-coast similarities of our educational system, in textbooks, curriculum, and in the training of teachers and administrators. One should also look at the similarity of college entrance requirements, at the standardizing influence of professional associations of teachers and administrators, and at the increasing role of the federal government in education. As a simple matter of fact, we already have a substantial degree of centralized control in American education.

True, we do not have a specific national curriculum, and we do not have large numbers of students studying exactly the same syllabus. But many states stipulate the syllabus in detail. And, whether we have a national curriculum or not, most students wind up taking many of the same courses and reading many of the same books. Look at a syllabus for, say, sophomore-year English or junior-year French or senior-year Problems of American Democracy in a hundred or in five hundred schools across the land and what will impress you most is their similarity. We may not have a national curriculum, but we have plenty of uniformity. What we have not got are any sort of national standards.

If American educators really fear that national exams would further erode local initiative and the freedom of the teacher, there are many ways around the problem. Such exams could be regional, or state-wide, or merely system-wide, or even school-wide, if the necessary precautions for external assessment or external moderation were taken. If these arrangements were made effective, we would have what would amount to a national exam but with protection for local control. A brief look at school-leaving examinations in Europe will emphasize two points: that almost all advanced nations have found it necessary to require a "national" exam of some kind at the end of the academic secondary school; and that the variety of successful methods of doing it suggests that no one way of organizing and administering such an exam is demonstrably superior to others. Most of the European leaving exams involve about the same percentage of the age group, but no one knows whether their standards are comparable. The Council of Europe is now sponsoring a study to determine in a more systematic fashion than has been done before what degree of equivalence actually exists among the leaving certificates of European countries. And an American foundation is sponsoring a study following up on work done at the International School in Geneva to determine the feasibility of developing a leaving certificate for the international schools of many countries.[30] Meanwhile, one naturally assumes from the other similarities of Europe's educational systems that their leaving exams must be roughly comparable.

There is one basic difference to be noted between England and Europe.

Universities and other institutions of higher education in Britain set their own admission requirements, just as they do most of the time in the United States. Although the national exam, the GCE, is the main criterion used in higher education for admission, requirements can vary a good deal as to scores in A-Level subjects as well as in the number of subjects needed. As we have already noted, Oxford and Cambridge impose their own admission exams on top of the GCE. But in most of Europe the school-leaving exam is also an admission exam to higher education, and passing it gives more or less automatic rights of entry. European countries, that is, reserve to the state the authority for deciding who goes to institutions of higher education, and not, as in English-speaking countries, to the institutions themselves. Neither approach is necessarily superior: England, by virtue of giving admissions authority to the institutions, has one of the lowest dropout rates in the world, whereas the United States, perhaps by virtue of the same policy, has one of the highest.

In most of Europe, the leaving exam is "internal" to one degree or another. Individual teachers and schools have a voice in writing, administering, and grading the exam, again in contrast to Britain. In West Germany, for example, the leaving exam, the *Abitur*, is done in a variety of ways depending on the *Land* involved, but it is usually prepared by state school inspectors from questions submitted to them by teachers. The actual exam is then sent in confidence to the schools, where it is given at the appointed time. The exam is a good deal longer than the GCE, covers four or five subjects, and is designed, in contrast to American notions of Germanic scholarship, to test, not the student's stock of facts, but his abilities to order his thoughts and to analyze ideas. The student's teacher in each subject then reads and assesses his paper, which may also be read by still another teacher of the subject; the final grade is the average of these two assessments. In cases of substantial difference, an oral exam is also given. School inspectors also sample the graded papers at random as a check on standards. Possession of the *Abitur* entitles one to admission to German universities. In Switzerland the *Maturité* is prepared, administered, and graded by the individual school. Each school wishing to give the exam is visited and approved by the Federal Maturity Commission, a body made up mostly of university faculty members that exercises general supervision over the leaving exam. The *Maturité* gives admission to all Swiss universities.

The Dutch *Eind Examen* is an interesting combination of internal freedom and external control. By invitation certain teachers suggest questions each year to the central inspectorate of schools, which then writes the exam and sends it to the schools. Each school gives the exam and grades it according to a grading guide from the inspectorate. The papers are then sent to the school's Visiting Committee, a group of university faculty members appointed for each school. The committee reads the papers before visiting the school, where it conducts oral examinations of all candidates. In the end, it is the committee rather than the teacher that decides on the final grade, a responsibility that many teachers are glad to yield. Belgium has a similar system with its *Certificat d'Humanités*, although the outside "jury" does not have quite so much authority. However, Belgium is not entirely satisfied with the results of this exam and in 1965 imposed a second exam on those students seeking admission to the universities. The Danish *Studenteksamen* is a wholly external affair like the GCE, though required in a number of subjects; there seems to be very little dissatisfaction with it.

Perhaps the closest system to that of the English GCE is the French *Baccalauréat*. It is far more external than internal. Each of the twenty-three regional *académies* in France prepares its own exam and through the university in each region supervises the grading of it by classroom teachers. Since there is also an oral test involved, the *académie* appoints outside oral examiners, but from the ranks of local teachers. Individual teachers, however, as in Holland or Britain, have little or no control over the assessment of their own students.

Discontent certainly exists in Europe with these leaving exams, but it is not general. There is very little support in any country for abolishing the system (with the possible exception of Sweden), but there are important reforms in almost all countries. In Germany, where the *Abitur* has traditionally involved a large number of subjects to be passed simultaneously, recent criticism from the schools has resulted in a decrease in required subjects. On the other hand, the *Baccalauréat* has recently been expanded beyond the somewhat rigid and specialized exam that it once was. In response to a growing body of criticism a major reform of the "bac" will be completed by 1968, allowing for more science and economics and for a greater number of options. Sweden will soon do away with her traditional *Studentexamen* and will thereafter base university selection on a broader range of criteria. But she is not likely to be followed in this respect by many other nations.

In view of the consequences that flow from a student's performance in leaving examinations throughout Europe, it is surprising that one encounters so little criticism about standardization of grading. Since these exams are essay-type and in most cases are not centrally read and graded, the possibility seems great that standards among schools and districts will vary. Arrangements of some sort are made everywhere for external moderation, but if one probes very far into the actual operation of the system, one cannot help but have doubts about how well this particular problem is met. In talking with teachers and administrators in many countries about the possibility of injustice because of the lack of standardization, I was often told that, yes, such injustice probably did occur. Nobody worried much about it, feeling that it was not a major problem. But chance probably plays a large part with students on the borderline between pass and fail, always the most troublesome group in examinations, and perhaps with others as well. Comparability among the GCE boards, as we saw, is a problem, but it must be an even greater problem among the twenty-three *académies* of France or among the eleven *Lander* and the thousands of *Gymnasien* of Germany. Examiners cannot be "standardized" very well, and perfect justice is no more attainable in examinations than in anything else, but more attention to the problem of minimizing variation in grading is needed in most of Europe. Certainly a major effort to ensure comparability would be called for in the United States if we were to inaugurate any kind of national examination administered from multiple centers.

Should we inaugurate such an exam? As I have said, I believe that the United States, as the only major advanced nation in the world that lacks a leaving exam, should at least undertake one on an experimental basis, and the basis should be broad enough to give us reliable information about the probable consequences of expanding it to cover the nation. At the risk of repetition, let me list some of the advantages that accrue to countries that have a leaving exam and the disadvantages that accrue to us for not having one.

*First*, a leaving exam means that students taking it have worked to a syllabus that is developed and refined year after year on the basis of experience. This in turn means that they have been exposed for a period of years to a course of study that is sequential and integrated. I submit that there is a *prima facie* case for this kind of study in secondary schools and for its superiority over the haphazard and assuredly unsequential collection of courses often found in our own secondary schools. I do not mean only that the elective system of our schools is deficient, allowing as it does many good students to make many bad choices; I also mean the lack of close relationship between one year's work, elected or obligatory, and the next, and the failure to build systematically on what students have done before. In a word, students working toward a leaving exam usually follow a syllabus that represents a progression over a number of years in each subject of the exam.

*Second*, a leaving exam means that students have an incentive to work—or, as some would say, a prod. Libraries have been written in the United States about student "motivation" and how the absence of it prevents learning and how it should come from within the student rather than be imposed from outside. And I would agree that it would be nice if all of us were motivated by a pure love of knowledge rather than by examinations and other pressures. But I am assuming that between now and the time we reach that happy state, it will be necessary to continue to assist motivation by means of external pressure. Students themselves are quite frank about the incentive value of the GCE and the fact that without it their work would deteriorate. The following comment from a group of students at Marlborough College, one of England's leading Public Schools, is commendably frank and I would think highly representative in its attitude toward examinations:

> . . . it is still probably true to say that although schoolmasters may scorn examination syllabuses and long for an opportunity for true education, the fact remains that the existence of O and A level, entrance and scholarship, and their very great importance, is for the vast majority the driving force behind all intellectual exertion. If the exams did not exist, the status of work would drop, and few people would do more than jog nicely along.[31]

And few people, I should think, in the United States would claim that large numbers of students, lacking a national exam to work toward, do more than "jog nicely along." We have never exerted very much pressure in the United States. Nor do I think we do today, not at least by European standards. People in American education talk a lot about the mounting pressures on students, but most of this pressure is not, as it is for the European child, on whether he will go to college at all, but only whether he will go to the "college of his choice."

*Third,* a leaving exam means that teachers as well as students have a yardstick against which to measure their own performance. We have no such check now in the United States, with the result that endless educational research has been undertaken into something called "teacher effectiveness" and ways of judging teaching, all of which has left us about where we started. The one criterion of the effectiveness of a teacher that is imposed by an external exam—the pupils he turns out—is the one that has never been invoked in the United States. It is the one that will be opposed the longest by poor teachers and by professional associations of teachers.

*Fourth,* a leaving exam means that schools as well as students and teachers have a means of judging themselves, and the public has a means of judging schools. For some reason any suggestion that schools should be judged like other institutions in our society is anathema to our professional administrators. They seem to feel that any kind of national standard against which their own schools could be measured would be the onset of an educational Dark Age; but one suspects that their concern is more with status and the avoidance of criticism than with educational quality or institutional freedom.

Schools are constantly being judged by parents and professionals alike, but mostly on impressionistic and often irrelevant grounds. Ask any superintendent of schools, for example, about some "good" schools of his acquaintance, and he will mention a number without the slightest hesitation and seemingly without suffering in the making of such judgments.

Then ask him for his reasons. He will say something about the amount of money spent on the school, that the principal and staff are excellent people (more judgments that he makes without the slightest hesitation), and that parents think well of the school and support it. In other words, he is perfectly willing to offer you a judgment about a school so long as the evidence can be limited to what goes into the school (in money, staff, good will, etc.) and not extend to what comes out. Except in cases where a school has a particularly good record of sending its graduates to well-known colleges, one rarely finds that the criterion of achievement is the one used in the evaluation of a school. Obviously, I am not suggesting that a leaving-examination system would give us a perfect yardstick for judging schools or for schools to judge themselves. What goes into a school *is* important to what comes out, and nobody would expect a down-and-out slum school to compete in exam results with a well-heeled palatial establishment in suburbia. Moreover, the achievements of a given school are not to be judged solely in terms of examination results. But when all the cautions are in, it must still be clear that a public examination system provides a better means of institutional evaluation than anything we now have. Not the least of its virtues is the pressure it would bring to bear on school boards to improve schools with consistently poor results.

*Fifth,* a leaving exam means that some kind of continuing national assessment can be made of our educational system. Again, we are alone among the major nations in having no way of judging where we are as a nation in the quality of our schools. Since we have no national standards of achievement, we must settle for opinion instead of knowledge about this most important of educational questions. Our professionals are scandalized at the whole idea of a national standard, but they are not very clear about precisely what the dangers of having one are. They grumble about the schools being dictated to by outside agencies, about "freezing" the curriculum, about hamstringing teachers, about eroding local initiative. (The same professionals who thus defend this kind of decentralization in education will be found on other occasions attacking the local school board as obsolete.) But as I mentioned earlier in this chapter, there is already a far greater degree of centralized control in American education than most people realize. To the extent that we want or need that kind of control, I am sure we are better off to have it overt than covert. Also, there is no reason why a leaving exam must be administered at some remote distance from schools and teachers; it can be as closely related to, and as closely controlled by, teachers as one wants to make it.

*Sixth,* and last, a leaving exam means that both employers and institutions of higher education have a better instrument than they now have with which to make decisions about applicants. Granted that no single criterion is or should be used in making such decisions, a leaving exam, judging by English and European experience, is the best single guide to future performance. An American employer now has mostly his hunches to go on in hiring high-school graduates. He has a record of work done as measured out in hours and units of credit, but it may or may not mean something; he has no way of knowing. He has letters of recommendation that may mean nothing at all. He has his own impressions from an interview, which experience proves are exceedingly chancy. What he does not have is a comparative measurement, one that gives him some idea of how the applicant compares to other people his own age.

Likewise, the college admissions officer, who has one of the most impossible jobs in American education, is frequently little better off than the employer. If his institution is one that requires standardized tests of applicants, he will have these test scores, but they will not tell him a lot of things an essay-type leaving exam would tell him. Our College Boards are very limited in the subjects and the skills they can test, whereas the GCE is available in fifty or more subjects, many of which include oral tests and laboratory demonstrations. Using standardized tests, how does a college admissions officer decide, for instance, whether a student has any competence whatever in speaking a foreign language, not to mention the question of accent? [32] He doesn't, of course—any more than he can know much about a science student's laboratory techniques. I pass over the other criticisms of standardized tests that in recent years have been voiced in the United States, about both their validity and reliability, and the second thoughts about the use of these tests that a number of our leading institutions of higher education seem to be having.

What about "prediction"? Our professional testers like to say that their standardized tests are better predictors than other types of tests, but I remain very skeptical. The GCE in English, as we have seen, is a controversial exam in Britain, but it is a great deal better than, say, the multiple-choice, machine-scored aptitude and achievement tests in English that are commonly given in the United States. On standardized tests, it is possible, as one visiting British teacher observed, "to get a good mark . . . without being able to put two words together in original composition." [33] Whatever a given score means on machine-scored tests, it has a very uncertain connection with the student's abilities in his native tongue. So far as forecasting a student's general performance in college is concerned, the "coefficients of correlation," as the professional testers like to call such things, of our standardized tests are not impressively high, though they improve when combined with other measurements such as school records, just as the GCE also does.

Nobody knows how the GCE and our standardized tests might compare in predictability in American higher education. Actually the evidence available indicates, not surprisingly, that the best way to predict a student's record in college is the record he made in high school. The ability range of students involved in higher education in Britain and the United States is much different, as are the criteria of success. Also, the GCE is necessarily a prediction about a student's performance in the single subject in which he does his degree, whereas our College Boards predict on the much wider and safer base of how well a student will do in the extended general curriculum of the American college. Even so, if one looks at such a gross comparison as general success in college, then the GCE is rather better, since the dropout rate in English universities is among the world's lowest, while ours is about the world's highest. But if one tries to pin down the comparison to finer distinctions, trying to work out a comparison, for example, of grade-point average in American institutions with class of degree awarded in English institutions, one simply finds the available data insufficient or nonexistent.

The question is important, which is why I engage the reader in this tedious argument. If our College Boards and similar machine-scored tests are as good as, or better than, a European-type leaving exam for purposes of predicting college performance, the case for experimenting with a public examination in the United States is greatly weakened. It is by no means eliminated: college prediction, although the sole function of our College Boards, is only one of a number of functions performed by a leaving exam. As I indicated earlier, some educational psychologists in Britain are persuaded of the superiority of standardized tests over the GCE type. Here is a typical statement:

> We know and can precisely calculate the chance errors of [standardized] tests, their validity for the purpose for which they are designed, and their predictive efficiency; sixty or more years of research have been devoted to close critical examination of their strengths and weaknesses, and to the circumstances in which they may safely be used. Traditional examinations, interviews, assessments of various kinds have not had anything like the same sustained scrutiny; we do however know that the reliabilities of most public examinations and of the interview as it is usually conducted, are much lower than those of even moderately well designed tests and the margins of error very considerably higher.[34]

This seems to me to state the matter with more confidence than the evidence warrants, but the statement is representative of the attitude of a number of professional educators in Britain.

In education it happens with great frequency that professional knowledge does not take us very far in considering the desirability or feasibility of ideas. The predictive value of standardized tests compared to that of the kind of leaving exam found throughout Europe is simply not known. The question is important enough for us to try to find out. So I think we do need at least to experiment with a national leaving examination in the United States. I said before that I found myself in the middle on the theoretical question as to whether we should have such an exam nationally, by which I simply meant that it would be a mistake, even assuming it were possible, for us to adopt such a system without an extensive period of development to determine both whether and how it might be made to work effectively. One way in which such an experiment could be undertaken in the United States is suggested by a new national examination system now being developed in Britain as a complement to the GCE. It is called the Certificate of Secondary Education (CSE), and in organization it may well be more suited to American conditions than the GCE.

## THE CERTIFICATE OF SECONDARY EDUCATION

The reader may remember that a document called the Norwood Report was published in England in 1943. It was concerned with the whole question of examinations in secondary schools, and one of its main recommendations was that the School Certificate examination, the predecessor of the GCE at O Level, be dropped from British schools and replaced by an "internal" exam for sixteen-year-olds. The committee strongly felt that any exam at this age

> is best conducted by the teachers themselves as being those who should know their pupils' work and ought therefore to be those best able to form a judgment on it. . . . The direction therefore which change should take is sufficiently clear: it is towards placing the conduct of the examination in the hands of the teachers; they alone can best judge the needs of the mass of their pupils and they ought to be the best judges of the success or failure of the methods they employ.[35]

Two things might be noted about the Committee's basic position as set forth above: It was simply a statement of educational faith about the superiority of internal to external examining; and it was applied only to the lower level of national exams, though one would suppose the principle just as applicable to eighteen-year-olds as to sixteen-year-olds. My own feeling is that the most useful kind of national exam in the United States would be an external system with extensive provision for teacher participation. But this is probably not feasible in the United States, vested interests and ancient myths being what they are, and so a system of internal exams something like the CSE may be the most that an optimist could hope for. The CSE serves a quite different set of purposes in Britain from what it would in the United States, but its organization is quite adaptable to American conditions.

For twenty years the Norwood recommendation lay in limbo. Then came another report, sponsored by the same body that produced Norwood, the Secondary School Examinations Council. It is known as the Beloe Report and was concerned with secondary-school exams other than the GCE. It came out solidly for the old Norwood recommendation but developed it in much greater detail.[36] Beloe was better received than Norwood and led in a short time to further reports from the Secondary School Examinations Council setting forth detailed plans and proposals for a new examining system to complement, not to replace, the GCE and to be taken by students below the GCE level. Originally, that is, the CSE was proposed as an exam based on the Norwood principle of internal tests but chiefly for students below GCE ability; the idea was later modified and the range of students broadened to include those in the GCE range, the hope being that this new exam will eventually displace the O Level of the GCE.[37] An important report from the Schools Council in 1966 suggested the eventual merging of the two exams, at least at the O Level of the GCE, but thought that the separate systems would have to continue to operate for a considerable time. Meanwhile the GCE system, said the report, should move toward a more "internal" method of examining, similar to the new CSE.[38]

The main impetus to the formation of the CSE was the widespread feeling that more students should receive some kind of recognized qualification when leaving school than was being done through the GCE. Also there was great concern about the proliferation of dubious exams, especially in the secondary modern schools. It might have been possible to expand the GCE to take in a wider range of students than the top quarter or third of English students, but there was too much dissatisfaction with the existing exams at O Level in the nonselective secondary schools to permit this. Thus the idea of using the established system was rejected and an entirely new and separate national system of examining was created alongside or underneath the GCE. It was to take in a larger number of students than the GCE, the broad middle range of students between the fortieth and eightieth percentiles of ability, and was to depart from the old system in other important ways. The aim of the CSE designers was

> to attempt a new reconciliation of freedom and order by placing upon the teachers themselves full responsibility for syllabus content and methods of examining, but within a framework of discussion, guidance and information which recognizes that a national system of assessment must be, within reasonable limits, genuinely national in its descriptions of the content and caliber of attainment.[39]

Not all the experts and commentators liked the new exam. On the one hand were those who thought it would be "a pale imitation of the GCE," and those who said it was still another manifestation of the egalitarian frenzy that had overtaken Britain and that supported anything that did away with merit and promised to give everybody prizes. On the other were those who saw in the CSE just another demonstration of an old educational phenomenon, *plus ça change, plus c'est la même chose;* they were horrified at the creation of still another national examination in what they regarded as an educational system already riddled with exams. But I am sure it is true to say that the CSE received the support of the great majority of people in British education. It is still too early to know the reaction of employers and the public.

One idea recurs throughout the reports and the rest of the literature on the CSE: the importance of teacher control of the exam. A favorite slogan is that the CSE is to follow and not to dictate the curriculum. I discussed earlier my own skepticism about the degree to which external exams do dictate the curriculum. I should now like to record my skepticism, even though I would recommend the CSE approach to the United States, that this approach will produce the good effects claimed for it in Britain. Too much is made *a priori* of the virtues of teacher participation in the CSE. The following kind of statement appears often:

> . . . the C.S.E. examinations, with their emphasis on full teacher representation at all levels, were arranged so that power could lie in the hands of the actual teachers involved in teaching. The examination could thus constantly reflect the developing secondary school curriculum and not impose its own pattern on the schools. Delegation to local examination committees was an important arrangement which seemed likely to lead to more real teacher-control.[40]

It is one of the anomalies of education that teachers are often unreliable judges of their own students' abilities. One's first assumption is that teachers are the best possible judges, but experience fails to establish this as a general principle. A. N. Whitehead always made a great point of the absolute importance of examinations remaining the province of the individual teacher, and no doubt this is the best thing—if the teacher is a Whitehead. The principle, that is, is sound if one is talking only about the best teachers. But since there are lots of average, poor, and awful teachers, the idea breaks down when applied without discrimination. The few investigations that have been made in Britain do not lend much support to the accuracy of teachers' judgments,[41] and examining bodies as well as universities and colleges, not to say employers, find the accuracy of teachers' estimates extremely variable. Whether the problem can be met through what the CSE calls "external moderation" remains to be seen.

Briefly described, the CSE is a national system of exams operated through fourteen regional boards. Each board, like each of the GCE boards, has full control of its own examinations, though a national body, the Schools Council, exercises general supervision over the entire system and publishes guidance materials for use by the teachers and moderators of the regional boards. Some of the publications of the Schools Council are very good indeed on technical problems of this kind of examining.[42] The CSE is a separate-subject, free-choice exam; students pick the subjects they wish to attempt and the number they wish to attempt. Each of the boards, when in full operation, will offer a broad range of examining facilities that will allow teachers to choose for any given class of students one of three "modes" of examination. These modes represent a variety of internal and external examining techniques. Mode One is pretty close to the usual GCE (using an external syllabus and an externally marked exam) and Mode Three gives most of the control to the individual school (syllabus and examination written by the school, but with external moderation). Great emphasis is being placed by the Schools Council on flexibility, on experimentation, and on the use of various combinations of essay-type and standardized tests. Undoubtedly there will be many differences among the fourteen boards when they are in full operation, many more than among the GCE boards. But whatever the differences, British officials are clear that, as the Secondary School Examinations Council said in its first bulletin about the new system, "Effective teacher control of syllabus content, examination papers and examining techniques is the rock on which the CSE will stand." [43]

Although the GCE will remain the examination taken by students aiming at higher education, many administrators hope that the CSE in its highest grade (this exam, like the GCE, has a number of pass grades) will ultimately take the place of O Level of the GCE, thus at last putting the Norwood recommendation into effect of no external exams below age eighteen. This possibility is naturally a threat to the GCE boards and is a source of tension. The Beloe Committee in 1960 was quite clear that the new exam was to apply below the GCE O Level, not attempt to dislodge it; [44] but that aim was broadened by the developers of the CSE, many of whom were old critics of the GCE.

It is of course too early to judge the success of the CSE in Britain. As I write this, only nine of the fourteen regional boards have given their first exam, and it is still not clear how the system will develop. It can be said, however, that it will profit a great deal from the experience of the GCE, including the mistakes. An interesting fact in the early stages of the CSE is that most of the teachers using it have been choosing Mode One as their examining method, meaning an external exam externally graded, very like the usual GCE. A few schools even submitted their old GCE syllabuses to the CSE boards! So once again there would seem to be room for doubt about the claim that it is the teachers who are anxious to free themselves from the bonds of external exams. A major effort at research and systematic development is being made with the CSE, much more so than with any other examination in English education. Thus the exam promises to be at least a technical success. But no one yet knows whether it will be accorded an important place by employers and other "users," most of whom are still wedded to the GCE.

This alphabetically tangled review of the CSE may serve as an illustration of a system that is perhaps more relevant to anything that we might undertake in the United States than is the GCE or the French *Baccalauréat* or other fully external examinations. I suppose the Regents Examinations of New York State are the closest thing we have to a leaving exam in the United States. This system is fully a century old and should offer us a considerable fund of experience. It combines a number of external and internal elements: The syllabus is prescribed externally by the state; the examinations are prepared externally by committees of classroom teachers; and the exam papers are graded internally by the students' teachers, with a certain amount of external moderation (in practice not much) exercised by the State Education Department. Each high-school principal has the primary responsibility for maintaining grading standards within his school, and is assisted in this task by rating scales that are based on state-wide norms and issued to him by the state.

There are important differences between the Regents Examinations and either the GCE or the CSE. The Regents is a group-subject exam, in which the student is required to have completed a stipulated preparatory course throughout high school and to pass simultaneously in a number of both mandatory and elected subjects. The exam is aimed at the upper half of the high-school population and is usually taken at age eighteen, whereas both the CSE and the O Level of the GCE are taken at sixteen.

The Regents Examinations naturally have their critics, both those who would like to see them abolished and those who would like to see them strengthened. But they do seem to have the general support of teachers and administrators in New York State. How "successful" they are as a leaving certificate is a question that, as usual, reduces itself in the end to opinion. The State Education Department confidently says:

> In the area of academic achievement, Regents examinations provide a measure of quality that is valid, equitable, and easily understood. In the guidance of individual pupils, Regents examinations have been found to provide an excellent index for predicting future academic success, both in high school and in college. As supervisory tools, they are effective in encouraging good teaching and learning practices.[45]

Allowing for some bias on the part of those who administer such an exam, I would not quarrel much with this evaluation. It seems a justifiable assumption that a state-wide examination system that has evolved over a hundred years and continues to have the general support of thousands of schools does do most of the things claimed for it. I confess to some doubts about the internal grading arrangements. Unless external moderation is more effective than I believe it is in New York State, standards will almost certainly be low in many schools, in spite of rating scales or anything else. This means not only that the purpose of a public exam is defeated in those schools, but that injustice is done to students in other schools with a higher standard. I record this merely as a strong suspicion. One would need to have the answers to a great many questions about the Regents Examinations before using it as a model for a national exam, but the long experience of New York State with this leaving certificate would surely need to be assessed in any plan for a national certificate.

There is, then, a case to be made for the experimental development of a leaving examination in the United States. I have not tried to spell out the details of how it might be organized simply because there are a great many possible ways of doing it that could be equally effective; much would depend on the degree of support for the general idea that might be forthcoming from teachers and administrators. My own preference would be for a system that would involve teachers to the fullest possible extent, but that would be external to the individual school in the preparation of the syllabus and the exam. I would also like to see it a group exam requiring a pass in a number of basic subjects, perhaps with a number of pass grades. A group-subject exam represents a publicly known standard for the general education of children, not merely what might be achieved in one subject. It also reduces the margin of error in the assessment of a candidate, since the final grade is made on the basis of his performance over a number of subjects, not one or two. I hazard the guess that such an exam system, at least as an experiment, would receive strong support from the public, from employers, from colleges and universities, and, I would hope, from classroom teachers themselves.

## CHAPTER V

# The Status and Training
## of Teachers

ONLY ECCENTRICS would fail to share the conviction of the majority of people that classroom teachers and the way in which they are prepared for teaching are matters of supreme importance in education, perhaps the greatest importance of all. Statements asserting that these things are important abound from official bodies in Britain and the United States, and from laymen and educationists. Sometimes the statements are pious commonplaces; sometimes they take the form of political promises, as when the Labor Party in its 1966 election manifesto says, "We will raise the status of teachers"; sometimes they are so overblown as to claim, as does Britain's National Advisory Council on the Training and Supply of Teachers, that "the quality of successive generations will depend most of all on the intellectual and personal worth of the individuals by whom they are taught." [1]

While few Americans would deny the importance of the subject of this chapter, few are aware of the size and influence of the teacher-training industry in the United States and of the larger field of professional Education of which it is a part. Nearly one-third of all the bachelor's degrees awarded by all American colleges and universities are awarded to students coming out of teacher-training programs; about half of all the master's degrees awarded each year by all institutions are in Education; and more doctor's degrees are awarded in Education in a normal year than in any other single subject. All this makes Education by far the largest segment of our system of higher education. It is also one of the most controversial. It has been widely and justly criticized for low standards, anti-intellectualism, empire-building, and for certain monopolistic, not to say inquisitorial, tendencies. Fortunately things have improved in recent years, in part because of the hammering to which Education and teacher training have been subjected. There is still much to be done before these areas of higher education become what they could and should be, but perhaps a start has been made. The British and European systems of teacher training offer, I believe, a number of useful comparisons with our own.

Nowhere are the training programs for primary and secondary teachers as unified and similar as in the United States. In Britain and everywhere in Europe, the split system of secondary schools results in a split system of teacher training, just as it does in a split system of professional organizations and most often in a split salary structure. Teachers for primary schools and for nonselective secondary schools are usually trained in single-purpose institutions similar to our own disappearing teachers colleges. In France it is the *École Normale*, in Germany it is the *Pädagogische Hochschule*, the English call it a College of Education, the Dutch a *Kweekschool*, and the Italians an *Istituto Magistrale*. But everywhere it means about the same thing: It means training programs that combine some work in academic subjects with a large exposure to educational psychology, teaching methods, and practice teaching. Everywhere the prestige of the teachers college is low. So are the standards of admission compared to those of the universities, and the standards of work done, though improvement is now being made. On the other hand, teachers for the selective secondary schools are trained in one or more academic subjects at the universities through at least the first university degree; they may then move directly into the schools without further preparation or they may have a training course which includes a minimum of theoretical work in Education and a maximum of apprenticeship and practice teaching.

It is a curious fact that the social status of teachers in many countries has been inching downward since World War II, while the length of training and the requirements for admission to training have been inching upward. These factors combined with rising birthrates and extended schooling for many children, as well as earlier marriages and childbearing, have created a serious teacher shortage in almost all advanced countries. We have our own shortage for the same reasons. But we are better off than most of Europe, partly because teacher salaries in response to the supply-demand situation have risen disproportionately to those of the general population. In their efforts to solve the stubborn shortage of teachers, Britain and Europe are studies in frustration. In England teachers are paid on a national scale of fifteen steps, with modest differences in the scales for teachers who are university graduates and those who are not. The present basic scale stretches from a low of about $3,000 (in American purchasing power) to a high of about $6,500 for a university graduate with a "good honors degree." In addition there are supplementary payments of sundry kinds for a great many teachers.[2] As with us, this scale for beginning teachers, particularly for women, makes teaching fairly competitive with a great many jobs in industry, but the top of the scale is low and the best teachers are undoubtedly handicapped by it. Men with families, whatever their quality as teachers, are handicapped by it. I mention the salary in passing but hasten to add that I do not intend to try to compare educational salaries between the two countries on anything but a rough and general basis; more exact comparisons would have to be based on some kind of equivalency formula that would include Welfare State benefits in Britain, cost of living, length of academic year, and many other sensitive matters.

Although the quality of teacher training is not a major issue in most countries, nothing to what it has been in the United States, the practicality of trying to solve the teacher shortage by expanding the training colleges often is. The "wastage rate," as the British call the rate at which trained teachers leave the classroom, is so high as to suggest that merely increasing the enrollments of training colleges is an uneconomic answer to the problem. Estimates are that within five years of graduation from a British teacher-training program, seventy percent of the women and thirty percent of the men will have left teaching. Yet few countries insist that people who have been put through training colleges at state expense commit themselves to a certain period of teaching in return. France requires a pledge of ten years' service, but does not enforce it; Britain used to require one but gave it up as inhumane. The whole matter is one of the anomalies of teacher training. Efforts to meet the shortage by the use of untrained persons, or by reliance on technological innovations, or by the use of "auxiliaries," are met with a solid wall of opposition throughout Europe by the teachers' associations.

The English system of training teachers is the customary two-level system, but with some important differences from the rest of Europe. The bulk of teacher training is conducted under the general supervision of "Area Training Organizations," otherwise called "Institutes of Education." There are now twenty Institutes, all but one of which are parts of universities and all of which bring together in a kind of voluntary federation the Colleges of Education in their region. Britain now has about 140 general Colleges of Education, all associated with Institutes of Education, and another fourteen Colleges of Education that are also associated with Institutes but concentrate on special subjects like physical education and "housecraft." Teachers for the primary schools and most teachers for the nonselective secondary schools are trained in these Colleges, which are typical enough of the single-purpose teachers college that prevails throughout Europe. Additionally, the great majority of British universities have Departments of Education that are closely related to the Institutes but that keep their separate identity. Teachers for the grammar and other selective secondary schools are mostly university graduates who have taken a degree in which they specialized in one or perhaps two subjects. They are not yet required to have any further preparation for teaching, but those that do further work do it in the form of a one-year course in a university Department of Education. In this chapter I will look in some detail at these three elements of the British system of teacher training—the Colleges, the Institutes, and the Departments—as well as at certain problems of professional Education that are relevant to our own.

## The Colleges of Education

The training of teachers began in Britain as a private endeavor, an effort by the Church of England, and the Dissenters in a small way, to supply teachers to their own elementary schools. Not until 1904, well after Parliament had made elementary education compulsory, did an LEA establish its first training college. Now about two-thirds of all the Colleges are "maintained," not by universities or by the national government, but by the LEA's. The rest are still controlled by "voluntary bodies," mostly the Church of England and the Catholic Church. The Robbins Report in 1963 strongly recommended that the status of the Colleges be raised by, among other things, removing them from the control of local authorities; since then the matter of how the Colleges should be governed has been an important issue. Robbins also recommended a change of name for them from "Training Colleges" to "Colleges of Education," though how much this somewhat artificial provision will add to the status of teachers is not clear. Scotland made the change well before Robbins, in 1959, but the prestige of its general-purpose Colleges of Education seems to be about the same as before. However, the Colleges in recent years have begun to escape the traditional stigmata of teachers colleges: their very small size; their preoccupation with the training of primary teachers; their intellectual and often geographical isolation; their meager budgets. In 1944 a national committee whose report recommended fundamental reform in British teacher training found that "what is chiefly wrong with the majority of the training colleges is their poverty and all that flows from it." [3] Poverty is no longer the major problem. The Colleges are now being expanded and enriched at a fast pace. Few of them can yet boast the facilities of even the poorer range of American colleges, whether in amenities like swimming pools and bowling alleys, or in essentials like good libraries. Many are still quite small by American standards. All told the 154 Colleges now enroll only about 86,000 students; only in Scotland, in Edinburgh and Glasgow, does one find large American-type teachers colleges. The Colleges are financed through a central pool administered by the Department in London. All the LEA's contribute to this pool in proportion to the number of children in their schools, so that at least a rough equalization now exists among all the Colleges in Britain in the pre-eminent matter of finance. Qualitatively the Colleges still suffer from their heritage, but are now meeting these problems more effectively than in the past.

## WHO TEACHES IN THE COLLEGES?

Probably the greatest difference in teacher training between the United States and most other countries is in the kind of people who staff teacher-training institutions. In Britain and Europe the great majority of people who teach both academic and Education courses are themselves recruited from the schools. Such was also the case at one time with us; now, however, academic subjects are taught, even in our remaining teachers colleges, by people with advanced degrees in the subject who often have had little if any experience in schools. And on the professional side, the field of Education has become so specialized in the United States that even the pedagogical courses are often in the hands of people who have not taught in schools. But abroad, postgraduate degrees are much rarer among academics than with us, and Education is only now beginning to follow the American pattern; so that the Colleges of Education have not had the opportunity of recruiting staff from any other source than the schools themselves. The average teacher-training staff therefore represents in Britain and Europe a much wider fund of practical teaching experience in schools than is the case in the United States. On the academic side this means that staff members bring to their job a university training in their subject at least as deep as a master's degree from a good American institution and a number of years of experience teaching it to secondary-school students in the upper ranges of ability. On the Education side it means that staff members may or may not have had university training or formal work in the Education specialty they are teaching. The few studies of College staffs that have been made in England indicate that many of the theoretical Education courses are taught by persons without formal qualifications in the specialties involved. In 1965, for example, a leading educational psychologist reported on a survey done by a joint group of the British Psychological Society and the Association of Teachers in Colleges and Departments of Education. The survey found that in the Colleges,

> 185 out of 304 lecturers [i.e., regular staff members] teaching psychology had some formal qualifications in the subject, but in only 50% of the cases was this at the degree level. And this is too rosy a picture, since it derives from the 102 colleges which provided information out of the 139 asked. One suspects that the non-responders included a more than average proportion of very poor provision for the teaching of the subject. There seems to me no doubt that, at this present moment, the *majority* [his italics] of

those teaching psychology in our colleges have had no formal teaching in the subject. . . . Let me quote Hollins, reviewing the working party report: "The picture would be even blacker, I think, if the analysis had gone further. A closer examination of the qualifications of specialists in educational psychology would reveal that too many of them are inadequate. Too many diploma courses allow students to qualify by theses describing children's behavior on a basis of inadequate theory, and a lack of rigorous experimental design with appropriate statistics." [4]

Other studies have arrived at similar conclusions. William Taylor of the Institute of Education at the University of Bristol has done more work on the composition of College staffs than anybody else in Britain and has reported his findings in a number of places. Looking at the principals of the Colleges (that is, the heads), he found eleven percent of those heading LEA Colleges and forty percent heading private Colleges had had no training in Education. He also found:

> Forty per cent of the principals who completed questionnaires had four years or less experience of training college work before assuming their present appointments. Forty per cent of the men and nearly twenty per cent of the women had never worked in a training college prior to becoming principals. Fewer than one in seven men principals and one in four women had previously held a vice-principalship, which appears to be a terminal role for the majority of incumbents. . . . Of the thirty-five principals in the present sample who had no previous experience of college work, eleven had come from university teaching and eight had been heads of grammar schools. Educational administration and the local authority inspectorate provided three each, two had been engaged in religious work, one had been head of a primary school, three had been deputy heads or heads of departments of grammar schools and four had held other appointments. [5]

By contrast, the accepted thing until recently in the United States was to hire new presidents of teachers colleges only from the ranks of educationists. Elsewhere Taylor reported that data contained in a questionnaire sent out a few years earlier by the Robbins Committee indicated that almost thirty percent of the men who responded from College staffs and just over fifty percent of the women did not have a bachelor's degree in any subject; but adds:

> . . . a few of these have a Master's degree in Education, which can be worked for in some universities by non-graduates who have successfully completed courses for an advanced diploma or certificate. Of those with first degrees, 11 per cent of the men and 13 per cent of the women had obtained first class honors, 68 and 55 per cent respectively had second class and the remainder third class, pass or general degrees. [As compared, say, to teachers of the humanistic subjects in British universities, 68 per cent of whom have first-class honors degrees.] [6]

Despite their background of school experience, those who teach Education in the Colleges are often criticized by students and schools. They are accused, as they also are and with great justice in the United States, of being out of touch with everyday problems of schoolteaching, a criticism that goes back at least as far as the McNair Report.[7] In neither country, I am sorry to say, is it customary for such people to continue to teach part-time in schools or to do a period of full-time teaching every few years. This qualification should be an obvious one for people who teach other people how to teach but it will not be made a standard requirement in either country because of opposition from the staff itself; the fact must be faced that many people join a College staff precisely to escape the rigors of teaching in schools. One does find an occasional College staff member whose specialty is pedagogical methods and who also continues to teach in schools, but it is rare. The vast majority do not even demonstrate their theories to their own student teachers in an actual classroom situation. The head of the Department of Education at one of the new British universities, at York, is alone so far as I know in either country in requiring members of his staff to teach one afternoon a week in the local schools. He makes that requirement clear when he hires people for his Department. May his tribe increase.

Although their backgrounds and qualifications vary greatly, College staff members are paid on a standard national scale. The two staff ranks of "Lecturer" and "Senior Lecturer," corresponding roughly to our Assistant and Associate Professor ranks, make up about seventy-five percent of the total staff of the Colleges. Their teaching load is around fourteen or sixteen hours a week and their classes tend to be smaller than those of an American college, though the range in size is wide. The average staff-student ratio nationally is a generous 1/10, well below American ratios; and the Colleges usually run a thirty-six-week year. Staff members are under no pressure to publish, and most do not publish significantly or engage in research. A typical staff member in an academic department would have joined the College after seven or eight years of teaching in a grammar school. After a similar period, though often much less these days, on the staff as Lecturer he would move up to the next rank and probably be drawing a salary of perhaps £2,100 for the academic year, equivalent in purchasing power to perhaps $8,000. The College staffs are represented in salary negotiations and other professional questions by an organization called the Association of Teachers in Colleges and Departments of Education, which has a membership of about eighty-five percent of those persons eligible to join. It publishes a journal, *Education for Teaching*, and performs the customary functions of a professional association. In certain restricted ways, it can exercise a considerable influence over policy in teacher training.

The picture that emerges of the staff of the Colleges from what systematic information is available and from my own travels is this: There is a pretty clear division similar to that in our own institutions between the academic departments, which are mostly composed of university graduates with reasonable degrees who are chiefly interested in their subject and who have a fund of experience in the schools; and the Education department, where many people will be without degrees and probably without specialized work in the pedagogical subjects they teach, but also with a fund of practical school experience. Many from both groups, however, will not have done any teaching in schools for many years. A candid general assessment would have to be that the typical College staff in Britain does not compare particularly well with an average American institution. But the comparison is not very fair because of the accelerating conversion of American teachers colleges to general-purpose institutions requiring a larger and better academic staff than they formerly had. If we confine the comparison to a representative College of Education in Britain and a typical teachers college as it existed until very recent years in the United States, the British might come out well ahead on most qualitative considerations.

### WHO GOES TO THE COLLEGES OF EDUCATION?

The caliber of students entering the Colleges is naturally related to the status of the institutions. The best students everywhere in Europe head for the university. Those who cannot get in go to teacher-training colleges or other institutions. Even so the qualifications for entry to teacher training have been going up in most countries. Both France and Germany now require the leaving certificate of the academic secondary school for admission to training even for primary schools. Since many countries admit students to teacher-training establishments at an early age, often between fourteen and sixteen, the training programs are apt to be split between a "long" course for those that enter early and must complete their general education before doing their pedagogical training, and a "short" course for those who enter at perhaps eighteen with a school-leaving certificate. Thus France admits many sixteen-year-old girls to the *écoles normales* but puts them through the *Baccalauréat*, the tough leaving exam of the French *lycée*, before admitting them to pedagogical training for elementary-school teaching; Germany requires all prospective teachers to have passed the *Abitur* before their technical training; and other countries operate two complete and separate programs, such as Denmark, where the "seminaries" for training teachers offer a five-year course for graduates of the middle school who enter at about seventeen and spend the first two years in academic study, and a three-year course for graduates of the *Gymnasium* who enter at nineteen already in possession of the academic leaving certificate. Everywhere the training course itself is shorter than the American four years, with the result that elementary teachers are qualified a year or two ahead of ours—sometimes, as in Italy, two or three years ahead of ours.

Everywhere also, a good many elementary teachers come from the working classes, though this no longer means what it once did. In the United States it no longer means much of anything. Teaching was once the only way up for girls, and they were often the first generation of their family to get a post-elementary education. This is still true to a varying extent in European countries where elementary teachers still come from the lower classes of society, but not because teaching is the only way out of their condition: It is merely one way that often happens to have greater attractions than other ways, and their condition itself has greatly improved. In Britain there is the added incentive, a very great one, of grants from the LEA's with no strings attached for going to a College of Education. Thus the conclusion is unavoidable for anyone visiting the Colleges and talking to students that a great many students are not there out of any commitment to teaching. Many drift into the Colleges. They fail to gain admission to the universities, or they have nothing better to do and certainly nothing that pays them for doing it. These motives are plentifully in evidence in the United States also, but there are many other options open to American students that are not available to British students. In neither country is the failure rate in teacher training of any size; few students are flunked out of any program on either side of the Atlantic. But the "wastage" rates after training in the United States are lower than in Britain, possibly reflecting a stronger interest in teaching in the first place.

Whatever the motives of British students, their qualifications have been going steadily up as measured by their performance on England's main leaving examination. Only a few years ago the "standard" qualification for admission to the Colleges was a pass grade in five subjects at the Ordinary Level of the General Certificate of Education exam. This was well below university requirements and so the pattern of entry in higher education revealed that the more the GCE scores of any given group declined the more the students involved wound up in the Colleges.[8] This is still the general pattern, but government statistics now indicate that it is a small minority of students who come to the Colleges with only five O Levels. Now a quarter of them have two passes at the Advanced Level, which was the old standard for entrance to the universities, and another quarter have one A Level. This means that at least half the new students in the Colleges are from the top ten percent of all British students; the other half are among the top fifteen to twenty percent. On this kind of comparison alone, one would suppose that as a group they are better than American students in comparable training courses. This would also seem to follow from the fact that Britain has a much lower precentage of children of upper-secondary-school age actually in school than does the United States; since the Colleges supply some of the smaller numbers of teachers therefore needed in these grades, they are probably of higher ability. Certainly one would assume this to be true from comparing the percentages of the age group that finish any kind of higher education, including teacher training, in Britain and the United States. In Britain now, about six percent of the age group completes some form of higher education, and it is from this group that most new teachers come; in the United States, the figure is about eighteen percent. In part this only means that we have provided more facilities for the development of young people than Britain has, but that is not the principal difference; the main fact simply is that most of the new teachers in Britain and Europe come from a higher level of the population in ability and intelligence than in the United States. Whether these countries will maintain the standard as they expand their school systems to approach the quantitative scope of ours is another question.

Complaints are nevertheless common about the caliber of students in the Colleges. The men particularly, it is said, are poor. Also the rapid expansion of the Colleges is blamed for bringing in, along with some very good students, a lot of bad ones who somehow scraped through the exams.[9] Students themselves are often strongly critical of many of their fellows and feel that the status of the Colleges is reduced by the numbers of poor students. If there is validity in these complaints, one is then faced with the problem of how to relate the complaints to the rising examination records or to the other criteria of admission to the Colleges. One of the other criteria is one that American institutions also emphasize and that has always seemed to me eminently unreliable: the interview. It always seemed more than possible to me that American educationists when interviewing candidates for admission to teacher training could easily and even unconsciously screen out many good people who might be less conformist or docile than their interviewers would like but who might make excellent teachers. Conversely, the orthodox-minded interviewer could screen in all the nice, agreeable girls who would accept uncritically what they were told and who would never, never think of rocking the professional boat. Mostly, however, the stated objects of the interview always seemed to me laughably unattainable, even if desirable. The few English studies that have been done support the common-sense conclusion that there is no discoverable relationship between the interview and the subsequent performance of the student.[10] What is one to make of a statement like the following, by no means uncommon, from the Principal of a leading British College of Education? He says that the first thing he looks for in interviewing candidates for admission is their capacity to "exercise personal responsibility," and after deciding about that, "The other criterion by which I judge is, in girls,, an innate kindness and sympathy, and, in boys, a budding humanity which will, when they are three or four years older, enable them to give true service to the children they teach." [11] If the supernatural insight required to make any sort of useful judgment about such things in a short, or even a long, interview were possessed by many people in education, the interview might be a valid criterion for admission to teacher training; but since it is possessed by few people in any walk of life, the interview as used in both countries might have something to do with the complaints that are common about the quality of students in teacher training.

British educationists, echoing their American counterparts, frequently warn against raising admissions standards to teacher training, or for that matter imposing too high a standard of performance within the programs. There may be more substance in this view in England than in the United States since, as we have seen, the Colleges already draw their students from the upper range of ability. Nowadays American educationists, aware of the pressures for lifting admissions standards, might not state the matter quite so forthrightly as, for instance, the Director of the Oxford Institute of Education:

> . . . a high academic standard in "subject-matter" is not a necessary part of the professional equipment of all teachers in the same way as a high academic standard in engineering is a necessary part of the professional equipment of all engineers. If we demand it, we are demanding it for a different reason—as a kind of high level intelligence and attainment test. And it is doubtful whether there is a sufficient correlation between success in such tests and success in teaching to justify us in doing so. . . . Assuredly if we press on with the raising of academic standards until all [teacher-training] colleges are demanding two A levels for entry we shall both distort the school education of many teachers and lose to the profession many young men and women of no great academic talent who would make excellent and devoted primary teachers. It would be hard on them and no gain to the nation if they were to be debarred from teaching because of an inability to reach an academic standard which had no particular relevance to their professional ability.[12]

The last thought would seem strange to American academics who have been saying for many years that good people were being lost to teaching precisely because of the low standards of the training programs and the dreariness of the Education courses. In my opinion, that loss is still greater in the United States than any loss ascribable to the intellectual demands made on students.

THE STANDARD COURSE OF TEACHER TRAINING

Among the 154 Colleges of Education in Britain, there is obviously a great deal of variation in staff, students, programs, standards, buildings—

everything. Our concern is not to try to survey this variety but to look at the common elements of the principal program. This is a three-year course for students coming directly from the secondary schools and headed for teaching in primary and nonselective secondary schools. Some Colleges have other programs such as one- and two-year courses for mature students but most of the time adamantly insist that everybody take the three-year course. Britain has made a strong effort, with considerable success, to get mature people to return to teaching or to undertake training programs to begin teaching. We could well consider a similar effort ourselves if we could get the cooperation of the professional associations. The Colleges also offer a variety of "in-service" courses, and latterly a four-year course leading to a university degree in Education. But the "standard" course is our present concern.

First, we should note that there are important equalizing factors in the administration of the Colleges throughout England that are not found in our system. As I have already mentioned, the two most important such factors are the national pool for the financing of the Colleges, and the national salary scale for the staff of the Colleges; thus for better or for worse one does not find the enormous range that prevails in the United States in both these vital matters. There is a third factor making for a certain degree of standardization: the admissions requirements. They do vary with the College, but minimum standards are set by the central Department for all institutions. Finally, there are the Institutes of Education, which introduce a strong measure of standardization into the training programs. In spite of these equalizing factors, however, I would emphasize that variation is great among the Colleges. Not the least of the reasons for this variety is the absence of a large body of agreed-upon professional doctrine of the sort that gives American training programs the same look from coast to coast.

The standard training program in a College of Education takes students at eighteen or nineteen after twelve or thirteen years of schooling and puts them through a three-year course. The academic year is divided into three twelve-week "terms," longer than those of British universities, and much longer than Oxford or Cambridge. The three-year course is only recent. Training was increased from two years, which is still common in Europe, in 1960 in response to recommendations of national committees and to pressures from the National Union of Teachers and other bodies that were convinced, from faulty supply-demand projections in the 1950's, that a surplus of teachers was developing; also because many people felt as one national committee put it as early as 1944:

> A two-year course is not sufficient for students entering upon their training at 18 years of age. . . . An essential element in education at this stage is a reasonable amount of leisure and a personal choice in the use of it.

Many students in training colleges do not mature by living: they survive by hurrying.[13]

There are no fewer than seven teaching age ranges in which students can specialize in the three-year course, but in practice the differences among them are not great. Some differences can be seen if one makes a three-way division of the courses of study into those for Primary, Junior-Secondary, and Secondary teachers. But the similarities among the three courses are greater than would be found between the courses for elementary and secondary teaching in American institutions. Whatever the age range that they propose to teach, all students combine study in academic and pedagogical subjects in about equal parts. Some of the better-known Colleges, like Homerton at Cambridge, give more than half to academic study, and others give more than half the primary teachers' time to pedagogical study, but a national average for all groups would be about half and half.

"Concurrence" is the main organizing principle of the three-year course, in contrast to American practice. The English feel, that is, that the academic and professional work should proceed side by side throughout the three years, whereas typical American practice, especially for primary teachers, is to give over most of the first two years of college to general education and most of the last two to pedagogical training. Britain's National Council on the Training and Supply of Teachers strongly endorses the principle of concurrence:

> The essence of the case for concurrent courses of education and training is not merely that personal education and professional training are concurrent in time, but that they interpenetrate and reinforce each other over a period of at least three years, thus strengthening the student's personal education and increasing, by unforced growth, his understanding of children. It has been urged upon us that the concepts and the degree of human understanding required in a professional training course are not best developed when they are experienced as an aftermath, as it were, of a degree course; they must be lived with and evolved as part of the whole personal development of a student over a sustained period.[14]

It is an engaging theory such as one might expect to be produced by a national advisory body, but I confess to some doubts about the value of concurrence in and of itself. It is not done in most professional fields, though this may be unimportant since teaching is unique in many respects among the professions; but there is nothing much beyond speculation to support it. Students themselves would not always endorse it, for many would prefer specialization. Whether concurrence is a sound principle or not, it is one of the basic differences between the British programs and our own, and is strongly supported by the Colleges themselves.

Perhaps the best way I can illumine the standard course in a College of Education is to look at the ingredients common to a number of programs. This is a more complicated job in England than in the United States, since higher education in England and Europe is not neatly parceled out in hours of credit and units of study. But a typical three-year course would look something like this:

*First year:*

1. A week of observation in schools as an introduction to teaching in the age range the student has in mind.

2. A series of lectures, perhaps five or six hours a week, as a general introduction to Education, with some attention to psychology and child development, general methods of teaching, and contemporary issues.

3. A series of lectures and discussions in one "Main" subject chosen by the student, perhaps three hours a week; it may or may not be an academic subject.

4. A block of study in one or two "Subsidiary" subjects chosen from a wide range of possibilities, one or two hours a week.

5. A block of study in combined subject matter and methods of teaching in such common subjects as English, mathematics, physical education, and religious knowledge, perhaps four hours a week.

6. Three weeks of practice teaching.

*Second year:*

1. Continuation of No. 2 above, perhaps five hours a week of instruction in the history and philosophy of education, educational psychology, etc.

2. Continuation of No. 3 above, the Main subject, for three hours a week.

3. Continuation of No. 4 above, one or two hours a week for two of the three terms of the year.

4. Four weeks of practice teaching.

*Third year:*

1. Continuation of study in professional subjects but substantially increased in time during the first term and involving both further general study of Education and specialized study of one area.

2. Continuation of the Main subject in some Colleges for three or four hours a week, but dropped in others.

3. Practice teaching for seven or eight weeks, probably most of it in the middle term.

4. The last term of the year is given over to a special paper and to preparation for final comprehensive examinations.

A number of things are apparent from this kind of listing to anyone interested in comparing British with American teacher training:

*First,* the influence of the single-purpose institution is strong throughout the three-year course. This is a deliberate and a cultivated influence, and would be defended, I believe, by the majority of College staff members. They would not agree, that is, with what I suppose is the prevailing American view, which I certainly share, that the day of the single-purpose teachers college is past. The benefits of training teachers in isolation of the rest of the world of higher education are insufficient to counteract the limitations. There is some feeling about this in Britain also, but the general persuasion in both Britain and Europe seems to be that the single-purpose institution for preparing teachers for the nonselective schools offers more advantages than disadvantages.

*Second,* the principle of concurrence, good or bad, spreads the practice teaching over the three years, and often allows the student to teach in two or more schools with two or more age groups. Also, more time is devoted to practice teaching in the British three-year course than in the American four-year course. Since practically everybody in teacher education everywhere agrees that practice teaching is the most valuable part of any training course, I should think that we might consider the virtues of the longer and somewhat different practice-teaching arrangements common in Britain and most European countries. I might add the incidental note that practice-teaching arrangements everywhere get steadily more difficult as teacher-training enrollments grow. Britain is even stingier than we are in paying the host schools and the supervising teachers, nor are there many "demonstration" schools connected with either the Institutes of Education or the Colleges. Everybody may agree on the value of practice in teaching, but it often plays second fiddle to the theoretical work in Education in both countries.

*Third,* academic study is less, absolutely and relatively, in British programs for training elementary teachers than in American. I would hazard the guess that as much as two-thirds of the time of the prospective primary teacher over the three years of the British course is devoted to professional Education as we understand it and one-third to academic work. I should point out that the so-called "Main" and "Subsidiary" subjects studied by many intending primary teachers are from the soft side of the College offerings, even though the College may not consider them soft. To illustrate from one of the leading institutions, the City of Worcester College of Education: In 1965 it offered seventeen subjects as Mains, which were taken by 295 students, both primary and secondary. About half these students, 151 to be exact, chose either English, Mathematics, History, Geography, Physical Sciences, Biological Sciences, Sociology, or Rural Studies. The other half chose either Arts and Crafts, Divinity, Handicraft, Housecraft, Movement and Dance, Music, Needlecraft, or Physical Education. It does not necessarily follow that British teachers are less competent academically than American, since a number of complex factors, including the secondary education of the teacher, would have to be considered.

*Fourth,* the subject-matter training of teachers bound for the nonselective secondary schools is again less in England than in the United States. The obvious difficulty with this comparison is that we do not have a split system of secondary schools using different kinds of teachers. But if we look, say, at the training of our junior-high-school teachers and compare it with the three-year British course, the difference is clear enough.

How would one evaluate the standard three-year course in relation to the American system? As one who has criticized our own standards and practices in teacher training, I confess to similar feelings on the whole about the British system; it seems to me to suffer from the same deficiencies as ours. And students in both countries would, I believe, support this evaluation. I suppose I put more reliance than educationists would think wise on the opinions of students in teacher-training programs and of teachers who have been through the programs. For years I have been struck by the gulf between what students think and what their professors think they think; between what students say to me as a campus visitor and what the Education faculty, usually with great conviction, tell me their students believe. I have also been repeatedly struck by the reluctance of people in Education, which after all is a field that puts the greatest emphasis on student involvement, to solicit on some sort of systematic basis the honest reaction of students to the training programs of which they are a part. British educationists are no more anxious to make this solicitation, I found, than American. Having talked to a great many students in both countries, I would only record that most of them react about the same in teacher training. They have the same criticisms to make: The course is full of busywork and time-consuming trivia; staff members are nice, kind-hearted people but dull and ineffective; the course could easily be shortened but instead is becoming more inflated year by year; practice teaching is the best part of the course and the theoretical work in Education the worst. A survey of student opinion in the Colleges was published in 1966 by the National Union of Students. The Union reported that it had asked the cooperation of 151 Colleges in making the survey of their students but that only thirty-five had given their cooperation. Among the things found in this limited survey was a consistent vote by students against the number of lectures in the course, a vote for more practice teaching, and a vote for better supervision of practice teaching. The report also found: "A substantial proportion of the students felt that the course had not contributed as much to their intellectual development as it could have done. It should be noted that 70% of the students had Advanced level subjects before they entered college." [15]

Many a British schoolman would back up these judgments. There is a natural tension in many fields between people who employ specialists and those who train them, the former demanding practical skill and the latter demanding time for theory; but one would think this conflict could be resolved in Education. The usual answer is more time for training, and so we in the United States are now moving toward a compulsory period of five years of training as a beginning qualification even for elementary teachers. It is a wholly indefensible inflation of the academic currency—but it is, of course, the easiest answer. In Britain it was said a few years ago that the old two-year course was responsible for what one Director of an Institute of Education called the

> less than perfect understanding between the schools and the training colleges about the content and purpose of the course of training. The schools, which after all have to accept the products of the colleges and set them to work in classrooms, often under conditions of teacher-shortage and over-large classes, are inclined to reproach the colleges for sending out teachers with airy ideas but ignorant of how to make a register. The colleges are inclined to reproach the schools for demanding tricks of the trade.[16]

But the three-year course that was to resolve this conflict does not yet seem to have had the happy effects claimed for it in advance.[17]

Secondary school heads in particular seemed to me less than satisfied with the teachers they were getting from the Colleges. In 1964, for example, a conference of the heads of London's comprehensive schools produced a report of one of their discussions and called it "Teacher Training: Proposals for Reform." The main message conveyed to the Colleges by the heads, who collectively represented an extremely wide range of experience with students, teachers, and Colleges, was that the present three-year training course was not turning out people sufficiently competent in either the subjects that they had to teach or in methods of teaching them. The answer proposed by the heads was that the Colleges put greater stress on academic study during the first two years and much more on practice teaching in the last year; they also wanted a shift of responsibility for the supervision of student teachers away from the Colleges to the staff of the host schools. The theoretical work in Education was proposed for the cuts that would have to be made. Among other things said in this document, several main paragraphs of which I will reprint in the Notes for readers sufficiently interested, was this:

> Students now get their certificates and diplomas when they are one year older [since the start of the three-year course]; they come into our schools to that degree less immature and naive. But their personal education is often surprisingly shallow. The standards of their studies often seem to recede from those they achieved in the sixth forms of their schools. Their program in the first two years still appears to be unduly fragmented by teaching practices and by the formal Education Courses. In short, we felt that the interval of three years between the departure of our sixth form pupils into Training Colleges and their return to us as probationary

teachers might well be more imaginatively filled than it often is at present. Most of our conference assured us that in this view we were supported by a not inconsiderable body of opinion in the Training Colleges themselves.[18]

It has a familiar ring, though I do not suppose that a conference of American school principals would be likely to come up with such a statement; administrative solidarity is not so far advanced in Britain as in the United States, and it is still possible for one group of administrators to criticize another without the professional sky falling in. My own view as an outsider is that the London heads are substantially right and that many people in the Colleges would indeed agree. However, it is obvious that many, probably most, College administrators and staff members would not agree. (Following the London report came a similar one prepared by heads of schools in Kent, stressing the limited value of the three-year course.)

The standard of achievement actually maintained in the Colleges is as hard to define as standards anywhere, not only because the student varies quite a lot from College to College and Institute to Institute, but also because nobody has done any systematic study of this inflammatory subject. Britain has not yet had the kind of surveys of teacher training that we have had in recent years in the United States, and unfortunately there seems to be none in prospect. A few of the Colleges do not award grades, which might be some sort of guide to an outsider, but prefer "continuous assessment"; and most do not flunk out many students (in a three-year period, for example, Worcester had thirty-five "withdrawals" for all reasons). Also it must be a major problem within each College for lecturers to know where to peg their own standards: Some of their students will have studied any given subject to the O Level of the General Certificate of Education; some will have studied it well beyond that point to the Advanced Level of the GCE; and some will not have studied it to either level. So the range of student preparation is extremely wide. If all students are then to be brought to the same level in any given subject by the College in the same length of time, though starting from such different points, one suspects that the level is not going to be high on the academic side of the curriculum. I very much doubt that even "the ablest students," as one of the Department's publications asserts, "can reach a level comparable with that of a pass degree in their chosen subjects."[19] A pass degree is the lowest class of award in British universities and admittedly can mean very little, but students who take it have higher qualifications than College students and have studied fewer subjects at the university with tutors who are presumably more qualified than most College staff members. It therefore seems doubtful that the College student can reach the same standard with a different kind of tutor while doing all of the other work involved in the training program. What the actual standard is on the academic side one can only surmise; I would think it generally below that of American programs for both primary and secondary teachers in our better institutions.

On the Education side, since postgraduate work in Education is still relatively rare among College staffs, the Colleges rely on what American educationists would consider nonspecialists. This picture is slowly changing as British universities begin to offer a range of postgraduate work in Education, but most of the people now teaching pedagogy and Education in the Colleges are not formally trained in those subjects. In times past the Colleges wisely relied on experienced teachers to fill posts as "Masters and Mistresses of Method"; they still do under different titles. When these posts are filled American-style in the future with people who have postgraduate and perhaps undergraduate degrees in Education but who may be short of teaching experience, one wonders if the training programs will be strengthened. Again the standard of work in Education in the Colleges is hard to pin down, even though "external moderation" and other factors probably make it more uniform than in the United States. I can only record that what I saw was not impressive, especially in theoretical subjects like educational psychology and sociology. It is not impressive with us either, but I suppose that if training programs must require as much Education theory as they do in England and the United States, it is better to have it done by people with postgraduate work in it than by others. Perhaps the real answer is to reduce the theory.

In summary, looking first at the negative side, I would say that the teacher-training institutions in Britain are still the poor relations of higher education, just as they traditionally were in the United States. The difference in atmosphere between a single-purpose institution and a university or general-purpose college is immediately sensed by a visitor: The single-purpose college is more parochial; its head is likely to be more the benevolent dictator than would be conceivable in any university, and academic freedom means something different in the two types of institution; there is an undercurrent of anti-intellectualism in the teachers college, or at least a noticeable absence of intellectual intensity and drive; there is a tendency for the primary school to dominate the College, not only in the percentage of students headed for primary teaching, but in the outlook and ethos of the institution. The Colleges do attract to the staff good teachers from the grammar schools, but not as many of the outstanding ones as might be supposed, many of whom would not consider it a promotion. The Colleges are limited in their academic horizons by, among other things, the wide differences in background among the students and perhaps the staff; and their work in Education consumes large quantities of student time without a commensurate return in quality.

On the positive side, I would say that the Colleges are now getting students from a higher range of the intelligence scale than American teacher-training programs, and that students are academically well ahead of their American counterparts when they arrive, though that lead may diminish by the end of their three-year course. The emphasis on practice teaching is a strong point in the Colleges. (It might be even stronger if it were done in a continuous session during the third year rather than strung out in short bursts over the three years.) The practice of putting instruction in the methods of teaching, as well as supervision of practice teaching, in the hands of experienced teachers and subject specialists is a particularly strong point and is something that has long been needed in the United States. Supervision of practice teaching also means more, and student teachers are visited much oftener, in Britain than in the United States. However, programs in both countries suffer from the assignment of College supervisors to student teachers working in a number of different subjects.

Finally, the Colleges have, I believe, a considerable advantage over American training programs in being organized around university-based Institutes of Education. These Institutes are an outstanding feature of professional Education in Britain, and American educationists might well give them some serious consideration.

## Institutes and Departments of Education

Most countries have never really sought an answer to the old problem of how to cure the provincialism of small, usually impoverished teachers colleges that are scattered across the land, often in tiny villages that are geographically and intellectually isolated. We solved the problem in the United States only by allowing the colleges to evolve into general-purpose institutions. In Britain the problem was discussed as early as the 1890's, when a national commission recommended that the Colleges be affiliated in some fashion with the universities, but nothing was done for half a century more. In 1944 England's McNair Report finally galvanized enough people into action, and a peculiarly British creation, the Institute of Education, took shape in the universities. The McNair Committee was appointed to investigate the whole of teacher training in England and Wales (a job that should now be done again) and found the hundred institutions then engaged in the work not to be related to one another "in such a way as to produce a coherent training service. . . . It is clear to us that the idea of separate and self-contained training institutions must be abandoned."

The committee was opposed to creating a single centralized system to solve the problem but sought instead a formula that would respect the fundamental authority of the institutions while bringing them under the influence and control of the universities so that, as the Committee put it, those who intend to be teachers, or otherwise to associate themselves professionally with the young, have the chance to enjoy a period of education and training which, above all else, will encourage them to live a full life themselves so that they may contribute to the young something which arises as much from a varied personal experience as from professional studies.

The main recommendation was that British universities "should accept new responsibilities for the education and training of teachers," and at least half the committee thought the universities should do this by establishing Schools of Education. Such Schools were to be integral parts of the universities, and the Colleges were to affiliate themselves with whatever School they chose. Teacher training thereafter was to be controlled through the joint authority of the School and the College, but the committee was definite that the university "and no other body" was to be "the focus of the education and training of teachers in the future." The Committee concluded with this exhortation:

> We make this proposal for the major constitutional change at a time when fundamental reforms are being made in our educational system, when we are within sight of full-time education for every boy and girl up to 16 years of age, with compulsory part-time education up to 18, and when it is necessary to attract to the profession of teaching men and women of high quality and potentialities. We believe that in years to come it will be considered disastrous if the national system for the training of teachers is found to be divorced from the work of the universities or even to be running parallel with it. We are not looking a few years but twenty-five years ahead, and such an opportunity for fundamental reform as now presents itself may not recur within that period.[20]

Nearly twenty-five years later, the committee would be both pleased and disappointed. The universities did not respond with great alacrity to this trumpet call, but they did respond; Schools of Education were not established as fully integrated parts of universities, but Institutes of Education were established as affiliated parts of universities; in 1967 the academic departments of the universities were not much involved in teacher training, but teacher training was no longer divorced from, or running parallel to, the universities.

Some of the "Redbrick" universities like Bristol and Birmingham led the way in accepting the idea of an Institute of Education, while Oxford and Cambridge resisted. The arguments that took place in the late 1940's in the university senates over the issue would sound familiar in the United States. At Leeds, for example, another Redbrick university, a faculty vote was taken in 1947 after extended debate over whether the training of teachers had any relevance to a university. The faculty decided it did not and voted down a proposal for an Institute. After that a number of influential people began telling the university that it had a duty to accept the

Institute, and it became clear at the same time that there was a considerable body of national opinion in favor of the McNair proposals. Subsequently Leeds did accept an Institute, as did the other universities on varying terms. Cambridge was alone in refusing an Institute, and still is today. In contrast to Oxford, where at least a few dons actively supported the idea, Cambridge presented a united front against it. Consequently the central Department established an independent Institute of Education in the city of Cambridge and gave it more money than it would ever have been likely to get from the university. Today the Cambridge Institute is loosely associated with the university, but is still financed by the central government. What it lacks in prestige and other benefits from not being a part of Cambridge University seems to be compensated for by generous financing from the Department. In 1966 the University reaffirmed its earlier decision and with a substantial majority again voted down a proposal that the Cambridge Institute of Education become a part of the University.

Briefly described, an Institute is an administrative arrangement whereby all of the principal interests involved in the training of teachers are brought together under the aegis of a university to exercise a shared control over teacher training in the area. These interests are the employers of teachers (the LEA's), the central Department, the Colleges both LEA and private, and the universities themselves. All are represented on the governing body, usually a "Council," of the Institute, which also includes certain educational experts as "co-opted" members. Below the Council is usually an "Academic Board" responsible for general academic policy, and below that a number of "Boards of Study" representing the separate academic subjects and bringing together the subject specialists of the Colleges. The Colleges are free to affiliate with whatever Institute they choose, but in practice find the one nearest them the most desirable for ease of communication and for practice-teaching arrangements. Thus the number of affiliated Colleges varies widely among the Institutes; London's is naturally the largest with over thirty Colleges, and the Institute at the University of Hull the smallest with only two.

Over the last twenty years some Institutes have developed particular specialties. A few like Bristol and Birmingham stress educational research; some like Leeds emphasize service to teachers in the area; London is *sui generis* in this and most other respects and big enough to emphasize many things. But all strive to fill certain basic functions. They all attempt to encourage research within the Institute and to disseminate the results of research to the Colleges. They also maintain an educational library better than the separate Colleges can afford. And they all organize conferences and short courses and sometimes advanced degrees or diplomas for teachers.

But their main job is to unify and to some degree standardize the training of teachers in the Colleges. As the responsible body for organizing teacher training in their area, they seek to maintain common standards throughout their affiliated Colleges but without unduly infringing the freedom of the Colleges. Walking this particular tightrope is not easy, and the compromises made along the way are, in my opinion, one of the unsolved problems of the Institutes. Practices vary a lot, but the general machinery for controlling standards involves the cooperative development of syllabuses and examinations through the several Boards of Studies. Each department of each College, for example, might submit the syllabuses for its courses to the appropriate Board of Studies at the Institute for approval. Since membership on the Board is usually open to all teachers of the subject from all the affiilated Colleges, the size of a Board can be very large and unwieldy in the most popular subjects, and a certain amount of log-rolling probably takes place. The Board may have established a "core" syllabus that is used in all the Colleges but beyond that will allow great latitude. Changes in submitted syllabuses are sometimes requested by the Board of Studies; most syllabuses are approved without much alteration. In other words, the course of study in any given College in any given subject will have been scrutinized by a central body of specialists in that subject but will have been approved without change, unless it is plainly below a somewhat vaguely defined standard. Thus the Colleges of a large Institute will present a bewildering multiplicity of syllabuses that have something in common with one another but also individual features. In Education there is usually an Institute-wide syllabus, but not in other subjects.

Similarly, examinations and grading standards in each subject are rather loosely controlled through the Institute. Sometimes the individual departments simply prepare and grade their own exams without reference to the Institute Board of Study. But they must do so under the general supervision of an "external moderator" appointed by the Institute; that is to say, a supervising examiner from outside the College. Sometimes exams are prepared by the appointed moderator from questions submitted to him by the Colleges. The Colleges then read and grade the exams and return a sample of them to the moderator for comment.

The strong and weak points of this machinery for maintaining something like common standards are probably evident. The Institute does bring outside pressure to bear on the individual Colleges and probably does prevent a really low standard from developing in any of them; it does bring subject specialists from all the departments in a given subject together for an exchange of views and in a joint effort to define aims and content; it does bring a certain amount of university influence into the Colleges through representation on the Academic Board and the Boards of Studies of university faculty members; and it does leave the Colleges a large measure of freedom. By the same token, however, it suffers from

the large-committee approach to education and from the need for consensus. If a camel is a racehorse designed by a committee, an Institute
syllabus and exam are apt to reflect their own distortions for the same
reason. An Institute-wide exam in any subject, to be acceptable to all the
departments involved and relevant to all the syllabuses involved, is likely
to be so general as to be passable by almost anybody. And indeed this,
I feel, is often the case now.

But the greatest weakness of the English Institutes, I regret to say, is
precisely in the matter that the McNair Committee saw as the main reason
for creating Schools or Institutes of Education: the active involvement
of the university faculties in the training of teachers. Again, some Institutes are better than others at this, but the fact is that none of them has
really effected a happy and fruitful marriage between the educationist
and the academician or between the Colleges and the university departments. They still live in different worlds. The Institutes are still pretty
low in the university pecking order. Since they do not bring many fee-
paying students into the university (most of the students are in the
Colleges), they have to fight hard for money against the more influential
departments of the university; they do not have nearly the power of, say,
the dean of a big American School of Education whose division may put
more money into the till than any other division of the institution. The
academic departments do have a voice in the Institutes through their
representation on the Academic Boards and Boards of Studies, and they
do, I suppose, exercise a certain general influence within the Institutes;
but the academician's role is nothing like what was envisioned by the
McNair Committee. He almost never actually teaches a student from an
Institute or from any of the constituent Colleges, nor does he visit the
Colleges, nor does he visit students doing practice teaching, nor does he
participate in anything but a minor way in the preparation of syllabuses
or examinations. His role is advisory and too often perfunctory. It will
improve, however, in the near future as British universities begin to
award a "B.Ed." degree through the Institutes to the best students from
the Colleges. And relations will improve also as the Institutes at big
universities like Birmingham and Leeds are converted, as is now being
done, to Schools of Education with full university status.

We of course have had the same separation for many years of the departments of Education and liberal-arts departments, but a rapproche-
ment seems to be coming. It might be assisted by something like an Institute of Education. Even though our teachers colleges are disappearing, a
federation of the principal interests involved in teacher training along
the lines of an Institute might have much to be said for it. Until recently,
Institutes of Education were unique to Britain. Now they are being
adapted to the teacher-training system in Sweden and in parts of Canada
as well as in other Commonwealth countries. In the United States such

agencies would have to be voluntary bodies unless organized by state authority for state institutions, in which case they might do more harm than good. But they, or some adaptation of them, could perhaps be the means for raising the standards of teacher-training programs in general and eliminating egregiously weak programs in particular—something that is not done now by either the regional or national accrediting organizations. The progress made recently in teacher training in the United States has been made by individual institutions under their own steam; a regional Institute might regionalize the steam. I can think of a great many teacher-training programs in the United States that would be greatly helped if they were part of some kind of regional federation representing the interests of employers, teachers themselves, educationists, and academicians. Nobody should lightly suggest the creation of still another organization in teacher training, but I would suggest that Institutes might contribute more to the improvement of this enormous enterprise than a good number of agencies now operating in it. If they were effectively organized, Institutes might put some other organizations out of business.

DEPARTMENTS OF EDUCATION IN ENGLAND

Throughout Europe teacher training is really two worlds, the world of the teachers colleges where people are trained for primary and non-selective schools, and the world of the universities where people who subsequently teach in selective schools are educated and where they may or may not be trained for teaching. In Britain these worlds are more closely related than in most of Europe, not only through the Institutes but through Departments of Education. Almost all English universities have Departments of Education that operate jointly with the Institutes or alongside them. In a few places such as London the two operate as a single unit, while in other places they operate separately but under the same head; but in most universities the Department is a separate entity with its own head and its own faculty and its own job to do. The Departments antedate the Institutes, often by a long time. The Department at Oxford, for instance, is nearly seventy-five years old, whereas the Institute was established in 1951. The Departments have somewhat more status in the universities than the Institutes and are better situated to fight for their share of the university budget, and so they are prone to guard their separate identity lest they be submerged in the Institutes. The Departments' days are probably numbered, however, for it seems certain that Schools of Education will eventually be created in most of the universities and will merge the existing Departments and Institutes.

Although the Departments have always made an effort to promote research, being departments of universities, their main job has been and continues to be the training of university graduates for teaching in grammar schools. A one-year postgraduate course in Education for such people is offered throughout Britain's universities. At the end of the course the student is granted, not a graduate degree as in the United States, but a "Diploma" or "Certificate" in Education that gives him the status of a "trained" graduate teacher. Traditionally, any graduate of a British university has been eligible to teach without further training, and most of the staff of the selective schools in Britain did not train. Today the one-year course is still voluntary but over half of all new grammar-school teachers are taking it immediately after completing their degree. If they do, they receive a stipend adequate for all expenses, and they start teaching at a higher salary than "untrained" graduates. Since a large percentage of each year's university graduates enter teaching, about one-third of all those in humanistic subjects, the one-year Diploma course is a large operation in British universities.

It may surprise American readers to know that the typical Diploma course involves no further study whatever in the individual's academic subject (in which he has specialized for the previous three years). He is enrolled in the Department of Education and does all of his work there. Perhaps two-thirds of his year is spent in the study of the usual Education subjects. He will attend a large number of lectures by members of the Department on educational history, philosophy, and psychology, on methods of teaching, and inevitably on current issues in education; he will do an extended essay during the year on a pedagogical subject; and he will have comprehensive exams at the end of the line, except at a few universities where "concurrent assessment" prevails. The other one-third of his year or a little more will be spent in practice teaching in one or two blocks of time.

Like the Institutes and the Colleges, the Departments of Education are staffed by what American educationists would consider amateurs; that is, teachers. Most staff members are former classroom teachers, and thirty percent of them began their teaching careers in state grammar schools. A recent survey of the staff of the Institutes and Departments of Education indicated that "Only 13 percent of the staff surveyed had not worked in schools for at least two years; 4 percent had twenty years experience or more and the remainder had spent between two and twenty years in the classroom." [21] However, the field of professional Education in Britain is rapidly following the American lead and in the future will supply a variety of specialists in Education rather than academic subjects to the staffs of teacher-training programs. At present the practice-teaching work of the one-year course, like that of the three-year College course, contrasts sharply with the customary American approach. People who supervise student teachers in most American programs are Education specialists, often far removed from classroom teaching; in Britain they are subject-matter specialists who, in most cases, have fairly recent classroom teaching experience and who visit their student teachers much more often than with us. They also teach the methods courses in their academic fields. I was sorry to see, however, that subject-matter specialists were too often in charge of student teachers in other subjects. True, we are even worse when we allow, as we often do, specialists in Education without advanced work in academic subjects to teach others how to teach these subjects and to supervise their practice in doing so; but the solution is surely not to put subject specialists to doing the same thing outside their own field.

As might be expected, pressures are building up for making the one-year Diploma course compulsory for university graduates who propose to teach in grammar schools or in any other type of school. This seems to me an unfortunate, if inevitable, development. I can see some virtue in professional training for, say, a university graduate who has himself been through only the English independent schools and who intends to teach in a comprehensive or a secondary modern school, but even then his training might best take the form of an extended apprenticeship rather than further university-based theoretical study. For many grammar-school teachers, professional training is of doubtful value. But in any case, the usefulness of professional training is not perhaps the main reason for the drive to make it compulsory. The question is one of status as much as anything. The National Union of Teachers has always been somewhat bitter about the fact that university graduates could teach without having any pedagogical or professional training. The NUT sees this as a threat to the professional status that teachers seek, and so has been bringing its very considerable power to bear on the Secretary to change the rules. Likewise British educationists almost to a man are behind the NUT's position, for obvious reasons. And of course visiting American educationists are scandalized at the whole idea of England's allowing graduates, sans Education courses, to "enter the profession"; as one characteristically puts it:

> The significant thing to the writer is that neither in English educational literature, nor on his visits to English schools of all types, nor in his discussions with headmasters and other officials has he ever come across more than half-hearted defense of optional training for university graduates.[22]

He must have visited different schools from those I visited, for my impression from grammar-school visits and talks with headmasters is precisely the opposite of his: I found nothing but half-hearted defense of mandatory training for university graduates. Also he might have got a surprise if he had talked with some students taking the one-year course.

In all probability, it is merely a question of time before the Diploma course is made obligatory. Delays may be necessary because of the teacher shortage, as they have been in the professional training of teachers for the technical colleges in spite of a contrary recommendation of the National Advisory Council on the Training and Supply of Teachers,[23] but it is coming. Like so many of our own training courses for teachers, the Diploma course is based on faith, hope, and supposition, as well as professional protectionism. Nobody knows in any demonstrable way whether it makes a graduate a better teacher than he would otherwise have been, though one can certainly find a great many grammar-school headmasters of wide experience who can see small difference between trained and untrained graduates. If one were to go only by the opinions of the students themselves, one would have to bring in something less than a hearty vote of confidence in the Diploma course. Their opinions of professional training, like those of many students in the Colleges of Education, just about parallel those of American students in teacher training. Which is to say, they are consistently negative, and for about the same reasons. British students have an incentive, however, for taking the course that is not found in most other countries: a government grant adequate for all fees and living expenses. Many students therefore do the Diploma course as a year of relative leisure after the rigors of their degree, and about 12 percent of them do not enter teaching at the end of the course. The National Association of Schoolmasters, speaking no doubt for a brasher group of teachers than the NUT, said in its testimony to the Robbins Committee:

> Departments of Education have all too often had one serious defect in the past. After a hard course of study leading to a degree the Professional year in the Department has tended to be a year of relaxation for the students and the tutorial staff have let it be so.[24]

As usual, students praise the practice-teaching part of the course but are unenthusiastic about the rest. One of them, writing in an educational journal, seems to me to echo pretty well the opinions that came my way from graduate students taking the Diploma course:

> Most students agree with me, saying it is wonderful to get out of the Education Department into a real school. . . . Nearly everyone is critical of the course, usually in a general way: the various subjects are considered badly taught or not worth teaching; there are complaints at lack of contact with the staff. This sort of talk is often just, but is also the result of a general feeling of frustration. I think this arises because a student feels that his intellectual academic skill is disintegrating because no rigorous demands are being made upon him, and that no comparable practical skill is being given in exchange.[25]

Students themselves seem to have as little effect on changing or reforming the graduate course as students in the Colleges have on their courses, or as they do in American programs. Only one Department of Education in England, so far as I know, has undertaken to survey the opinions of its students and former students about the Diploma course. I have seen the results, but unfortunately the Department regards them as top secret and is extremely anxious that they not be published. In 1963 the Ministry of Education, as it then was, sponsored a general survey of the attitudes among all kinds of university students toward certain careers, including teaching and the Diploma course. Nearly two-thirds of the students questioned are reported to have said they thought the course would be

> very useful or fairly useful, particularly on the practical side. Where students had reservations about the training offered, these were mainly on the score that it was too theoretical. The chief improvements suggested for the course related to practice teaching: that there should be more of it and that it should be better organized. There was also some feeling, especially among women students, that the course was too long and that shorter or optional length courses should be introduced. There was no evidence that any substantial number of students was deterred from training by the form and content of the present course.[26]

Unfortunately, the Ministry did not follow up on this sampling of opinion to find out what students thought after they had actually been through the course or while they were in it.

Within the Education field in England, which is not yet so monolithic as ours, I found some pretty frank assessments of the Diploma course. Even when educationists want to make the course compulsory, they often recognize the need for a major reconstruction of it. H. C. Dent, former Assistant Dean of London University's Institute of Education and former editor of the *Times Educational Supplement,* regards the Diploma course as "the weakest form of training we have" and thinks that students are justified in regarding it as "a soft year with no intellectual demands." Similar opinions were expressed to me by educationists at a number of British universities, who would agree, at least in private, with this assessment from the dean of the School of Education and Social Work at the University of Sussex:

> Departments of Education, with their responsibility for providing a one-year postgraduate course for the training of teachers, have not looked much like "genuine" university departments. They have pursued very little research, most of it in psychology, and virtually none of it in sociology; they have carried a staff many of whom seemed by university standards, non-academic; they have usually been housed "down the road"; and they have generally suffered from an inferiority complex. If there is some truth in the assertion that historically training colleges were committed, as a matter of policy, to mediocrity, it is also true that university departments of education have been committed, as a result of university policy, to much the same lack of distinction. And thus it is hardly surprising that many undergraduates have preferred to go straight into

schools without attending a department of education or acquiring a certificate in education.[27]

In Europe, however, the training of teachers for the academic secondary schools is in somewhat better repute, mostly because of an emphasis on academic ability and on pedagogical apprenticeship rather than theoretical study. Since teachers in the selective secondary schools of Britain and Europe are university graduates, they come from what in most places is the top two or three percent of the age group, possibly four percent in Britain. With us they come from the eighteen percent of the age group that completes the bachelor's degree. Again one might say that we simply develop more of the native ability of our people, and we do, but the main fact is that most of our first degrees do not and cannot reach the qualitative level of first degrees in Britain and Europe. In a word, there can be little doubt that teachers, taken as a group, in the selective secondary schools of England and most of Europe are better educated and of higher native ability than in our senior high schools.

For teachers going into the selective schools of most countries, formal instruction in pedagogy is a minor element in their preparation. In France, for example, professional training for teaching in the *lycée* is only about a dozen years old and is still strongly based on practice. The first requirement is the degree, on the strength of which one may be admitted directly to teaching if a more qualified applicant is not available. Normally one studies before or after the start of teaching for one of two further qualifications: the CAPES (*Certificat d'Aptitude du Professorat de l'Enseignement Secondaire*), or the *agrégation*. Both are highly competitive examinations administered nationally and therefore with a national standard. The CAPES involves a year's work under the supervision of a regional training center. It includes some study of Education, but at least seventy-five percent of the work is in the form of practice teaching under close supervision. Because the number of people passing the exam for the CAPES is controlled by the number of posts available in the *lycées* for holders of it, the failure rate is much higher than in any teacher-training program in Britain or the United States.

The highest qualification normally sought by teachers in the *lycée* is the *agrégation*. The prestige of being a *professeur agrégé* in France is very real, and the Association des Agrégés is one of the most influential bodies in French education. After his university degree, a teacher who wishes to study for the *agrégation*, which also leads on in many cases to university teaching, must first spend a year or more doing a thesis in his academic specialty under the supervision of the appropriate university faculty. After a successful oral exam on his thesis and related matters, he is awarded a *diplome d'études supérieures*. After that he continues the study of his academic specialty, frequently for a number of years, until he feels qualified to attempt the *agrégation*. This examination, too, is sharply limited by the number of posts available in the *lycées*. The competition is more severe than for the CAPES and the failure rate is high; it is not uncommon for candidates to attempt the exam five or six times. The standard for the *agrégation* is, I would judge, somewhere between the master's and the doctor's degree at our best institutions. By the time he passes the *agrégation* a French teacher will have had little if any formal study of Education, but he will be in full command of his subject. Before anyone says that such people might be good scholars but bad teachers, he should note that the French *lycée* puts a higher percentage of the age group through the academic leaving certificate, the *Baccalauréat*, than is true in any other country of Europe.

Germany has what must be one of the longest teacher-training systems in the world for teachers that go into the *Gymnasium*. A German student, having passed his *Abitur* from the *Gymnasium* at age nineteen or so, goes on to take a university degree that requires five to six years of academic study, in the course of which, if he intends to teach, he will also pass a preliminary exam, the *Philosophicum*, in philosophy and Education. After his degree he will do a well-organized apprenticeship of two full years on a small stipend from the state. The first year consists of practice teaching, seminars with other teachers, and a variety of work in his academic specialties (he must have two) and in Education; the second year he is assigned to a seminar with ten to fifteen other *referenda* from the same area, in which mutual problems are discussed and some papers written, but in which most of his time is again given over to supervised practice teaching. At the end of his second year, he has a comprehensive exam that includes, as is common in Europe, two or three demonstration lessons before a panel of judges. After that, the student still has several years ahead of him of probationary teaching. Thus a *Gymnasium* teacher is often in sight of thirty before he becomes a fully qualified teacher in Germany. Proposals have been made recently for reducing this protracted training system, partly because of the severe shortage of teachers in Germany, where an advertised vacancy even in a humanistic subject may produce only two candidates and in the sciences only one. But the long course will probably be kept and a shorter one, comparable perhaps to the French CAPES, introduced alongside.

In the United States we have had suggestions in the past and even a few scattered movements to create some kind of superior qualification for teachers, perhaps a kind of American *agrégation* that would qualify successful candidates for admission to a senior professional association of some prestige. Whether it might be called a Master Teachers Association or a Schoolmasters Guild or, most recently, a Society of Academic Teachers, a senior qualification for the best teachers could be a more powerful incentive for them than any number of piled-up "in-service" courses in Education, the prestige value of which might best be left undiscussed. Let us be frank: One of the reasons for the low status of American teachers is the refusal of teachers themselves to make any distinctions in their own ranks and to give appropriate recognition to the fact that all teachers are not equal; some are better than others, and a lot of the better ones, having stayed for a number of years on the professional plateau of equal pay and equal if low public esteem, abandon the field entirely for the more mountainous country of industry.

Why do American teachers, one of the largest professional groups in the nation, have so small a voice in educational policy? Why so weak a voice in public affairs of any kind? Why do they allow themselves to be exploited so often? Why do they accept so uncritically the shifting doctrines of professional Education? Why do they submit so meekly to having their professional association run by administrators instead of teachers? Why, if reforms are needed in education, are not teachers themselves the voices of change instead of the voices of silence? Why, in a word, are they so far down the social and professional totem pole? For many complicated reasons, no doubt, but one of the big ones is that they lack effective leadership and a hierarchy based on merit. A prestige qualification for teachers might be one way of mitigating this condition. I for one wish that such a qualification could be established or at least seriously explored in the United States. For years we have heard the lamentations of teachers' associations about the lack of control that teachers themselves have over "entry to the profession" and similar matters, but surely one of the reasons for this situation rests with teachers themselves.

Quite apart from the question of why teachers are professionally weak, we in the United States have surely reached the point in the education of teachers where we should be able to train at least as large a percentage of people to as high a standard as is done in much poorer countries abroad for their academic secondary schools. A growing percentage of our high-school teachers have the master's degree, but it would be a brave man who would claim to know what standard that represents; for it represents, of course, a great many different standards. Like so much about our educational system, we have to make a speculative judgment about the substantive qualifications of our teachers, in the absence of any sort of publicly known and recognized standard. Without pressing any particular solutions to the problem, I feel that the education of teachers for the academic secondary schools in Britain and Europe is a subject that would repay the careful attention of those who run our own teacher-training programs.

A RECENT STUDY OF BRITISH AND AMERICAN TEACHERS IN TRAINING

Late in the preparation of this book the report of an interesting study became available comparing the teacher-training students of the United

Kingdom and the United States. To my knowledge it is the first study of such scope to be done and as such is relevant to our present discussion, though it is on the whole a disappointing piece of work. It was carried out by the Research Foundation of the University of Toledo (which also conducted the comparative study of pupil attainment that we looked at in Chapter III), under the Cooperative Research Program of the United States Office of Education. Its object was "to assess and compare the intellectual and personal characteristics of pre-service teacher education students in the United Kingdom and the United States." [28] A total of 2,175 students in the United Kingdom were tested out of a sample originally stipulated as 2,762. But out of a sample of 5,000 students in the United States who "were assigned to be tested" on the basis of a comparable sample, only half that number were actually tested because of the failure of many institutions to carry out the testing arrangements—a situation that, one would suppose, would have suspended any very definite conclusions until the reasons for such an attrition rate could be determined.

In 1964 and 1965 these students, at three different points in their training programs, were given a series of six tests in three sittings, taking altogether twelve hours to complete. All the tests, as in Toledo's other study, were American machine-scored tests; the investigators report that they could not "locate British tests appropriate to the purposes of the study." Half of the tests measured native ability and achievement in a number of academic subjects, and half of them measured "professional knowledge" and various kinds of attitudes or personal characteristics that American educationists think are measurable and important to teaching. To get to the conclusions of this report, one must hack one's way through a couple of hundred pages of Educanto, dense with brambly patches like: "The visits tended to reveal a commonalty of orientation," or "Teacher education curricula has been mainly derived from a philosophical-historical and not an empirical base." But I will spare the reader all that and move on at once to the conclusions, of which there are six and which I will reproduce unsequentially and comment upon:

> *Conclusion I:* United Kingdom teacher education students tend to have, generally, as indicated by the test data, higher general intelligence and verbal comprehension than do United States teacher education students.
>
> *Conclusion IV:* United Kingdom teacher education students appear to be better prepared in the academic fields of study measured than United States students, except for the area of science, wherein United States elementary education students appear better prepared than their counterparts overseas.

Both conclusions seem to agree, or at least to be compatible with, our earlier discussion. Certainly No. I would seem to follow clearly from what we have already said about the academic backgrounds of British teachers. No. IV is, unfortunately, not as useful a conclusion as it might have been if the study had made some further distinction between College of Education students in the United Kingdom preparing for non-selective secondary schools and university graduates preparing in Departments of Education for grammar schools and other selective secondary schools. With both groups lumped together in the study's conclusions, and only the average identified, important differences are obscured in the kinds of students involved in the various training programs. For example, we are told elsewhere in the report that "United States and United Kingdom secondary teacher education students were evenly matched in the fields of English composition, biological science and physical science." But such a statement is meaningless until we know how many British university graduates were involved and what subjects they "read" for their degrees. If they read English, history, or a physical science, they should be far beyond their American counterparts in that subject; if they read something else, they would probably be behind. What is illuminated by treating them in a bunch? As it was constructed, this piece of educational research simply ignores one of the most fundamental differences between the teacher-training systems of the two countries.

> *Conclusion II:* United States students tended to be more learning centered, while their British counterparts tended to be more child centered permissive [*sic*]. Interestingly enough, the findings, on which this conclusion is based, remained stable over the three stages of preparation (years) examined in the study and held for both elementary and secondary education students.
>
> *Conclusion III:* Teacher education students in the United States hold more favorable opinions of administrators and other school personnel than do students in the United Kingdom.
>
> *Conclusion VI:* American students appear to be better prepared in the measured areas of professional education than their counterparts in the United Kingdom.

I find it difficult to evaluate these three conclusions because of the difficulty of knowing precisely what they mean. Looking at the first one, I readily confess to a strong bias against the pervasive attempts of educational researchers to quantify what cannot be quantified, or at least against their drawing "conclusions" from machine-scored tests that claim to show whether people are "warm" or "understanding" or "egocentric" or that claim to be able to predict how well future teachers will get along with pupils "in interpersonal relationships." In fairness to the testers, I should record their admission that on some of these tests it is possible "to identify the 'nice' or the 'right' answers according to what one has been taught in professional education courses"—or perhaps taught by one's common sense. But the testers add, in a spectacularly unscientific moment: "However, the nonthreatening situation under which these inventories [of attitudes] were taken should have encouraged truthfulness of response." One can only admire the audacity of researchers who are willing to base "conclusions" on this sort of stuff, an audacity that is not, I should think, a "nonthreatening situation" for American teacher training. The investigators make quite a lot in their report of their "finding" that British teachers are more "child centered" than American teachers. It may well be so, especially among elementary and secondary modern teachers, though the idea may be differently interpreted in Britain. But anyone who is willing to base such a conclusion on the kind of machine-scored "inventory of teacher characteristics" and "behaviors" that make up the tests used in this study is much more sanguine than I believe most people would be about the reliability of educational research into personality and attitudes. I think it significant that the actual tests used in this regard, taken from an extended "teacher characteristics" study done some years ago in the United States, are not regarded with great reliability even by the man who created them.[29]

Conclusions Nos. III and IV are unsurprising. Educational administration is not much revered in Britain, and it is impossible to take advanced degrees in one or another aspect of it. British teachers have plenty of respect for headmasters of schools but think of them more as "head" teachers than as professional administrators. As for the superiority of American students in "measured areas of professional knowledge," I would not dispute it. As we saw earlier in this chapter, work in pedagogy and Education plays a very large part in the three-year College of Education course in Britain, but it is done in a vast variety of ways quite unlike the standardized Education courses among American institutions. Former classroom teachers, many with no advanced professional study, teach most of the Education courses in the British Colleges of Education. Because postgraduate study in Education is relatively undeveloped in Britain, no large, codified body of professional doctrine is passed on in all the training programs. Therefore, if one subjects British students to tests prepared by American educationists to measure the grasp that American students have of American professional doctrine, I should think it probable that American students would know more of the answers. But whether that has any discoverable connection with the kind of teachers they become is a wholly different question.

> *Conclusion V:* The changes in measured academic competencies which occur across the three years of preparation reflect the recency of course work in the particular content area being examined, the basic sequential differences in teacher education curricula in both nations, and the performance of Scottish and English graduate students.

I would not dispute this conclusion either, but, again, it does not mean very much as it stands. It only reinforces my earlier suggestion that this study would have been more useful if it had made clear distinctions throughout between teachers headed for nonselective and selective schools in the United Kingdom, thus respecting the major difference between the American system and those of both Britain and Europe.

## THE GROWTH OF PROFESSIONAL EDUCATION IN BRITAIN

So often the present developments and controversies in British education echo the old, evanescent ones of the United States. A visiting American feels as though he has seen the whole movie before. I often felt that way in looking at the field of professional Education in England and listening to familiar quarrels. In the past, what little research was done in university Departments of Education was grounded in psychology. Now educational sociology, after a long struggle, seems to be an accepted specialty on about the same limited terms that it has been accepted for years in the United States; and the other subspecialties of Education are beginning to flower in England very much after the established American fashion. British educationists still feel it necessary from time to time to defend in rather idealized terms the general idea of Education as a university study,[30] but not many academics continue to resist the idea that universities ought at least to train teachers; and when that proposition is accepted the next step inevitably is the development of research in Education and the creation of advanced degrees in it.

Thus one finds a growing number of in-service courses for teachers offered by the Institutes and Departments of Education as well as by the LEA's and the central Department. Many are summer or weekend or vacation courses. In contrast to American practice, they are not compulsory for teachers in Britain as a condition of advancement, and are probably better courses for not being so. They are taught by HMI's as well as by teachers themselves and members of the Education staff. They are over-subscribed most of the time. Some teachers undoubtedly take them as a possible qualification for a higher post; but the fact that many teachers travel considerable distances at their own expense to take such courses out of their own interest is a marked difference from American experience. For full-time further study by experienced teachers, both the central Department and the LEA's make arrangements that are far more generous than an American authority would make: Each year a number of the best teachers are given a leave of absence on full pay by their LEA's to study at a university Department of Education, with no commitment or only a hazy one to return to their sponsoring authority. A good many do not return or only long enough to secure a better post on the strength of their advanced certificate. The variety of longer courses of study is also increasing: full-time diploma courses in educational psychology, in guidance, in educational sociology, educational philosophy, and a fair number of courses of study in Education leading to a master's or doctor's degree.

Educational administration, however, is still mercifully absent from the professional offerings throughout Europe, though one suspects that this too will change before long. In 1965 a survey by the OECD turned up a wide variety of courses in public administration among the universities of the European member nations, but significantly found only a few offerings in things like educational guidance or sociology; it found only one in all of Europe in educational administration, a one-year course at the University of Reading, in England.[31] In this regard Europe is far more likely to move in our direction than we in theirs, and as a result is quite likely to develop in time the same sort of fragmented, overspecialized and undernourished graduate degrees in Education found throughout the United States.

Not many years ago even schoolmen in England tended to be skeptical about the value of educational research for the solving of education's most important problems. The volume of research done in the Departments of Education was small and its influence even smaller. They tell a story in Britain about the hiring of the first professor of Education at one of the prestige universities after World War II. The examining board that was charged with interviewing candidates for the job had a difficult time finding suitable applicants because it was not sure what was suitable, but finally interviewed one HMI who looked promising and asked him if he would engage in research if appointed. He said yes, that he was extremely interested in the medieval sermon and would continue his research into that subject. The board thought it would be better for everyone concerned if the university's Professor of Education were to do real research into a real subject rather than imaginary research into imaginary subjects, and appointed him. The reputation of educational research in Britain is now higher than that, though it is only stating the facts to say that such research is still regarded with contempt by some academicians and condescension by many. More money is now given to educational research than at any previous time, but it is still a tiny fraction of what is spent in the United States. One Institute head says:

> Of a total expenditure of 800 millions [pounds] on education, the amount devoted to research is one-fiftieth of one per cent. We spend over 20 times as much on medical research, 30 times as much on agricultural research. The Department of Scientific and Industrial Research has a budget of over 80 times as large as that for educational research. D.S.I.R. spends more on research into glue than we do on research into education.[32]

For a long time educational research in the United States was also in this invidious position, and surely for the same reason: It could not produce the kind of tangible and usable result that research into glue, grass, or gall bladders could. It still can't, but it now gets a very ample supply of funds in the United States, so much so that the principal problem is to find enough really first-class researchers to spend it. Although the British Institutes of Education were intended to encourage research as one of their main functions, they have as yet done little. They have been in a unique position to sponsor cooperative research among themselves and through their affiliated Colleges, but the only Institute to make even a small beginning was at the University of Birmingham.[33] As to individual research projects, a survey conducted in 1964 among the staff members of Departments and Institutes of Education suggested that a shortage of time and not money was the principal limiting factor in educational research.[34] Britain does support one national research organization of some consequence, the National Foundation for Educational Research in England and Wales. This agency is financed jointly by the LEA's, the Department, the universities, and various other bodies and is now carrying on more projects than any other agency in Britain. Oddly enough, England is in the same position now as is the United States: Whatever the sums spent on more frivolous things, there is more money available than ever before for educational research (through the central Department, the Schools Council, the foundations, and the universities), but a paucity of well-trained men and well-conceived projects.

Any reader familiar with the development of American teacher training will recognize that Britain is now going through the same kind of status battle that has gone on for many years in the United States. Professional Education is still perhaps the least distinguished of American academic pursuits, but reforms and improvements are now beginning to change its status. Like the United States, England will probably find that reform precedes respect. The Robbins Committee and other bodies have made numerous proposals in the last five years for raising the status of teaching and Education. Some of them may be based more on hope than reality, as I will discuss in Chapter VIII. Here I would only mention the two most important recommendations, both made in the Robbins Report.

The first one was to raise the status of the Colleges by removing them from the control of the LEA's and making them entirely the responsibility of the universities to which they were already affiliated in academic matters—in short, a return to the original McNair proposals in that Robbins wanted the universities at the same time to create Schools of Education to unify the Departments, the Institutes, and the Colleges. Many educational arguments were set forth in support of this idea, but the main object was to free the Colleges from what the Robbins Committee regarded as the old-fashioned and oppressive restrictions imposed on them by the LEA's. So long as the Colleges were tied to the apron strings of education committees, so long would they be regarded as parochial institutions set apart from the world of higher education. (In Scotland, by contrast, this problem does not arise, since the Colleges of Education have independent governing bodies.)

The Robbins recommendation was strongly supported by most educationists and most Colleges, though quite a lot of people in the Colleges looked with misgiving on the idea of university control. The LEA's and their Chief Education Officers, having watched much of their authority drift out of their hands since World War II, opposed the whole idea and wrote abrasive letters to editors in defense of the record of the LEA's with the Colleges. The LEA's also lacked faith in the ability of the universities to train enough of the right kinds of teachers fast enough to meet the teacher shortage; nor did they feel the universities were equipped by interest or experience to sponsor the kind of expansion of the Colleges that was needed. The Labor government listened to the LEA's and, to the surprise of many Labor supporters, upheld the claim of the LEA's against the Robbins recommendation. However, a year later another national committee brought in alternative proposals. It recommended that (a) the governing bodies of the Colleges should be changed to make them separate from the local education committee, and have representation from the College staffs, from the LEA's, and from the schools and universities; and (b) the Colleges create their own "Academic Boards" composed of senior staff people to enlarge the academic freedom of the staff and its voice in policy.[35] Both recommendations, which will probably be adopted, have as their aim to diminish the control of the Colleges by the LEA's.

The other and closely related proposal will seem curious to Americans. It was for the creation of a "Bachelor of Education" degree, the kind of degree that has been in such poor repute for so long in the United States and that many American colleges would like to jettison. But as we have seen, most British teachers and almost all of them that train in the Colleges do not take degrees. Instead they are awarded certificates, which are lower in esteem. Robbins proposed that the upper range of College students should be allowed to take an extended course of training of four years in collaboration with the academic departments of the universities and to be awarded a B.Ed. degree at the end. This too was debated in the educational press and to some extent the general press, with the discussion reminding one College Principal "of a bomb-disposal squad debating how best to deal with a particularly dangerous-looking object slowly emerging above the surface."[36] After the initial caution, however, this recommendation is now being put into effect in a number of British universities, and will probably be adopted in all of them in time. The B.Ed. is developing in as many different ways as there are Institutes. It is too early to judge whether it will accomplish what is hoped for it, or whether it will suffer the same fate as ours.

I regret not having found more to praise in the system of teacher training in England. It was, frankly, one of my disappointments; I had somehow expected it to be better than it is. At the least I did not expect to find it in such hot pursuit of so many of our own bad practices. It has its strong points and we should study them—the Institutes as a means for bringing into a cooperative federation the employers of teachers, teachers themselves, academicians, and educationists, all under the university umbrella; the emphasis on teaching experience in the staffing of the Colleges; the emphasis on practice teaching and the supervision of it; the depth of preparation in subject matter of teachers in the selective secondary schools; and the high standard of academic preparation of those who enter teacher training. And in Europe we should look in particular at the high admission requirements to training, the dominance of apprenticeship in programs for secondary teachers, and the importance of a senior qualification publicly esteemed for the best teachers. This is quite a lot from which our own teacher-training industry could profit.

## CHAPTER VI

# Universities in Britain

TO SERVE A NATION of just over 54,000,000 people, the United Kingdom now has forty-two universities. Enrolled in full-time or "sandwich" courses in these institutions are about 185,000 students, which is roughly four percent of the age group. These numbers compare pretty well with most of Europe and will increase rapidly over the next decade. To serve our own country of 200,000,000 people we have about 1,200 accredited, degree-granting institutions in which there are about 3,500,000 full-time students. But a comparison of ourselves with other nations does not mean very much until many other factors are taken into account. British and European universities accommodate a much narrower range of ability than ours and have nothing approaching the variation—in organization, finance, curriculums, standards, faculty, equipment—found among American institutions. Most universities in Europe are financed by and controlled in varying degrees by the central government; most are urban nonresidential institutions whose component faculties are scattered around the cities; and admission to them, as we have seen, is controlled by the state through the examinations for the leaving certificate of the academic secondary school. Britain departs from both Europe and the United States in these matters: Her universities function in a kind of limbo between state control and full independence, more of the latter than the former. They all operate under Royal Charters and get most of their funds from the central government. But they are not directly answerable to anybody. They are self-governing, they establish their own admission standards, and most are residential in some degree. Thus British universities in a number of important respects are unique among those of the major nations.

One can distinguish several basic types among British universities, leaving aside a few one-of-a-kind places like Durham and Wales. At the top of the heap socially and in many other ways are, of course, antique

Oxford and Cambridge, whose origins reach back to the twelfth and thirteenth centuries. Although other universities are now breaking away, often noisily, from the Oxford and Cambridge traditions, one should keep in mind, as the Dean of London's Institute of Education has pointed out in several places, that all English universities continue to owe a very great deal to the two ancient establishments—in curriculum, in teaching methods, in student housing and social amenities, and perhaps most of all in the high percentage of faculty members that were themselves educated at Oxford and Cambridge. Then, after an enormous leap in time, came the four Scottish universities in the sixteenth century, at Glasgow, Edinburgh, Aberdeen, and St. Andrews, that are still quite different from English institutions; then, after another leap in time, came the beginnings in 1826 of the University of London, still an institution quite distinct from all the others; and then, in the late nineteenth and early twentieth centuries came a number of "provincial" or "civic" universities like Manchester, Birmingham, Liverpool, and Leeds—"Redbrick" establishments built, not in the Elysian Fields and of the handsome gray stone of the ancient foundations, but in the middle of smoking Midlands cities of the unlovely red brick that advertised their liaison with industry and technology. Then came the postwar spate of new universities like Keele, Sussex, Lancaster, Essex, and Warwick that have tried to shun the academic legacies of both the Redbricks and of Oxford and Cambridge; finally and quite recently has come the conversion of the "CAT's," formerly Colleges of Advanced Technology, to the status of technological universities. None of these institutions compares in size with the American multiversities of New York or California, or even with the big state universities like Minnesota and Wisconsin. Only London with about 26,000 students dispersed among its many constituent colleges that include such semi-autonomous institutions as Imperial College and the London School of Economics, as well as a variety of institutes and schools, compares in size or complexity with state universities like Pennsylvania, Washington, or Maryland. Some British institutions like Hull or Reading are the size of medium American liberal-arts colleges. Most British universities follow an unhurried three-term academic year of about thirty working weeks (only twenty-four at Oxford and Cambridge), stretching from late September to mid-June, the standard offering being a three-year course leading to a bachelor's degree.

Like British schools, the universities are under the effective control of appointed laymen (except at Oxford and Cambridge) and of the teaching staff. Professional administration is a small and rather unadmired vocation; its ascendancy may be unavoidable in the future, but right now *homo bureaucraticus* is still a subordinate species. Universities are usually governed by a triumvirate of bodies, the Court, the Council, and the Senate, the first two being made up mostly of lay members and the last of senior members of the faculty. Together or sometimes in conflict they rule the affairs of the university. The highest administrative post is that of vice-chancellor. There are chancellors too, but purely honorary (Queen Elizabeth the Queen Mother, for example, is Chancellor of London University). The vice-chancellor's powers are rather vague and indeterminate; in some cases heavily ceremonial; in others, especially among the new universities, substantial. Faculty power and academic freedom are great in both British and European universities, greater than in many American institutions. The rights and privileges of senior faculty members are extensive, though junior members everywhere complain of an inadequate voice in policy.

The independence of British universities, however, is not total. Since they get most of their funds from the government, they are subject to the financial decisions of both the Chancellor of the Exchequer about overall university expenditures and more directly to the University Grants Committee. The UGC is a body peculiarly English (now exported to Australia, India, and Hong Kong) that stands between the government and the universities and protects one from the other while at the same time representing both. Briefly, the UGC is an agency created in 1919 to which are appointed mostly men who are active in teaching and research (no vice-chancellors, since they are the clients of the UGC) and who take whatever funds the government has decided can be spent on universities and distribute them according to their wisdom to the several institutions. Being a kind of inner circle of senior university people and a few selected outsiders, the Committee seems to conduct a good deal of its business in the somewhat funereal lounges and dining rooms of the Athenaeum Club, a renowned but gloomy London establishment for writers, intellectuals, and academics. The whole operation requires a strong degree of confidence from all interested parties in the integrity and fairness of the Committee.

It is often said that the UGC is only a middleman to keep the government from oppressing the universities and the universities from badgering government ministers, but with no real power over the institutions. In fact, it has a great deal of indirect power over university policy simply by virtue of having continuously to make decisions about what proposals will receive financial support and what will not. The universities submit their general operating budgets for approval to the UGC as well as special proposals for buildings or other expenditures. Thus if an institution has decided that it wants, say, a school of architecture, it might well be prevented from having it by the UGC or told to wait ten years. It can still have its school of architecture, but not on government funds, which in effect in Britain means that it will not be created. Although widely praised and respected, the UGC gets the brunt of considerable university criticism when building budgets are cut or salary raises are not approved;

it is also accused of being too small and too haphazard for the needs of the universities of a modern nation; and it is sometimes thought of as authoritarian, or too remote from the universities even though its membership is weighted on the side of active faculty members, or too much under the thumb of the central treasury. But mostly it is praised and supported as an effective buffer between the government and its often stubborn or unruly children, the universities.

## The Robbins and the Franks Reports

At the center of most of what is now happening in the British universities is a document that must be one of the most exhaustive of its kind and most noteworthy in modern educational history. It is the 1963 report of the Committee on Higher Education, with Professor Lord Robbins of the London School of Economics as its chairman. It was the main impetus three years later to the publication of another report, the Franks Report, confined to Oxford University. Together these reports tell a great deal about the past, present, and future of universities in Britain. The Robbins Committee, though not strictly speaking a Royal Commission, was appointed by the Prime Minister and was another in a long line of national boards of inquiry whose reports we have had occasion to review in a number of places. The Robbins Committee was charged with considering the state of all full-time higher education in Britain and its long-term development, a job that had never been attempted before. One of the first things the committee discovered, no surprise to any outsider who has tried to track down information on British institutions of higher education, was the paucity of statistical and other data with which to set about its deliberations. Accordingly the committee undertook a number of special investigations to collect its own basic facts. And it conducted six other inquiries into particular questions for which data were not available. It conducted an extensive series of statistical analyses, made trips to seven other countries, took oral and written evidence from ninety organizations and thirty-one individuals, collected 400 documents of written evidence, and held 111 meetings over a period of two years. After duly meditating on all this, it produced six big volumes: the "Report" itself, and five volumes of supporting information.[1] It is perhaps the most thorough discussion of a nation's institutions of higher education, and the most complete compilation of data about them, that has been produced anywhere (Sweden has done a similar but smaller job), and is clearly important reading for anyone interested in English education. It would also be good reading for people interested in higher education anywhere. Let me try to summarize as briefly as possible the essential content of the report:

The committee's assignment in 1961, "seventeen years after the passing of the great Education Act of 1944, which inaugurated momentous changes in the organization of education in the schools," was to consider "whether changes of a like order of magnitude are needed at the higher level." The committee finished by deciding that changes of a like order of magnitude were indeed called for. The main message of their report was that the entire structure of higher education in Britain was in need of reform and of massive and continued expansion. The committee found England holding its own at the moment in these matters with most of the countries of Europe but in danger of falling badly behind in the future. The committee's basic attitude was that British higher education needed to be "rationalized," liberalized, modernized, and greatly enlarged. Certain ideological principles seem to have guided the Robbins Committee before or during their deliberations:

*First:* The committee began with an attitude toward supply and demand in higher education that forms the entire bedrock of its report: ". . . we have assumed as an axiom that courses in higher education should be available for all those who are qualified by ability and attainment to pursue them and who wish to do so." The committee felt this principle to be almost self-evident on grounds both of national economic need and the personal development of individuals.

*Second:* The committee assumed throughout its report the principle of equality of status in higher education; that is, that equal performance should be given equal recognition throughout the field, though it found this equality badly lacking. Thus the familiar English problem of "parity of esteem" that has so bedeviled secondary education was found to be similarly a problem in higher education, where some institutions were accorded greater prestige than others on nonacademic or irrelevant grounds. The committee made a number of recommendations for removing what it thought of as invidious distinctions among degrees, certificates, and institutions.

*Third:* The committee recognized that different types of institutions of higher education would continue to serve different purposes, but felt that they should all be of equal importance; the only "morally acceptable" thing, therefore, was to make transfer between types of institutions easy for those students who might want to change.

*Fourth:* The committee strongly felt that deliberate long-term and continuing national planning on the basis of adequate research information was essential in British higher education, something that had never before been attempted. At the same time it felt that institutions, within the limits of national planning, should be left as free as possible to experiment and to take new paths according to their own desires.

*Fifth:* Finally, the committee established as a guiding principle that the radical expansion it recommended should not entail any lowering of standards. There was no incompatibility, it felt, between "the claims of numbers . . . [and] the claims of achievement and quality. . . . Equality of opportunity for all need not mean imposing limitations on some. To limit the progress of the best is inevitably to lower the standard of the average."

Without reviewing the exhaustive statistics and the detailed argument of the Robbins Report, we should note its main recommendations, most of which were immediately accepted by the government, the general public, and the educational community. Proceeding from the above five principles as a sort of *a priori* philosophical base, the committee brought in these major recommendations:

*First:* In accordance with the idea that higher education should expand to meet the level of qualified demand, the committee foresaw the need for nearly tripling the number of students in higher education by 1980— an expansion from 216,000 full-time students in 1962 in all types of higher education to 560,000 in 1980 (350,000 of them in universities). The committee thought this increase a minimum projection of need, without entailing any lowering of entrance standards.

*Second:* Tied to the "massive expansion" of higher education was the recommendation that many more students be encouraged to take a broader course of study for their degrees than was customary. In other words, the committee thought the kind of specialization normally required for the British first degree, one of its distinctive characteristics, was not suitable or desirable for a great many students who would be attending institutions of higher education under the recommended expansion.

*Third:* The committee thought that a significant percentage of the students in the teacher-training colleges were capable of doing degree-level work but were denied the opportunity under the existing system of LEA control of the colleges. It therefore recommended that all the colleges, which it thought should be renamed Colleges of Education in an effort to raise their status, should be removed from local control and given independent governing bodies, and should become constituent members of new university Schools of Education. Thereafter, those students in the Colleges of Education who showed themselves capable should be encouraged to take a university degree, a new one to be called the Bachelor of Education degree, at the end of a four-year course of study.

*Fourth:* The committee found technology to be one of the most neglected areas of higher education and one of the ones most in need of expansion. It recommended that the Colleges of Advanced Technology, then giving a "Diploma" at the end of a four-year "sandwich" course, be given status as technological universities and be allowed to award degrees. (Sandwich courses alternate between blocks of full-time study and full-time work in industry, similar to the "cooperative" programs in American institutions.)

The committee also recommended the development of five "SISTER" institutions, "Special Institutions for Scientific and Technological Education and Research comparable in size and standing and in advanced research to the great technological institutions of the United States of America and the Continent."

*Fifth:* Among the new subjects England was most in need of, the committee felt, was "Management Studies," and it recommended the creation of two postgraduate schools in the subject to accompany the growing number of colleges and universities offering undergraduate work in it.

*Sixth:* The committee recommended that students studying at the many Regional and Area Colleges—part of Britain's extensive system of "further education" mentioned in Chapter III—be allowed "the same opportunity for degrees as those in university institutions." To make this possible, the committee thought that a new and wholly independent agency outside the universities, a Council for National Academic Awards, should be created and empowered to oversee such work and to grant degrees to successful candidates.

*Seventh:* Doubtful that the scale of expansion it thought necessary could be accommodated entirely by the existing institutions, the committee recommended the creation of six new universities, and the "advancement to university status of some ten Regional Colleges, Central Institutes, and Colleges of Education."

*Eighth:* It recommended that the traditional autonomy of British universities be modified to the extent necessary to bring all of them into a coordinated system of higher education and in particular that Oxford and Cambridge either set their own houses in order so that they would be no longer outside such a system or be made the subject of a special investigation.

*Ninth:* The committee found the University Grants Committee "one of the significant administrative inventions of modern times" but recommended that its scope be enlarged and that it be changed in various ways to make it simply a "Grants Committee" with "oversight of the entire body of autonomous institutions" that were to make up the field of higher education in Britain.

Considering the magnitude of the Robbins recommendations and the liberalization of higher education that they entail, one might have expected the report to be received with some restraint in government and university circles. But such was not the case. The reception of the Robbins Report was enthusiastic, though the enthusiasm became somewhat dampened with time. Many of the above recommendations as well as many minor ones I have not mentioned have in fact been adopted and are now being put into effect. Some others have been quietly dropped. The most important recommendation, to increase the number of students in higher education according to a specific timetable, has already been surpassed. Among the important recommendations that were definitely rejected by the government was the proposal to remove the Colleges of Education from LEA control, also the proposal to create the SISTER institutions, and also the committee's strong recommendation that all of higher education be given an independent voice in appropriations and national policy by being put under a separate, appointed education minister. Although these rejections have been bitterly condemned by Robbins and others who served on the committee, the report as a whole has had a very great measure of success. Perhaps the most lasting of its effects is that it brought the idea of national planning in higher education, of deliberate long-range policy-making for the entire field on the basis of reliable data, into public and professional consciousness.

At least a few observers thought that a fundamental weakness in the report was its seemingly uncritical, or perhaps unexamined, view of the function of universities—its acceptance of the idea that whatever universities were doing was about what they should be doing, only they should be doing more of it. I suppose this criticism is justified though a little unfair in that the report does give some attention to the content of courses in higher education as well as merely to the logistics of the expansion. Even the British Socialists, who would be expected to endorse the report without much question, thought:

> The greatest criticism one can make of the Robbins Report is that it lacks any basic educational philosophy. It makes little attempt to define what exactly a system of Higher Education is meant to achieve, and gives very little support to any measures to try to find out.[2]

But perhaps national investigating bodies cannot be expected to grapple with such abstruse questions, much less reach agreement about them. Philosophical reflection is not done well by committees; at any rate, it rarely informs committee reports in education on either side of the Atlantic. Other important criticisms of the report were that (1) it failed to take account of the vast array of professional and higher education done outside the universities; (2) it seemed to have learned little from its study of higher education in other countries; (3) it succumbed to pressures from the Colleges of Education for transfer of control to universities; (4) it made little attempt to forecast manpower needs apart from teachers; and (5) its definition of academic freedom placed universities above and outside the kind of national planning the committee itself wanted to see developed.

Among the report's notable passages was its no-holds-barred criticism of the academic *apartheid* that seems to be enjoyed by Oxford and Cambridge. The report said:

> . . . the number of times when it is necessary to except Oxford and Cam-

bridge from general statements about British universities, the difficulty both universities have in reaching rapid decisions on matters of policy with their present constitutional arrangements, and the general obscurity in which so many of their administrative and financial arrangements are shrouded are not compatible with a situation in which they, like other universities, are largely dependent on public funds. Continuance of such anomalies may well endanger not only their own welfare but also the effectiveness of the whole system of higher education in this country, of which they are and should be so splendid a part. . . . We recommend that, if Oxford and Cambridge are unable satisfactorily to solve these problems within a reasonable time, they should be the subject of an independent inquiry.

Oxford, the oldest university in the English-speaking world, has more than its share of liberals of any type, but not so many in regard to the institution itself. Oxford has never been what one would call adventuresome about its own administrative or other arrangements. It has probably produced a greater percentage of the nation's Prime Ministers and politicians, senior civil servants, churchmen, judges, businessmen and assorted intellectuals of renown than a single institution of any other major country. Harold Wilson, Sir Alec Douglas Home, Macmillan, Eden, and Attlee were all Oxford men, as were half of even the Labor Cabinet in 1966. Founded by Englishmen driven out of the University of Paris during the quarrel between Becket and Henry II, Oxford had a stormy time of it for many years during which its relations with the town could only be described as ferocious. On one occasion a student killed a townswoman and the townsmen in return hanged two or three students, whereupon a number of other students fled to the northeast and founded another academy at Cambridge, which was to become Oxford's historic rival. On another occasion, when the great English reformer John Wycliffe was master of Balliol College, the townsmen were so inflamed about the university that they sacked the halls and massacred about sixty students. Over the centuries things quieted down and Oxford became increasingly devoted to its own traditions. In the middle of the nineteenth century, Emerson observed in *English Traits* that "Oxford is old, even in England, and conservative."

Oxford has not taken kindly to change and innovation during most of its 800 years and did not take kindly to the Robbins comment that seemed to threaten it with a Royal Commission. Nevertheless it acted and in 1964 appointed a commission of its own to investigate itself under the chairmanship of Lord Franks, then provost of one of the Oxford colleges and a former ambassador to the United States. The Franks Commission listened to the diagnoses by innumerable people of Oxford's ills. It also collected a million or so words of written testimony and then produced its own Robbins-like report in May of 1966, a two-volume, 900-page document that publicly washed more Oxonian linen than had ever before been seen in the long history of the institution.[3] Hereafter, the old complaint, echoed by Robbins, will have to be dropped that adequate information about what goes on at Oxford is unobtainable; these two volumes are a full statistical record and a full general exposition of the University and its constituent colleges. The testy comment of the Robbins Report, and the appointment of the Franks Commission itself, implied the need for reforms at Oxford, especially reforms that would bring it into a coordinated national-university plan. Actually, the Franks Commission struck a middle way in its recommendations between the radicals who wanted to see Oxford's status leveled to that of other universities and the stand-patters who wanted to preserve the old ways without any compromise with modernity. Before proceeding to a more general discussion of British universities, I think it will throw light on the whole subject if I extract some of the key passages from the Franks Report and summarize its most important recommendations:

*First:* The Franks Commission rejected, as had the Robbins Committee, the idea that Oxford should become either a wholly postgraduate institution or should restrict its role to that of an ordinary university. The commission thought it essential that Britain have at least a few universities of world reputation and that Oxford was obviously one. The commission said:

> Oxford has duties and obligations that extend beyond national boundaries, for it is an international university, comparable to the great centers of learning in Europe and across the Atlantic, attracting scholars and students of the highest quality from all parts of the world. . . . The world of scholarship is as competitive as that of commerce, and it has no protective barriers. Oxford must show results and must attract resources in an international arena in which there are many ancient foundations, some vigorous new experiments, and many institutions which dwarf it in size.

*Second:* The commission thought Oxford should continue to expand, but not beyond medium size. From its total enrollment in 1965–66 of 9,824 students in all categories, it should grow to perhaps 13,000 by 1980 or 1985. Stress should be put during this growth on the applied sciences and "social studies"; stress should also be put on increasing the percentage of women at Oxford. The commission also wanted a major effort to increase the number of postgraduate students, not too many of them "home-grown"; while commending the traditional preoccupation of Oxford dons with the education of undergraduates, the commission thought it past time to expand and develop postgraduate study.

*Third:* Regarding admissions to Oxford, one of the most sensitive topics, the commission recognized the justice of some complaints and not of others. It agreed that students from state grammar schools were put to some disadvantage by the special entrance exams for Oxford, not because they were discriminated against by the colleges, an idea the commission rejected, but simply because their schools could not offer them the same kind of special preparation, a third year in the sixth form, that the Public Schools and direct-grant schools could offer. Actually many state schools do have a third year in the sixth form, but not often of the quality of that of the independent schools. The commission did not agree that the special exams were in themselves deleterious. It thought them a "well-tried instrument [that] has acquired a refinement given by years of practice. It is so constituted as to be a searching test of promise." I think it significant that the commission found, as I mentioned in Chapter IV in connection with regular GCE exams, that the schools using the special entrance exams the most had the least quarrel with them. The commission reported:

A general attack on the entrance examination was leveled by the representatives of the Association of University Teachers . . . who criticized it as responsible for fostering gratuitous competitive pressures, premature specialization, and the narrowing of the curriculum in the schools. But although the representatives of the teachers' associations and those heads of schools who met the Commission were divided among themselves in their opinions about the educational implications of the examination, there was no dissent from the vigorously held view of the schools accustomed to prepare and submit candidates for the examination that it exerted a liberalizing effect on the curriculum and stimulated the teachers and pupils involved.

Nevertheless, the commission thought it would be undesirable for Oxford to continue indefinitely to impose a special entrance exam, but at the same time did not think the present A-Level exams used by most of the universities for entrance purposes were at all adequate for that job. It therefore recommended that Oxford take a leading role in trying to reform the university admissions process throughout Britain and to create a new examination to be run by the universities and used by all alike. That will take some time to do, if it is ever done. Meanwhile, the commission thought the Oxford entrance exam should be reorganized on two levels in order to equalize opportunity between students coming mostly from state schools with the usual two years in the sixth form, and those coming mostly from independent schools with a third year; the former would be allowed to take one part of the exam designed for them and the latter the customary one. If this recommendation is adopted, it will probably mean a change in the Oxford student body, with many more state students in residence representing a kind of home background different from that of the independent-school students who have dominated the student body in the past.

*Fourth:* The commission came out strongly in support of the traditional teaching method of Oxford, the tutorial. "We intend," they said unequivocally, "that reading and writing, rather than listening, should continue to be the salient characteristics of the Oxford system." But the commission was distressed by a certain amount of "overteaching" suggested by the number of tutorials that students were getting. Instead of the pattern of the past, with each student doing one tutorial a week, the commission found the university average to be one and a half. Many students, that is, were doing two a week, which the commission thought would "debase the concept of the tutorial as it has been understood in Oxford." It strongly recommended a return to one a week and it rejected the tendency to increase the number of students attending a tutorial session:

> If in any group one pupil has written an essay and one or two others merely listen and perhaps throw in an occasional opinion, they are not experiencing a tutorial but merely attending a class. For the tutorial means that the undergraduate has to try his hand at creation under correction.

The commission also rejected suggestions that less attention be given to research by Oxford dons, and put no faith in the movements growing elsewhere in British universities and in Europe that research and teaching can be separated:

> The representatives of the colleges, like those of the faculties, were agreed, as can be seen in their oral evidence, that research and teaching were best done by the same people. The teaching in the colleges would not be so good unless those doing it were also engaged in original research. . . . A divorce of teaching from research would be a loss to the nation directly in its effects upon the majority of undergraduates: it would also adversely affect the academic succession in retarding the development of their minority who aim at becoming research workers in their turn.

But because of the emphasis on tutorials at Oxford, the commission found the staff badly overworked with a more unfavorable student-staff ratio than at other universities. It recommended a twenty-percent increase in Oxford's teaching staff.

*Fifth:* Contrary to the hopes of some people outside Oxford, the commission strongly supported the continuance of the system of self-governing colleges, which it wanted developed further and improved. However, it wanted also some basic reforms to restrict the freedom of the colleges and to increase the power of the central university. Among other things, it proposed a major redistribution of wealth among the constituent colleges (some of which are much richer than others), by requiring the colleges to contribute to a financial pool in accordance with their means, the funds then to be redistributed among all up to a certain minimum figure. It also thought that the chief administrator, the vice-chancellor, should have a longer term of office and more power over the colleges. In a series of recommendations about the complex government of Oxford, the commission in effect thought that the time had come when the colleges, although remaining independent in many ways, would have to yield a good many of the powers they have carefully guarded in the past to the central authority of the university.

In brief, then, the Franks Commission's recommendations would make a number of quite fundamental changes in Britain's oldest and most famous university, changes that reflect the same social and educational movements that we have noted throughout this book. But they would leave the general structure of Oxford fairly intact. The commission itself thought: "If our recommendations are followed, we believe that a series of balances will be preserved: that of college freedom and university planning, that between new subjects and the established disciplines, and, for the staff, that between research and teaching." The Franks Report was not as well received as the Robbins Report, though it was launched with a great deal of fanfare ("bombast," as the head of one Oxford college called it). Few commentators gave it a wholehearted endorsement when it appeared, but most found themselves fundamentally in agreement. My own impression is that most of Oxford is ready for change but not necessarily of the sort recommended by Franks. The colleges naturally want to retain their independence, and there are many honest doubts about the workability of the Franks recommendations in regard to admissions, tutorials, and other matters. At this point, it is impossible to know how much of the report will be adopted, but whatever its fate it remains a most thorough and illuminating exploration of that venerable institution.

Cambridge for its part did not respond to the Robbins challenge as speedily as did Oxford, but eventually it too was left with little choice but to indulge in some organized introspection. In April 1966, Cambridge appointed a body similar to the Franks Commission to look particularly at the tangled web of university administration. Although it will not be heard from for some time, it seems safe to predict that it will recommend substantial changes that will improve the external relations of the University but, like Franks, will retain most of the essential Cambridge. Change is, as they say, very much in the university air in Britain and much of it will come to the oldest institutions.

## Admissions, Degrees, and Student Life

The complicated question of who should be admitted to universities is answered in only a few basic ways in Western countries. There is the European way, which, as we have seen, gives more or less automatic admission to anyone in possession of the leaving certificate of the academic secondary school. Although this limits the potential entry to a small minority of the age group, the experience of European countries is that the dropout rate even among this select group is high. The United States, on the other hand, maintains an open-door policy, letting almost anybody have his chance at a higher education, and also has a high dropout rate. Britain selects carefully among students who have passed a certain number of subjects of the leaving exams, and has a low dropout rate. Probably most countries, whatever their admissions policy, find themselves somewhere between the ludicrous dropout rate of French universities, seventy-eight percent, and the English rate of fourteen percent. The British "wastage" actually ranges between a low of about five percent at Oxford to a high of thirty percent in some of the technological universities. Not much study of this wastage has been done, and so one can only guess at what portion of it results from factors other than academic failure. One cannot, therefore, say much about what the rate should be, but in the view of the vice-chancellors of British universities, "wastage rates could not reasonably be expected to be less than 10 per cent. A figure below this would be capable of the interpretation that selectors were playing for safety, which we should regret." [4]

One of the criticisms of the Robbins Report came from people in the universities who felt that the quality of the British degree would inevitably drop as the numbers of candidates went up. The novelist Kingsley Amis led this criticism with the cry "More Means Worse" and brought down an avalanche of countercriticism on himself. The report had devoted a good deal of space to "the so-called pool of ability" and had decided that it was a lot deeper than was implied by admissions standards to British universities; but even then the report was careful to reiterate the claim that its recommended expansion need not mean a lowering of the usual entrance standards. Lord Robbins himself thinks these standards are probably too high: "I personally think it would be a good thing if entrance standards were lowered a bit—two or three A Levels is an excessively high standard—but that would mean even more expansion." There was so much talk after the Robbins Report about the pool of untapped talent that Amis was moved to say at one point that he was not so much worried about that as about the pool of tapped untalent already in the universities. Surveying the situation worldwide for UNESCO not long before Robbins reported, Frank Bowles found admission standards frequently too high. He concluded that

> the selection methods now being used at the time of entrance to higher
> education should be regarded with grave concern. They affect the validity
> of secondary school credentials, constrict the programs of secondary
> education, choose students on the basis of small differences in their per-

formances, reject students who are prepared to do the work of higher education, create examination burdens, and lead to the establishment of special supplementary but undesirable school programs.[5]

Whether or not more will in fact mean worse in British universities, it will certainly mean different. A different sort of student, with a different home background, from what has been usual in British universities is going to appear in force. About the same numbers as before will presumably be coming from the upper and middle ranges of society, but many more from families lower down the scale, from the brick-row houses of the cities and the mock-Tudor bungalows of suburbia. And that will mean in all probability a strong movement toward American-type programs and attitudes, and perhaps even, as the Franks Report suggested, standardized machine-scored tests on the American pattern for admission. It will mean a new emphasis on the practical and the useful, for the new strata of students will have scant interest in the leisurely cultivation of the intellect that has always been found in European universities, though rarely in American. These students are not going to accept required work in philosophy placidly, as people like Sir Richard Livingstone thought should be done,[6] nor are they going to contribute to the survival of subjects like Greek and Latin. Shortly after the Robbins Report, an American classicist wrote this comment to his English colleagues:

> I have little doubt that Robbins or the tendencies and authorities it represents will mean a diminution of classical studies as they are now carried out at Oxford, Cambridge, London, and the older universities generally. In America I believe the classics have been cut away from below, in the schools . . . Greek has almost vanished from the secondary schools, and Latin has vanished from some, while the amount available has been reduced in almost all. The student who wants to be a classicist can still be one, if he goes to the right college, but he will be doing work at eighteen which, forty or fifty years ago, was being done by school children of fourteen. The teachers at the university level have had to streamline their methods as best they can. Britain is still far from such a situation, but it might serve as a warning of possible things to come.[7]

The new emphasis will be on science and technology, which provide "the main hope of our recovery," as one British physicist put it, now that the colonies are gone with their "easy markets and easy supplies."[8] The Robbins Report itself was unabashedly liberal (or "frank" or "realistic," whatever term one chooses) about the fact that first-generation university students would be interested most of all in their careers. Quoting Confucius, who said that "it was not easy to find a man who had studied three years without aiming at pay," the report thought:

> We deceive ourselves if we claim that more than a small fraction of students in institutions of higher education would be where they are if

there were no significance for their future careers in what they hear and read; and it is a mistake to suppose that there is anything discreditable in this.

A greater concern for utility will be felt even at Oxford and Cambridge, particularly if the Franks Commission recommendation about a broader entry from state schools is put into effect. There was a time when the tradition of gentlemanly study dictated that the student shun anything that might be connected with grubbing a living. But even now many undergraduates at Oxford and Cambridge know, as two dons observe in a recent book,

> that, unlike their wealthier, more socially established predecessors, they will not be able to afford such detachment, that compromises will be forced on them. They cannot follow the advice of those dons who tell them to read their Plato and stop worrying about jobs; they feel quite rightly that though the dons may know all about Plato they know very little about how one earns a living.[9]

Until 1966 Oxford and Cambridge, names that, since the two universities are so alike in so many respects, are often contracted to "Oxbridge" (or "Camford," as one don suggested who was unhappy about the contraction), remained outside the Universities Central Council on Admissions— the organization established by the University Grants Committee to bring some order into the chaos of university admissions, which are infinitely less chaotic than our own, and to ensure that all vacancies are filled. Now all undergraduate applicants for admission to all universities must go through this organization, which in turn forwards applications to the institutions named by the applicant. The institutions still control their own admissions, but the machinery has been simplified through UCCA, and the government is in a much better position than formerly to keep abreast of the supply-demand situation.

At Oxbridge ninety percent of the intake still comes through the special examinations that these institutions insist on giving on top of the usual A Levels. Many people, including the Franks Commission, have criticized this practice and have held that it makes a hash of the Robbins recommendation about achieving a national system of higher education and particularly about achieving "parity of esteem" among institutions. One of the recurring themes of the Robbins Report, which I should think would strike many Americans oddly, was the importance of doing away with any hierarchy of institutions and establishing all as equal in the public mind. This leveling of reputation clearly is inconsistent with the Oxbridge scholarship exams, which require a longer preparation than is required by the other universities. In the eyes of some dons these exams also deepen the already serious gulf between the arts and sciences, since they require a high degree of specialization. Moreover, any talk about equality among British universities is nonsense as long as Oxbridge takes in such a lopsided entry in favor of the Public Schools and direct-grant schools. The pattern is changing, but it was still true in 1964 that the Cambridge men's colleges, for example, filled sixty-three percent of their vacancies with students from Public Schools and direct-grant schools, and the remaining thirty-seven percent from state grammar schools, despite the far greater number of students in the state schools.[10] As I mentioned before, the main reason for this seeming injustice is simply that the state schools cannot compete with the others in preparing students for the Oxbridge scholarship exams. An element of social distinction no doubt continues to be present, if in no other way than the fact that middle-class families are more likely than working-class families to provide the desirable environment for Oxbridge preparation; but the principal criterion for entry remains ability, and this certainly means, Robbins notwithstanding, a continuance of a hierarchy among British universities, as exists in many countries, notably the United States.

In all of the dramatic expansion of higher education, few of the old European fears about overproducing intellectuals or highly trained people are in evidence. The Robbins Report based its expansionist position not on statistical projections about the British economy and the probable future demand for manpower, as we are prone to do, but simply on the level of probable demand for higher education. After struggling with the uncertain evidence available about manpower requirements, the report said simply that

> we have not found it practicable to make trustworthy estimates of the aggregate demand for the products of higher education twenty years hence, and our recommendations for the provision of places are based on estimates of potential supply.[11]

Actually, manpower studies did play a large part in the committee's deliberations, but one senses in reading the report that the committee itself was uneasy about them. Even so the report was criticized for not being a little more humble about the reliability of its projections.[12] The chief statisticians of the Robbins Report later commented on the "bluntness of the instruments" at the disposal of people who try to make such predictions.[13] Malthusian fears are still justified in underdeveloped countries like India or developed countries like Italy, but they now seem to be absent from Britain, the United States, and most of Europe. The time is still not in sight in either Britain or Europe when the scope of higher education will be anything like our own or when students will be admitted as freely over as wide a range of ability, but everywhere the pattern of admissions is being widened and liberalized, bringing into the universities large numbers of practical-minded students who are going to have a strong influence on future programs. We may live in an age of the greatest leisure and comfort in the world's history, but the leisurely and detached cultivation of the mind is a vanishing luxury.

## DEPTH AND BREADTH IN BRITISH DEGREES

Following up on the specialized work of the grammar-school sixth forms, the programs of study in English universities in the past have been relatively specialized compared to Europe and extremely specialized compared to our own typical undergraduate program. A great many still are, but again the pattern is changing. At the older universities, most students still "read" a single subject, though the work they do within that limitation is both broad and deep; many also spend a certain amount of time in a second subject that may or may not be taken very seriously. Thus the broad general education of many a university graduate in Britain ended when he passed his O Levels at sixteen, and often earlier. One result of this specialized education, as we noted before, is the early and effective divorce between the world of the arts and the world of science and technology. The same kind of controversy that swirls around sixth-form specialization is now seen in reduced intensity at the university level. Almost all the new universities in Britain have made an effort to move away from the single-subject undergraduate degree. None of them, with the possible exception of Keele University, has adopted anything like the breadth of the American degree, but programs of study that cover a number of related fields are common. The Robbins Report, consistent with its liberal views in general, argued for the creation of broader honors courses in all the universities, being careful at the same time to say that it was not advocating "the creation of soft options." It held out as a basic principle:

> The essential aim of a first degree course should be to teach the student how to think. In so far as he is under such pressure to acquire detailed knowledge that this aim is not fulfilled, so far the course fails of its purpose.

Perhaps so, but the fact is that a good honors degree from a British university has always demanded a great deal of "detailed knowledge" and has clearly been aimed at something more than teaching the student to think. In Scotland, the universities have always required study on a broader front than the English, just as they have required broader preparation for admission. They are probably closer to the American pattern than the universities of any other country in Europe, though they still fall short of the conglomerate collection of courses that make up the American first degree. "General education" as it has developed in American institutions since World War II is not now and probably will not become very common in Britain; but, looking the other way, I would think our colleges might well consider some adaptation of the degree courses in British universities, which would certainly mean a tightening up of undergraduate study.

The most radical departure from tradition, one that does not seem very promising, was undertaken by the first of the new universities, Keele, which opened in 1950. Keele set out to create a self-contained academic community, and is now the only university to house all of its students on the campus. The somewhat isolated effect of its being built in a semirural area in the middle of England's Potteries region near Stoke-on-Trent causes some of its students to call it "Kremlin on the Wall." Keele is well known for its mandatory first year, the Foundation Year, of extremely broad study. It is in fact so broad as to surpass any American institution of my acquaintance. There are no fewer than 230 lectures that make up the first year's work, covering the length and breadth of human knowledge! One's first look at the lecture schedule suggests a gigantic smorgasbord, except that the element of choice is lacking. All the sciences, all the arts, all the offshoots of both are covered in what are necessarily sweeping mass lectures. On the basis of this all-embracing tour of knowledge, students then begin to narrow their study in the second year and narrow it still further in the third and fourth years. Keele was allowed to develop a standard four-year undergraduate program only as an exception, which is one reason it can afford to spend the first year the way it does. The University Grants Committee will not permit such an expensive departure from the usual three-year course in other places, another illustration of the policy-making power that is reposed in the UGC. The students themselves seem to react fairly well to this kind of super-general education, though a survey of student opinion in 1965 found that "There seemed to be a general consciousness of the superficiality of the F.Y. [Foundation Year] course." [14] There is a considerable amount of switching of major subjects on the part of Keele students between the time they arrive from their sixth-form work and the time they have finished the Foundation Year, suggesting that the first year may be responsible or that Keele attracts students who are undecided about their specialization when they come.

Perhaps the most notable, or at least the most noted, experiment among the new universities has been at Sussex, which committed itself from the beginning to the development of an alternative to the single-subject degrees of the older universities. The first thing it did to break down the usual departmentalization of knowledge was to eschew departments and instead to create Schools—a School of Physical Sciences, a School of Education and Social Work, a School of English Studies, a School of European Studies, etc. Then it set about creating courses of study that involved concentrated work in one school but included mandatory work in others. Similarly, the new University of Lancaster has attempted to escape the specialization problem by creating "boards of studies" alongside the usual academic departments and by allowing students to study in at least three fields during the first year before choosing a more specialized course for the last two. Likewise the new universities of East Anglia, of Kent at Canterbury, and of Warwick at Coventry, all present variations on the Keele-Sussex theme of broadening the undergraduate course. However, none of them, again excepting Keele, has created anything as broad and as indiscriminate and with so much choice as the ordinary American undergraduate degree. In one way or another they all accept the twin principles that the first vice-chancellor of Sussex described as the base upon which that university built: "the need for disciplined study in depth; and . . . the need for the major study to be set within the context of related subjects." [15] No university in Britain or Europe would accept the rationale, if there is one, for the American first degree. But of course none of them yet accepts students from such a wide range of ability and background.

The specialization issue is by no means settled in Britain. Many if not most of the faculty members of the older universities still favor the traditional courses. Some of these courses in any case are very like the much-touted programs of the new universities. The University of Manchester, for example, has had a broad degree course in American Studies for a long time. For a very long time Oxford has had its "Greats," involving the study of classical languages, literature, philosophy, and history; it has also had its "Modern Greats" a long time, one of its most popular courses, involving study in philosophy, politics, and economics. Cambridge similarly has had its "Economic Tripos" in sociology, economics, politics, and history. But the distinguishing feature of most honors degrees in the older universities is that they require concentrated study in one subject by carefully selected students, a form of higher education that would still be stoutly defended by these institutions. The vice-principal of one of Oxford's women's colleges, after an extended look at some of our better institutions, returned to Britain reassured about the specialized English degree and felt that we paid a high price for our broad degree:

> Three points of criticism may be levelled at the average [American] liberal arts education. First, too much is attempted in the general course, so that the only way to cover the ground is by handing out pre-packaged information at a desperate rate. . . . Reading rarely goes beyond set pages of textbooks, and discussion, though lively, is limited to what was in the hand-out. Secondly, subject-matter is snipped up into too many little courses, which means, with the operation of the elective principle, that students can jump continually from one subject to another. It is common, for instance, to drop a language after one or two years and move to another. Knowledge is not sufficiently structured for mastery to be obtained anywhere. The third weakness lies in methods of testing. "Objective tests", such as quizzes of the right/wrong or multiple-answer type, are

used at frequent intervals to test mere information. The announcement "Next week there will be a quiz on Dante's *Inferno*" suggests a somewhat ludicrous form of test. At the other end of the scale, fourth-year students write lengthy term-papers, with their books around them forming a strong temptation to incorporate large chunks. What rarely appears, for obvious reasons, is the short essay question which we value so much, both as a method of training and as an unseen examination exercise. . . . The cardinal issue is whether we are going to think of liberal education as "exposure" to a somewhat fortuitous collection of required and elective courses from which it is hoped something will adhere, or as the training of minds through the exploration of fairly wide but adjacent territories. The first leads almost inevitably to the lecture course in the form of a passive aircraft trip in which the pilot only requires one to note the chief landmarks. The second can give a real, though limited, experience of hacking one's way through the jungle on the ground. If we wish to retain something of our original conception of university education, while broadening it to include a wider variety of ability, it is the second conception we must follow.[16]

In Europe the same pressures that are now felt in England against specialization, or rather in favor of more general education, are also evident. Even though the French *Baccalauréat* is broader than the A Level of the GCE, French universities are not happy with the general knowledge of their incoming students. In an attempt to remedy this lack, as well as to reduce the burgeoning numbers of students, the French universities instituted some years ago a tough introductory year, *année propédeutique*, of general education for all students. It has not worked well, however. It has a very high attrition rate, is disliked by both students and staff, and delays specialization for the best students who are ready and anxious to begin their professional work. In Germany the new large university at Bochum, the University of the Ruhr, is attempting an integration of traditionally separate disciplines a little on the Sussex plan. Sweden is moving in the same direction, both in secondary school and the university. In Britain it is still too early for the universities to know how well their modified general education will work or even how the students themselves are going to react to it after the specialized work of the sixth form. But it seems to me very much the wave of the future, for better or for worse.

## STUDENT LIFE IN BRITISH UNIVERSITIES

Along with a few things like the sixth form in the secondary school and the tutorial in the university, the college system as the organizational principle for student life is one of the outstanding contributions of England to education. Again, the college system comes out of Oxford and Cambridge, which between them now have about fifty-five separate, independent colleges ranging in size from under fifty graduate students at Oxford's Nuffield College to over seven hundred undergraduates at Cambridge's Trinity College. Not all Oxbridge students live in colleges, which can hardly accommodate modern enrollments, but university life is still organized around the colleges. Like the tutorial system, which I will discuss presently, the college system is an effective but rather lavish way of going about higher education. It breaks up large institutions into units in which the individual student can feel he has a genuine place of importance. As members of a college with its own traditions, its own individuality, its own tutors living in the college, its own special academic interests, its own quarters, quad, chapel, library, and dining hall—as members of a close-knit community within the larger university—students rarely feel, as so many do at big American universities, that they are faces in the crowd.

But not many of the other British universities have colleges on the Oxbridge model. Among the older ones, Durham and St. Andrews have something like an Oxbridge college system, and several of the new universities, such as York and Kent, are trying to create one. Others have also tried but usually wind up with a pale imitation of Oxbridge, for the college system requires more money than the University Grants Committee is apt to allow for such pleasant but extravagant matters. The college system is at its best when colleges can be grouped physically around a university core and not, as in London, scattered around the city until some of them, such as the London School of Economics, become in effect autonomous institutions. At its best, in Oxford and Cambridge, the college system is a many-splendored and very expensive thing. But the fact remains that outside Oxbridge most British students do not live in colleges. They live in "digs" in the nearby towns or in university dormitories and halls of residence.

Still another unique element of British higher education makes student life very pleasant indeed: a system of local-government grants that guarantees every student who secures admission to either a university or a College of Education a sum of money sufficient to meet all his educational and personal expenses. These grants are subject to a means test and are scaled down as the parents' income goes up, but the means test is not severe and practically all students in British institutions of higher education receive full or partial government grants throughout their course of study. The grants are designed to cover all institutional costs, living expenses, travel to and from home, and even vacation allowances. The system is, I suppose, the most generous in the world, and ensures, among other things, that no person in the United Kingdom needs to forego a higher education because he is poor; he has only to be admitted to an institution to be assured of adequate support. Postgraduate maintenance grants are even more generous. They are higher than for undergraduates and are not subject to a means test. Despite the grotesque complaints of the students themselves, student grants in England, plus the usual medical and other benefits of the Welfare State, make for a kind of student life in the universities that is far more secure and carefree than one finds possibly in any other country of the world. (There is even a system of "Mature State Scholarships" for a limited number of people over twenty-five who missed their academic chances earlier—another unique element of English higher education.)

Academic life, on the other hand, can sometimes be complicated at those institutions that retain the traditional specialized degree, for this system forces on the student an immediate choice of fundamental importance to his future. The "lost" first year is one of the commonest phenomena in higher education in both Europe and Britain, a time when the student makes a basic choice of career and at the same time must adjust to the great difference between the closely supervised life and work of the secondary school and the freedom of the university. American students escape these experiences because of the postponement of final choice until the junior year or so and because the first two years of college are so like the last two years of high school. But a British student going, say, to Cambridge is confronted with a bewildering range of "Triposes" about which he knows little and among which he must choose. He may not get a lot of help from his college or from the university or from the secondary school he left. Many change their course of study as a result of poor decisions, but it lengthens their university career. Of course, in many of the new universities, a firm choice can be postponed until the end of the first year.

Most British students, I believe, do not have to work very hard to gain a reasonable degree, though I obviously will not endear myself to them by saying so. The examination system, especially at Oxbridge and the older universities, allows students extremely long periods in which self-discipline is the main impetus to work; but many students lack self-discipline. And the big examinations themselves are not as demanding as one might suppose except for the top degree classifications. A national survey in 1962 of students' work habits indicated that, according to the students themselves, they worked an average of 36.7 hours a week. The range was from 29.5 to 44.4 hours. The survey also indicated that very little work is done in the long vacation periods given by British universities, despite the state grants theoretically designed to cover such work. Eighty-six percent of the students said they studied less than one hour a day during such periods.[17] I doubt that American students of comparable ability study much harder than British students, but they are busier because of the mandatory class schedule and also because so many of them take part-time jobs. Students anywhere would probably look with horror and unbelief on the kind of work schedule followed by an American,

George Ticknor, when he, like a number of Americans, studied at a German university in the early part of the nineteenth century. The following entry from his diary was recorded recently in a German publication:

> I rise precisely at five, and sit down at once to my Greek; upon which I labor three mornings in the week until half past seven and three days till half past eight. On Mondays, Wednesdays, and Fridays, at the striking of eight o'clock, I am at Professor Benecke's for my lesson in German. . . . At nine, every day, I go to Professor Eichhorn's lectures on the first Three Evangelists. . . . At ten this lecture breaks up, and I catch a walk of 15 minutes as I come home; and from that time until dinner at twelve I go on with my Greek. After dinner I take a nap of half an hour, which refreshes me very much, and then half a cup of coffee, which wakes me up and gives me spirit for the afternoon. At half past one I read passages in Blumenback's Manual which he will expound in his lecture and at three I go to his lecture on natural history which would be amusement enough for me, if I had no other the whole day. After this I take a walk, and at five go to Dr. Schultze's, a young man, but at least to me an extraordinary Greek scholar, held to be decidedly the best Greek instructor in Gottingen, and recite to him in Greek.[18]

Such a regimen would not commend itself to many students anywhere, for it demands a devotion to learning for its own sake that is out of fashion even in Oxbridge and Europe.

As for the extracurricular activities in sex, drugs, and politics that are so much discussed in the United States, British students seem to me even freer, if that is the appropriate word. One's judgment is necessarily impressionistic, so to speak, but I would say that drug taking among students is fully as great a problem in Britain (though not in Europe) as in the United States, and that sexual experience is practically universal. Nobody has any very clear ideas about how the social ethos of university students is created, but it does not seem to have much to do with institutional organization in either Britain or the United States or with the relations between staff and students or with the quality of instruction. Political and general protest activity is also increasing among students in both countries, with the left wing naturally predominant. Britain's National Union of Students had a strong Communist element for some years, but repudiated it at its annual conference in 1966. Student politics nevertheless remain further left in Britain than in the United States, as is British political life nationally.

## CLASSIFIED DEGREES

The overwhelming majority of British students take a three-year course ending in an extended comprehensive examination that is of the greatest importance for the kind of degree they are awarded. The classified degree is still another distinguishing element of British university education. Some variation in degree classes is found among the universities, but most award their undergraduate degrees in five categories: First Class Honors, Upper Second, Lower Second, Third Class (Oxford adds a Fourth Class), and Pass or Ordinary. The final comprehensive exam is the principal criterion for establishing the class of degree. At Oxford it is the sole criterion: The undergraduate at the end of his three years undergoes during a period of perhaps ten days a series of exams over the entire range of his subject; it is the culmination of his university career and his opportunity to demonstrate his mastery of the subject, or the lack of it. In most institutions, First Class Honors go to perhaps five percent of the candidates and are therefore of considerable prestige, not to mention professional value. They are the standard qualification for university teaching. Top Seconds are not far below but go to a wider percentage of candidates; they sometimes qualify their holders for postgraduate study and university teaching as well. Lower Seconds, Thirds, and other awards are distributed in a variety of patterns among the universities, so that it is not easy to know if standards are comparable from one institution to another. The Pass degree is a kind of safety net into which in the old days many a gentleman scholar was tossed and into which today go students who for whatever reason are barred from taking an honors degree. The Pass-degree standard can be very low indeed at British universities, including Oxbridge, where it could conceivably have something to do with the low dropout rate.

The idea of classifying degrees works best, I suppose, in a country with a relatively small number of universities and a highly selected student body. These conditions permit something like a publicly known standard to be established, so that the distinctions made in degree classes mean something. External moderation in British universities also helps to achieve some comparability of standard. But I would guess that the classified degree in Britain, at least those classes below First, will mean less as the numbers of institutions and students and degree subjects increase. However, Britain will never have the problem we have in our colleges and universities of not knowing what standard is represented by the degrees of many of our institutions. Our problem might be alleviated by a classified-degree system, but not a great deal unless steps were taken at the same time to define in some public way the standard represented by the classes; and this would probably be impossible in view of the variety of our institutions and methods of control. We, I fear, will have to continue to live with the fact that both the undergraduate and graduate degrees from a great many of our institutions of higher education do not in themselves say very much since they are not related to any generally recognized standard of excellence.

At the same time I would record my belief that graduate study in our best institutions is apt to be better than in England. Partly this is due to the fact that we have had to develop graduate study more fully in order to give professional work that is given in British undergraduate study; but it is also partly due to the fact that graduate study can be pretty loose and unorganized in Britain, where until recently it has not been stressed and is still not regarded as a requirement for university teaching. The British graduate degree may require no course of lectures or seminars whatever, but merely the preparation of a thesis. (Of course the Oxford and Cambridge M.A. requires only the ability to pay a fee of five pounds, which most Oxbridge graduates can manage, and the ability to survive for twenty-one terms, or about five years, after one's original matriculation—like the Scottish M.A., it is considered a first degree for which the B.A. is a sort of probation.) Not that our graduate work is what it should be. I have great sympathy, for example, with the reforms that are suggested from time to time for the American Ph.D. degree, and I am certain that the multitude of subjects in which the master's degree is earned is badly in need of an overhaul. Also, I am pretty certain that the standards for either degree can be very low in some subjects in most institutions and most subjects in some institutions. But the mandatory course work, particularly in the sciences, and the supervision of dissertation that usually prevail for doctoral study in our best institutions produce a better-trained professional than is often produced through the leisurely, relatively unsupervised and undemanding doctoral work of British universities. I am talking about the general pattern, not about the really outstanding individuals who would probably emerge from any system. I think the following comment from an academic who knows both American and British graduate work a just one in advocating more and better graduate research in England but in saying that Britons

know all about the quality of many American first degrees—and higher degrees too for that matter. Do we really want to parallel that vast sea of mediocrity that is American post-graduate work? Can we afford it? . . . To say that much of American post-graduate work is mediocre—which is true—is to neglect two vital points. First, the best American work is superb—and rests, pyramid-like on a mass of research no better than competent. Second, those participating even in work of mediocre quality *are better for it.* The discipline, the constant exposure to the hard pressure of facts are provided by no undergraduate course. Are we so sure of the quality of our bachelors that we can say, disdainfully, in Britain that they do not *need* to find this discipline in post-graduate work? [19]

## Faculty Members and Teaching Methods

American influence is also at work in the conditions under which the staff of English universities work. First there is the "brain drain" that brings many of the faculty members of British universities to work in the United States; now there is a noticeable drain the other way, with an increasing number of American faculty members going to British universities, particularly the new ones. Then there is the American publish-or-perish virus that is rapidly infecting the British universities; some observers even think they found it in the Franks Report on Oxford staff. There is also the growing habit of outside consulting, the effects of which can be considerable on the instructional program. And there is even a small movement toward giving university teachers some training in pedagogy.

Professors are far fewer in English and European universities than American. The typical department in a British institution will have but one professor, the head of the department, who is almost a law unto himself. Below him in descending order are "Readers," "Senior Lecturers," "Lecturers," and a few other subaltern ranks. Their teaching "load" is difficult to compute, since university study is organized in a quite different fashion from the American credit system. What studies have been done indicate that the average university teacher may spend about thirty percent of his time in teaching and another thirty percent in his own research. The range is wide and varies by rank and institution, but in almost all cases I would judge that the Briton does a good deal less teaching than his American counterpart (except at Oxbridge, where he does more). What he does do may be mostly in mass lectures, characteristic of European institutions. The student-staff ratio of English universities is one of the most generous in the world, seven or eight students to one teaching member if the new universities are taken into account. But I very much doubt that this provision can be maintained throughout the kind of expansion that Robbins has recommended. The Robbins Committee thought that the expansion could be made "to feed itself" in staff but they based their calculations on some singularly tenuous reasoning in which the assumptions were, as one scientist later commented, "naive" and the mathematics "trivial." [20] But at the moment the lavish ratio of staff to students in British universities is a distinguishing feature.

It is said that the chief reason for the brain drain is salary. The University Grants Committee establishes the percentage of faculty ranks that can prevail in the universities; hence less than a quarter of the total staff below professorships can be in the top grades of Reader or Senior Lecturer, which means that most faculty members are in the lower ranks and pay scales. Typically a man of forty will be in one of the two top grades and be paid perhaps $11,000 a year, calculating his base pay in American purchasing power. In the sciences it will be a little more, and in medicine still more. The upper ranks are below American salary standards, but not far below when one considers Welfare State benefits and other matters; but the lower ranks compare less well with American institutions. At least as important as salary, I believe, in the drain is the diversity of opportunity in the United States, the generous provision for equipment in the sciences, and the higher status of technological and engineering work. Consider, for example, this embittered comment from a Reader in Physics at one of the University of London's colleges:

> When I leave this country it will be because (a) I have not had a rise for three years and my car is getting old—say what you like prestige and comfort depend on salary even in a university; (b) promotion is slow, senior posts too few and the universities run on a mixture of medieval democracy and high-handed inefficiency—when I was applying for jobs one university took seven months to decide I was second best and another took six months to decide not to make any appointment; (c) in the United States one's work is appreciated or at least evaluated—here you have to get a Nobel Prize before anyone notices you have been living in a shed in the Cavendish yard; (d) finally, we are continually told that the best of our scientists go to and stay in America—which is rather depressing for the ones who are still here.
>
> Well, why don't I go? Because I am too lazy to change countries at my time of life and it is rather cozy in England. I shall sleep on it for another year; no one will notice.[21]

But things are rapidly improving and the brain drain is not as serious a problem as it was a few years ago. Britain in her turn gets a good many university staff from Commonwealth countries, and, as I say, a number of Britons are returning from the United States as well as an increasing number of Americans going to Britain. The staffing of Oxbridge colleges is a particularly inbred affair, much more so than the American Ivy League, though the Franks Report did not regard inbreeding as a problem at Oxford. Appointments at Oxbridge pay more than other universities and are a lot more sought after. They say that the politics of Oxbridge in appointments and other matters are still admirably summed up in the classic little satire of F. M. Cornford, *Microcosmographia Academica,* published originally in 1908. Cornford divided Oxbridge dons into five categories: Conservative Liberals, Liberal Conservatives, Non-placets, Adullamites, and Young Men in a Hurry. The first three were obstructionists, the last two revolutionists. Whether it still applies or not, the whole machinery for the running of the two ancient universities is extremely democratic but is also built for inbreeding and maintaining *in statu quo* the undeniably attractive life of the colleges. The Oxford and Cambridge self-studies will probably change the rules.

As to the pedagogical training of university teachers, at least three institutions have experimented with some sort of organized program. Leeds University has operated such a program through its Institute and Department of Education for some years, though with what success is not clear; the University of Sheffield has recently tried organizing panels of senior faculty members to whom young lecturers could repair for advice; and the University of Leicester has experimented in similar fashion. Such training was somewhat warily supported in the 1964 report of a national Committee on University Teaching Methods, which following up on data from the Robbins Report, said that a majority of university teachers surveyed were

> in favor of the view that "newly-appointed university teachers should receive some form of organized instruction or guidance on how to teach." Overall, 58 per cent of respondents took this view. Among university groups it was least current at Oxford and Cambridge (48 per cent) and most in Scotland (65 per cent). . . . We discussed with most of the university delegations who came to see us the question what training a university teacher should receive. We are clear that any proposal to make a full-time course of training lasting for, say, a year a necessary qualification for a university appointment would receive no support at all. Any arrangements which were obligatory, and which occupied much of the time of prospective or newly-appointed university teachers, might act as a serious deterrent to the recruitment by the universities of men and women whose primary interest was in scholarship and research. On the other hand, the present arrangements, if such they can be called, seem to us to be more haphazard than is desirable, and result in much university teaching being less effective than it should be.[22]

I am reminded of a study of graduate schools in the United States some years ago in which the investigator found many graduate-school administrators in favor of some sort of pedagogical training for new staff members, but were all agreed that it would not be given by the Department of Education. A number of experiments by our colleges and universities have been tried in the past, but without much success. I doubt that the English will have any more luck.

TEACHING METHODS IN BRITISH UNIVERSITIES

The standard American teaching method in higher education, the lecture-discussion method with groups of twenty or twenty-five students, if it is a method, is not found very much in the older British universities and even less on the Continent. It is found in the newer universities in Britain and has always been used in the Colleges of Education. In Europe, the usual practice is mass lectures without tutorials or discussions or much of anything else. Before World War II and the rapid expansion of higher education, a tutorial in a British university was a weekly person-to-person meeting between a student and his principal teacher or advisor, his tutor. With the increase in student numbers, the one-to-one tutorial is decreasing; one-to-two and one-to-three or more is now becoming common, especially at less than affluent universities than Oxbridge. According to a recent national study, eighty-six percent of the tutorials at Oxford are still given to one or two students and fifty-nine percent of those at Cambridge (where they are called "supervisions"). This study strongly endorsed the tutorial method and favored the one-to-one type: "The case for the one-to-one tutorial rests on the hypothesis that each student differs from his fellows to an extent which requires individual treatment in some of the teaching he receives if his powers are to be developed to the full extent of which he is capable." [23] The Franks Commission, as we saw earlier, took the same position.

To an American student from one of our typical academic factories, a tutorial would be a strange experience. He would prepare an essay for it that might take twenty or thirty minutes for him to read to his tutor, giving it the stress and intonation to carry his meaning, and then, depending on the tutor, be subjected to a kindly or merciless grilling to defend his argument, or perhaps listen to an extension of it by the tutor into new areas. It is the classic method of Mark Hopkins on one end of the log and the student on the other; it is a restricted Socratic dialogue. For a student to write a defensible essay every week for three academic years and have each discussed and challenged in a private session with his tutor can be a rare intellectual discipline and a rare privilege indeed anywhere in the world of higher education. "What are tutorials like?" ask two Oxbridge dons in a recent book, and answer their question this way:

> It is almost impossible to say. They are as different as each don, each undergraduate who goes to make them. Some last for several hours, conversation coming in odd bursts while the don dresses, fries an omelette, sings snatches of Italian opera, dusts the knick-knacks on the mantelpiece. Some start and stop dead upon the hour and are marmoreally silent bequests of the mind. Some take place in panelled, gilded chambers where one sits on antique chairs sipping sherry and eyeing priceless works of art. Some take place in sparsely furnished offices with metal filing cabinets standing shivering in the corners. Some take place far out along the road to Banbury or Cherry Hinton in untidy sitting rooms with the shouts of children and the smells of cooking coming through the kitchen. The don may be a grisled senior, a Reader or a Lecturer, though never a Professor, or he may be a young man, a junior Fellow of his college, without a university appointment, or a research student, scarcely older than his pupil. [24]

If a student has the same tutor throughout his university career, as is often the case, it means a prolonged association not only intellectually but personally. Tutors get to know their students' private lives in great detail and can often afford the student a kind of guidance impossible in most institutions of higher education. Of this often overlooked aspect of the tutorial system, one Oxford don writes:

. . . the main outward stress of the modern tutorial system at Oxford thus falls on the educational side: it is recognized that the primary function of the tutor is to instruct. But it must not be supposed that the other side, which played so large a part in the relations of tutor and pupil in earlier days, has been lost sight of in modern Oxford. In some colleges an undergraduate is assigned for all his time to a "moral tutor," who is often not the tutor to whom he is going for his reading, but one who undertakes to keep in touch with him generally in his life. In most colleges the two functions are combined: the educational tutor is also a moral tutor, and, though this may mean that a man may often pass from one tutor to another during his years of residence, it has the advantage that the relation is less artificial and springs naturally out of the intimacy over work.[25]

Although the tutorial system is widely praised in the new as well as the old universities, some experienced people like to point out that it can be a resounding failure with some students and some tutors. If either the student or tutor is an intellectual bore, the tutorial process is a failure. Also there are naturally personality clashes on occasion. And there are nowadays a great many young and inexperienced tutors. But the tradition of undergraduate teaching by the tutorial method is rightly regarded as one of the most valuable contributions of Oxford and Cambridge to educational practice. When the *Spectator* ventured to suggest a few years ago that "Of the many things peculiar to Oxford and Cambridge, the tradition of undergraduate teaching is hardly the first that comes to mind," it got a number of hot replies, of which the following was typical:

. . . you, sir, must be perfectly well aware that students at Oxford and Cambridge receive far closer and more comprehensive personal tuition [i.e., tutoring] than their counterparts elsewhere, that Oxford and Cambridge dons spend most of their teaching time (at least twelve, and sometimes twenty, hours a week in this University), giving individual tutorials, and that nearly all of them regard teaching as their most important work, and as the principal function of universities. You ought to know that this tradition is admired universally, and that it is beginning to be followed not only in this country but in the United States . . .[26]

Nor is the tutorial necessarily best done with the kind of student one expects to find in the Oxbridge colleges. David Daiches, an experienced professor in both British and American institutions, now of the University of Sussex, pointed out in 1963 the relevance of the tutorial method to the more job-minded students now coming into the universities:

If . . . the Government responds to Robbins with a crash program of utility higher education, it is important that the voices of those who really know about teaching the young in universities should be heard and listened to. The more our universities attract first-generation students (and they are bound to do so in increasing numbers); the more we discover, as we shall, that whole classes of youngsters who previously never thought of the university can in fact profit by a university education; the more necessary is intensive individual tutorial teaching. Oxbridge, the home of the tutorial system, in a sense needs it least. It is the student from the "culturally impoverished" home, who has not absorbed from his background any notion of reading or studying on his own, who needs tutorial teaching and who will be educationally destroyed if subjected only to the large lecture course.[27]

I doubt that the tutorial system could be adopted very widely in American institutions as they are presently organized even if the will to do so existed. The student-staff ratio of many of our institutions is at least twice that of Britain. Also, the lack of specialization on the part of American students, as remarked by the president of the University of Minnesota after a visit to Cambridge a few years ago, would suggest that tutoring should wait until the student at least begins serious work on his major.[28] Even then, he might be behind the British student in specialized knowledge and might require a different kind of tutorial. But the advantages of this method are so clear that it might well be considered seriously by our wealthier institutions (some of which indeed already have modified tutorial arrangements), and might even be adaptable to some of those less wealthy. It is hard to see how it could mean much or be economically defensible as long as the undergraduate is in the elementary stages of his subject, but it could be invaluable later on.

The lecture system is not, I am afraid, in particularly good repute in British or European universities, although it is the primary system. Even in England, it is now a minority of students who get any significant amount of tutorial work; most students get most of their education by lecture. Pressures from students are being felt everywhere, including the United States, for fewer lectures, more seminars, and more personal contact with teachers, though the typical university student in Europe is far worse off in this regard than the American. The lecture is in poor repute everywhere for the same reason, for being dull, sometimes inaudible, for failing to do what a lecture should: bring together the fruit of years of study and research, range over reading the student could not hope to do, bring mature judgment to bear on the subject; in short, do for the student what he could not possibly do for himself in the library. When a lecturer does this, students do not complain. "No discipline is ever requisite," as Adam Smith pointed out in 1776 in *Wealth of Nations*, "to force attendance upon lectures which are really worth the attending, as is well known whenever any such lectures are given. . . ." But such lectures are apparently as infrequent in Britain as in the United States. Every survey of any size of student opinion that I have seen in either country criticizes the lecture, or at least fails to give it any positive vote of confidence. A roundup of student opinion in Britain in 1961 found repeated criticism of teaching methods. There is a general condemnation of lectures, and some [student] unions support the idea of having printed lecture notes—perhaps the most pointed comment they can make on some of the lectures which students have to sit through.[29]

A larger survey done the next year brought in the same finding:

> The general tenor of the student memoranda is very similar. It is highly critical of the lecture. The principal desiderata are fewer and better lectures, closer staff-student relations, and more teaching by tutorial and seminar. There are two strands in the criticism of the lecture. The first is that too much emphasis is placed on lectures as a method of teaching; the second is that the quality of some lectures is lower than it should be.[30]

The survey of Keele University students to which I referred earlier found that, of the students responding, thirty-nine rated the lectures of the Foundation Year "Very Good," eighty-one rated them "Moderate," and seventeen "Poor." [31] Not a bad showing as student opinion usually goes. Oxbridge does not escape by any means. Oxford students for years have consistently and noisily criticized a great many lectures and lecturers, and have reinforced the point by avoiding them, and at Cambridge a survey of undergraduates in 1964 concluded:

> Many found the lecturers uninteresting. Scientists went to them because they comprised the essential syllabus. Arts students tended to go to very few (three or four a week) and only to those which they found stimulating. Those reading law usually went to ten a week. One undergraduate found all English lectures uniformly uninspired and stopped going to them after the first fortnight. . . . All thought that lectures could be made much more interesting and useful if they were given only by those who enjoyed and excelled in lecturing. . . . Some lecturers should be relieved of the burden of giving courses, for their own sake and for their students' benefit.[32]

What relevance does all this have for American problems? At a minimum it might be a small reassurance to those students and academics who incline to think that lecturing is better somewhere else. The plain fact is that few people anywhere have the ability to lecture well, though when the lecture is well done I am sure that it is superior to our system. In most of our institutions, we have adopted a kind of compromise between the mass lecture of Europe and the tutorial of Oxbridge, the lecture-discussion method with groups of students; this method is successful, in my opinion, only in the hands of an outstanding teacher—and we need to face the fact that most members of college faculties are not outstanding teachers. Too many of our undergraduates spend too much time in rambling and incoherent discussions that pass for classes. They are probably better off there than in a French lecture amphitheater if the lecturer is poor but not if he is good. What one always comes back to in this matter as a goal to be worked toward is something approaching a tutorial system, even with tutors of only moderate ability, in combination with large, voluntary lectures limited to the best faculty members available.

As in so many other areas of British education that we have examined, we now find university education moving rapidly toward a number of American practices at the same time that we might well consider the advantages of British practices. Some of the distinguishing elements of British universities are expensive enough to make higher education in that country about the most costly in the world at a time when the English economy is weak; and these elements would make our own system infinitely more expensive if we were to adopt them. But others, such as the specialized three-year degree for certain able students, the modified and broadened degree programs of the new universities, the comprehensive examinations at the end upon which much depends, perhaps classified degrees among some of our institutions, perhaps tutorials among some that can pay the bill, are all matters to which our colleges and universities could give attention as they continue to expand and the distance between students and staff continues to grow.

## CHAPTER VII

# Some Final Thoughts on English and American Education

THE READER will be glad to learn that I do not propose to devote this brief chapter to recapitulation or to summarizing the main points of the book. I think the main points of the book are made well enough in the appropriate places in the foregoing chapters. Here I would like only to record a few final thoughts comparing British and American education. Some readers by this time may have concluded that these systems are so unlike that fruitful comparisons cannot really be made. This was the feeling of Sir Geoffrey Crowther at the end of his committee's three years' work on upper-secondary schooling in England, when he told an American audience:

> For the past three years, I have been engaged, with my colleagues of the Central Advisory Council on Education in England, in a comprehensive study of the English educational system. I had some of my own education in the United States, and I have been a frequent visitor to America ever since. This double experience has bred in me a growing sense of astonishment that two countries which share the same language, so many of the same cultural traditions and ways of life, whose political, religious, and social aspirations are so largely identical, should have educational systems so utterly different as to provide almost no basis for a comparison between them.[1]

But he went on to make a number of useful comparisons, as I hope this book has also done. Still, his basic point was well taken. British education is much more easily compared with European systems, with which it has a greater affinity. As we have seen so often in this book, the split system of schools and teacher training that prevails in England and Europe has ramifications throughout these systems of education and makes comparisons with the unified American system extremely complex.

Thus there are no simple answers to simple questions like: "Is English education better than American?" It is better in some ways, worse in others, and incapable of comparison in still others. Having said that, I hope it will not seem contradictory if I add that general questions can legitimately be formulated and answered about how these two systems compare in quality. We might ask, for instance: "Does British education serve that country better than the American system serves ours in relation to investment?" The answer is "Yes." Or we might ask: "Are the English as a nation better educated than the Americans?" The answer is "No." If we ask: "Is British education as good as its reputation in the United States?" the answer is "No." If we ask: "Is American education as bad as its reputation among British schools?" the answer is again "No." If someone were to ask me: "Is British education as good as you thought it was before going to England?" I would answer, "In parts, yes, but mostly no." If someone were to ask me: "How does American education seem to you after looking at it for a couple of years through English and European glasses?" I would answer, "Better in most ways, worse in a few."

But the effect of an extended exposure to other educational systems is to sensitize oneself to the danger of sweeping comparative statements that do not really compare anything, like this one in 1966 from the Superintendent of Schools of St. Paul: "American schools are doing the most outstanding job of educating its youth that has ever been done by the schools of any nation in recorded history." [2] This sort of absurd braggadocio, which is still common enough among our educational administrators, is simply meaningless until one makes clear what it is that American schools are being compared to. Or consider such an unthinking idealization of American schools as the following, from the hand of a leading British propagandist for the comprehensive school:

> The large American high school is no longer primarily a part of the local community, but a self-sufficient community on its own. The staff are fully absorbed in their important, ever-changing, and always demanding work. Not only are there departments staffed by specialists for all the normal subjects; there is also a guidance department run by qualified psychologists whose job it is to assess the personality and ability of each pupil and to help him to choose both the right path through school, with its multitude of options, and the right career on leaving school. . . . The great educational debate in North America . . . is about the grouping of children *within* the common school. At present there is little more than the occasional attempt to put the clever children in one class or stream, the average in a second, the slow in a third, and so on. . . . Within a broad curriculum, there is room for much individual choice. Rapid progress in a favorite subject can take a pupil into a class one or two grades higher for that subject, while he pursues others at a more normal pace. . . . [America] believes that the great contributions to human life have come from indi-

viduals who were allowed or were determined to assert their unique view-point, often flatly against the weight of orthodox opinion. Copernicus, Martin Luther, Charles Darwin, and beyond them Jesus of Nazareth—theirs is the spirit that inspires the thought and works of America's educators, from Dewey to Conant.[3]

Not even the American Association of School Administrators would suppose that such an uninformed assessment, sans any mention of standards or achievement, of the American school has any resemblance to reality.

But more important in my view than general questions about whether one system is better or worse than the other are questions about whether we seem to be doing as well with our resources as other advanced nations are doing with theirs. If we ask, for example—and we should: "Is American education better than British or European in relation to the amount of time and money spent?" the answer, I am afraid, is "No." Looking at what Britain and the United States get for their respective investments in education, we Americans have no reason whatever for satisfaction. I wish people like the Superintendent of Schools of St. Paul would temper their happy chauvinism with some consideration of comparative educational "output." If they did they might make fewer grandiose claims for their own schools and might even find themselves asking why American education is not a great deal better than it is. As I mentioned in Chapter I, Britain and the United States now spend roughly the same portion of their gross national product on education, but this means that we spend nearly twice as much money per student as do the English. Industrial productivity, that is, in Britain is only about half that of the United States per head of population, and the gross national product is only about half that of the United States per capita. A lot of complicated historical, geographic, and economic reasons account for the difference, but the result is that we spend a great deal more money on every child in school than do the English, or for that matter the French or Germans or Swedes or Swiss.

Of course, we cannot say that because we spend twice as much money as the English we should get twice as good an educational system, since the difference in costs and standards of living cannot be ignored. But even so, it seems pretty clear ~~to me~~ that there is an imbalance between what we get for our investment and what England and Europe get for theirs, and the imbalance is not in _the_ ~~our~~ favor. ~~Our~~ professional educators have been telling us for as long as I can remember that to get better education we have to spend more money, lots more. They have never left the nation in any doubt about the proportional relationship between educational investment and educational quality. If they are right, if it is true that more money should produce better education, then it seems to me we compare badly with other nations. Britain gives every child ten years of education, which in classroom time would come to about eleven American years, and gives at least a quarter of its young people twelve and many thirteen years of education, which in classroom time would come to thirteen or fourteen American years. She does this for just about half the money we invest to give seventy percent of our children as much as twelve American years of schooling. I wonder how our educational achievement would compare to the British if they spent twice as much money on their schools as they now do or if our respective investments were truly equivalent. It is not a simple comparison, but even a rough estimate of what we and other nations get in education in relation to investment cannot be reassuring for us. This is why I am puzzled at the comfortable conclusions our educational researchers reach, who should know better if anyone does, when they discover that American children manage more or less to hold their own with English and European children on American standardized tests. Surely the obvious question is why American children do not do a great deal better. If educational quality follows educational investment, American children should presumably leave the children of every other nation in the world well behind in achievement. That they do not is a fact that needs attention.

### THREE LESSONS WORTH REPEATING

Still more important perhaps for most of us than the comparative efficiency of American and foreign schools is simply the question of what we can learn from the educational practices of other nations. Since we have talked a lot about this in the foregoing chapters, I would like here to reiterate only three points about English education that we might seriously consider adapting to our own system.

The first point concerns educational evaluation. We should take no pride in the fact that we remain the only advanced nation of the world that has no means of regularly determining the achievement of its educational system. We are the only one that lacks a school-leaving exam related to some kind of publicly known educational standard. Many of our educational administrators recoil even at the idea of a one-time national assessment, apparently feeling that we ought simply to float along indefinitely on a sea of doubt and confusion about just what the measureable results are of the massive American investment of time, money, and people in education. I do not know whether an examination system like the GCE is feasible or desirable in the United States, but I am certain that the half century of experience that Britain has had with large-scale, essay-type public examinations is something we should look at very carefully. The time has come for us to give serious attention to creating some means of measuring educational results.

In the absence of such means, what evidence we do have about results leaves the question of the quality of schools in considerable doubt. Imperfect as any attempt to pin down the performance of our schools must be, we are surely given pause when we remember that our own armed services, applying what in all conscience are undemanding standards, must regularly reject at least a quarter of their potential recruits as functional illiterates, most of whom have had at least eight years of public schooling and twenty percent of whom are high-school graduates. Nor does one easily forget the results of educational polls, with all of their attendant uncertainties, such as the one conducted some years ago by Gallup on a nation-wide sample of high-school and college graduates, the findings of which were both ludicrous and unsettling in the depth of ignorance revealed. Or consider the more concentrated experiment devised a few years ago by a visiting British educator: he prepared, in consultation with American teachers, a General Knowledge test in Science and Mathematics, English, and Social Studies, to be given eighth-and ninth-grade pupils in a sample of Michigan schools. He reported the main facts, charitably, as follows:

> Results were received from twenty-three groups in seventeen schools, the schools being chosen on a random basis, except that they included both large and small school systems, and both urban and rural, scattered throughout the State. . . . While the test was intended for Eighth and Ninth Grades, some schools returned samples from Tenth, Eleventh and even Twelfth Grades. The age range was thus considerable, the median being around 14 years.
>
> Results showed an average mark varying from school to school of from 15.6 to 40.3%. Individual marks ranged from 0 to 69%. Little significant differences in attainment were detected between grades. . . . No question lacked some right answers, and few questions were unattempted; answers showed, in general, *some* acquaintance with the subject matter; the level at which the test was pitched appeared, on the whole, reasonably correct. On the other hand, full and accurate answers were extremely rare; the great majority were imprecise, loosely or wrongly worded, and presented in a slovenly way. Standards of handwriting, spelling and ability to frame a simple sentence were in general considerably lower than those of the average English school child of 8 or 9 years—and this applied no less to children of 17 who attempted the test than it did to children of 13. . . .
>
> It would be easy, and unfair, to attach overmuch importance to the results of a single general knowledge test, set to a limited age-range, and set without warning to children unused to tests of this kind. Nevertheless, the results appear to offer certain points, and to suggest certain general conclusions which contemporary American educators cannot afford to ignore. First, the results were remarkably consistent, and consistently low; no school achieved an average of 50%, and the differential range between school and school was within 25%. Secondly, there was nothing in the test with which any class was *wholly* unfamiliar; the general level of potential attainment estimated for this age was evidently approximately correct. . . .

The standard of English, whether in knowledge or power of expression or the elementary skills of handwriting and spelling, must give cause for concern. . . .

Finally, the results revealed in the section of the test devoted to Social Studies show an alarming unawareness, on the part of normally intelligent 13–16-year-olds, of their own country's history and geography, and of the fundamental ideas for which America stands in the world. . . . I am quite sure, from all that I have seen, that there is nothing wrong with either the abilities or the attitudes of American children generally; all that is wrong is a failure, very often, on the part of educators, to bring out the potential that is there. I cannot forbear quoting the message from one child, which would be inconceivable for an English child to write to a visiting teacher, but which epitomizes all the candor and vigor that is so good in American youth; it ran, "Mr. Wales, have a blast!" [4]

Or more recently and much more authoritatively, we have had "Project Talent," a massive study of certain aspects of American schools. The first major report out of this project was published in 1964. It was admirably summarized and interpreted by George Weber in a lead article in the *Bulletin* of the Council for Basic Education; and because this volume bears directly on the question of national assessment, I think the article worth reprinting here in its entirety:

For those who wonder why reform in education is still necessary let them consider some of the startling information contained in *The American High-School Student,* the latest and most important report issued by Project Talent. (This tome of 736 pages, roughly the size and shape of a large-city telephone directory, is available from the Project Talent Office, School of Education, University of Pittsburgh, Pittsburgh, Pa. 15213, $8.50.) The prospector in its pages will find the going rough, but patient searching will reveal nuggets of information about the typical high school student that will show why the reform of American education is unfinished business.

Project Talent is a massive series of studies done by the University of Pittsburgh for the U. S. Office of Education and some other government agencies, with an expenditure of more than $2,500,000 of Federal funds. In the spring of 1960 a two-day battery of tests and questionnaires was given to a stratified, random sample of 440,000 students in 1,353 different public and private high schools throughout the nation. The number represented five per cent of the total number of students in grades 9–12. The undertaking was the largest and the most representative testing of high school students ever done. The students took tests on their knowledge, aptitudes and abilities. They also filled out questionnaires on their interests, activities and backgrounds. Finally, they wrote two paragraphs, one on "My views about an ideal occupation," and one on "What high school means to me."

In *The American High-School Student*, item-by-item responses are shown for the 394 questions covering interests, activities and backgrounds. Some of these questions—such as the ones on family income, the value of the family house, the year model of the family car, and the club activities of father and mother—may seem to some people an invasion of privacy. Other questions seem trivial. But the report contains the answers to all 394. You can learn that girls don't like hard manual labor and that 93 per cent of the senior boys expect to have children. You can learn the number of dates per week the seniors said they had (median for boys was 1.3; for girls, 1.8), and the number of rooms in their homes (median was 7.7).

More significantly, the number of semesters taken in various fields was reported by the seniors. *Forty-eight per cent of the boys and forty-one per cent of the girls took no foreign language at all in high school.* These are the percentages of boys and girls who took *two semesters or less* of the fields shown while they were in high school:

|                   | B    | G    |
|-------------------|------|------|
| Science           | 58%  | 77%  |
| Foreign languages | 87%  | 83%  |
| Social studies    | 44%  | 43%  |
| Mathematics       | 50%  | 73%  |

Turning to the tests that measured knowledge and abilities, unfortunately the item-by-item responses are not shown. Detailed scores—with means, percentiles, standard deviations, and correlations—are listed for tests whose exact nature is not given. Some samples are cited, however. In English, 56 per cent of the twelfth-graders saw nothing wrong with "neither of them are"; 15 per cent went along with "couldn't hardly"; 26 per cent said "like he should"; 17 per cent saw no need to capitalize "British"; and 36 per cent wanted to stick an apostrophe somewhere in the possessive "its."

At first glance, spelling looks much better; we are told that the average senior could spell 93 per cent of the test words, which were a representative sample of the 5,000 words used most frequently in published materials. But then we find that almost all of these words are very easy, such as *corn, five, pages, rain, sang,* and *tea,* all of which were spelled correctly by all seniors. On the other hand, over half of the twelfth-graders could not correctly spell *breathe.* To illustrate the "difficulty" of the words given in the tests (which are not actually shown), the authors report that the test results mean that the average senior would misspell about four words in the preamble to the Constitution, which contains only about forty different words.

Other subjects fared as badly. Eighty-three per cent of the seniors had no idea of what "double jeopardy" meant; 88 per cent did not know what "indictment" was; and 86 per cent could not choose the correct century for 1002 A.D. Twenty-four per cent of our high school seniors could not select the first words of our national anthem from five possible answers. Out of 16 very simple arithmetic reasoning questions (the testers tell us that "a bright elementary-school student should not have any trouble with most of them"), the average high school senior boy missed 6, the average girl 7. Previously released material on the two one-paragraph themes showed that 99 out of 100 high school students committed errors in spelling and usage, a revelation which "shocked" the test administrator.

For reasons unexplained, no data on how individual schools or states did on these tests will be released. But the report does say that Northeast students were above the national average, Southeast students below. Also, we are told that twelfth-graders generally did better than ninth-graders. (We should hope so!) But differences within regions and within grades were far greater. For example, 20 to 30 per cent of ninth-graders knew more about many subjects than the average twelfth-grader.

An important clue to one of the weaknesses of American education—the quality of classroom teaching—is contained in another part of the report. Project Talent followed up the seniors of 1960 a year later to find out what they had done, their attitudes towards college, and so forth. One of the findings: Education was a far more popular choice for college specialization among young people in the bottom quarter of the aptitude distribution than among those in the top quarter. In fact, there was a strong inverse relation between aptitude and choosing an Education program.

We are convinced that if the results of Project Talent were widely and properly disseminated they would shock the nation. Although *The American High-School Student* gives only partial results and its cumbersome organization does not make for easy reading, its findings leave no room for reasonable doubt that we need a drastic improvement in our schools. There will still be differences over how the improvement should be accomplished, of course, but it is imperative that we have a strong national consensus on the need for it.[5]

Perhaps that indeed is still what we most need in American education a decade after *Sputnik*—a strong national consensus on the need for reform. But until we have a reliable national assessment to tell us where we are in American education, it is difficult to produce a consensus in favor of change or against it. Whatever the outcome of the present project in national assessment, which might at least give us an accounting at one point in time, we should examine carefully the question of whether we want to continue in our lonely role as the only industrialized country of the world without a national system of public examinations or some other means to give us systematic knowledge of the performance of our schools.

The second point that I would reiterate concerns the typical course offerings of the American secondary school. We should put an end as soon as possible to the smorgasbord curriculum. We should, that is, drastically curtail the elective system of our schools (and colleges too, for that matter). I readily admit to a bias against this system before looking at the English or European systems, but it is even stronger now. We really should stop taking pride in being the odd man out in this regard also. We are the only advanced nation of the world that refuses to recognize the central importance of a stipulated curriculum, and not just for good students, but for all. However much other countries may envy us our educational system—what they most envy is our wealth and greater investment in education, not our educational results—not one of them is proposing or would tolerate anything as loose and indiscriminate and wasteful as the American elective system in either secondary or higher education. Even the Newsom Committee, that most progressive of all Britain's national boards of inquiry, would balk at the degree of freedom of American students to be badly educated. One of the most experienced members of the Newsom Committee, after a good deal of visiting among American schools, wrote in a memorandum to the committee:

> The abiding impression the visitor gets in an American school is that this is a place of *enjoyment*. The pupils have a free choice of subjects and an immense variety to choose from; they can try anything once and whatever the economic and social sanctions which keep them in school, they undoubtedly stay happy. . . . The system of free electives operated in the senior high school has some grave faults particularly for the more academic pupils; it can lead to a lack of intellectual self-discipline; no proper sequence of learning skills; and ill-directed and aimless acquisition of snippets of knowledge producing in the more intelligent pupils a "Reader's Digest Mind"; the possibility of underdevelopment because gifted students choose undemanding or seemingly vocationally relevant courses; and too much emphasis is laid upon the acquisition of social skills rather than intellectual development. It may be vital for girls to be popular but it is a pity if they cannot be intelligent as well.[6]

I am certain that these sentiments would be echoed by the vast majority of educators in Britain and Europe, who would subscribe to the idea of a stipulated curriculum for the average and below-average students as well as the able; they might make the curriculum broader for the lower ability range of students, but they would see nothing but disaster in the American program. They are right, and it is we who are wrong and should make the change in their direction.

The third point follows from the second. After consigning the smorgasbord curriculum to its well-deserved oblivion, we should put in its place a program of basic studies that reflects a little more faith in the intellectual capacity of American students than we have shown before. We could learn from British and European schools that subjects like physics, chemistry, mathematics, and foreign languages are not beyond the grasp of average students, as we have been told so long by our professional educators as well as by people like James Bryant Conant. We should note, for instance, that all Swedish children study English for four years and most of them for at least six; and that in many British schools, including secondary modern and comprehensive schools, French is a required language for all students; and that in fact the study of one or more foreign languages is found with great frequency in the schools of Europe for students well down the ability range. The point is not whether

European children use other languages more often than we do, a doubtful proposition in itself with British as well as other children, but whether, as our educationists have always told us, children of even average intelligence are innately incapable of learning another language.

Similarly, the study of physical sciences and mathematics are often mandatory for practically all students in European schools, certainly for three-quarters of the student body, whereas we persist in saying that only the top quarter or so can "profit from" the study of these subjects in high school. We could also reexamine other subjects of the curriculum from looking at foreign practice. We are about the only nation to have abandoned the study of geography as a separate subject. It remains a standard requirement in British schools, primary and secondary, and in most of the schools of Europe. We are almost alone in our addiction to that amorphous amalgam, "Social Studies," in which geography and history are often submerged in a tide of "current events." It is time we acknowledged that the vast majority of students can and ought to do creditable work in basic subjects through the secondary school, and we should reconstruct the curriculum accordingly.

There are many other lessons we could learn from the British. Above all, we should strive to do as much for our best students as Britain and Europe do. In spite of all the talk of the last ten years about educating our "academically talented" students, we are a good deal behind what other countries in fact accomplish with theirs. We are committed for social reasons to the comprehensive school, but the least we should be able to do after more than half a century of experience with this school is to stop penalizing our best students in the imagined interests of the average. That we do penalize them is clear from looking at Britain and Europe; there is surely no excuse for our continuing to do so today. Teacher training might be the best place to start an attack on the problem.

We should also consider the advantages of the longer school year and the longer school day in Britain, especially since most American children have not been needed on the farm for thirty years or more. We should also note the emphasis in British schools on the headmaster as the *head* master, the principal teacher, who is respected for his teaching ability and experience and is thought of first as an educator, not as a report-writing, record-keeping, office-bound, nonteaching administrator. We should note the British emphasis on the classroom autonomy of the teacher and the teacher's freedom from administrative trivia and domination—no small point. We should note that the British conviction that adults know better than do children what subjects should be studied in school means that a coordinated curriculum can be created to stretch over a period of years and not be shot full of holes by electives; and this allows a sequential study of basic subjects from year to year, and it also allows study to proceed on a weekly timetable offering some variation for teachers and students rather than the monotonous daily round of subjects of the American school. We should note the greater emphasis on practice teaching in British programs for training teachers as well as the pressures from schools and trainees for even more of it; also the practice of putting courses in pedagogical methods under the direction of experienced teachers. We should note that the British university degree ensures, in three years, that people who teach after taking it have a much deeper knowledge of their subject than the American teacher after his four-year bachelor's degree.

All these and numerous other points discussed in the previous chapters are things that American education should consider, not with a view to accepting them uncritically or imitating them, but with a view to the possible adaptation of them to the particular conditions of American education.

## CHAPTER VIII

# A Candid Message to the English People

*My main concern in this book has been to describe the present situation in English education for American readers and relate it to American problems and practices. But I hope the book will also be of interest to people in the United Kingdom. In the past the English have shown no great curiosity about the educational systems of other countries, nor have we Americans, but like most peoples we both have always been interested in what visitors think of our own institutions. Before bringing this book to an end, therefore, I would like to turn the transatlantic telescope around and offer to my British readers some thoughts on their educational revolution and how it might profit from American experience. I trust that I may address them with a collective "you," even though I know very well that Britishers are anything but of a single mind on the matters I want to discuss. If some of my comments seem harsh or presumptuous I can only hope that Britons, who were my generous and delightful hosts for the better part of two years, will accept them in the spirit in which I offer them—the worried reflections of a grateful admirer.*

THE GREATEST QUESTION facing you in your present educational turmoil is the one that has also faced us for many years and to which we have never really found an answer acceptable to a large majority of people. It is, quite simply, the ideological or philosophical question of educational purpose. I don't know whether you will be any more successful in answering it than we have been as you move into a period of unprecedented change and expansion, but you might give it a little more conscious attention than you do. What is it that you want your schools to accomplish? You appear to me to be in great confusion on this absolutely central point. Do you want your schools to be places where children and young people become literate in the basic subjects of human knowledge, and where they try to equip themselves to live their personal and professional lives as wisely as possible? Or do you want schools to be adjustment centers where curative psychological theories are tried out and young people trained in tribal manners and habits? Do you want to use your schools as primary instruments of social change, as the means of reforming your social institutions—which means that there are no limits to what they might be asked or ordered to do for political and other purposes? Or do you want them to concern themselves with developing and furnishing the minds of future citizens who might then be able to change society in whatever ways seem to them, not necessarily to teachers or educational experts or social theoreticians, to be desirable? Or do you want schools to become an arm of the Welfare State, acting as child-minding centers, taking the place, by order of the government, of inadequate parents, ineffective churches, and uncaring communities? Or do you want them to become job-training centers, taking the place of industry and trades, which can do the training better?

The question of priorities is paramount. It is not just a financial question: Finances follow more important decisions, taken deliberately or merely allowed to happen, about the function of educational institutions. If you do not reach some kind of consensus about that, you can still make educational progress, but it will be to the accompaniment of confusion and controversy and great waste. Let me discuss under four headings what seem to me the major problems of your educational revolution and what you might learn about them from American experience. They are "Expansion and Status," "Politics and Professionalism," "Lessons from the American Comprehensive School," and "The Newsom Report and Half Your Future." With each of these topics, the first order of business for you ought to be to decide what you think is the basic function of the educational institutions involved.

## Expansion and Status

The need for expansion is hardly controvertible. With seventy-five percent of your young people still leaving school by the time they are sixteen, with four percent in the universities and another four percent in other kinds of higher education, there can be little doubt that the expansion and extension of your educational service is necessary if your island economy is to thrive and the quality of life is to improve. But the absence of defined objectives at the various levels of your educational system threatens to undermine the expansion. You want to keep everybody in school longer, but you are not sure why or what it is you want to do with them. You want to make, as Harold Wilson vaguely announces, "a grammar-school education available to everybody," but you don't seem to know whether this means an abolition of "meritocratic" education, as some of your sociologists call it, or a genuine extension of high-quality academic education to more young people. You want lots more students in higher education, but you sell the idea, as we do in America, on the basis of the earning power of a higher education. Your post office hasn't yet started franking envelopes with the slogan, "To Earn More You Must Learn More," as ours did a few years ago, but there is little effort in all of your expansionist activity to suggest to students that more education might be good for them as people.

At the same time, you convince yourself that the pool of ability is much deeper than you thought before and that more will therefore not mean worse, instead of frankly recognizing that the second proposition does not follow from the first. The pool of ability is certainly deeper than you have thought before, but the chances are that an expansion on your present scale will indeed mean worse, if for no other reason than that good education does not expand in direct proportion to the student population; it involves things like buildings, libraries, institutional experience and reputation, and student traditions, and most of all it involves teachers and their dedicated efforts over a period of years. You should face the fact that more *will* mean worse, at least for a while, and try to ameliorate the effects of radical expansion as best you can while you are waiting for quality to catch up with quantity. Meanwhile, why kid yourself?

As you expand you seem to be obsessed with matters of status. You seem seriously to believe that you can achieve "parity of esteem" among educational institutions by declaring that it exists or ought to exist, despite your experience with secondary modern and grammar schools. Instead of accepting, even relishing, the rich diversity of your schools and colleges and universities, you spend time deploring the educational pecking order. The determination of the Robbins Committee that there shall be no hierarchy in higher education, that the public shall put all institutions on a plateau of prestige, is simply silly, and would not be given a hearing in any other country, certainly not America, that was so fortunate as to have some world-renowned institutions. Actually, the Robbins Committee was ambivalent on the matter, deploring the lack of equality on the one hand and recognizing its virtues on the other. Would a Frenchman say that the *grandes écoles* are now to be no more prestigious than a provincial teachers college, or that an unselective technical institute is fully the equal of the *École Normale Supérieur* or the *École Polytechnique?* Would the most sanguine of American levelers say that Harvard is no more important to the nation than Slippery Rock State College or that the Oskaloosa School of Osteopathy was to be regarded just as highly as the Johns Hopkins Medical School? It is surely obvious in Britain if anywhere in the world that equality of prestige among educational institutions is unattainable, even if desirable. I would suggest that you take the following sort of conclusion, from one of your well-known comparative educationists, with great skepticism:

> Our study of England and Wales makes one point startlingly clear: the manner in which institutions, with deservedly high prestige, may by their very existence complicate and distort the whole of the admissions process. There is a ladder of desirability, all the steps of which are clearly marked and well known. The most fitted want to go either to Oxford or Cambridge, and even to particular colleges. Refused admission, they try London or Bristol and down the line of the newer colleges or colleges of advanced technology. Thus it turns out that only a small minority are truly satisfied and proud. It seems as if one had built into the English structure of higher education a mechanism for producing maximum irritation and frustration.[1]

I doubt very much that the majority of British university students are neither satisfied with nor proud of their institutions simply because they failed to get their first choice. I noticed that the Franks Commission reported that "we learned from our witnesses that the majority of their pupils from the maintained schools concentrate on a university place rather than a place at a particular university."[2] Most students in the United States would also like to go to a handful of our most famous colleges and universities, which can take only a small minority of students, but the rest do not seem to suffer traumatically from going elsewhere.

There is a good chance that the concern of the Robbins Report that equal performance be awarded with equally valuable degrees will backfire. What may well happen, for example, with the degrees of the Council for National Academic Awards or with the new B.Ed. degree is that, far from rewarding equal work with equal degrees, the work will not in fact be equal and the degree will not in fact be regarded as equal. Perhaps it is not so much a question of equal ability. Some students outside the universities and some in the Colleges of Education are no doubt capable of degree-level work, but it is a far different matter to provide such work through outside study or through the kind of programs being put together for the B.Ed. If it should turn out in five or ten years that the B.Ed. and the degrees of the CNAA are regarded as inferior by employers and the public, will this not have aggravated the problem Robbins hoped to solve? At this point, I would give the CNAA degrees a better chance of success than the B.Ed. But that question apart, why worry about putting all institutions on the same level; why not rejoice that you have so many institutions so highly regarded in the rest of the world? It seems to me that the recommendation of the Franks Commission that special efforts be made to keep Oxford an international university with a world reputation is only common sense. The same might be said of some of your other institutions and of some of your schools. By all means try to raise the status of institutions, but by genuinely improving their quality, not by artificially lowering your best. Take for your text the comment of Thomas Arnold in his Rugby days: "Our concern is to raise all and lower none."

Another pawn in the status game is the independent schools. You have some of the best in the world but now you seem to be more concerned about the fact that only some people can afford them than about raising your other schools that are open to everybody. You fuss and fume about the Old Boy Network as if it were something created by schools instead of by people. You seem to think you can defeat it by changing the schools, whereas you will probably only rechannel the Network, which in any case is going obsolescent under the larger social developments of postwar Britain. You denounce the independent schools for having the best teachers and more of them in relation to the numbers of students than the state schools, but envy is a poor basis for educational reform, and the punitive leveling of all schools in these matters would have very little effect on the state system. You get exercised about the "social divisiveness" of the Public Schools and denounce them as "nurseries of privilege," but you seem to ignore the fact that these schools have also been of great service to the state system: They have demonstrated to the state schools the inadequacy of the 11-plus and the need to provide for the later development of many who fail it, no mean contribution to British education; they have been the academic models, and no bad ones, for a great many state grammar schools; and they have saved the taxpayers a lot of money that will otherwise have to be found in the future if they are to become semi-state comprehensive schools.

Perhaps you ought also to ask yourself if denying freedom of educational choice to the minority of people involved in the independent schools in the supposed interests of the majority is not a high price to pay in an age that is already closing the gap between the classes with great speed. You ought also to ask yourself if you really want an exclusively government-controlled system of schools, with the restrictions on experiment and dissent and the enforced regard for bureaucratic orthodoxy that are inevitable in a monolithic state system. Ask yourself what you have to lose as well as what you think you will really gain by continuing to attack the independent schools on the grounds that they are too rich (most are quite poor by American standards with no endowment and no financially active alumni groups) or too divisive or that their status is too high. And ask yourself if at least some of the advantages of independence are not worth preserving—for example, the fact that parents, having bought, often at some sacrifice, what they regard as a high-quality education for their children, take a more active role in that education than do parents in the state system. Yes, I know that lots of parents send their children to independent schools from less worthy motives, but lots more are genuinely interested in the quality of education offered there. One of the greatest factors making for excellence in private education in both our countries is not that such schools are so much better off financially than state schools, but that they are obliged to satisfy the customer or go out of business; whereas a monopolistic, no-choice state system could ignore the customer, since he cannot opt out. Granted that many British parents cannot opt out of the present state system, what is gained by preventing everybody from doing so? I believe that one of the greatest needs in American education is for *more* private education to offer some challenge and competition to the state system that in many areas is monopolistic. Nothing is easier than for the schools in such areas to grow fat and complacent, unresponsive to the consumer who has no other place to go, and above all to become somewhat authoritarian. Your politicians and educationists who want an exclusively state system for Britain might find themselves less enchanted if they were to contemplate the dangers as well as the imagined glories of such a system.

I would not defend many of the practices in your independent schools. They have their outmoded traditions and their trivial snobberies, and some of their students probably do emerge with an offensively superior attitude. Moreover, I would admit to some uneasiness about English boys who never see the inside of a state school, who go from private nursery schools to private primary or prep schools to Public Schools to Oxford or Cambridge. This is a highly exclusive route that probably gives some protected students a distorted view of life (though I doubt that this would be a problem in the United States). But there are ways of mitigating these effects without abolishing independence in education. Even if there were not, abolishing independence would be too high a price to pay to save the country from a few snobs, which in any case it would not do. You have far more pressing problems in education to worry about.

One such problem in connection with your present expansion is that of educational efficiency and productivity. You talk a lot about efficiency in industry, where low productivity is undeniably your severest problem, but your educational authorities seem to be less than receptive to the idea that they too could be more efficient and productive with the limited funds available. Unless you can persuade the electorate to spend even more money on education than you already spend, which is about as high a percentage of your gross national product as any major country in the world, and if you are to continue your existing program of reform and expansion, you will have to get greater productivity from both industry and education. So I would be inclined to take a harder view than you have up to now toward, for example, the NUT's protectionist policy against alleviating the teacher shortage through "ancillaries" and "auxiliaries." I would call the NUT's policy protectionist because it is mostly concerned with maintaining professional status and not with the educational effects of that policy, as becomes perfectly clear whenever the NUT tries to shore up its position by logical argument.[3] I realize that the NUT can swing a lot of political weight, and I do not suppose it is possible or desirable for the government to take a hard and fast position opposite to theirs, but there is such a thing as public opinion that might be rallied to move the NUT to a more reasonable position. The problem is aggravated by your single salary scale for teachers, which overpays the transient young woman for the one or two or three years she is in the job and underpays the people you need most, the experienced career teachers. I am not suggesting that you should meet the uncompromising line of the NUT with an equally uncompromising one of your own, for that would be a fruitless exercise, but you could certainly take the initiative in the matter and carry your case to the public more effectively than you do.

Similarly in teacher training, greater productivity is an entirely reasonable expectation. The thirty-six-week year of the Colleges of Education is a good deal better than the thirty-week year of the universities and much better than the laughable twenty-four-week year of Oxford and Cambridge, but it is still a poor yield on the investment involved. You have had some overdue luck recently in moving the Colleges to a greater concern for efficiency, and they have responded pretty well to the need for expansion, but they could do still better by a considerable margin. I would not take too seriously their dire descriptions of the administrative and other difficulties of year-round operation. Such difficulties exist, of course, but they are not insurmountable, as can be seen at a number of American institutions that now operate eleven months a year. Nor would I take at face value the argument of the Colleges about being unable to give the same quality preparation to greatly increased numbers. They are probably right about this, but I very much doubt that the decline in quality would be all that important; and it may simply be necessary, as in other areas of education, in the interests of greater numbers.

The more important question is whether expanding the Colleges is in itself an efficient way of meeting the continuing shortage. The wastage rate of College graduates is so high as to suggest very forcibly that other routes to the teaching license ought to be developed. For instance, the shortened courses for mature women could be even shorter and a good deal more flexible without any serious loss of quality, and they could be made more generally available rather than restricted to a few cases. In addition, it must be clear that a great many women of intelligence and education are not going to submit in middle life to two or three years of full-time training in a College of Education in order to teach; nor do they need such protracted training. Apprenticeship courses of preparation in the schools themselves could be created and might prove to be a good deal better for such persons than the usual training course aimed at young women of nineteen or twenty. You ought to explore the possibilities of differential salary scales for men and for career teachers. Salaries respond to supply and demand in most areas of society, but are not permitted to do so in the state schools because of the female-dominated NUT, which has everything to gain by insisting on equal pay. Actually, I doubt that you can win this particular battle, but you could surely develop some better ways of beating the teacher shortage than the extremely wasteful procedure of expanding the customary three-year training programs overpopulated with girls in the Colleges of Education.

At the least you might reexamine the system of payments to students in the Colleges. It is perhaps the most generous system in the world and is more appropriate to a country so wealthy that it wishes to pay people to get a higher education merely as a measure of national improvement. You now pay in personal grants over £1,000 to many such students during their three-year course, in addition to another £2,500 or so to maintain a place for every student in a College of Education on the presumption that she means to be a teacher. What would be a reasonable return to the state on this investment? France requires a pledge of ten years of teaching from such people, without anything like the British system of maintenance grants, though admittedly such a pledge is not easy to enforce. Admittedly too, one cannot do much about the biological facts of life that take young women out of classrooms and into marriage and maternity wards (hopefully in that order), but that does not mean that the state should support them through the three years of a teacher training course. I think it is generally agreed that out of every hundred women put through a training program, eighty will have left teaching before the age of twenty-five, meaning that they have given under three or four years of service, many of them only one or two. I know you hope to lure them back after their families are grown, but that is an uncertain forecast indeed, and won't you find yourself with some sort of retraining job in any case with women who have been out of education for twenty years? I find my own experience echoed in that of Sir John Newsom, who records the response to his questions of a number of girls in a training college he visited in 1964:

> I asked why they were there. After a while, when we had got to know each other and were talking a bit more freely, one girl spoke and then others chimed in supporting her. They hoped they were going to get married, they said—engagement rings were flashing all round—and there could not be a better preparation for marriage than going into a teachers' training college. Nice long holidays, civilized surroundings, doing the subjects you like doing, giving up the ones you don't, plenty of art work, pottery, dancing and music and instruction in child development and child psychology. I think this girl was perfectly right and that teacher training for primary schools is a very good preliminary training for marriage, but this is not the argument advanced to support the considerable annual expenditure involved.[4]

Certainly my impression from the Colleges of Education I visited is precisely the same.

In the United States, when the government helps finance prospective teachers through their education, it does so in the form of a loan, half of which is abolished if the individual teaches at least five years. I know of only one place in Europe that finances teachers in training as generously as you do and that is the Canton of Geneva, a rather wealthier state. I am sure you do so from laudable intentions, but at a time of such shortage of both teachers and money, perhaps intentions are not enough. With your present policy, you not only fill up the places in your Colleges with girls who have no intention of teaching as a career, but you may be keeping out others who would not be deterred by a teaching commitment. I noticed that the National Association of Head Teachers at their 1966 annual meeting called for a new policy requiring teachers trained at state expense to fulfill a contractual obligation to teach or to refund the state's investment. You should listen to this lonely voice.

You might also reassess the system of student grants in the universities. You might even consider replacing the present system of grants, which is based at least partly on the fallacious assumption that students will thereby keep their entire year free for study, by a system of low-interest loans similar to systems used in America. Our scholarships and student grants cover less than three percent as a national average of a student's expenses in higher education.[5] But loans to serious students are easily available, and ensure a serious commitment on his part to his own education. This generation of British students certainly does not suffer from the psychological scars of the dole of the 1930's, with its hated "means test"; it is only their elders who do. Loans are the best "means test" possible, for they ensure that funds go to the students who really need them. I noticed that the Robbins Report thought the student-grant system would have to continue as long as so many first-generation university students were coming into the institutions, but this same pattern of entry is found all over the world, especially in America, without having a serious deterrent effect. I think we do lose some able students through inability to pay in higher education, but I doubt that they are very serious about going to college in the first place; if they were both serious and able, there is no financial reason for them to forego a higher education in the United States.

I have been struck by the attitudes of expectancy that you have engendered in university students by your payments system. Far from being grateful to a generous government, they seem to be quite ill-tempered about the fact that it is not more generous still. Inevitably, they have come to regard not only a university education as a right but the comfortable financing of their private lives as well. When I visit your ancient universities or your new establishments like Sussex and York and see the splendid provision you have made for the students lucky enough to be admitted to such institutions, and when I remember that practically all of them are paid to attend, I think of these students as some of the most privileged persons in the world—in an age and a country where privilege has become a bad word. So if I were you I would cast a cold eye on the regular demands of the National Union of Students not only for bigger grants to everybody but for abolition of the means test. Instead, I would give some thought to whether the present system makes the most of the public funds available for education. I might be especially tempted to a little surgery on such wasteful grants as those given to anyone who signs up for the one-year postgraduate Diploma in Education, with no commitment on their part to teach. They have already had a three-year degree course on the taxpayer, and I am pretty sure that a number of them sign up for the graduate year for reasons other than their interest in either the course or in teaching; and in fact some of them never teach. My feelings on this point may be colored by a certain lack of enthusiasm for the course itself, but it is hard for me to see the rationale for supporting for another year all graduates who get themselves admitted to this course.

## Politics and Professionalism

As I mentioned in Chapter II, the balance of powers that you have evolved in eductaion between central and local authority seems to me to work very well. Many people are uneasy about the present drift of power to the center, and I certainly share their fear when I consider the enforcement of such policies as the one about comprehensive schools. It may be useful for the central government to enunciate general policy in education, but to subordinate education to partisan political doctrine is another thing. One of the reasons that it is so important for you to define as clearly as possible the purpose of education and the function of schools is the inevitable temptation of politicians to use schools for the realization of doctrinal ends. No one can draw a clear line between political decisions that try to effect the will of society through educational change, which I suppose is how many people would look at the comprehensive issue, and decisions that distort or exploit that will and use education to effect partisan goals. Even so, and in spite of the comprehensive issue, the balance of powers in British education between the national government and the LEA's seems to me an effective one, with enough built-in checks to prevent any long-term abuse of power.

But I am less sure that you will maintain a wise balance in the future between the layman and the educational expert. This relationship too has its twilight zone where rights and responsibilities are blurred. Defining the role of the public and the professional in education is an old and sensitive question in my country, and I foresee it developing in yours.

The traditional respect for the amateur in Britain, the attitude that the expert should be on tap but not on top, is being subjected to the same pressures that have been at work for years in America. We have many more such experts than you have and many more kinds of them, but you are now confronted with the same problem of trying to keep clear the function of the experts in the making of basic educational policy. The problem is created mostly by the imprecision of knowledge in education. In fields where the extent and significance of the specialist's skill and knowledge are more manifest, in medicine, or law, or engineering, conflicts do not arise so often, for the layman knows the limits of his knowledge quite clearly and the expert the extent of his. In education, however, the limits of knowledge and verifiable fact are reached very quickly by both laymen and experts. Education as a subject of special study is still a new and very uncertain enterprise, far more impressive for what it does not know than for what it can say with confidence. Thus it is extremely important for people who must make educational decisions affecting large numbers of children to realize how tenuous are the answers that experts can legitimately give to most of the questions that can be asked in education. There is scarcely a question beyond statistical matters to which education committees must address themselves that can be answered definitively by educational experts or by evidence from research. Whether the question is one about training teachers, streaming, comprehensive schools, examinations, boarding, coeducation, specialization, teaching machines, or any of a hundred other subjects, the decision must finally be made on the grounds of what seems plausible, probable, or possible, or made as an act of faith, hope, or charity; but it cannot be made on the grounds of clear and incontestable evidence.

This should not be surprising. Education, being something that happens internally to human beings, does not lend itself to precise analysis, at least not yet. The educational researcher can almost never find or create a research situation in which all of the important variables of "human nature and conduct" (as John Dewey called one of his best books) can be taken into account, even assuming the researcher knows what they all are, which of course he doesn't. Even if he did, he would still lack techniques of proved worth for measuring them and for eliminating his own biases from his research. Whether educational research will at some point in the future attain any high degree of reliability is a moot question, but it assuredly has not reached that point now. Hence, laymen and politicians should not look to the educational expert for answers he cannot or should not supply, much less for any special wisdom on questions of educational purpose and priority. I thought that your Secretary of State for Education and Science made his point very well, even though he may not always have followed its logic himself, when he said in a 1966 speech in defense of the government's position on comprehensive schools:

. . . the "waiting for research" argument betrays a misunderstanding of the nature both of educational research and of our political system. Educational research, in any case a very new tool, can give us new facts, illuminate a range of choice, tell us how better to achieve a given objective. But it cannot tell us what the objective ought to be. For this must depend, as I tried to make clear earlier, on judgments which have a value-component and a social dimension—judgments about equity and equal opportunity and social division and economic efficiency and all the other criteria which I have mentioned in this speech. These judgments cannot be made in the National Foundation for Educational Research. They can be made only in Parliament and the local Council-chamber.[6]

Just so. It may be that an even humbler role for educational research at this point in its development is appropriate, for there are not many questions upon which it can really illuminate a range of choice or tell us with much certainty how to achieve a given objective.

A problem, then, arises that you should be more conscious of than I think you are when people who must make the primary decisions in education demand more of the expert than he can supply, or equally when the expert claims more than he can deliver. Take, for example, the whole tormented question of secondary reorganization that the Secretary mentions above. The amount of expert knowledge useful to those who must decide whether or how to reorganize is meager, tentative, and conflicting. In other words, nobody really knows whether this way of organizing schools in Britain will achieve more or less than is achieved in the present system; such knowledge does not exist. What does exist, of course, is the extensive experience of the United States in comprehensive education— which can be variously interpreted. In these circumstances education committees should not look to the expert for an answer and he should not attempt to foist one on the committee, at least not in his capacity as an expert. No doubt he has as much right as the next man to stump the country banging the comprehensive drum to his particular tune, but he is exceeding his right if he does so in his role as an educational expert claiming special wisdom on the question. One can multiply examples with ease. If one thinks of any of the major educational issues now under discussion in England, one sees how limited is the evidence that can be called on from research, and how difficult it must be for the layman to tell whether the expert is speaking on any given occasion out of genuine knowledge on an issue where knowledge should dictate the conclusion, or out of personal conviction on an item where his feelings are perhaps of no more consequence than those of anyone else. What is therefore needed in both your country and mine is not a denigration of educational specialists or their research, but an effort to restrict the role of both in the determination of policy. It may not be as easy as you think.

As your Institutes and Departments of Education expand in the universities, they become steadily more professionalized and specialized. Following the American pattern, they are now beginning to offer a range of postgraduate degrees in new educational specialties, and this growth, if American experience is any guide, is likely to feed on itself, creating still more specialized degrees and thereby creating special-interest groups within the field of professional Education, each of which is a kind of lobby for more of the same. Courses of study will begin to multiply with great speed. As these developments take place, you will probably find that expert opinion is always on the side of more of everything, not on the side of retrenchment, economy, efficiency, and productivity.

If, for example, the old two-year course in training colleges was good, three years are better, and four years better still, as can already be seen from reports of official bodies.[7] Ultimately, it may well be five years as the standard preparation for teaching, as it quite unjustifiably is becoming with us; what we mostly need in America is to render the fat out of the existing four-year program. You may also find that as training time increases, the extra time is used for professional and pedagogical study. My opinion is that if more training time is to be created it should go to more and better subject-matter preparation, especially for teachers going into secondary schools. One of the major weaknesses of your secondary modern schools, and your teacher-training courses for the people that staff them, is the failure to distinguish adequately between future primary and secondary teachers in the Colleges. Secondary teachers are turned out with rather weak subject specialties and in fact are misassigned frequently when they get to the schools. You will also find that the professional pressures will continue to build up for making mandatory the year of teacher training for university graduates. I have already commented on this matter in Chapter V, and here would only reiterate my feeling that it would be a mistake for you to require this kind of training for all graduates without an examination of what the training now consists of, what graduates think of it, and what experience schools actually have with those who have been trained and those who have not. In the meantime you might be well advised to build some flexibility into the ways that graduates can become "qualified," including apprenticeship arrangements in the schools themselves. What is to be avoided is what the professional wants most: a rigid, across-the-board ruling for everybody.

Professionalization usually means some degree of centralization of authority and standardization of requirements. As professional fields develop, their practitioners organize national associations which in turn establish national patterns of professional training and qualification, encourage professional solidarity, pursue professional status, and lobby for the interests of their special group—all of which means that they must establish in the public mind that a large body of expert knowledge exists in their field that requires extensive special training and that gives people with this training a voice of authority. The experts turned out naturally find it easy to persuade themselves of the extent and importance of their expertise, and take an increasingly dimmer view of the amateur and layman. They are almost always found on the side of restricting the role of the parent and the layman in education, on the no doubt sincere belief that experts know better than the public what is good for it and its children. Thus you found, for example, most of your professional educators solidly on the side of the Robbins recommendations to remove the training colleges from LEA control on the assumption that such control was capricious, amateur, outmoded, and exercised by elected officials without expert knowledge; that the thing to do was to free them from all this and attach them to highly professional Schools of Education in the universities.

I do not suggest that the increasing professionalization in education is all a loss or that you ought to oppose it. I merely want to sound a warning about the possible usurpation of authority in the future. I merely want to suggest that you keep American experience in mind. Educational experts for a long time in the future are not going to be in a position to solve most problems or make most policies; until they are, you should indeed keep them on tap but not on top.

## Lessons from the American Comprehensive School

Perhaps the time has passed when a visitor could have said anything useful to you about your present comprehensive-school policy. The decision to "go" comprehensive is apparently irrevocable, but there may still be room for the accommodation of minority views in the execution of the policy. I am puzzled at your persistent failure to look abroad to see what might be learned from other people about comprehensive schools before making such a far-reaching change in your secondary system. We have probably had more experience with comprehensive secondary education than any other nation in the world, and you could do a lot worse than make a careful study of that experience. Such a study might not change your mind about going comprehensive, especially if it were conducted by people who had made up their minds in advance, but it might at least permit you to avoid some of our mistakes as you put your comprehensive policy into effect. Not that you are uninfluenced by American education. Far from it. I often get the impression that, as one of your educational writers commented, "anything Transatlantic tends to be welcomed as an aspect of an inescapable future." [8] That is just the problem: You take too much from American education without questioning or examining it and without considering the much different circumstances under which our respective educational systems have developed. Your professional educators are especially prone to this habit, though they should be the very people to know better.

Let me therefore outline under a few appropriate headings some of the lessons that you might learn from the lengthy experience of America in comprehensive schools. I shall try to do so as dispassionately as I can, but dispassionate analysis, as we both know, is an illusion in education; so perhaps I should make my own bias clear. In assessing the twentieth-century history of American education, people often find themselves taking one of two fundamental positions for each of which a good case can be made: That our educational development in these years has been an unprecedented record of success and achievement, in which the imperfections are minor beside the accomplishments; or that it is a record of confused purposes and unredeemed promise, in which the imperfections loom very large beside the accomplishments. Both statements are "true" depending on one's general views and expectations of universal education. I lean toward the latter position, believing that we should have done a great deal better in American education than we have, and that even today there is a wide gap between our claims and our performance, between the assumptions upon which we proceed in American education and the realities of our accomplishments. It is true that we have more of our young people enrolled full-time in educational institutions, and that we keep them there longer, than does any other nation, but we have yet to resolve the conflicting demands of quantity and quality in mass education, and this conflict has ramifications throughout our system of schools and colleges. On the specific question of secondary-school organization, I assuredly do not feel that our experience in comprehensive education proves this to be a superior way of going about secondary schooling; I think it is right for us for reasons that do not have much to do with education, but it seems to me an export item of very doubtful value.

First, a quick reminder about the politics of our educational system. The role of the central government is not at all what it is in England or most of Europe. It is or has been up to very recent years a quite restricted role. Each of the fifty states continues today as it has in the past to be a sovereign power in educational matters, theoretically answerable to nobody but its own citizens. To carry out its responsibilities, each state has a department of education in its governmental apparatus, and such departments in the larger states rival in size your Department of Education and Science. By long tradition the states relinquish many of their educational powers to local school authorities, who are mostly elected on a nonparty basis similar to the way your local boards were elected before the 1902 Act. The finance of education, then, is a shared responsibility between the state and each local community, with the federal government involved only in special, although rapidly increasing, programs.

In practice this seemingly chaotic system works better than you might expect. There are irresistible forces operating on both the states and the local authorities that make for a large measure of uniformity and centralization in such critical matters as curriculum, teacher training, and general organization. The qualitative and financial differences among American schools and school systems can be tremendous, far greater than in your system, but I would guess that one of the lasting impressions you would get if you traveled around America visiting schools would be the degree of standardization that exists among them rather than any degree of difference that might be suggested to you by our extended chain of command.

1. *Social factors in the comprehensive school:* I begin with this matter because of its importance in your own thinking. Whatever the educational arguments for the comprehensive school and whatever the proclamations of minority groups (like the CND banner that mindlessly exclaims, "Comprehensive Schools for Peace"), it is clear to me that your politicians based their decision about going comprehensive mostly on theories about the social effects of such schools. The main assumption is that the comprehensive school will bring greater equality into English life, that it will overcome social barriers and snobbery and put an end to the social divisiveness of separate schools. But this seems to me the weakest and least tenable ground upon which to base the comprehensive movement in Britain, for two reasons.

First, comprehensive schools, because they are comprehensive, serve relatively small catchment areas in precisely those parts of the country where problems of inequality are greatest—in and around cities. Here the comprehensive school becomes indeed a neighborhood school, and thus the quality of a given school is often dictated by housing patterns. Housing patterns are becoming more, not less, homogeneous in both our countries, with middle-class families continuing to flee the cities to the desirable suburbs and lower-class families concentrating more than ever in the undesirable areas of cities. The result, as can be seen in a thousand cities of America, is socially homogeneous schools that are called comprehensive. They can be very impressive in, say, Grosse Point, Michigan, or Scarsdale, New York, or in any suburb that may spend £500 a year on each child, and they can be appalling fifteen miles away in a downtown slum. The social effect of such schools is to reinforce rather than combat class consciousness. We could debate the causes and cures of this condition, but the immediate point is that neighborliness between classes is not a function of the comprehensive school, as you seem to think it is, where neighborhoods are themselves homogeneous. Confident claims are sometimes made in England that the neighborhood limitations of the comprehensive school can be overcome by redrawing school lines. I think you will find that redrawing school districts along artificial lines or busing children from "underprivileged" neighborhoods over long distances to put them in somebody else's neighborhood schools is not as simple as it may look in prospect. And transporting middle-class children into underprivileged schools only embitters their parents, who then opt out of the state system altogether.

Second, it is very doubtful that schools, no matter how they are organized or what the neighborhood patterns are, can create such a thing as social equality. They can strengthen it, but only if the driving force comes first from the community at large, as it has in America. To be sure, there is plenty of distance remaining today between the theory of American society and the practices we all know about, but equality is still a major characteristic of American society. Our comprehensive schools represent the answer to one of the principal historic problems of America: the need to find some means for unifying an extremely heterogeneous collection of immigrant peoples speaking many different languages and having few traditions in common. But even more important, the comprehensive school reflects the egalitarian impulse of this assortment of peoples, their dislike of artificial barriers and unearned privileges, and their desire to give everybody equal access, as it were, to life, liberty, and the pursuit of happiness. This is the essential theory, the ideology if you like, of the American comprehensive school. But it probably does not work the other way around. If there is no real consensus in British society in support of the equality of classes, you can hardly expect institutions so closely related to homes as are schools to do the job. People, not institutions, decide what a community will be. I think you might be disappointed if you look to the comprehensive school to surmount the barriers erected by the English people themselves.

Moreover, you might remember that there is still plenty of snobbery in American life also, despite the length of our experience with the comprehensive school. Our kind of snobbery is tied more to wealth than to family or background, but it is often reinforced, as you perhaps surmise from what I have already said, by the neighborhood school. The word "exclusive" can be applied to more areas in and around New York City or San Francisco or Detroit than London, and the comprehensive schools serving such areas are similarly exclusive. Apart from that kind of obvious distinction, the degree of social mixing that actually takes place in a comprehensive school with a heterogeneous student body is often smaller than you seem to think. Mixing occurs in America in such activities as games and assemblies and clubs, as well as in unstreamed classes, but in general students tend to associate, when there is a choice, according to social and economic status. They do so even more as soon as they leave the school and go home. One can talk of schooling dustmen and dukes together in a brave new Britain, but it is doubtful if they would ever find themselves in the same neighborhood school and even more doubtful that, if they did, they would hobnob around or otherwise develop attitudes toward each other not supported at home or by the community. So again, don't expect the neighborhood comprehensive school to be a social-leveling device or to make everybody respect everybody else because they happen to be thrown together under the same roof. If British society is to be more egalitarian, as it obviously is, I doubt that schools will play the major role in that development.

2. *The problem of size:* There *is* a problem of size in comprehensive schools, even though your comprehensive votaries may pretend that it is not important. I don't know what the ideal size of a secondary school is or if there is one, but when schools get to a thousand and more students there is a loss of that intimate spirit and rapport that are often found now in the English school. The typical comprehensive school in the United States is an informal, friendly, happy place; but it is also a large place where the head may not even have met many students to whom he hands graduation certificates after three or four years in the school, and where the general problems of logistics and organization often block the development of the kind of close contact between students and staff that is a distinguishing element of your schools. Also, a comprehensive school is a place in which students of widely different abilities and interests are working in many different ways for many different purposes. It is a school without a single, clearly defined goal shared by all. Thus a great many American students never develop a real identification with their school, certainly nothing to what an English student commonly does. American students may participate in all the school-based rituals, from "pep rallies" (a phenomenon perhaps unique to America that in itself says something about the *esprit de corps* of schools) to charity dances; but they do not feel about their school the way your students often do. One almost never has occasion in America to cite one's school in later life, to follow it or to identify oneself with it in any important way after leaving. When two educated Englishmen meet, one of the first things they manage to discover is each other's school. When two Americans meet, this might be the last item of conversation that would occur to them.

I don't know whether this loss of intimacy can be avoided as you move to comprehensive schools. I have visited some of your larger schools that seem to retain a measure of it, though they were not comprehensive. And I know that your comprehensive schools attempt through the house system to solve the impersonal factor introduced into them by sheer size, but those I have seen are not greatly reassuring on the point. The house system may have much to be said for it on other grounds, but I do not think it solves the problem of size in a comprehensive school the way that colleges do at Oxbridge. It may be that the loss of rapport and close identification with the school cannot be solved. It may be that this is simply part of the price you will have to pay for comprehensive schools. But you would be better off doing so with your eyes open than telling yourself that size is not a problem.

3. *The administrative problem:* Still another problem of the comprehensive school is its tendency to create a professional class of school administrators quite apart from the teaching staff. I have already mentioned the Parkinsonian growth of Education as a field of study in America and its effects. American Schools of Education now offer a bewildering number of postgraduate programs, that seem to increase at a sort of geometric rate, leading to master's and doctor's degrees. At last count there were no fewer than eighty subjects of specialization in which a doctor's degree could be earned in Education in the United States. Many of these fructifying specialties are in educational administration, a subject not yet discovered for postgraduate study in most of Europe. Not only can one take, for example, an Ed.D. degree (Doctor of Education) in Educational Administration, but one can take it in at least half a dozen subspecialties of that subject. The graduates of these programs then become the nonteaching heads of large comprehensive schools where they may have several full-time, nonteaching administrative assistants, several more full-time, nonteaching "guidance counselors," and perhaps other oilers of the educational machinery. To back up these administrators— that is, to administer the administrator—one naturally needs a large central administration for the school system as a whole or for parts of it. A few years ago one writer calculated that New York City had more educational administrators than all of France. I don't ascribe this situation solely to the comprehensive school, nor do I mean to say that an administrative apparatus is unnecessary. But the comprehensive school has been a major impetus to the pseudo-professionalism as well as the growth of the nonteaching staff now found throughout our secondary system.

The problem created thereby is not merely financial, draining funds that might better be used in other ways. It has had strong effects on educational quality as well. People with a master's degree in something called Guidance Counseling who do no teaching and are pretty well removed from the students they counsel are not always better than teachers in that role. Administrators who keep secretaries busy mimeographing reports, forms, questionnaires, and sundry other documents that flood the life of the American teacher are not necessarily contributing to education. Most of all, nonteaching heads who by virtue of their position dominate their staff to the degree that many do in the United States, where the individual teacher's authority is far more circumscribed than with you, are diminishing the standard of education in their schools. Can it happen in England? It certainly can; one can see the beginnings of it now. Generally, your headmasters are well respected for their experience and ability by your teachers, who themselves retain a great deal of authority, but what the situation will be when they are all in big comprehensives with big nonteaching staffs whose members have done a postgraduate course in a nonteaching specialty is another matter. In 1965 a fact-finding committee of the California legislature published the results of a survey that had been made of a vast sample, 15,000, of teachers throughout California, a state that is so often cited in Britain as an educational utopia. The findings of this survey indicated among other things that forty-three percent of the teachers involved were not teaching the subject in which they specialized in training (we both have misassignment problems, as I mentioned earlier). Practically all of them were strongly critical of the Education courses they took in training, and their sentiments on school administrators are summarized in the report this way:

> With virtual unanimity the classroom teachers responded that, if given reasonable class sizes, uninterrupted classrooms [by administrative announcements, etc.], and fewer nonteaching duties, they could do immeasurably better at that which most of them seem to want desperately to do—teach. . . . In America the quaint tradition has developed whereby the nonteaching personnel have become spokesmen for education in general.
> It is surprising that classroom teachers have with such docility surrendered their role as spokesmen even for what goes on in the classroom. . . . It is shocking that these views [of classroom teachers] seem to be obtainable only under the shelter of anonymity as was provided by these questionnaires.[9]

The administrative problem is another one to which I do not have the answer. I merely call it to your attention in the hope that, as the comprehensive school grows in Britain, you will at least be conscious of the dangers of overadministration and of raising up a professional class of nonteaching administrators who will proceed to centralize and consolidate administrative power and to abridge the traditional rights and responsibilities of teachers.

4. *Pedagogical problems:* I suppose the issue that generates the most heat among Britishers is the education of high-ability students in a comprehensive school. An answer to the question of whether such students can progress as well in comprehensive as in selective schools cannot yet be based on experience in England, since most of your comprehensive schools do not have an adequate representation of able students. Nevertheless, defenders and opponents alike make confident claims about it. I don't know whether you will find that you can educate your better students just as well in comprehensive schools or not, but our experience does not lend much support to the idea that you can. I would come to the heart of the matter at once and say that, yes, the high-ability student has always been penalized in our comprehensive schools. One of the principal findings of a study of American secondary schools by James

Bryant Conant a few years ago, which only confirmed what was generally known, was that too many of our able students were being undereducated:

> If the fifty-five schools I have visited, all of which have a good reputation, are at all representative of American public high schools, I think one general criticism is in order: The academically talented student, as a rule, is not being sufficiently challenged, does not work hard enough, and his program of academic subjects is not of sufficient range.[10]

I think that most American educators, in moments of complete candor, would be willing to admit that the education of high-ability students has been one of the least successful aspects of our secondary schools. This condition is now recognized as indefensible by a lot of schoolmen, and many efforts at reform have been made in recent years—after, that is, half a century of experience with the comprehensive school. But it is still doubtful that our good students are being educated according to their talents. One can speculate about how this problem relates to parental attitudes in the United States, or to the values of American society at large, for these are important influences on the school. But my own conviction is that the main cause of this waste of ability is in the school itself. Nobody can say how much of it is due to comprehensiveness as such, though it seems logical to assume that a similar waste of talent would not occur in selective schools whose whole reason for being is to educate the able student.

Contrary to a good deal of opinion in Britain, many if not most American secondary schools are streamed in one way or another. Streaming is roughly but not wholly according to ability, since the element of choice is always strong; but rarely are American schools streamed in the degree that yours are. Characteristically they have only a few basic streams. They will have, for example, a college-preparatory stream that in a middle-class suburb might include fully half or more of the student body. There may or may not be a further division of these students by ability. There will be a stream for "commercial" students, perhaps one for secretarial skills, perhaps a general stream. But the chances are that any given class in one of our comprehensive schools will exhibit a much wider range of ability than a class in an English grammar school, or for that matter in a good number of your secondary modern schools; sometimes an extremely wide range. These mixed-ability classes create very tough pedagogical problems that are not at all solved by the new techniques we hear about. The simple fact is that the vast majority of teachers are not able to cope with mixed-ability classes and do justice to all their students. Inevitably the tendency in such heterogeneous classes is for the standard to become that of the average, and for the better students to suffer.

It is also the same group of students, the multitudinous average, that tend to set the entire ethos of the comprehensive school. By virtue of sheer numbers, the voice of the average becomes the dominant one, setting the intellectual tone and the goals of the school and limiting the influence of the better students. It is also true, I am sorry to say, that not a few of our educational administrators set their own sights on the average instead of the best. In short, the academic pressures in an unselective school are far more often downward than upward. It has become fashionable among your comprehensivists to claim that putting everybody together in the same school means that good students can encourage poor ones by their example; the effects of propinquity, it seems, are in one direction only. But it seems more than possible to me that such effects might take the opposite direction, as they often do in our schools, with the average and below-average exerting their influence on the able. To be brainy is not as hazardous in our schools as it used to be, but it is still a serious question whether these schools unavoidably militate against the bright student.

A major cause of our wasting the talent of good students is our elective system that allows so many good students, and indeed all students, to make bad choices. The smorgasbord curriculum so typical of our schools was created by our decision to universalize secondary education and the consequent assumption on the part of our schoolmen that something besides the traditional academic courses had to be offered to the new kinds of students coming into secondary schools. Over the years, the number of offerings steadily increased until it became possible for students of high ability or low to hop, skip, and jump all over the curricular landscape in response to whatever impulse was in possession of them at the moment. We have had some tightening up in recent years, but it is still entirely possible for good students to make a great many bad decisions and to come out of high school with an incoherent, unsequential, and unrelated collection of courses. It is even more possible for average and below-average students. You are fortunate that this problem is not yet a serious one in your grammar schools. Nor is it as serious in your secondary modern or comprehensive schools as it is with us, but I would guess that the pressures within these schools for electives and a "broadened" curriculum are going to grow apace as you raise the leaving age. The Newsom Report, which I will presently discuss, is an unmistakable sign of these pressures.

Another factor that has penalized the bright student in our schools has been the lack of first-rate specialist teachers. For a lot of reasons I won't detail here, we have trained teachers badly in the United States and even now do not turn out secondary teachers comparable to your graduate teachers in their knowledge of their subject. It is anyone's guess how much the comprehensive school as such is responsible for this failure in teacher training. Probably the failure has been a two-way affair between the school that, being geared to the wide band of average students, has failed to demand high-quality specialist teachers, and the training institutions, which have failed to raise their own standards on their own initiative and thus ultimately to raise the sights of the schools. Again, your grammar-school example may save you, but I would suppose that the movement of the best teachers to industry and to institutions of higher education will be exacerbated by the conversion of grammar to comprehensive schools.

And still another way in which comprehensive schools have handicapped bright students is in restricting their opportunities when they come from lower-class families. As I have mentioned, one of the greatest limitations of our schools in countless communities, which ironically is one of their greatest advantages in countless other communities, is their function as neighborhood schools. Almost all nonboarding schools in any country are necessarily neighborhood schools, but the size of the catchment area is vital. Many a small English grammar school serves a catchment area larger than a big American comprehensive school, and thereby serves the cause of educational justice better for the able student. Consider, for example, the consequences of the relatively small catchment areas that prevail for the schools serving many depressed or backward communities or high-density slum areas of American cities. These schools tend to be badly financed and badly housed, and they find it hard to attract good teachers. Is justice being done the able boy or girl who must attend such a neighborhood school, especially when the state-school system may be the only means he has for lifting himself out of the slum? On the other hand, the neighborhood school can be splendidly housed and financed if the neighborhood happens to be Palo Alto, California, for example, or Newton, Massachusetts. It is this latter kind of school, I am afraid, that most people in Britain take to be typical, especially visiting British educationists who have their tours put together for them by government officials. In truth, the typical school is somewhere between the two types. But many a gifted child has been lost in a poor neighborhood comprehensive school. You might ask if lots of less gifted children are not also lost, and of course the answer is yes; but what justice or wisdom is served by making gifted children share the same fate because they happen to live in the same neighborhood?

All this does not argue against comprehensive schools. I am myself a graduate of a quite typical comprehensive school in a quite typical city of the American Middle West and my sympathies are with this kind of school. Although we still have serious problems of the kind I have outlined to solve in our comprehensive schools, I am certain that our best course is to solve them without the cataclysmic effects of converting to some other system. But our situation is not yours. For you I would argue against what I can only call the ill-considered, headlong rush into a monolithic system of comprehensive schools now being encouraged, indeed commanded, by the government. Not only are there the basic uncertainties about comprehensives that I have mentioned, but quite apart from these there is a strong case to be made in Britain for maintaining multiplicity in types of schools, for avoiding massive standardization as though you were a heterogeneous nation of immigrants as we were, for leaving room for heterodoxy, choice, and dissent even within the state system. And surely there is an even stronger case to be made for the survival of those many schools, both independent and maintained, that have earned over many years a reputation for academic excellence, some of them the envy of half the world. By all means, have comprehensive schools, and do not wait for research to tell you how to do it. But why assume that one type of school, with which you have had little experience, is so superior that it must be made to prevail at all costs throughout the country? Until you can accumulate some experience, why not be content to build comprehensives (as we did in America) in new towns, or in places where for special financial or geographical reasons they offer clear and concrete advantages, or in places where existing institutions of established quality do not have to be sacrificed?

Instead you seem perversely bent on dismantling the whole system you have been building these many years. Your comprehensive spokesmen seem to be saying that the wisdom of going completely comprehensive in as short a time as possible is so self-evident and incontestable that no reasonable man could disagree. The certitude of your comprehensive zealots fills me with awe. You should know even better than America that good schools are not created overnight or by government fiat; they are the end result of many years of work by many people. You should set about reorganizing them and all of the people in them with great care. It is both bizarre and tragic to me to see you now attacking and threatening to destroy your best schools in the name of comprehension. Apparently, not even those unique institutions, the direct-grant schools, are to be spared by this juggernaut. Academically these schools must be among the best the world offers, and socially they are fully as mixed and democratic as thousands of schools in America or anywhere else. For the English people now, with forethought and deliberation, to set about destroying the flower of their educational system seems to me, if I may put it candidly, sheer masochism. It is the triumph of purblind political dogma over educational common sense. I ventured to say as much when I was a visitor to your shores and was accused by John Vaizey, one of your leading comprehensivists, of "intervening" in your politics. There is a long tradition, he thought, of Britons and Americans not doing this—which seems to me a singularly obtuse and unhistorical observation. If anything, there is a long tradition, stretching back at least to the Founding Fathers and beyond, of both parties commenting quite vigorously on one another's politics, a healthy tradition. Any American who was in

England, as I was, during the Goldwater–Johnson presidential campaign would be in no doubt about the volume or the vigor of British comment on American politics, much of it from academics like Mr. Vaizey.

So I find it hard to take very seriously this cant about butting into your political affairs. It is precisely because the decision to go comprehensive was a political decision that you should examine closely the educational arguments put forward to support it. Although it is perhaps too late for you to avoid putting all your eggs in the comprehensive basket, you should at least disabuse yourself of your faith in the magical or curative powers of the comprehensive school. Your expectations of this school may turn out to be wholly unrealistic. You expect it somehow to correct all of the deficiencies that you have for years refused to correct in the present system. The comprehensive school will rescue, you say, those children who would otherwise have been misjudged at 11-plus; it will make for fluid movement within and among streams; it will equalize and extend educational opportunity for all children; it will allow good students to move ahead as well as they would in a grammar school and at the same time encourage the less able by their example; it will develop everybody's capacity for intelligence and make the most of Britain's pool of ability; it will allow economies in buildings and equipment; it will make the services of the best teachers available to all instead of to a narrow band of top students. Most of all, of course, it will bring social equality to England.

But the comprehensive school, as I have suggested, will not necessarily do any of these things, certainly will not do all of them, and probably can never do some of them. Moreover, none of them really has much to do with how schools are organized and administered; let us face the fact that when you have established a monopolistic system of comprehensive schools across the land, you will not have created out of the insubstantial air a lot of new educational resources but only redistributed or rearranged those you already have. Most of the things that need doing in your educational system *could* be done through the existing system of schools and without the upheaval now taking place. For example, the mistakes inevitably made at 11-plus, which you should long ago have done something about, could be corrected just as well, perhaps better, in the present system as in one that is comprehensive, if you would bend your energies to that task. The pool of ability could be plumbed just as deeply, perhaps more so, in separate as in comprehensive schools. The "Newsom children" could be educated just as well, perhaps better, in secondary modern as in comprehensive schools, especially if a number of your educationists, sociologists, and politicians would stop telling the modern schools how awful they are and get busy trying to make all of them as good as the best of them. But all that, I realize, is probably not germane to the present situation. I do not suppose you will modify your comprehensive plans, but I hope you will at least be able to avoid some of our mistakes.

## The Newsom Report and Half Your Future

I summarized the Newsom Report in Chapter III and discussed those aspects of it that are probably of most interest to American readers: the report's unfortunate assumptions about the proper education of what it calls "Half Our Future," by which it means half of the children in school and half of your future adult population. I thought American readers would be interested in comparing the report with similar ones in the United States and with the way in which we in the past have set about educating rather more than half of our future. Here I would like to return to the subject long enough to sound a warning to you again to look at our experience and profit from our mistakes instead of repeating them. Let me again lead with my own biases: I believe that education through the secondary level should stress the basic academic subjects, the primary fields of human knowledge, and in doing so should stress the intellectual development rather than the vocational training or social adjustment of all children, bright, average, and dull. My belief assumes that all children, except the small minority of mentally retarded, can respond to a systematic basic education when it is in the hands of able teachers, and that they are in far greater need of it for the life they must live in this age than they are of training for particular jobs or of school activities designed to adjust them in one way or another to society.

Your Newsom Report is based on precisely the opposite assumption, and my disappointment at reading it was deep. As I made my way through this interesting but verbose and convoluted document, I kept asking myself if it was really going to be necessary for American educational history to repeat itself in every other advanced country of the world. I kept asking myself why you, like the Swedes, should now be proposing to commit all of the mistakes that we committed in the education of our own "Newsom children." I was even more disappointed to see the uncritical reception that this report enjoyed throughout Britain. A few people did comment here and there adversely on it, saying that it had failed "to formulate a basic theory of the educational process" (the same accusation that was made of the Robbins Report) and that it was "obsessed with Technique"; [11] and a socialist publication said of it rather surprisingly:

> While welcoming its focus on the education of more than half of Britain's adolescents, many people deplore the assumptions made about "our children" (as the Newsom Committee queasily calls them) in the report's terms of reference. Paternal, patronizing and wordy, this report has been subtitled "Platitudes for Proles" in at least one staff-room: although rather

alarmingly in some areas it seems to be regarded as breaking new ground.[12]

I would doubt that many people "deplore" the assumptions of the report. On the contrary, most people seem to share the sentiment of the *Guardian* editorial that thought "this report on the twilight children was one of the most powerful and moving documents in the history of British education." [13] And indeed the report is full of strong emotional appeal, calling attention to the need to do more than you have done about the education of the average and below-average student. But what the report recommends you do is pretty much what we have been doing for many years and what we are now beginning, I hope, to undo.

The report seems to me in fundamental conflict with itself. It begins admirably enough by supporting the idea that children in the lower half of the school population have been underrated by the schools, but it then goes on to spell out an education for them that is certainly no compliment to their underrated powers. The report also begins, less admirably, with the highly dubious hypothesis that intelligence is "largely an acquired characteristic" and that the abilities of half the school population have lain undeveloped because of the school's faulty beliefs about the innate limitations of these children; but it then devotes the remainder of its pages to exploring and recommending exactly the kind of education that schools would undertake if they did indeed believe in these limitations. In this curious way the report goes well beyond the now-condemned premise of the old Spens Report of 1938, not to say the Hadow Report of 1926, that children could be divided with reasonable accuracy into groups based on their inherent abilities and then given different educations appropriate to these abilities. Far from believing that intelligence can be acquired, the Newsom Report, so it seems to me, is based on the idea that the Newsom children are different not in degree but in kind from the upper half and must therefore have a different kind of education. The fault, it seems, is not in themselves but in their stars that they must settle not only for something less in the way of education but something quite different. The report might well have been subtitled not "Platitudes for Proles," but with an old Spanish proverb about the University of Salamanca: "What God does not give, Salamanca doesn't either." The Newsom assumption is that God does not give enough to at least half your children for them to be able to profit much from a secondary education centered on the fundamental subjects, which, in fact, are the most vocational of all and which they may never study again if they fail to do so in school.

Far too many of your educators accept this assumption themselves. Here is the head of one of your Institutes of Education saying:

If enough teachers of the right quality and right training (for this is clearly at fault to a large measure) cannot be found at present, it is far better for these adolescents in Secondary Modern Schools to escape at the age of 15 from the clutches of the mock-academics who are feeding them with a mild and water version of the Grammar School syllabus, and go out to work.[14]

Here is a Public School man musing on what might be done in the independent schools with lower-class, lower-IQ kids if they are to be "integrated" into these schools:

> To suggest that there is nothing which we *can* teach to children of this type after a certain age seems absurdly pessimistic: the difficulty is rather that owing to our narrow view of education we are bankrupt of ideas. If, for instance, there is a strong desire amongst adolescent children of this group to learn a skilled trade which will bring them in good money when they leave, let them be taught this at school—in a community which will enable them to develop psychologically at the same time—by being part-time apprentices. Every child has something in which it is really interested: the important thing is not to exclude this interest from the system. This is perhaps most obvious with adolescent girls. Most adolescent girls are interested in men, clothes, and cosmetics. This seems very right and proper; very well, let them be taught about these.[15]

Once accept this view of educational purpose and you will join a lot of yesteryear's educators in the United States, who were, as one of our distinguished clerics and educators, Canon Bernard Iddings Bell, said a few years ago, "as confused as the rest of mankind about the nature of the good life. They cannot civilize the Common Man's children because they have surrendered to the Common Man." [16] You and most of the countries of Europe now face the same enormous problem that faced us in America when we universalized upper-secondary education: What kind of schooling should or can be given the masses of children staying on in school for another year or two or three? We were not ready to meet the problem in the earlier part of the century, and neither is Britain or Europe now. We jumped to the wrong conclusion because it was the easiest one, and so is England. We decided that the majority of students being kept on by law to sixteen and then to eighteen, whose parents had not stayed in school that long and who had no particular educational help from home, had neither the ability nor the desire to "profit from" (the usual phrase) the traditional academic curriculum. Obviously, said our educators, they needed something else. But what? Well, the reasoning went, they were interested in jobs, clothes, cars, movies, and the opposite sex, and so we should teach them something constructive about these things; and, since they were all future citizens and founders of homes, they must be made interested, if possible, in "Citizenship" and "Home-making." This blinkered view of the educational potential of the majority of children was shared alike, I regret to say, by great numbers of parents, teachers, and educational administrators. The underlying assumption was a kind of modernized Platonism that divided children neatly by their IQ's and that many of your educators possibly deplore when it appears in other places in the educational system. The assumption turned out to be what in the current sociological jargon would be called "a self-fulfilling prophecy."

Over the first decades of this century, but particularly between the two world wars, American schools followed this dim, deterministic philosophy and created an ever-increasing variety of offerings for the American Newsom children whose abilities were allegedly too limited to permit them to grapple with geometry or physics or French. Our educators began to broaden the curriculum at the secondary level with many subjects never before found in schools and with which teachers had no fund of experience upon which to draw. Soon in the typical secondary school, instruction was available in a galaxy of vocational, secretarial, homemaking, and "distributive" skills, some of which stretched the word "skill" a very long way. There was also an array of courses or units of study that were neither vocational nor academic, but that dealt with personal problems, with adjusting to oneself, one's family, one's friends, one's community, and one's future husband or wife or children. We developed, that is, the smorgasbord curriculum complete with a free choice of items.

What was it like for the Newsom children going to such schools? For that matter, what was it like for a great many others? The smorgasbord curriculum was by no means limited to the lower half, but allowed countless of the best and the good students to make bad choices. Well, my own career as a student in a typical Midwestern American comprehensive school at the end of the 1930's illustrates as well as anything I can think of the lengths to which the new, or perhaps I should say the Newsom, education had gone by that time. Without inflicting on you the details of my secondary education, which you might find hard to believe, let me just set forth the salient facts. My secondary school was exactly the type that Britain is busily building, a large comprehensive institution serving as the neighborhood school for virtually all children within a residential radius of two or three miles. The catchment area encompassed all kinds of lower-class and middle-class homes, more naturally of the former than the latter but representing a pretty good cross section of American society. The education I received there was quite typical of that received by most of my friends and by at least half, I should think, of the students in that school and in most schools of its kind around the country.

My program of studies, which was not so much a program as an indiscriminate potpourri, was one to warm the heart of the Newsom Committee. Throughout my years at the school I spent perhaps forty percent of my time in subjects that had academic titles like English, History, Biology, and "Civics." The titles, however, were misnomers—in America we often confuse the names of courses with their contents—for the work had little connection with any sort of organized study of any knowledge of consequence. Both the staff and the school administration assumed that most working-class students by definition had no need of serious study, no ability for serious study, were not interested in it and could not be made interested in it. These were just the facts of life and not to be altered by man. I was in what was called the "Commercial" program. This was, I think, the largest stream in the school, into which went most of the students who were not taking a secretarial-clerical course or not headed for higher education. The aim in the Commercial program was to keep students engaged in something that might be called purposeful activity, hopefully related in some tenuous way to the name of the course. In English we rarely wrote anything but we read newspapers, magazines, and third-rate short stories and talked about our favorite radio programs. In History we read cowboy stories to learn about how it was in the West in the old days, but actually spent the bulk of class time in a sort of generalized bull session on "current events," that ubiquitous friend of all teachers; since we had no historical background to tell us how an important current event came to be important, we often wound up talking about sports. What was essential in the eyes of the school was to keep us occupied, off the labor market for a few years, out of trouble, and as happy as possible.

The other sixty percent of my time was spent in courses that were considered by the school to be "vocational," a euphemism to cover activity in everything from the repair of cars to the repair of "personal relationships" (a topic I seem to recollect). Again, I think the Newsom Committee would applaud my vocational studies, which were related, as they recommend throughout their report, to my outside interests and activities and which therefore changed with great rapidity. If the object, that is, of the Newsom-type of education is to relate schoolwork to life outside the school, I suppose that object was achieved in my case, for my school counselor, a kindly man, insisted always on finding something in the school's offerings to complement my life outside. One term I would do a course in "Salesmanship" because I had a job peddling ice cream after school; another term I would do a course in "Bookkeeping" because I had a job after school busing dishes in a hotel (my staff advisor saw some relationship between these two activities that always remained rather mystical to me—anyhow I flunked the course, and that was not easy to do); another term I would do a course in "Merchandising" because I had a job in the incoming freight department of a dime store. I will not trouble the reader with a discussion of the content of these courses, for in all honesty I cannot remember a single thing of importance that transpired in any of them.

I stumped my advisor on one occasion. In answer to his invariable question at the beginning of each term—"What do you want to be?"—I can still remember answering, having got a job several weeks before as an usher in a theater and having picked up a new word there, "I want to be a theater magnate." He said that maybe I had a practical bent, and so signed me up for a course in "Shop" (that is, manual training). I stumped him even more when I went on later to a job as a lifeguard at the local swimming pool, for there was nothing in even the smorgasbord curriculum that seemed relevant to that; and he finally gave up altogether when I started working in an abattoir for chickens. During my last year in the school it became clear that the United States would get involved in the war in Europe and I, having a passionate interest in airplanes, decided that I would join the Army Air Forces and become a pilot. My advisor thought this a wholly irrational ambition in view of my scholastic record and nonexistent prospects for college, but he signed me up anyhow for a new course in "Aviation," in which we all had an extremely pleasant time making model airplanes, chatting about things aviational, and visiting the airport. Presumably the school was thereby allowing me to continue to relate my studies to my "felt needs," as the Newsom Report everywhere urges.

Thus I emerged from my secondary schooling with no work whatever in mathematics (not even algebra, not even "general math"), no work in physics or chemistry, and no work of substance in English, history, a foreign language, or any other basic subject. My "academic" program of studies in the secondary school turned out to be about the least useful possible, having a highly negative relevance to higher education. (At the same time, I am profoundly grateful for the range of opportunity and the open-door policy of American education that allowed me to proceed to college and later to doctoral study and a university career.) Of the allegedly vocational work I did I can say with great certainty that none of it contributed in anything but a negative way to anything I have done since leaving school. As far as I can recall, I took two courses throughout my four years of secondary school that subsequently proved of value, the one in "Shop" where I learned something useful about tools, and one in "Typewriting" where I learned the rudiments of a skill upon which I am now hopelessly dependent. A debater might say, I suppose, that this only proves the wisdom of "practical" courses, but two good dishes out of twenty from the smorgasbord would close most restaurants.

I review this appalling history of miseducation with you not because it is unusual, but precisely because it is typical of the education received by countless numbers of students of my generation and because you seem to me in great danger of going the same way. Don't think this kind of schooling was a temporary aberration or that in these more enlightened days it has been eradicated from American schools. Once established, the Newsom approach to education has great tenacity, for over the years it creates, among many things, some very powerful entrenched interests among teachers, administrators, and professional associations. The Newsom education is still very much with us. We reached a kind of educational nadir at about war's end. In 1945 the United States Office of Education called a national conference in Washington to consider the education of the same part of the student population that was to be the concern of the Newsom Committee nearly twenty years later. Toward the end of its deliberations this conference adopted unanimously a resolution now known as the "Prosser Resolution" after the man who introduced it. This resolution took about the dimmest view possible of the intellectual abilities of American students. The gist of it was that only twenty percent of American students could profit from an academic, college-preparatory course of study in our high schools; that the next twenty percent should be given extensive vocational training for skilled trades; and that the remaining sixty percent, something more than half our future, could do little in the way of either academic or vocational study, but instead they were to get a good deal of what was significantly called "life-adjustment training."

If you are still in doubt about what life-adjustment training is, you could refer to a volume published a short time later by the Office of Education, *Life Adjustment Education for Every Youth* (note the "every"), and based on this and subsequent conferences. There you would learn, for instance, that

> every youth must learn to shop effectively, but economically, and use well what he has bought . . . [students should learn in school to use leisure time and this embraces] developing and matching of skills in boxing, wrestling, and fencing: games such as checkers, bridge, billiards, ping-pong, chess, horseshoe pitching . . . [students should] participate in a wide variety of coeducational activities to establish relationships which will lead to intelligent selection of mates and to living happily with them . . . to understand the function of the family . . . to use skills and understandings related to the budgeting, decorating, and furnishing of the home . . . the school should be responsible for meeting many of the immediate social needs of students. Social interrelationships should be planned and help should be given in the pursuance of these interrelationships. Parties, dances, teas, luncheons, picnics, clubs . . .[17]

Elsewhere in the book, which was supposed to be and which unfortunately became a sort of guide to curriculum development in the same way that the Newsom Report is now being used in Britain, we learn that training was to be given in schools in things like "safe living," "personal grooming," "hospitality," "boy and girl problems," and a legion of other nonsubjects. Thus the school, the only institution of society equipped to give organized instruction to all children in the basic subjects of human knowledge, was no longer to confine itself to this task, but was to become a social-service center taking over many of the functions of industry, of the home, the church, the youth club, and the community. If you hear echoes in all this by now, you are merely remembering the similar recommendations of the Newsom Report.

I can hear many British parents and schoolmen asking with raised eyebrows just what is wrong with it. I can hear them sniffing at the idea of inflicting Shakespeare or French or magnetic fields on future barmaids and bus drivers. They may feel that dustmen and dukes should go to school in the same building but are sure they should not get the same education. So let me say, first, that, yes, it is a perfectly sound and worthy goal for schools to help bus drivers read Shakespeare and barmaids to read French. But second let me also say that I am not suggesting the Newsom approach is without merit, nor am I suggesting that the Newsom children should have an exclusively academic diet. There is room and need for many of them, as well as many brighter students, to get some training in the basic skills of working with wood or metal or cloth or food if it can be kept subordinated to their academic studies, which they need far more, and can be well-constructed work in principles and fundamental processes (which it often is not). Nor would I attempt to gainsay the Newsom program for those students who have a persistent contempt for school and who repulse with surliness if not violence every attempt of the school to educate them. And I am sure that for the foreseeable future the school in any mass system of education will not be able to get through to some students, no matter what activity is invented for them.

What I am saying is that the basic attitude of the school toward the Newsom children is all-important, since it conditions everything that happens to them in the school. If it is negative and based on the assumption that they cannot really be educated but only trained and entertained, then that becomes probably the most reliable "self-fulfilling prophecy" one can make. If it is positive and expectant, based on the assumption that the vast majority of children can respond to an academic program when it is in the hands of good teachers, that too would become a self-fulfilling prophecy, as indeed it has proved to be in a number of slum areas of American cities. In short, the contrary assumption to that of the Newsom Report seems to me the only one that holds any promise for half of Britain's future: that education through the secondary level should stress the basic subjects, the primary fields of knowledge, the most truly "vocational" knowledge possible in this age, and in doing so should stress the intellectual development rather than the job training or social adjustment of all children, bright, average, and dull. I think your wartime Norwood Report put the matter admirably when it said:

> We believe that education cannot stop short of recognizing the ideals of truth and beauty and goodness as final and binding for all times and in all places, as ultimate values; we do not believe that these ideals are of temporary convenience only, as devices for holding together society till they can be dispensed with as knowledge grows and organization becomes more scientific. . . . We have no sympathy, therefore, with a theory of education which presupposes that its aim can be dictated by the provisional findings of special Sciences, whether biological, psychological, or sociological, that the function of education is to fit pupils to determine their outlook and conduct according to the changing needs and the changing standards of the day . . . our belief is that education from its own nature must be ultimately concerned with values which are independent of time or particular environment, though realizable under changing forms in both, and, therefore, that no programs of education which concern themselves only with relative ends and the immediate adaptation of the individual to existing surroundings can be acceptable.[18]

I would urge you to look carefully at the evolution of theory and practice in American schools before deciding on the future of the Newsom children. Look, for example, at the record of our attempts at "citizenship education," which we based on the un-Socratic idea that virtue in its various aspects is something that can be taught. You might listen to the cogent observations of one of your own educators after he had spent some time looking at American schools:

> . . . you cannot teach patriotism by adjurations to be patriotic; you cannot teach citizenship by moral homilies; you cannot teach democracy by setting up microcosms of local government in school; you cannot teach equality by including children of diverse abilities in the same class. These, and other desirable qualities, like truth, honesty, justice, and generosity, are learnt if they are learnt at all, in the ambient atmosphere that should, through the personalities of parents and teachers, pervade the school and the home; they are learnt gradually, from infancy, in ten thousand instances of precept and example, often far removed from the immediate moral. A child will learn—and, contrary to the Rousseau school, he has to learn—to be good by being surrounded by people who are good and who expect goodness in return; he will learn to develop his intelligence by being surrounded by people who are intelligent and who keep him up to the mark. To use the school as a vehicle for imparting moral attitudes is not only morally wrong—what Bernard Shaw called abortion—it is socially self-defeating . . .[19]

You might also look at our vocational education, which is far more extensive than anything yet found in your secondary modern schools, and ask yourself if the Newsom Committee is really right in putting this kind of instruction at the head of the list for the average and below-average students in the age of automation and lightning technological change when the advanced nations are all worried about "retraining" large segments of the labor force whose skills are outmoded. You might listen to Robert Maynard Hutchins commenting on what we can expect in America if we persist with the vocationalism that has become a major characteristic of our secondary-school system:

> . . . education has never been as job-oriented as it is today. This is a melancholy instance of the general truth that a doctrine seldom gains acceptance until it is obsolete.
>
> The doctrine never was any good. In any country that has a highly mobile population and a rapidly changing technology, the more specifically education is directed to jobs, the more ineffective it is bound to be. Today such education is patently absurd. Everybody is aware that the official rate of unemployment among young people is double that among adults. The actual rate is undoubtedly higher, because many young people have thought it useless to apply for work. The general reaction to this situation borders on fantasy: it is to propose widespread extension of vocational training. In short, the cure for the disease of no jobs is training for them.[20]

The question of priorities is always preeminent in education. It is even more important in Britain than America since you have less time available in which to educate the majority of your people. Among the hundreds of good and useful things that people would like to have done to, or for, or with, secondary students, you must decide what are the most important things that should be attempted in the limited time available. To come at the question negatively, I submit that the kind of vocational training plumped for in Newsom is obsolete and self-defeating; even if it were not, schools are not the best places for it. I submit further that the adjustment courses the Newsom Committee recommends in such unlimited variety are a travesty of its own deeply felt desire to do something to combat the "underprivilege" of the Newsom children. These children deserve better of the school than a patronizing program of amateur therapy or busywork on hobbies or phony social graces: Even the dullest of students does not really need to come to school to be instructed in such tribal trivia as how to comb his hair, behave on dates, eat in restaurants, use the telephone (which, come to think of it, is not a simple skill in Britain), pick out neckties, or come in out of the rain.

Before it is too late, you should try to decide why you are determined to raise the leaving age to sixteen in 1971, a fearfully expensive step that will consume funds badly needed elsewhere in education. I applaud the step, but cannot help wondering what is really going to be gained if the added year is to be governed by the educational philosophy of the Newsom Report. Let the school worry less about adjusting the Newsom children to the modern world; let the school unadjust them, show them something better than they know outside school, and develop their mental resources so that they have a chance to cope with the speed of change in modern industry and with their equally changing social environment. Let the schools, in the words of your Michael Sadler, "give children and youth new things to love and admire," not seek to recapitulate the last forty years of American experience. In a word, let the school give the Newsom children bread and not stones.

These, then, are some of the important problems upon which American education might throw some light. There are many others I would like to discuss with you: your failure, for instance, to educate your women as well or as long as you should; your failure to involve parents in the work of your schools to anything like the degree you should; your failure, like ours but greater, to make elementary information about your schools and universities easily available to parents, most of whom have not the slightest idea about how to secure such information, if indeed it exists; your failure to give a higher priority to school and college libraries; and sundry other subjects upon which I have not touched in this book. But I began this chapter by talking about priorities, and I repeat that the most important thing for you to do as you advance toward the last quarter of this apocalyptic century is to give thought to what it is you want your schools to accomplish. In the process of doing that, I hope you will redirect your welcome sense of urgency in education.

You should stop being intimidated by those sociologists or politicians who invent words like "meritocracy" and who attack your schools for fostering an "intellectual aristocracy." You can take pride in the quality of your "meritocratic" schools that have already gone a long way toward creating an intellectual aristocracy to which the gentlemen who denounce it happily and prosperously belong. You should be indulgent, I suppose, when your educationists say, for instance, that you "need to create a much wider aristocracy—of those who excel in the art of social living. This the American school consciously sets out to achieve." [21] You should forget about teaching people unteachable or incomprehensible things like "the art of social living" and concentrate on trying to bring all of your schools as close to the level of your best ones as possible. You should stop sweating so much about where snobs and rich men send their sons to school, and where many not so rich, and not so snobbish, and even Labor Lords, send their sons to school. You should stop attacking the best of your maintained, independent, and direct-grant institutions, which include many schools that any other nation would be delighted to have. You should stop quarreling with educational excellence as though it were a reprehensible thing, or merely because everybody can't have it right now. In a word, you should take the revolver from your own head and save yourself for the greatest of all the problems that confront you: how to get and keep first-rate teachers—in decent classrooms—with classes of reasonable size—throughout the country—for the extended schooling in fundamental subjects of all children. That problem will dwarf any others for a considerable time to come.

# Sweden — Paradise for Planners

INSPIRED by both economic necessity and political conviction, Sweden over the last twenty years has put into effect a vast program of educational reform, well beyond anything yet attempted by other countries. She is reconstructing and expanding her selective and very traditional school and university system in order to open as many academic doors for as many students as possible. In doing so, she hopes not only to meet her requirements for skilled manpower but to make Swedish society even more democratic and egalitarian than it now is. Her success or failure has great implications for the rest of Europe, which looks at Sweden with admiration and envy, not only in education but in economic development and industrial relations, and regards her as the most modern and progressive state in Western Europe.

Let me first describe the reforms themselves that are taking place in Swedish education, so as to give some idea of the magnitude of change involved, and then examine how and why these reforms were adopted. The first and most important reform is in the compulsory common school. Before World War II, Sweden had a dual educational system in the familiar European mold, a six- or seven-year *folkskola* that for a minority of selected students led at the end of either four or six years to an academic secondary education in a *realskola* and later in a *gymnasium*. Most children, however, remained in the folk school to the end and after that received training in some kind of part-time continuation school. Later, at perhaps age eighteen, a few went on to further general education in a folk high school.

In 1950 the Riksdag, the Swedish parliament, made a preliminary decision and in 1962 a final decision to supplant the folk school with a nine-year comprehensive school compulsory for all children. This school was to be free of external examinations (that is, national tests), was to stress freedom of choice for parents and pupils, and was to make use of "modern" teaching methods in place of what some would regard as a traditional *ex cathedra* methodology. The Swedes call it a *grundskola*, literally a "basic" or "foundation" school, although the last three years of it can be considered a kind of lower secondary school. For convenience, suppose we call it simply the comprehensive school. By 1970 virtually all children between ages seven and sixteen will be in the comprehensive school and will follow it to the end before moving on to secondary education or to the labor market.

In brief, the nine-year comprehensive school is organized in three "departments" of three years each. Swedish and mathematics predominate in the Lower Department; music, art, handicraft subjects, history, civics, and geography are given an increasing amount of time in the Middle Department. English, by the way, is a compulsory subject for all students from grades four through seven, and the great majority elect to continue with it after that. No tracking or grouping by ability as well as by choice is permitted in either the Lower or the Middle Department. This homogeneous pattern is broken, however, in the Upper Department. Pupils are divided by ability in the seventh and eighth grades in English and mathematics and divided further according to certain elective subjects. They are divided still further in the ninth grade, divided in fact in a way that to many people inside and outside Sweden seems ludicrous. There are nine tracks into which pupils can go, chiefly on the basis of choice. Five of them are classified as "theoretical" tracks with a compulsory academic program for about eighty percent of the time, and four are "practical" with compulsory academic subjects only forty percent of the time. This atomization of the last year of the comprehensive school reflects a political compromise, the "Agreement of Visby," wherein the Liberals and the Socialists resolved in 1960 their political rather than their educational differences over the reform of the common school.

In 1964, the Swedish parliament, having completed this reform and faced with the fact that by 1966 half the sixteen-year-olds in the country would be finishing their compulsory education in the new comprehensive schools, passed into law an extensive reform of secondary education. This is a reform of great complexity in which many details are still unclear, but it is built on the same social and political ideas as is the comprehensive school. The present secondary system in Sweden is divided between a *gymnasium* offering several different and specialized academic programs to a selected student body, and a profusion of other schools and programs, often part of the same *gymnasium*, offering vocational and technical training to an unselected student body. The reform will:

1. Expand the selective secondary school to accept thirty to thirty-five percent of all children coming from the comprehensive school.
2. Reorganize the selective secondary school by abolishing separate

programs as they now exist and creating in their place a common curriculum that will extend in diminishing fashion through the three-year
course and consume about half the total time, with five lines of specialization for the other half. The hope is to increase thereby the amount of
general education and postpone specialization, two complementary steps
that are given great emphasis by the planners.

3. Create a number of two-year *fackskolor,* or continuation schools, that
will offer a combination of practical and academic subjects to twenty to
twenty-five percent of the age group finishing the comprehensive
school.

4. Expand an existing system of vocational schools to offer a variety of
training to twenty to thirty percent of those completing the comprehensive
school.

This reform technically came into effect in the autumn of 1966, and by
1970 the Swedes confidently expect the vast majority of young people to
enroll voluntarily in full-time secondary education after their compulsory
schooling.

The third dimension of Sweden's reform is teacher training. Realizing
that school reforms could succeed only to the extent that teachers were
able to put them into action, the Swedes appointed a national committee
in 1960 with instructions to examine the organization of teacher training;
these instructions were later extended to include the content as well. In
September 1965 this committee brought in a report that, like the Robbins
Report, can only be called massive, and whose recommendations were
described by the committee's secretary, Sixten Marklund, as "radical."
The main report was 714 pages. There were five supporting volumes
printed for distribution and discussion in Sweden, and there were further
volumes of data not distributed. Marklund spent three years of full-time
work on this report and had a staff for much of that time of up to fifteen
persons. And all this for a school system that has about 50,000 teachers
all told.

With minor variations, teachers are now trained in Sweden in a dual
system characteristic of Europe: Teachers for the compulsory grades are
trained in one of twenty-four teachers colleges and in programs that vary
according to the age and schooling of the entering students. Teachers for
secondary schools are trained at the universities in the several academic
departments or faculties. Marklund's committee, again a little like the
Robbins Committee, recommended that all teachers at all levels matricu-
late in Schools of Education that would be affiliated with universities,
thus in effect recommending the dissolution or conversion of the teachers
colleges. Teachers for grades one to six of the comprehensive school
would receive all their training in the School of Education, with the
cooperation, one hopes, of the academic departments of the university;
teachers for grades seven through the last year of the secondary school

would receive their subject-matter training in the university and their pedagogical training in the School of Education.

A further recommendation was for the creation of a policy committee, a *skolämneskollegium,* for each subject in the teacher-training curriculum, with representatives from the academic department involved, from the School of Education, from practicing teachers, and from students themselves. It would probably not occur to an American institution to have students or for that matter classroom teachers represented on such a body, but it is traditional in Sweden. A similar kind of policy committee was also recommended for each of the larger divisions of school subjects, such as the humanities or the sciences.

The Director General of the Royal Board of Education, Hans Löwbeer, who can best be described as the chief educational administrator of Sweden, expects the parliament to approve most of the Marklund committee's recommendations. When it does, the principal changes in teacher training will be those that most of the nations of Europe discuss but find more difficult to realize: an end to the intellectual and geographical isolation of the small, single-purpose college for teachers; the beginning of a training for teachers specifically designed to meet the problems of the new and expanded common school; an active role in teacher training for members of the academic faculty; and the imposition of pedagogical training on teachers headed for the academic secondary schools.

Finally, to ensure that its reforms stretch from the bottom to the top of its educational ladder, Sweden has a number of committees now working on changes that need to be made in the universities if these institutions are to play the kind of enlarged role that is implied for them in all the other reforms. Universities in Europe are always the hardest nut for the planner to crack. Their faculties tend to disapprove of the liberalizing reforms of the lower schools and certainly of the academic secondary schools, they have little interest in teacher training as such, they are not fond of educational bureaucrats and administrators, and they have plenty of independence and power with which to oppose what they don't like. All these conditions are perhaps as true of Sweden as of Germany or Italy. Moreover, the universities in Sweden were not closely involved or consulted in the previous reform decisions in Swedish education. But typically the Swedes have now created a new national planning agency for higher education, run by Nils Gustav Rosén, who came to this sensitive job from many years of experience as Director General of the Board of Education. He has money and authority and political backing.

Among the reforms that Rosén and his supporters have in mind for the universities are these: (1) an admissions system based on the student's general performance during the last year of his secondary education, including his scores on a number of standardized tests, and not, as it is now, on a single comprehensive national test, *studentexamen,* at the end of the selective secondary school—this reform is already adopted and will come into effect in 1969; (2) a reduction in the time needed to take the first degree, which can now extend to six or seven years; (3) a reduction in the high attrition rate of students; (4) an overhaul of university teaching methods, though nobody in Sweden knows how *that* can be done; (5) introduction of a new faculty rank specifically designed as a teaching rather than a research post; and (6) expansion to make room for fully sixty percent more students within the next four years.

These, then, are the bare bones of the Swedish reforms. Taken together they are an astonishing phenomenon. Other countries may have put into effect a reform similar to one or another of those in Sweden, but I can think of no nation that has done so much in so short a time or that has any prospect of it. By 1970 Sweden in the space of twenty years will have effected a fundamental reconstruction of every level of her educational system. One should emphasize that these reforms go far deeper than organizational matters. That at least is the planners' intention. They involve both a change of purpose in Swedish education and a change of teaching method. It is therefore important for one to look not merely at what the reforms are but at the reasons Sweden undertook them.

Despite her neutral status during World War II and her freedom from bomb damage and Nazi occupation, Sweden was driven by that conflagration to the same kind of searching examination of her educational institutions that engaged some of the Allies. But in contrast to, say, France, she had both the will and the resources to act as well as to contemplate and discuss. The prosperity of postwar Europe, which had strong implications everywhere for education, was especially apparent in Sweden. Her economy was booming, she had full employment and unsatisfied demands for skilled labor, she had the ingredients of severe industrial conflict of the kind that has plagued Britain since the war, and she had a socialist-welfare state whose share of the gross national product continued to grow until it stabilized at about thirty-five percent. To Swedish politicians and planners, all this meant, if Sweden were to continue to prosper in a strife-free atmosphere, that the remaining sources of class distinction and social privilege had to be eliminated, the virtues of cooperation and communal life emphasized more than ever, and the supply of trained manpower increased. All this in turn meant the reform of her education system, which they felt continued to reflect elements of an outmoded society of restrictions and artificial barriers, and to be controlled by a curriculum too narrow and a pedagogy too rigid for a modern system of mass education.

Many reformers saw the new education in a more reciprocal relationship to society than do most Western nations. They saw the new education, rather like some American reformers of the 1930's, as both a reflection of society and as a major instrument for changing that society. Thus Jonas Orring, Deputy Director General of the Board of Education and a central figure in the reform movement, puts it this way: "For both the individual and society, the school reform is thus in effect a radical social reform." In talking with many Swedes about the reasons for the reform, I found that certain themes kept recurring. The most common one was the importance of developing a democratic school system. "Democratic" was not sharply defined but it was clear that most of them had in mind a kind of homogenized educational system in which all children would attend the same school and in which as many distinctions as possible—whether of dress, position, home background, *or* of intelligence and accomplishment—would be blurred. Other themes repeated themselves: the importance of achieving social justice in Sweden; of equalizing educational opportunity among classes and regions; of giving students and parents as much freedom of choice in as many ways as possible; of teaching Swedes to respect all occupations equally and to live cooperatively and harmoniously with themselves and all other nations.

If some of these lofty ideals strike a reminiscent chord, circa 1935, to an American ear, it should be recorded that American influence has been considerable in Swedish educational reform, as it has been in Swedish life generally. The sound of American education is heard, for example, in the range of elective subjects of the new comprehensive school and in the stress given to parental choice; in a policy of automatic promotion; in the increasing use of standardized tests; in the formation of the new continuation schools, which take much from the American junior college; and in the ascendancy of electronic education and the new technology of education. Sweden even has a "Trump Committee" at work investigating the possible adaptations to Swedish schools of the organizational ideas of the American educationist J. Lloyd Trump. But most of all, the influence of American education comes through in any discussion of aims for the comprehensive school and of the teaching methods by which these aims are to be realized. Even the terminology in which the discussion goes on seems borrowed. One feels the shock of recognition when reading, for example, from an official Board of Education pamphlet on the new schools of Sweden, that "the right of every person to an all-round development of his personality, talents and interests is fundamental to the aims of the new comprehensive school . . . [and that] the school must contribute towards making young people worthy members of a rapidly developing society." [1]

Or consider these thoughts, which I string together from a book by Jonas Orring. The book is his summary of the findings and philosophy of the 1957 School Committee in Sweden, of which he was secretary, and which was the most important single body involved in creating the new comprehensive school:

. . . the school should be more pupil centered and rather less subject-matter oriented than formerly . . . the work of the school must be based on respect for the personality and individuality of each pupil. This is in keeping with the fundamental democratic conception that all human beings are equal in value, regardless of their capabilities in one direction or another . . . The aim of the school must be primarily to help each pupil to achieve an all-round development of his gifts and interests—his personality . . . To strengthen the feeling of responsibility, duty and pleasure in family life should also be one of the tasks of the compulsory school . . . The aim of the school is also to foster good social habits. One of its most important tasks is to help young people to learn the difficult art of corporate life . . . This teaching should, starting from the pupil himself, include the home, the school, intercourse with school-fellows, societies and associations, work, and community, the State and the world. Social training should be organized with due regard to the rapid changes that are a feature of modern society . . . Social and human factors are just as important for the individual and society in the world of today and tomorrow as are intellectual ones. The greatest of current problems is the inability of people to live and work happily together—not to attain new and greater intellectual performances.[2]

Reading this, one is reminded of nothing so much as the airy doctrines of yesteryear's progressives and life-adjusters in the United States. One can only wish the Swedes more luck than we have had in their efforts at "citizenship education," "education for democracy," "education for international understanding," "education for social competence," education by way of pupil-centered pedagogy and the unfettered development of personality. But I confess to an unhappy feeling that they are far more likely to recapitulate the last thirty or forty years of American experience.

The basic decision in Sweden to create the comprehensive school was a political decision, no doubt properly so. "Every big school reform," as Hans Löwbeer observes, "is on the first hand social and political." This decision was taken by the parliament in 1950 with a substantial majority vote and was not based on educational or psychological research. Describing the reasons for the introduction of the comprehensive system, Torsten Husén, of the School of Education of the University of Stockholm and one of the leading and most prolific spokesmen for the reform of Swedish education, quotes this statement from the then Minister of Education:

A work of reform which is intended to bridge the old gaps between social classes must see to it that the school system appears to all groups in society as a unitary construction, within which there are available and open ways for all young people and where each growing individual, independent of his social starting point in life, will have the opportunity to learn how he can best utilize his potentialities for his future tasks. Such a goal cannot be compatible with an overt or disguised parallel school system. A differentiation into separate schools should not, according to my conviction, take place until it is necessary with regard to vocational choice.[3]

The same statement could have been written by the Ministers of Education in England or Italy or France. Implementation of the decision to create a comprehensive system, however, was delayed for political reasons and to give time for research into how, not whether, the comprehensive school could best be created. The order of events, that is, was similar to what it has been in England, where the big debate about comprehensive schools is now going on in the same way that it did in Sweden in the 1950's. In England, the decision to "go" comprehensive has also been a political decision, taken at first by a few Labor-controlled Local Education Authorities, notably London and Leicestershire, and followed fitfully by others over the last twenty years. In November 1964, comprehensive education was enunciated as national policy by the Labor government. In July 1965, the same government issued a directive to all the local authorities to submit plans by the summer of 1966 for going comprehensive. And in September 1965, the same government announced the first major research project to be undertaken in Britain on comprehensive education. To those who feel that this reverses the logical order of things, British supporters of the comprehensive school are apt to point to certain Swedish experiments which are often cited as evidence of the superiority of the comprehensive system.

What are these experiments? One of the most interesting and important was done over a five-year period in the Stockholm schools, under the direction of Nils-Eric Svensson, who now heads a new "Research Planning Bureau" in the Royal Board of Education. In the mid-1950's the Stockholm schools offered the educational investigator a very rare commodity: a clear-cut research situation, at least more clear-cut than the so-called behavioral sciences can usually find or create. Because of teacher and classroom shortages, the Stockholm school board in 1954 divided the eight-year public schools of North and South Stockholm in such a way as to create three distinct patterns, in one of which pupils were tracked on a competitive basis after the fourth grade, in another after the sixth grade, and in the third not at all. In other words, the situation made possible a comparison of comprehensive, untracked education with two different tracks of pupils separated by ability at different times, all between grades four and nine within the same system and among pupils of comparable home background. The research took the form of machine-scored intelligence and achievement tests in each type of class over an extended period of time.

The results, as I read Svensson's report of the experiment, indicated very little difference among the groups tested.[4] However, some experts, like Husén, interpret the results more optimistically and say that while the brighter pupils were not in the end handicapped in untracked classes, the duller ones were helped.[5] Either way, the results suggest, or perhaps "prove" if you have faith in the reliability of educational research in the present state of its development, that separation of children by academic ability does not pay off—up to the tenth grade, in a school population like Stockholm's, with a staff of similar training and outlook to that of the Stockholm schools, and with the other principal conditions of the experiment duplicated. The trouble of course is that these things never can be duplicated in the behavioral sciences, and findings cannot be "proved out" by other researchers in other places.

Further research projects were undertaken at the same time in Sweden to compare the "efficiency" of the comprehensive school with that of the traditional one. The results were indefinite. Some experiments that seemed to favor tracking are said by Husén to be flawed in technical ways that make their conclusions "almost completely irrelevant." [6] Others were never finished. In short, Swedish research comparing comprehensive with selective education produced little concrete or compelling evidence for or against. The parliament nevertheless considered the social and political arguments in favor of the comprehensive school far more weighty than any educational arguments against it, and in 1962 confirmed its 1950 decision and gave final form to the comprehensive school. Sven Moberg, Under Secretary of State in the Ministry of Education, puts the chronology this way: "We tried to get a clear picture from the psychologists and scientists, but they could not give an absolutely clear picture. So we politicians acted on what we considered desirable grounds and created a unified school for Sweden. Most of us feel that our experience since then supports the wisdom of the decision."

How well the Swedish reforms are working is an unanswered and as yet unanswerable question. To the planners in Stockholm they are of course working very well. It is true that most Swedes now accept the reforms, some with enthusiasm, some with resignation. Very little of the embittered debate that filled the Swedish press in the 1950's remains today, except occasionally on special problems like compulsory religious instruction. Perhaps I should add as an aside, however, that a number of people with whom I talked felt that faith had so far outstripped evidence in the reforms that any negative conclusions that might be indicated by research would not be permitted—that is, that the new education would simply not be allowed to fail. In most countries the view from the center of educational reform is apt to be rosy; the view from the provinces often turns gray. Whether the distance between the dreams of theoreticians and the realities of the classroom can be satisfactorily bridged in Sweden remains to be seen. It is one thing to say, for example, that the first degree must be taken in a shorter time but that its quality must not be allowed to drop; but it is another to make this come true, especially if at the same time one reduces the specialized preparatory work of the secondary school. It is one thing to make a law bringing teacher training within, to use a favorite English phrase, "the orbit of the universities," but it is a far different thing to make the law a reality. It is one thing to formulate new aims and purposes, and new methods to go with them, for the comprehensive school; but it is an immeasurably more difficult thing to make this reform something more than organizational. In education, the best-laid plans of planners who sit at the center of power "gang aft a-gley" with great frequency.

On the central question of whether the reforms will lower standards in the primary and secondary schools, particularly for the bright, it is simply too early to tell. A visitor cannot even know whether a consensus exists in Sweden on this question. But whether it exists or not, it was clear to me that both the planners and the politicians involved are prepared to take the risk of lower standards for the best in the interests of more schooling for the average and the dull, and especially in the interests of greater social mixing and uniformity. Experience so far with the new comprehensive school indicates an interesting pattern: pupils are not dividing themselves up in the ninth grade in anything like the way the planners supposed they would. No less than eighty-five percent of pupils have been choosing the "theoretical" tracks. Nobody knows why, but a plausible explanation is surely that they do so for reasons of status. They may do so in the reformed secondary school as well, despite the determination of the planners to achieve "parity of esteem" among the academic, technical, and vocational programs of this school when it is reconstructed. In this regard the Swedes might consider the English experience with grammar and secondary modern schools. English planners after World War II were also bent on parity of esteem for all schools, but parents and pupils quickly decided that the new secondary modern schools were grossly inferior to the traditional grammar school—which is one reason the Labor Party is now determined to abolish the secondary modern school. But when they are all abolished and comprehensive schools prevail in both England and Sweden, the chances are, unless the planners can change people as well as schools, that an academic pecking order of some kind will flourish anew.

Whatever the reasons for the lopsided pattern now evident in the comprehensive school, Sweden will soon find it necessary to reorganize the ninth year. It will have to reduce the number of options, which were too many anyhow for schools in the north and in other remote areas of the country. Whether it will make further changes to meet the criticisms of some teachers and others is more doubtful. One cannot know how general is the condition described in 1965 in a letter to a London newspaper by a Swedish professor in which he said, "The nine-year compulsory schooling of every young person, whether capable of profiting from theoretical education, or not, has created an almost unbearable disciplinary situation in most of the higher classes: the non-capables are compensating their failures through obstructive behavior to the disadvantage of those who are able and willing to learn. This situation . . . infallibly leads to a lowering of the standard of education." [7] But one can say with reasonable certainty that, whatever the negative experiences, there will be no very great retreat from free-choice, comprehensive schooling in Sweden.

In considering the exportability of Swedish reforms, educational planners might well ask themselves whether the conditions which allow Sweden to make such sweeping and expensive reforms in such a short period of time can be matched elsewhere. To begin with, Sweden has a political structure peculiar to herself and Finland. Government ministries are deliberately kept small while a great deal of power is delegated to national boards that operate with civil servants under or alongside the ministries. Thus Sweden's Ecklesiastikdepartementet, actually a Ministry of Educational and Ecclesiastical Affairs, has a staff of about ninety persons, and at that is Sweden's second largest ministry, while the Royal Board of Education in Stockholm, which is operated under it by career administrators and educational experts, has nearly six hundred and is by far the most important agency in Swedish education.

Although Sweden has a good deal of seeming decentralization in education, through its twenty-four elected regional school boards and its more than one thousand appointed local school authorities, it is in fact as highly centralized a system as one can find. The Board of Education exercises enormous authority over all Swedish schools up to university level. It carries out the policies of the government and the Ecklesiastikdepartementet, but it also has extensive powers in its own right. It closely controls school timetables, national examinations, teacher training, and it stipulates the curriculum in detail. On the last point, the Board of Education issues a *Läroplan*, a comprehensive learning guide, for each type of school. The *Läroplan* for the selective secondary school, for instance, is a 772-page volume spelling out not only the syllabus for each subject and each program of the school, but details of scheduling, methodology, and testing.[8]

Combined with this machinery for making decisions and then putting them into effect is a unique habit the Swedes have of acting on the reports of national advisory bodies. Since World War II, Sweden has had a number of "royal commissions" that have studied her educational problems and that together have pretty well blanketed the system. The most important one in connection with the comprehensive school was the 1957 School Committee, which prepared the way for final legislation in 1962, but several others were involved at various times. Sweden also had a *gymnasium* committee at work for some years, which reported in 1963 and led to the major parliamentary action of 1964 reforming the whole structure of secondary education. In September of 1965 its teacher-training committee brought in its enormous report, which led to parliamentary action in 1966. Other committees are now at work on vocational education and higher education, and still another has recently been appointed on what can only be described as questions of status among the new types of secondary schools. Many countries appoint committees of this sort, but rarely are their recommendations made into law with such dispatch and with so few changes as in Sweden. Perhaps the Swede's high regard for action based on negotiation, orderly procedure, and communal judgment has something to do with it. Whatever the explanation, national attitudes in Sweden clearly make major reform easier than it is in most countries.

One should remember also that Sweden has other rare if not unique advantages: She has a small population in a very big country (she has almost twice as much space as all of the United Kingdom, for example, but only about thirteen percent of the population); she has relatively great natural resources; she has been free of war damage; she has had a stable government, indeed the same Social Democratic government, for over thirty years (the same Premier for over twenty); she has redistributed her wealth so that the income spread of the population is small; her gross national product has been increasing by five percent a year since 1960; she now has about the highest standard of living in Europe and probably the highest wage rates in the world outside the United States. But most of all, she has a monoracial, highly homogeneous population sharing the same traditions and ideals as well as a devotion to collectivism and conformity. Under such conditions, educational planners can do many things that might be neither possible nor desirable in other countries. Not the least of the dangers of planning in larger and more heterogeneous nations is the conclusion so easily reached at the seat of government that there is a single solution possible to a major educational problem and that the planners know what it is and how to put it into effect. Of course the companion danger is the difficulty of undoing or even mitigating mistakes inspired from the center. It is especially important, therefore, that other nations looking at the Swedish reforms assess them in the context of Swedish culture and society.

# English and American Schools as Seen by Exchange Teachers

FOR OVER TWENTY YEARS there has been an exchange program between the United States and the United Kingdom in which nearly 4,000 teachers have changed places. Every year, that is, roughly one hundred American teachers swap jobs with a hundred British teachers, in the interests of educational understanding and Anglo-American relations. Toward the end of their year abroad, these teachers are sent a sizable questionnaire on their experience by the agencies administering the program: the Office of Education in the United States and the British Interchange Committee in the United Kingdom. In addition to these questionnaires, statements are also collected each year from headmasters in England and superintendents of schools in the United States who have had an exchange teacher in their schools. To anyone interested in English and American schools, these reports make amusing and provocative, as well as neglected, reading. In going through the reports for the last several years, one naturally becomes aware of recurring themes that often throw an interesting light on the educational systems of the two countries. The teachers' reports contain a good deal of comment on the mechanics of the exchange program, which is of administrative interest, and a certain amount of comment on life in general in the host country. But I propose to look mostly at the educational commentary and to review, with considerable quotation from the reports themselves, the experiences these teachers seem to have in common.

The first thing that should be said is that for the great majority of both British and American teachers, the exchange year is a happy and successful one. Even allowing for the probable desire of both groups to respond favorably and to express appreciation in questionnaires that come from their sponsors, the consistency of their endorsement of the program is impressive. Some of this enthusiasm is no doubt due simply to being abroad for a year, with the chanee to travel in the United States or in England and Europe and to live in a different culture. The British teachers are, by their own testimony, regularly overwhelmed by the friendliness and hospitality of their American hosts; and Americans, when they have adjusted to the rigors of Britain, rejoice in English life and people. But more important, both groups seem generally to find the year a highly beneficial one educationally. In addition to the experience of simply teaching in, and talking with others about, a foreign educational system, they usually visit a variety of schools during the year. Thus they develop a view of the host country's schools not restricted to the institution where they happen to be teaching. In short, it should be said and stressed that this program for the interchange of teachers is heartily supported by the majority of teachers who have been a part of it.

However, one is naturally curious about the criticisms exchange teachers make of each other's schools at the end of the year. Their favorable reports, although reassuring for the sponsors in both countries, are not so interesting because they do not say very much beyond the fact that all went well, that the teachers involved made a lot of friends, learned a great deal, and had a jolly good time. It is the critical or at least the analytical reports that engage one's attention. Of course, most of the reports from American teachers are not exclusively one thing or the other; they are commendatory and critical, in parts. In contrast, a good many reports from British teachers are unreservedly commendatory, a fact that may reflect more a difference of attitude than experience.

Suppose we begin with four examples of general criticisms made by a minority of American teachers. Their reactions, that is, are not the customary ones; but they, and variations on them, occur often enough in the reports:

> My placement was unfortunate in that the head was abnormally insular. He was not interested in America, in new ideas in education or in anything unfamiliar. He said that I could use my own methods as long as they were the same as those he recommended. He was not unkind or antagonistic—just not interested or helpful. I was simply a member of staff and a rather suspect and substandard one because of my foreign-ness. Also we were dreadfully under-supplied and I lacked even the basic materials to do many things. I do not really consider my year's *teaching* a success in the sense I had hoped it would be.

> . . . I gave up shortly after school started. I'm used to working with children, not at them. The greatest of several difficulties was the complete difference between my personal philosophy, and that practiced in the school. To avoid problems I adopted their methods to a great extent, but this added to my own frustration.

> In almost every meeting which I attended in New York prior to leaving for the U. K., we were told that English education was ahead of ours;

so this is what I expected to find. From what I have observed this is untrue, unfounded, and impossible. How can unqualified teachers do as good a job as qualified teachers? How can children learn when teachers are drinking tea five and ten minutes after every bell rings? How can children learn when they are assigned to copy a song from the Hymnal for an English lesson day after day? How can children develop when the B, C, and D classes are neglected? By neglected I mean the teacher seldom gets out of her chair behind the desk; the children are assigned written work, this is checked and no discussion follows; history and science consist of copying from a book; and drawing is looking at a picture and duplicating it.

It is puzzling to me to comprehend the purposes the Interchange Commission had in mind in placing me in an ancient building without the barest amenities (no hot water, outdoor lavatories, no telephone, 40 degree temperatures in winter, leaky roof, no modern teaching equipment, 1938 geography books, no hall for P. E., no staff facilities, etc.) that was also in a state of terminal decay professionally! It was shocking to me to find an organization of 250 pupils in such a state of neglect. . . . I seriously question the fitness of a school of this type for an exchange teacher; it would serve only to create a distorted view in the mind of such a teacher about what British education is like.

And here is an embittered response that illustrates how negatively British education can affect a very few American teachers every year. This comment is from a secondary teacher in the Midwest who was assigned to a school in southeastern England and who was apparently so horrified by external examinations, among other things, that he is driven at one point in his report to this outburst:

I have visited all three types of State schools and am absolutely appalled at the completely undemocratic situation that exists as a result of the eleven-plus exam. Perhaps the greatest revelation has been the realization that the State system of British education promotes, in my view, one of the more rigid class and cast [*sic*] systems ever devised by man—and this in the name of democracy.

Elsewhere in his report, which I continue with merely to define the extreme position that can be reached on rare occasions by an American teacher, he says:

. . . I think it should be made clear that the British, as a whole, had and have no intention of profiting from their American teachers, as teachers. . . . I arrived unheralded, uniformed [*sic*], and unnoticed. For the most part, a state of status quo still exists. . . . I found the teachers with whom I was to work completely *dis*interested [*sic*—his italics] in me as a teacher or as an American. This attitude continues to exist at the present time despite my many attempts to remedy the situation. Of a staff of 33, more than half have yet to communicate with me, even to the extend [*sic*] of a morning greeting or a discussion of the weather. As a professional educator, I feel that my year in Britain has been a complete waste of time. I have tried without success to instill in my boys a love for learning and a dedication to responsible citizenship. They wish only to pass examinations—a completely useless activity in my opinion. . . . To break through this magnificent, invisible wall of narrow-minded goals in British education has been an impossible task. It is a credit to the British view of education that they are completely successful in blotting out any consideration, be it ever so small, of anything that is not British. Rule Britania! [sic]

One might have more confidence in the observations of this teacher, whose field was English, if he were a shade more literate and a lot less doctrinaire; but his comment does represent one end of the spectrum of response. More often, exchange teachers comment as do these three:

Mr. _____, my headmaster, was very helpful and professional. He wrote to me while I was still in America and sent me the schemes of work, etc. When I arrived he had us home for lunch on the first Sunday and took us for a tour of the city. During my time of teaching at his school . . . [he] was always friendly, helpful and professional.

It has been a privilege to work under Mr. _____ who is a dedicated educator. His interest in comparing educational systems, curriculum and methods has made the year a profitable and enjoyable one.

The exchange year has provided countless opportunities to develop professionally. I have been able to study new teaching methods and materials and to become acquainted with a new school system, its historical and philosophical basis and its organization, administration and curriculum. In terms of personal and professional growth the past exchange year has been one of the most rewarding in my lifetime.

British teachers, for their part, are almost always restrained and certainly never hysterical in their comments on American education. In fact, they are comparatively uncritical, perhaps because they are more willing than their American counterparts to accept the host school on its own terms. Of the few that offer general criticisms, here is a typical one, from a primary teacher:

[I] found the daily timetable tiring and think it bad for teachers and children, especially for the last-comers each day, when everyone is flagging. My records show difference in achievement between children in first group of day and those in last. . . . [It is] trying to be restricted to one textbook for all teaching purposes . . . A pity the status of American teachers is not higher. . . . Many American children do not appear to enjoy school as much as English counterparts. It seems a necessary evil—stepping stone to college. Marks and grades seem to be of paramount importance. In this area, pressure from parents is tremendous and "failure" of students seems to be regarded as a reflection on the parents and blamed usually on short-comings of teachers. Many parents seem to have completely unrealistic idea of children's capabilities.

One conviction is arrived at with great frequency by American exchange teachers: they go home convinced that English education is not as good as they had thought before coming. And English teachers return persuaded, though less often, that American education is better than they had thought. A typical comment from an American teacher is that "British schools are not superior to American ones—or at least the schools I have visited have been similar in methods and philosophies to schools at home." Another teacher thinks he may have got an unrepresentative view: "I have been quite disappointed in the standard of English Education as I felt it would be much higher. I have no doubt my feelings would have been altered had I been placed in a better school." Another one says: "I'd heard how the schools of the United Kingdom were of a very high standard and that in many ways were superior to American schools but I find that in many ways the American system of education is superior." Still another teacher makes this quite usual comment:

> Curiously enough, I had a higher opinion of British education before I arrived here. Perhaps I expected too much, but I'm leaving with the feeling that perhaps we in America do a far better job of general education for the greatest number of youngsters. There's no denying the very high standards for the most able kids, but I feel that far too many get lost along the way. . . . I'm beginning to appreciate what the American comprehensive high school is doing. The British system, with all its merits, leaves me still pretty lukewarm. I'll return home with far more insight and enthusiasm for my job, because I really feel that what we do in the U. S. is pretty remarkable.

On the other hand, a British teacher records his mistaken belief on going to America that "the standard in U.S.A. schools was below that of the standard of British schools. I have found from my experience here that the standards for similar groups of children are comparable." Another one, teaching in an American independent school of good reputation, says: "I understood that educational standards at comparative age levels were different, and that American seniors would be of a lower level of achievement and intelligence than English equivalents. I was wrong." Still another Britisher records: "I think some people at home have not a very high opinion of American education in general—I have been very impressed by my own school, and with those I have visited and shall sing their praises when I return home."

The most frequent problem encountered by American exchange teachers is the absence of close organization in English schools and the absence of any real introduction to the school or to their work by the headmaster, or any continuing guidance from him. A British teacher might think all this a virtue, an aspect of the traditional freedom and self-reliance expected of and by English teachers; but it is a new experience to the American. And because so many complain of it, let me record a number of different passages from their reports that will give the reader some idea of the variety of reaction involved:

> The Head gave me the scheme of work and *that was that!* From then on, he expected me to take over—be completely on my own.

> I was met at the bus the first morning and walked to the school. That is absolutely ALL. Not even shown around the building.

> The school is most casual in outlook and nearly anti-organization, consequently we (my wife was teaching also) were shown our classrooms, introduced to our pupils and left to do as we pleased with only a rough idea of any sort of schedule for the day and no knowledge of school rules. . . . Although we found this disorganization a bit difficult at first, we soon realized that it gave us unlimited freedom in our teaching methods as well as provided a relaxed atmosphere so necessary to the work with these handicapped children.

> There were no arrangements made for me. I was told to report to school on opening day. The headmaster showed me where the art room is, wished me luck and left. Not knowing anything at all about the school procedure, my mistakes came quickly.

> Nothing is ever clear-cut or organized so that it was like fighting my way out of a bag of feathers! The school seems to be in a constant state of confusion, with no one knowing where anything is or who is doing what. Most teachers and pupils take this for granted, apparently, and a teacher without a big voice and a tough manner is quickly at a disadvantage. . . . The lack of supplies (in a supposedly modern school) was shocking.

> I have enjoyed teaching here, but truthfully must say, I won't use the methods when I return home. I am accustomed to a more organized curriculum and sometimes felt "at sea" as far as teaching methods are concerned. There is also a lack of textbooks and materials in many of the schools. One certainly learns to use one's own initiative and to make the most of a situation.

> My introduction to my teaching assignment was vague, almost non-existent. What I learned about school procedures, my specific responsibilities, school facilities, textbooks and teaching materials, etc. came as answers to my endless questions.

> There were no arrangements made for my arrival and because my headmaster would never make himself available, I found out my teaching

assignment the first day of school. I also discovered that I had a first form, but no one provided any information as to what I was to do with them. To add to the chaotic scene, the former teachers had checked out the complete sets of books, leaving me with outdated ones and incomplete sets. I have yet to see a syllabus for the courses I am teaching.

At no point were we ever told directly what a Secondary Modern School was like. To people coming from Comprehensive schools the transition is a tremendous shock. An adequate report from an American and British teacher who has spent time in one of each of the types of English schools would be more helpful than the official versions of the British government which tend to be more idealistic than realistic.

The introduction to my teaching assignment never materialized. If I may be allowed to elaborate: (a) No syllabus, except for a handwritten list of a few novels, poems and plays, ever came my way; (b) My "timetable" reflected a lack of confidence in my ability to cope with the mysteries of preparing sixth formers for "O" and "A" levels (although all my teaching experience in the U. S. A. has been with 17–18–19 year old students); (c) No explanation of "examinations" was offered, and my questions regarding examinations were all but fruitless; (d) No kind of introduction of me to students was made  . . .

Perhaps it is unsurprising that American teachers, accustomed to more definite direction and a tighter administration than their British counterparts, should complain that they are left too much to their own devices. The director of the British Interchange Committee always suggests to the receiving schools that special attention be given the American visitor, and the results are often better than those indicated above. Here are a few more favorable extracts:

I really feel my Headmaster went out of his way to help me in any way he could. He took over a class for me one day and also let me take my class in to observe another teacher in the system. I never did feel like an alien in a foreign school but rather as an educator trying to adapt to a new school and a different type of organization.

I never expected to receive the great amount of freedom I was given to *grow* on this assignment. I never expected to be given the Christmas play and the opportunity to work with very talented children and "create" my own drama. I never expected to be given a special poetry class to teach "according to your methods." I never expected to be allowed to break down old, in-bred attitudes towards the classroom and substitute other attitudes, newer, more contemporary, more communicative.

. . . when we arrived we were met by my exchange's family. My headmistress invited me to tea at her home before school opened. She gave me samples of the books used for my teaching assignment as well as individual folders of the pupils. The Chief Education Officer invited me to tea at the Council offices and explained the school system. My headmistress offered tactful assistance during the first week of school regarding music and movement, library procedure, house meetings, etc. There were no difficulties.

British exchange teachers almost never complain about any lack of orientation, information, or equipment. If anything they get too much. Some comment on the excessive organization of the American school and the crowded school day:

> Conforming to a set rigid pattern, with every day alike was my greatest difficulty. Lack of variety and creativity in the classroom, led to boredom. Following manuals and workbooks left little to one's own initiative.

> . . . since I have been here I have filled in more forms, come up against more rule and regulations (written—and unwritten) than ever before in my life.

Other British teachers comment that "The pace is very different. I became tired very quickly. Every minute of the school day has to be used." Or that the work load was "very heavy indeed . . . Bus duty at 7 a.m.!" Or that he "loved it all except the 26 minute lunch." Still another refers to "the vast system of form-filling and clerical work in existence here."

Another condition sometimes remarked upon by American teachers is that the British schools to which they go show little interest in or curiosity about American education. Also, a certain number complain of indifference or hostility on the part of the head to the idea of having an exchange American teacher. And a few complain of outright anti-Americanism. One teacher remarks that while young Britons were interested in life outside England "others didn't want to hear." Another says that "only one teacher was interested in me or in the United States." Another puts her case strongly:

> . . . during the fifth week, Mr. _____ berated me for not following the English curriculum—How could I? I had never been told what it was! On the same day, he came into my classroom and berated me *in front of my class* for not using English teaching methods. . . . He simply isn't sympathetic to the exchange program. Why he agreed to it in the first place I cannot understand!

Another comments:

> One feels a lack of interest in ideas of American education; in fact, a conviction, almost, that we have nothing to offer in particular that the British would be interested in. . . . I have had only *one* colleague ask me any direct, interested question about American education—and not much on any other subject either.

Still another comments from Wales:

> Very few pupils ever asked questions or showed curiosity about me and
> America unless I prompted them. Furthermore, their general lack of
> interest in everything concerning school eventually led me to become a
> mere disciplinarian rather than a source of information and inspiration.
> . . . there could have been an arrangement to use me somewhere as a
> "teacher" rather than a "guard"!

Two further comments on these themes:

> It is surprising how little interest there is here in America, in education
> and in other subjects. Occasionally people ask about some highly pub-
> licized *criticism* of America—the race problem, etc. There is almost no
> interest among teachers here in education in America. They are quite
> set in their ways. . . . I feel that I have gained a great deal, but that
> they have been cheated by their lack of interest.

> We were told over and over that we were to be "ambassadors of good
> will" in this country. In order to attain this title, than [*sic*] I would have
> had to accept all untruths, jeers, jokes, unkind remarks about the U. S. A.
> with a smile and passive attitude. I have too much respect for my country
> (which I respect even more now) and for myself to accept the treatment
> I have received.

British teachers, on the other hand, rarely comment in this vein. The
following observation, by a Britisher assigned to a school in Texas, is practically unique: "Many students were charming, intelligent and pleased to
meet a foreign teacher but quite a large number were unbelievably rude,
insular and ignorant." If they encountered any significant anti-British
feeling or lack of interest in themselves or English education, they do
not discuss it in their reports. It is possible, of course, that their experience in these matters is similar to that of their American counterparts, but
that they do not feel it important enough to record or that it should be
recorded.

"Misassignment" is sometimes experienced by both groups. Secondary
teachers in the United States, although licensed to teach particular subjects and not, as in Britain, without subject specification, often wind up
teaching subjects for which they are unqualified. Visiting Britons have
the same problem occasionally. One British teacher, for example, found
himself teaching an entirely new subject, Anthropology, in an American
junior college. Another says she "spent two-thirds of the year teaching
subjects I know nothing about to senior students." Still another teacher
from a selective secondary school in England was rather spectacularly
misassigned when he was given three low-ability classes to whom he was
expected to teach "Problems of American Democracy." Another had no
fear of misassignment but blithely reports, "Considering my field is

religious instruction, I was prepared to teach whatever was offered." And another says charitably about his work in a Chicago comprehensive school, "I have always taught in a selective secondary school, but here I was allocated two of the lowest track levels. However for this I have no regrets. The hair shirt was bad for my back but good for my soul."

Two fairly typical comments from American teachers suggest how it works from the English side:

> I had hoped to be able to teach a subject at the level of my past experience: i.e., English to the sixteen and seventeen year old. Instead I was given an assignment teaching English to the first and second form, an age group I had never before taught. It was maintained that it would be easier for me to teach these forms since I would not have to then teach toward an exam.

> I was given very little advice about what subject matter to include in my classes. When I objected to teaching a class in mathematics (because I have never taught math) I was told this was one of the bottom sets and all I had to do was keep the students happy.

Discipline is a surprise to both groups. Before going to America, many British teachers fear that American schools are all blackboard jungles in which discipline is the major problem; and many American teachers suppose that English children are all models of deportment. In practice, Americans seem to have more disciplinary troubles in Britain than British teachers have in America. Here is a typical comment from an American teacher in a secondary modern school:

> I found the discipline very lax, by comparison to the school I am used to, and this presented the greatest problem. . . . There seemed to be no effective means of punishment and the result was that any sort of behavior had to be fought constantly—to this day. It is practically impossible to *teach*, especially classes above the first year.

On the British side, here are two comments, the first from a teacher assigned to an American East Coast school, the second from a teacher on the West Coast:

> The students in the school had the attitude that they were there to be entertained and were not prepared to make any mental effort. They were most friendly and pleasant as individuals but utterly lacking in normal good manners. Students were not given responsibility. There was little respect for the teacher on the part of the student, parents, or administration. I learned to ignore these things but would, I hope, never adjust.

> Discipline is undoubtedly the main difficulty. This was *not* a problem with me, but the inadequate means of enforcing it I found always tiring and tiresome, and a waste of valuable time by a minority of the class. In my own school in Scotland there would have been a "sorting-out" the first

week of school which would have resulted in a better teaching-listening atmosphere and better use of time throughout the rest of the year.

All this, then, encompasses the principal adverse reactions that both groups of teachers have with some frequency by the end of their exchange year. Their reports are also full of interesting minor items. A British teacher relates, for instance, that he had "only one shock: saluting the Flag, nobody warned me of this"; or another reports that his beard was not always "acceptable" but that he persevered. Many comment on the general interest shown in them by their American hosts who did everything from putting a new teapot (with a large supply of teabags) in the staff room for one exchange teacher to holding a benefit concert and producing $1,000 for another after being told that he was living in the United States on his British salary.

Americans have their problems, of course, with British housing and climate. One managed to blow up the water heater in his flat; another reports that she "simply could not believe I could be cold *inside*." But most get themselves adequately adjusted psychologically if not metabolically. A number have difficulty with heads of schools to which they are assigned, or perhaps, as I will discuss presently, the heads have trouble with them. From the teachers' point of view, these troubles stretch from the trivial (such as an argument over whether the window blinds in the classroom could be pulled or not—the head insisted that the blinds were not "used" in his school until June) to those that had a fundamental importance to the instructional program, such as is indicated in the following comment from an American primary teacher:

> . . . in a situation where the children had so very much freedom as to how, why, when, where they did what they wanted to, I felt chained.
> . . . I finally got used to the noise that is inevitable when each child is following through his own project such as practicing the recorder, modelling clay, reading, dramatising, etc. The freedom that bothered me was the fact that many didn't push on academically as I know they could have. . . . *Many* times I wished that I would not have so much formal informality. Because of my Head's wish that *his* school be known for this and not that, I was more or less bound to his methods and always felt frustrated because I couldn't exchange ideas and methods.

The above comment might seem bizarre to many Americans who have always supposed that the kind of elementary education here described is rampant in the United States, the land of progressive education, but not abroad. It merely emphasizes a final point that might be made about the teachers' reports. They illustrate a genuine multiplicity of experience, so that the observations of any one teacher can often be countered with those of another. One American teacher will report, for example, "The unwillingness [of British teachers] to try something new was overwhelming," while another one will say, "I had been misinformed about the austerity of the educational system. In actuality I found conditions here much more experimental, modern, and changeable than I had expected." The same kind of contradiction can be seen with most of the other problems mentioned in the reports. But it is not so much a contradiction as a simple illustration of the qualitative range and the diversity found in any educational system. It does not invalidate generalizations, though it may serve as a useful caution against taking the experience of any one teacher as general.

Heads of schools also make their reports on exchange teachers. Although their comments suggest that the quality of the exchange groups can vary greatly from one year to another, patterns of experience are again evident and do not always match those of the teachers. First, it must be said that there is a consistent difference between the reports of British and American heads. American heads are eulogistic the vast majority of the time about their English exchange teachers. Most often they speak in superlatives, praising teaching ability in particular. British heads, on the other hand, are much more critical of American exchange teachers. They too speak in superlatives and praise teaching ability, but not nearly so often. They are more apt to speak well of the personal qualities and the sociability of American exchange teachers than they are of teaching competence. Both groups have the occasional teacher who is hypercritical or chauvinistic, or one that is lazy or uninterested in the school. But there remains a marked difference in assessment between English and American heads.

Some comments are merely the obverse side of the teachers' complaints. American teachers remark very often on the lack of direction from the head, but to the head it may look merely like a teacher's lack of enterprise. As one says: "I felt that she required every subject to be presented in detail to her and she did not seem to be prepared to use any initiative in interpreting the syllabus." American teachers comment frequently on the absence of records and teaching aids, but an English head might see it only as an inability to adapt "without the manuals to which the Americans cling and the vast amount of duplicated material . . ."

American teachers complain that they are underrated, given the lower-ability tracks, and not allowed to teach GCE classes; but when they are so allowed, the head might report as this one did:

> I think it must be true to say that our G.C.E. classes must have suffered a little, particularly the A level ones in Pure Maths and Applied Maths where a difference of one grade may mean failure to gain university acceptance.

Or as this one:

> We feel that in both Mathematics and Physics he could have done

more than he in fact did to come to grips with the problems of selective teaching on a closely integrated syllabus.

Or the head might say, as this one did, "He was adequate up to Ordinary level, but not beyond"; or, as another comments, "The American method of teaching does not wholly suit our examination classes but is admirable for the lower streams."

Typical of the more general evaluations made by British heads is one that says of the American teacher: "I would grade him as B on a five-point scale, tending towards A from the social point of view and C with regard to the success of the actual work done." Another said that the teacher "made a very good first impression on everyone he met, but I am afraid that he did not come up to expectations in the classroom." Other adverse comment from heads takes various turns: One says that "To be perfectly frank, I was not satisfied with his work, but for the sake of Anglo-American relationships, I said nothing at first." Another comments, "I regret to say that the work in basic subjects in this class deteriorated considerably and of course I had to tax her with this fact." Still other heads comment this way:

> . . . Home Economics is very definitely not the same thing as our Domestic Science. . . . it will now take two years for the teaching of domestic science in this school to recover from the effects of this exchange.

> Her bright and breezy manner, her desire to establish a kind of equalitarian relationship from the outset, her broad, slick American humour, and her rather strong accent, have all combined to make the classroom situation a little difficult for her at times.

> We have had many visiting staff (French and German every year, Canadian, Swedish) but we have never had one which made us feel so inadequate. There seemed nothing we could do.

> In the staffroom, on the other hand (and it's a very happy staffroom), her attitude became almost intolerable. She became aggressively critical of things British, glorifying and magnifying everything American. Instead of the "good ambassador" she started out as, she became the American blowhard of the cartoons.

Occasionally a head will suggest that selection procedures in the United States are not what they might be. One says, "I cannot imagine how she got past even the most superficial screening," while another comments: "The two American exchange teachers I've had is too small a sample to generalize from, but these two should not have been sent over here. It seems to me, from these instances, that selection is not so carefully done in the U.S. Certainly the two _____ teachers who went from here were first class." Still, it is important to keep the proportions right. General approval of American teachers is very frequent in these reports from

British Heads, and unqualified praise comes on occasion. One says, for example, "I can honestly say I have never seen a class respond to a teacher in such a wonderful way." Another says, "I cannot imagine a more admirable exchange teacher. . . . has made a great impact here . . . we have the highest respect for his ability, integrity, and humour." Still another says of his American teacher, "We shall be extremely sorry when the time comes for her to leave us."

Nevertheless, when the heads' reports from both sides of the Atlantic are put in the balance, and allowance made for both the requirements of diplomacy and the probability of bias, the conclusion is hard to resist that the English send more good teachers to the United States than they get in return. Certainly it is not a secret that American officials involved in the program in London are dissatisfied with the screening procedures by which the American teachers are chosen. And I must admit that these doubts are reinforced in my own mind, however impressionistically, after reading through several hundred reports from American teachers. The awkwardness of expression that so often characterizes these reports, the grammatical and spelling errors, the tortured syntax, do nothing to shore up one's faith in the selection procedures used in the United States. One finds misspellings like "noisey," "preplexed," "straight jacket," "tri-patre system," "embarassment," "braggard," "roomate," "ocassionally." More important is the frequency of clumsy, unidiomatic English demonstrated in such a passage as this: "It is difficult for Americans coming from hyper-organized and written curriculum schools, to be faced with a basically local internal class situation"; or this: "Europeans by the factor of being traditionally leaders can still manipulate American foreign policy by expression of verbel [*sic*] natures." Although I would not want to make too much of this kind of loose, not to say incomprehensible, writing (perhaps one *should* make something of it!), there is enough of it in these reports to make one cautious in assessing the judgments of such teachers.

How much validity is there in the observations and criticisms of exchange teachers? First, I would say that both groups are right in modifying their general view of each other's educational system. American education *is* better than it is thought to be by a great many educators in England, especially those in grammar schools—although, ironically, it is not as good as professional educators and the *avant-garde* of educational sociologists in England are apt to think. And English education is not in fact as good as it is widely believed to be in America. These are discoveries worth making, and I wish more people besides exchange teachers would make them.

Each system has a good deal to learn from the other, and we in America now seem at least willing to consider the possibility that other nations might have something to teach us. However, I am not sure that Britain is similarly ready to look abroad for ideas. National groups like the Plowden Committee and other advisory bodies have of late traveled to the United States and other countries in the course of their investigations, but I believe our exchange teachers are generally right in feeling that British teachers and heads are not much interested in the American, or any other, educational system. They have always been comparatively oblivious even to the Scottish educational system, which at least offers sharp contrasts with their own. British schools exhibit a substantial lack of curiosity about what other people do in education.

As to the frequent American complaint about the disorganization of the English school and the lack of equipment and the unhelpfulness of the head, one could wish that American teachers were more adaptable. They could simply take the host school on its own terms and set about discovering for themselves what they need to know instead of waiting for someone to fill them in on all matters, great and small. Many American schools are overadministered and perhaps overequipped, and teachers have grown so accustomed to this superfluity that they have lost much of the authority and self-reliance the English teacher still retains. I wonder if some of their complaint is not resentment at what seems to them an inhospitable reception in general, and the consequent feeling, probably just in some cases, that the school did not really want an exchange teacher in the first place.

Their further complaint about being assigned too often to the lower ability groups raises a more difficult problem, on which I find it easy to sympathize with both parties. The American understandably feels that the head shows a lack of confidence in his ability by assigning him only or mostly non-GCE classes, and feels that his status among his colleagues is thereby diminished. But the head's position is surely understandable also. Whether the GCE system is good or bad, he has an obligation to his pupils that he cannot ignore. If I were a British head, I too would be reluctant to put GCE classes in the hands of a visiting teacher who had no experience with this or any other external examination system, who had not taught or perhaps even seen the syllabus involved, and whose level of specialist training might well be lower than that of the British graduate teacher he had replaced. In short, there is a case to be made both ways, and it may not be possible to satisfy both parties as long as the GCE plays the role it does in English education.

By contrast British exchange teachers do not register so many complaints as their American counterparts. One feels in reading their reports that they may be a bit more adaptable, more versatile, certainly more literate, and perhaps more restrained in voicing dissatisfaction than American teachers. Also, they may be more carefully selected for the exchange program. Whatever the reasons, they seem as a whole to have a highly enjoyable time of it in America, with few problems of adjustment.

# *Note on an Important Failure —*
# *Religious Education*

THERE IS ONE DIMENSION of English education that I have left unexplored in the main text, and that to some Britons would seem the most important of all and may also interest some American readers: religious worship and religious instruction in English schools. Although religious education is no longer directly relevant to our public schools and colleges, British experience with it seems to me to have implications for education everywhere; it presents a fascinating religious and educational problem. As in most of the countries of Europe, education in England was predominantly a church affair until the latter half of the nineteenth century, and the influence of the established church continues today to pervade British life despite a declining church attendance. In sharp contrast to American tradition, both religious worship and instruction are mandatory in Britain and in most of Europe (France excepted). The 1944 Act in England, far from following the wartime trend and diminishing the place of religion, strengthened it by requiring for the first time that the school day everywhere "begin with collective worship" and beyond that that "religious instruction in accordance with agreed syllabuses" be given everywhere.

Religion is thus the only subject of the curriculum to be dictated by the central government. Provision is made for parents to "opt out," as the English put it, but few in fact do. The act of collective worship with which the school day opens takes a great many forms, most of them quite inoffensive and doctrinally neutral. Religious instruction usually takes an hour a week according to a syllabus that varies with the LEA. Every LEA is directed in the 1944 Act to draw up its own syllabus according to a stipulated procedure that guarantees an equitable representation of religious denominations. What, then, is the result of this universal religious instruction? The universal experience of modern nations that require schools to try to teach universal religious truths is apparently universal failure. Great effort and time and money go into religious instruction in Britain and other countries, with the commonest observable result being the flight of more young people and adults from religious practice. It is arguable whether Marx was ever right in thinking that religion was the opium of the people, but he would be wildly wrong today; the people in almost every country of the West are more indifferent to traditional religion than ever before, although not to religious questions.

If any other mandatory subject of the curriculum produced such consistently poor results as religious instruction apparently does, reform would be urgently called for. And it is being called for by many voices in England. In 1965 seven faculty members of the Institutes of Education who were engaged in training teachers of religion for the schools signed a public statement claiming:

> There is growing concern about the apparent ineffectiveness of religious education. That this concern is not unfounded is confirmed by recent research which shows that many children are leaving school with a gross misunderstanding of the nature of religion, and rejecting it as childish and irrelevant.[1]

Another investigator, surveying the situation throughout Britain, reported findings that are pretty well summed up in the title of her book, *Backward Christian Soldiers*. She found that there was

> no evidence that more than a few children receiving compulsory religious education in the State's day schools are leaving school inspired by religion, or with an embryonic faith in God, or with some knowledge of the Bible, or with even the flimsiest basis on which to build Christian lives. On the contrary, recent research shows that most children see only a vague relationship between religion and twentieth-century living, and little if any connection between the church and Christianity.[2]

One of the leading journals in England devoted to religious education editorialized on the problem this way:

> The depressing conclusion of all the assessments that are beginning to appear is that few of our children know anything of value about the Bible; and not many more know anything at all. Those whose last contact with the Bible is at school are being given nothing that makes it of service in the depths of the personality. The old Puritan faith that a man could go out with the book and be safe has not been justified by its fruits.[3]

And the Bishop of Woolwich, that celebrated shaker of the Christian foundations, thinks religious instruction in British schools suffers from a "malaise of irrelevance and lack of bite . . ."[4]

Many and varied are the diagnoses. Some say the syllabuses are poor, many say the teaching of religious knowledge is poor, some say the examinations are poor, some say religious instruction is obsolete because religion is obsolete, some say the time is out of joint. The Crowther Report, looking at religious instruction in the upper secondary grades, thought that "there is no period of life when young people more need what the Education Act means when it refers, perhaps rather unhappily, to 'religious instruction', and no period when it is more difficult to give." [5] Certainly one reason for the ineffectiveness of this required subject is the cavalier way in which people are assigned to teach it. It is surely a sad irony that the one subject thought important enough to be made mandatory in every state school is handled in whatever way is most convenient in the timetable. A survey of secondary schools conducted jointly in 1963 by the British Council of Churches and the National Union of Teachers indicated that most of the staff members teaching the subject had no specialized preparation for doing so.[6] But a Gallup poll in 1965 in Britain found the overwhelming majority of British parents in favor of continued religious instruction in school. Of those interviewed, sixty-five percent classified themselves as members of the Church of England, thirteen percent as Nonconformists, and nine percent as Catholics, but less than half said they prayed regularly and less than twenty percent went to church regularly. Paradoxically, in the United States, where no religious observance or instruction is permitted in state schools, church attendance is very much higher. One can only speculate about the reason, and the pedagogical implications.

Religious instruction, or at least religious exposure, is also a marked characteristic of non-state schools, especially the Public Schools and the older universities. A number of the Public Schools began as monastic foundations where the chapel was the first building erected. The chapel remains today the most striking building on the grounds of many an English independent school. Oxford and Cambridge have what I suppose is as elaborate a provision for religious observance as could be found anywhere in the world, with each college having its own chapel, some of which, like King's at Cambridge, are known around the world. By the time a student from a Public School finishes his Oxbridge degree, he has had a kind of continuous religious exposure in resplendent religious surroundings for the better part of twenty years. But I would suppose that for most of them the result is similar to what Tolstoy records in his *Confession:*

> I was baptized and brought up in the Orthodox Christian faith. I was taught it in childhood and throughout my boyhood and youth. But when I left the second course of the university, at the age of eighteen, I no longer believed any of the things I had been taught.

Tolstoy recovered his faith with a vengeance, one might say, in later life. But the outlook does not seem promising for the present generation, who are assaulted not only by their own doubts, which is traditional, but by those of their parents and their own churchmen, which is not so traditional. The disintegration probably began during World War II (perhaps much earlier) and has grown steadily since. Lord Eccles, a postwar Minister of Education under the Tories, remarks in an interesting book about his own spiritual journey on the state of the churches during the war:

> The blast of the bombs did great damage to buildings which were old and in a bad state of repair. Among such rickety structures the war found out the weakness in organized religion. As far as I could see the churches did not supply the courage and the spirit which brought us to victory. My best friends were living with the paradox of behaving better, more bravely and less selfishly than in peace-time, and at the same time they were turning away from organized religion. They enjoyed the daily sense of being all in it together and doing a tough job under orders. More than once those I was working with contrasted the emptiness of the 1930's with the comradeship and definite purpose of the war, regretting that the church and a good place in society failed to provide a meaning for life.[7]

One thinks of Bonhoeffer's comment from his Nazi prison that "education which breaks down in face of danger is not education at all. A liberal education which will not enable us to face danger and death does not deserve the name." [8] One would suppose that a religion that similarly failed would be even more strongly condemned. And so it seems to be these days in Britain. Here is a distinguished British theologian, the Dean of King's College, Cambridge, introducing a volume of essays by a group of Cambridge theologians:

> The authors of this volume of essays cannot persuade themselves that the time is ripe for major works of theological construction or reconstruction. It is a time for ploughing, not reaping; or, to use the metaphor we have chosen for our title, it is a time for making soundings, not charts or maps. If this be so, we do not have to apologize for our inability to do what we hope will be possible in a future generation. We can best serve the cause of truth and of the Church by candidly confessing where our perplexities lie, and not by making claims which, so far as we can see, theologians are not at present in a position to justify.

And here is the Dean of Emmanuel College, Cambridge, taking the same kind of sounding for himself and presumably for many other members of the Anglican clergy in an essay called "Beginning All Over Again":

> The great problem of the Church (and therefore of its theologians) is to establish or re-establish some kind of vital contact with that enormous majority of human beings for whom Christian faith is not so much

unlikely as irrelevant and uninteresting. The greatest intellectual challenge to faith is simply that thoroughly secularized intelligence which is now the rule rather than the exception, whether it expresses itself in science or philosophy or the arts. It is by no means clear that anything like Christian faith in the form we know it will ever again be able to come alive for people of our own time or of such future time as we can imagine.[9]

And here is the editorial policy with which a journal called the *New Christian* was launched in 1965 to appeal to what might be called the Angry Young Clergy:

Since we shall in days to come be accused of propagating "heresy and schism" it may be as well at the outset to affirm our belief in the fundamental truth of the Christian Gospel. *New Christian* is not designed to be an organ of secular humanism. Yet, having made this affirmation, we must hasten to add that we feel under no necessary obligation to spread those interpretations of the Christian Faith which were undoubtedly of enormous value to people of other ages and other places, but which speak no longer to the Europe of the 1960's. It seems to us of the greatest importance that the ultimate truth of the Christian religion must be distinguished from interpretations of that truth and it will be our aim to present readers with a creative theology appropriate to life in the world of today.[10]

The "creative theology" turned out for the first year or so to be a vigorous attack on the lethargy of the Church of England and on contemporary social problems, but the theological content of the argument, significantly, was nil. I wonder what shape education would be in if teachers of other subjects were as unsure of their subject matter as Britain's churchmen seem to be of theirs; with this kind of atmosphere of rejection and confusion to work in, teachers of religious instruction in Britain might be forgiven their failures.

The new look in Anglicanism centers, of course, on John A. T. Robinson, the Bishop of Woolwich, who produced in 1963 the iconoclastic and, to me, exceedingly muddled manifesto *Honest to God*. To my surprise, I learned that the Bishop's position, whatever it is, has a certain amount of support within the Anglican clergy. Having refined his position as spokesman for the New Left in religion for a couple of years, he produced a "clarifying" volume in 1965 called *The New Reformation?* In it he redefined his position this way:

. . . I have not the least desire to weaken or deny the distinctive affirmations of the Christian faith. Among these I should certainly wish to assert: (1) The centrality of the confession "Jesus is Lord", in the full New Testament sense that "in him all things cohere" and "in him the whole fulness of the deity dwells bodily"; and (2) the centrality of the utterly *personal* relationship of communion with God summed up in Jesus' address "Abba, Father!" As long as these affirmations are safeguarded, I am glad if my questioning of the necessity of the "supranaturalistic" cast of thought (by which the *reality* of God in human experience is represented by the *existence* of gods or of a God in some other realm "above" or "beyond" the world in which we live) appears to Hindus, as well as to modern secular men, to make Christian truth less alien to them.[11]

Whether because of the Bishop's influence or the difficulties of the subject, the new British theologians seem to favor this sort of impenetrable prose, perhaps because their thoughts are also impenetrable. At any rate, in these days when words like "religionless Christianity" and "Christian agnostics" are thrown around as though they actually mean something, it is perhaps understandable that religious instruction in schools is something less than successful.

In place of religion, American educators talk a great deal about "values," and how to organize instruction to promote values in students. But I wonder if we are any more successful than the English are with religion, particularly in the secondary school. In higher education, one gets the strong impression that student values, while they may change *in* college, are not changed *by* it, at least not by their instructors or studies. A few years ago, an American investigator attempted to find something out about how or whether student values change in our colleges; and while I doubt that anyone can measure such matters very precisely, his basic conclusion seems to me to agree with ordinary observation:

> Students, for their parts, have demonstrated a capacity for shrewdly evaluating the performance of instructors. They particularly value the teacher who couples high respect for students as persons, with a capacity to arouse interest in his subject.
>
> Yet by and large the impact of the good teacher is indistinguishable from that of a poor one, at least in terms of his influence upon the values held and cherished by his students. Students like the good teacher better, and enjoy his classes more. But their fundamental response is little different than to any one else teaching the course. With important individual exceptions, instructors seem equally *in*effective in tingling the nerve centers of students' values.[12]

No doubt Socrates was right in holding that virtue could not be taught, but the assumption upon which liberal education in the United States is based is that it affects the values of students for the better. And so it does, I believe, when it is done well; but done poorly it probably moves students about as far as religious instruction in British schools.

How often one comes back to the question of priorities and purposes in education! Many people find it a tiresome question because agreement is difficult to reach and the question therefore frustrating. But how many of our failures are traceable to the absence of defined goals in education?

Is it not possible that the main reason for Britain's failure in religious education is, not teachers or syllabuses or timetables, but the absence of an agreed and realistic rationale for undertaking this kind of education in the first place? Before writing religious instruction into law, Britain might have asked herself what precisely was the reason for requiring such instruction in public schools; what the expectations were, whether schools were equipped for such instruction; whether they were the best places for it. And these questions always lead back to a prior question about the general function of schools. The 1944 Act did not define the function of schools or of compulsory religious instruction. We are no better off. We are still in the same position remarked on by T. S. Eliot in 1932:

> If education today seems to deteriorate, if it seems to become more and more chaotic and meaningless, it is primarily because we have no settled and satisfactory arrangement of society, and because we have both vague and diverse opinions about the kind of society we want. Education is a subject which cannot be discussed in a void: our questions raise other questions, social, economic, financial, political. And the bearings are on more ultimate problems even than these: to know what we want in education we must know what we want in general, we must derive our theory of education from our philosophy of life. The problem turns out to be a religious problem.[13]

Education in both Britain and the United States now lacks a bedrock of principle, religious or otherwise, upon which to build programs of instruction. We both therefore go from improvisation to improvisation, controversy to controversy, stopgap to stopgap. We in the United States are devoted to secularized public education, but we have yet to hammer out a national consensus about what it is we want our vast educational machine to achieve. We assume that means and ends are related in education, but we spend a lot of time quarreling about the means because the ends are still unclear. It is precisely because education demands a philosophy that it is as controversial and confused as it is. The formation of an educational philosophy, acceptable to a modern nation that is shorn of the religious anchor of other ages, may turn out to be impossible. If it is, we, like the British, will have to be content for the indefinite future to work for whatever improvements are immediately feasible in an educational system of immense size, variety, and energy, but no philosophical center. But I do not believe that we have to be content with this mildly melioristic prospect. I believe that with the right kind of national leadership we could arrive at a consensus about educational purpose. By the right kind I mean simply leadership that recognizes the importance of specific and limited goals in a mass educational system and the futility of looking to such a system to be all things to all men or to instill a view of life incompatible with society. The unhappy record since World War II of religious instruction in British schools ought to act as a useful reminder to us, not only of the supreme importance of defining our educational goals, but of restricting them to what schools can realistically be expected to do. I for one do not feel that they can realistically be expected to reform the community or the government or the church or the world, or that they can be expected to solve the emotional, psychological, or social-adjustment problems of young people. They should serve more specific and less grandiose purposes. They should be content to make an indirect contribution to these worthy matters through concentration on the limited job they are uniquely fitted for: instructing all students in the fundamental subjects of human knowledge, which have allowed our civilization, however imperfect, to become what it now is. That, I believe, is the most promising way of turning out students equipped to solve their own problems and an electorate equipped to solve the larger problems of our society.

# Notes

I HAVE TRIED to spare the reader the usual baggage (of questionable utility) of *ibid., op. cit., loc. cit.,* and *passim;* when I refer more than once to a work, I simply repeat the reference. The only abbreviations that might need clarification are: *Hansard*—the agency that prints the daily verbatim record of the House of Commons and the House of Lords (corresponding to our *Congressional Record*); *HMSO*—Her Majesty's Stationery Office, the official government printing and publications office; and *TES—The Times Educational Supplement,* a major weekly publication read throughout Britain and the Commonwealth.

## CHAPTER I

1. Maurice Reuchlin, *Pupil Guidance, Fact and Problems,* Council for Cultural Cooperation of the Council of Europe, Strasbourg, 1964, pp. 31–32.
2. Baroness Phillips, *Hansard* (House of Lords), Feb. 10, 1965, p. 165.
3. *The Uses of Literacy,* Penguin, 1958, 1963, p. 132.
4. Quoted in W. O. Lester Smith, *Government of Education,* Pelican, 1965, pp. 115–116.
5. *The Education of the Adolescent* (Hadow Report), HMSO, 1926, reprinted 1962, p. xix.
6. Two of the best sources: Miss M. M. Wells and P. S. Taylor, *The New Law of Education,* Butterworth's, 5th ed., 1961, is the most complete exposition. H. C. Dent, *The Education Act, 1944,* University of London Press, 11th ed., 1966, is a much briefer but excellent treatment.
7. Interview in *The Listener,* Jan. 14, 1965, p. 46.
8. *Statistics of Education, 1964,* Parts I, II, and III, HMSO; *Annual Abstract of Statistics,* Central Statistical Office, HMSO, 1965; and *Digest of Educational Statistics,* 1964 ed., U.S. Office of Education.

## CHAPTER II

1. *Curriculum and Examinations in Secondary Schools* (Norwood Report), HMSO, 1941, p. 53.

2. "The Inspector's Lot," *TES*, Oct. 14, 1966, p. 875.

3. *Hansard* (House of Lords), Feb. 10, 1965, p. 132.

4. Quoted from the speech of the incoming President of the National Association of Divisional Executives for Education, in *Education*, Sept. 17, 1965, p. 499.

5. Kathleen Ollerenshaw, "Sharing Responsibility," a speech reprintel in *Public Administration* (Journal of the Royal Institute of Public Administration), Spring 1962, p. 44.

6. *The Future Pattern of the Education and Training of Teachers* (Eighth Report of the National Advisory Council on the Training and Supply of Teachers), HMSO, 1962, p. 19.

7. One Public School headmaster who has worked with the organization has described it this way: "Whatever its declared pretensions of objectivity ACE is quite clearly a pressure group. Beneath its appearance of detachment the prejudices and opinions of its managers are plain from the tone and approach of most of the articles in its magazine *Where?* [The question mark has now been removed from the magazine's title.] Their dislike of all forms of independence in education is evident. I have no doubt that the intention of ACE's Director, Mr. Brian Jackson, is to assist in the abolition of independent schools and to direct change within the maintained system on preconceived lines." Alan Barker, "Independence and the Public Schools," in *Rebirth of Britain*, Pan Books, 1964, p. 188.

8. Christopher Chataway, "Education and the Parent," in *The Conservative Opportunity*, Batsford, 1965, p. 64.

9. "Report of the Working Party on the Schools' Curricula and Examinations," HMSO, 1964, p. 11.

10. *Encounter,* July 1963, p. 8.

11. *Equality,* Unwin, 1964, p. 26. First published in 1931.

12. From "I Spy Strangers."

13. J. Wilks, *TES*, May 22, 1964, p. 346.

14. Robin Pedley, *The Comprehensive School*, Penguin, 1963, p. 11.

15. E. R. Taylor and Sir John Lockwood, in *The Times*, Dec. 31, 1964.

16. *The Sunday Times,* Jan. 3, 1965.

17. "Socialism and Education," a pamphlet reprinted from the *Journal of the Socialist Educational Association*, March 1964.

18. Quoted in *The Guardian*, Oct. 7, 1965.

19. Harry Ree, from an interview printed in *Where*, Spring 1965, p. 18.

20. *TES*, Sept. 25, 1964, p. 457.

21. Stewart said: "The form of organization which we have had until recently, and which is still usual, can, I think, best be described by the word 'separatist.' The word 'tripartite' is now out of date. The word 'selection' does not adequately describe it, because the essence of the system is not merely that it tries, when the children are 10 and a half, to judge what their abilities are and one might have to decide, within a single school, what courses of study they should pursue. The essence of the system which generally prevails today is that, first, one tries to make, by one means or another, a judgment, when the children are 10 and a half, as to what their abilities are, and on the basis of that judgment one puts them into separate

groups and sends each group to a school designed to cater for the needs of that group and that group only. That is why I think the name separatist is the most accurate description of that approach to secondary organization. . . . In the Government's view we ought now to accept that the reorganization of secondary education on comprehensive lines should be national policy . . ." *Hansard* (House of Commons), HMSO, Nov. 27, 1964, pp. 1778, 1786.

22. *Hansard* (House of Commons), HMSO, Jan. 21, 1965, p. 416.
23. Sir William Alexander, in *Education*, March 18, 1966, p. 561.

CHAPTER III

1.  Data derived from *Statistics of Education, Part One, 1964*, HMSO, p. 22.
2.  *The State of Our Schools*, 2 vols., NUT, 1964.
3.  *The School Building Survey, 1962*, HMSO, 1965, p. 3.
4.  J. W. B. Douglas, *The Home and the School*, MacGibbon & Kee, 1964, p. 113.
5.  See, for example, both J. W. B. Douglas (above, p. 118); and Brian Jackson, *Streaming; an Education System in Miniature*, Routledge and Kegan Paul, 1964, p. 30.
6.  Brian Jackson and Dennis Marsden, *Education and the Working Class*, Routledge and Kegan Paul, 1962, p. 119.
7.  P. E. Vernon, in *Secondary School Selection*, Methuen, 1957, p. 22.
8.  "Educating the Individual Child," PEST Education Series 1, 1966, p. 5.
9.  Flann Campbell, *Eleven Plus and All That; The Grammar School in a Changing Society*, Watts, 1956, p. 133.
10. Brian Jackson and Dennis Marsden, *Education and the Working Class*, Routledge and Kegan Paul, 1962, p. 211.
11. Stephen Wiseman, *Education and Environment*, Manchester University Press, 1964, p. 155.
12. "Procedures for the Allocation of Pupils in Secondary Education," National Foundation for Educational Research, Sept. 1963, pp. 4–5.
13. J. W. B. Douglas, *The Home and the School*, MacGibbon & Kee, 1964, pp. xiv–xv.
14. One of the most detailed analyses of the margin of error is Alfred Yates and D. A. Pidgeon, *Admission to Grammar School*, published for the National Foundation for Educational Research by Newnes, 1957, p. 192.
15. Michael Armstrong and Michael Young, "New Look at Comprehensive Schools," Fabian Research Series 237, 1964, p. 1.
16. A. F. Watts, *Can We Measure Ability?*, University of London Press, 1953, p. 78.
17. John Brown, "Teachers for the New Large Schools," *Forum*, Summer 1963, p. 92.
18. Philip L. Masters, *Preparatory Schools Today*, A. & C. Black, 1966, pp. 34–35.
19. *A Comparative Study of the Academic Achievements of Elementary Age Students of the United States and the British Isles*, mimeographed report of the Research Foundation of the University of Toledo, 1965, 191 pages.

20. William Taylor, *The Secondary Modern School*, Faber, 1963, p. 91.
21. John Partridge, *Middle School*, Gollancz, 1966, p. 147.
22. J. Cornwell, "The Probationary Year," mimeographed report of the Institute of Education Training Colleges Research Group, 1964, p. 14.
23. See, for example, Michael Argles, *South Kensington to Robbins*, Longmans, 1964, p. 137.
24. *Fifteen to Eighteen* (Crowther Report), Vol. I, HMSO, 1959, pp. 464, 494.
25. See *Day Release* (Henniker-Heaton Report), HMSO, 1964. Actually, the amount of "day release" is not great in relation to the numbers of apprentices, as the Henniker-Heaton Committee sternly makes clear.
26. H. L. Elvin, *Education and Contemporary Society*, Watts, 1965, p. 177.
27. *Change and Response*, HMSO, 1965, p. 6.
28. M. V. C. Jeffreys, *Revolution in Teacher-Training*, Pitman, 1961, p. v.
29. Michael Armstrong and Michael Young, "New Look at Comprehensive Schools," Fabian Research Series 237, 1964, p. 12.
30. John Partridge, *Middle School*, Gollancz, 1966, p. 153.
31. Cyril Hughes, "Stones Instead of Bread: the Secondary Modern Mistake," *TES*, Oct. 16, 1964, p. 651.
32. *Half Our Future* (Newsom Report), HMSO, 1963.
33. *From School to Further Education* (Brunton Report), HMSO, Edinburgh, 1963, pp. 9, 10–11.
34. *Hansard* (House of Commons), Jan. 21, 1965, p. 424.
35. "Raising the School Leaving Age," Working Paper 2, Schools Council, HMSO, 1965, p. 13.
36. "Some Curriculum Developments—the Newsom Report" (printed document of the London County Council's Education Committee), 1964, 18 pages; it is now the Inner London Education Authority.
37. *Fifteen to Eighteen* (Crowther Report), 2 vols., HMSO, 1959–1960.
38. "The State of Our Schools," NUT, Part II, p. 19.
39. However, one writer pointed out a few years ago that the picture is much better if all post-secondary education is considered: "The large majority of young people over the age of fifteen who are receiving full or part-time education are specializing in scientific or technical studies of one kind or another. This is true irrespective of whether they are being educated in secondary modern and grammar school, in technical and trade colleges, or in universities." Harold Dowling, "Science in Education," *Crossbow*, July–Sept. 1962, p. 27.
40. Denys Thompson, "Another Hurdle," *Cambridge Review*, April 25, 1964, p. 350.
41. *Fifteen to Eighteen* (Crowther Report), Vol. I, HMSO, 1959, p. 259.
42. *Examiners' Reports*, Joint Matriculation Board (Manchester), 1965, p. 1. See also this board's "Occasional Publications" No. 3 ("An Experimental Examination in General Studies"), 1955; and No. 5 ("The Joint Matriculation Board Examination in General Studies"), 1957—for reports on the validity and reliability of the board's General Studies exam compared to its customary exams.
43. "Arts and Sciences Sides in the Sixth Form," Oxford University Department of Education, 1960.

44. "University of Keele Students' Union Academic Research Project," 1965, p. 28. Keele makes an effort to attract students who want to do a year of general study before university specialization, thus suggesting that they get many students who are dissatisfied with their sixth-form subjects.

45. *Where*, March 1966.

46. "Change and Response; the First Year's Work of the Schools Council," HMSO, 1965, p. 9.

47. A. D. C. Peterson, in *The New Statesman*, March 5, 1965, p. 358.

48. Quoted in "The Direct Grant School; a Memorandum Prepared by the Direct Grant Committee of the Headmasters' Conference," 1965, p. 8.

49. *Hansard* (House of Lords), Feb. 10, 1965, p. 188.

50. John Wilson, *Public Schools and Private Practice*, Allen & Unwin, 1962, pp. 74–75.

51. Philip L. Masters, *Preparatory Schools Today*, A. and C. Black, 1966, pp. 91–92.

52. P. L. Masters and S. W. Hockey, "National Reserves of Ability," *TES*, May 17, 1963, p. 1061. The authors also point out: "A word must be said to counter another argument sometimes heard. Since the Common Entrance Examination is sometimes thought to be more 'difficult' than the 11-plus, it is believed that boys like this, who passed the C.E. at 13, are thereby shown to have been underestimated at 11. But this argument is based on a misconception. Whereas the 11-plus is a test of ability, the Common Entrance is rather a test of attainment; it is obviously possible, therefore, for one boy's results in the two examinations to be widely divergent, and specifically for a boy of modest ability, who has been well taught for five years at his preparatory school and has worked hard there, to pass C.E. though he has failed the 11-plus."

53. John Dancy, *The Public Schools and the Future*, Faber and Faber, 1963, p. 57.

54. Howard Glennerster and Richard Pryke, "The Public Schools," Young Fabian Pamphlet 7, 1964, p. 7.

55. Daniel Jenkens, *Equality and Excellence*, SCM Press, 1961, p. 122.

56. Tom Pritchard, in *The Guardian*, June 26, 1965.

57. *Hansard* (House of Lords), Feb. 23, 1966, p. 276.

58. Published by Hodder and Stoughton, 1962.

59. See, for example, the yearly compilation that appears in *TES* of the schools from which entrants to Oxford and Cambridge come. The February 4, 1966, issue, pp. 322–323, contains a particularly informative survey for the years between 1956–57 and 1964–65.

60. *Where*, Spring 1965, p. 5.

61. *Hansard* (House of Lords), Feb. 10, 1965, pp. 160–161.

62. Graham Kalton, *The Public Schools; a Factual Survey*, Longmans, 1966.

63. Dora Pym, in the *British Journal of Educational Studies*, May 1965, quotes this passage from a letter written by Clarendon in which he is declining an invitation to head still another educational commission: "At this moment it would be impossible for me to fix a sum that would induce me to get into a Middle Schools drag. . . . I am very glad, however, that you meditate such a commission, as I know it is wanted. . . . Lyttelton would

make a very good chairman—the only one of the late [Clarendon Commission] lot who would. Devon is weak, Northcote pedantic, Thompson idle, Twisleton quirky, Vaughan mad; yet they all had merits and worked usefully together, except Vaughan who, tho' a man of real genius, is unmanageable."

64. *The Public Schools and the General Educational System* (Fleming Report), HMSO, 1944, p. 56.
65. Royston Lambert, "State Boarding," *New Society*, Oct. 28, 1965, p. 10.
66. *Hansard* (House of Commons), Dec. 22, 1965, p. 2108.
67. "Unity and Diversity in Secondary Education," *Harvard Alumni Bulletin*, April 19, 1962.

## CHAPTER IV

1. James A. Petch, *Fifty Years of Examining*, Harrap, 1953, p. 215.
2. Donald W. Dunnan, in a speech at the annual convention of the American Association of School Administrators, Feb. 1966.
3. *Curriculum and Examinations in Secondary Schools*, HMSO, 1943, reprinted 1962.
4. The two largest boards, London and the JMB, have published excellent pamphlets that describe their internal operations, and that could well be duplicated by the other boards. These two boards operate in a very similar fashion, but it is doubtful if the other boards are as well organized. See J. A. Petch, "The Joint Matriculation Board: What It Is and What It Does," JMB Occasional Publication 16, 1963; and "GCE London, the Work of the University Entrance and Schools Examination Council," University of London, 1964.
5. James A. Petch, *Fifty Years of Examining*, Harrap, 1953, pp. 131–132.
6. C. H. Dobinson, *Schooling, 1963–1970*, Harrap, 1963, p. 81.
7. H. Davies, "The Changing Grammar School," No. 2 of the Educational Papers of the Institute of Education, University of Nottingham (undated—1965?), p. 5.
8. D. R. Mather, N. France, and G. T. Sare, *The Certificate of Secondary Education; a Handbook for Moderators*, Collins, 1965, p. 15.
9. See *Examiners' Reports* for 1938, pp. 26–27; and for 1950, p. 1; both published by the JMB.
10. *Curriculum and Examinations in Secondary School* (Norwood Report), HMSO, 1943, p. 13.
11. R. A. C. Oliver, "An Experimental Test in English," JMB Occasional Publication 13, 1963. In 1964 Oliver also ran an experiment to test whether the JMB's "Test in English" was comparable in standards and grading with the Oxford and Cambridge "Use of English" test, with somewhat better results: 82% of the candidates were given the same rating by both examining bodies—but 15.5% of the entry passed one board while failing the other. See "Studies in a University Entrance Test in English," JMB Occasional Publication 19.
12. Brian Jackson, in *English versus Examinations*, Chatto & Windus, 1965, p. 12.

13. *The Examining of English Language* (Eighth Report of the Secondary School Examinations Council), HMSO, 1964, pp. 2–3.
14. See "The 1965 C.S.E. Monitoring Experiment," Working Paper No. 6, Part I, Schools Council, HMSO, 1966, p. 11.
15. "Fairer Examining," *TES*, Dec. 10, 1965, p. 1279.
16. Consider this waspish comment on GCE examiners: "Let us first dispose once and for all of this high sounding title, examiner. The typical assistant examiner examines nothing: he marks scripts under the direction of Chief Examiners who prepare the papers and the mark scheme. If it is a poor paper and a poor mark scheme there is little that the marker of scripts can do about it. . . . There is no trained cadre of examiners in the true sense outside the ranks of a select band of Chief Examiners relying on intuition and instinct. . . ." Dr. R. Mather, N. France, and G. T. Sare, *The Certificate of Secondary Education: a Handbook for Moderators*, Collins, 1965, p. 11.
17. See, for example, "How I Marked O-Levels," in *The Times*, March 20, 1965, p. 11.
18. P. Hartog and E. C. Rhodes, *An Examination of Examinations*, Macmillan, 1936.
19. *Secondary School Examinations Other Than the G.C.E.* (Beloe Report), HMSO, 1960, p. 17.
20. R. Irvine Smith, in *TES*, May 15, 1964, p. 1361.
21. *Sixty-second Annual Report, 1964–1965*, JMB, p. 12.
22. W. D. Furneaux, *The Chosen Few; an Examination of Some Aspects of University Selection in Britain*, published by the Nuffield Foundation by Oxford University Press, 1961. Furneaux comments (p. 97): "It is clear from the discussion above that school-leaving examinations provide by far the most useful and accurate information as to academic quality of any of the selection procedures which are used by the universities, but it is also clear that even at their best their accuracy is limited."
23. "The Effectiveness of G.C.E. Advanced Level as a Criterion for University Selection," JMB Occasional Publication 7, 1960, p. 3.
24. "G.C.E. and Degree, Part I," JMB Occasional Publication 10, 1961, pp. 63–65.
25. *Fifty Years of Examining*, Harrap, 1953, p. 216.
26. One psychologist, after giving the problem of university prediction considerable attention, says: "A great many small-scale studies have been carried out, many of them unpublished. Though there are wide variations from subject to subject, from university to university, and even from year to year within the same university, an overall correlation of between .3 and .4 seems a fair estimate [a pretty low correlation]. On the other hand, consistently high correlations can be obtained in certain subjects, particularly languages, between the matriculation examination and first year university marks." James Drever, "Prediction, Placement and Choice in University Selection," Godfrey Thomson Lecture, 1963, Moray House, Edinburgh, p. 11.
27. For example, the Artemis Press publishes a small volume of model answers in a dozen or so of the most popular GCE subjects, and some students,

certainly those on the borderlines of ability, might well be helped in both knowledge and approach to the exam by reviewing these "model" answers to past GCE questions.

28. James M. Charlton, *Model English Test Papers,* James Brodie, undated, p. 74.

29. "To expect examinations," says J. A. Petch with some justice, "to sort out large numbers of candidates into many groups, each group sharply differentiated from the two groups between which it is placed, is to run directly counter to the way in which nature has distributed human abilities. . . . Examiners dealing with hundreds of candidates in the limiting conditions of a public examination cannot bring to light the fine differences which those who deal with the small numbers of students in a school form or a university class may think they can find. There is fortunately another resource available. Blunt as the classification of performances in various subjects viewed separately must be, some sharpening may be achieved by laying less stress on what a candidate does in each subject considered separately and by looking rather to the level of his attainment in all the subjects he has simultaneously attempted." See "Marks and Marking," JMB Occasional Publication 8, 1960, p. 25. A problem arises of course with candidates who take only one or two subjects in the exam, which is one more reason for making national exam systems group and not single subject exams.

30. This study is described in a number of places. See, for example, D. Cole-Baker, "Towards an International University Entrance Examination," *Comparative Education* (Oxford), Nov. 1965, pp. 43–45. Cole-Baker is head of the Geneva school.

31. *Marlborough; an Open Examination Written by the Boys,* Kenneth Mason Publications, 1963, p. 32.

32. In fairness I should perhaps add that quite a few British teachers are less than happy with the way in which foreign languages are examined in the GCE, but this is not a deficiency of external exams as such, only of the way in which they may be done in a given instance. The following comment is not unusual, from a headmaster of a grammar school, who says that the GCE boards "obstinately refuse to encourage fluency. O level is a minor offender. The standard is so undemanding that success can be ensured by any reasonably competent teaching method. But few examinations could be more weighted against fluency than GCE A level. The papers are well set and marked; it is the emphasis that is wrong. . . . The genuine Language papers (prose, essay and oral) total 130 [possible points], of which the oral's share is 30." L. Bruce Lockhart, "Place of Fluency in Modern Language Examinations," *TES,* Nov. 12, 1965, p. 1019.

33. "Did Columbus Go Too Far?" *TES,* Dec. 28, 1962, p. 843.

34. "Procedures for the Allocation of Pupils in Secondary Education," National Foundation for Educational Research, 1963, p. 9.

35. *Curriculum and Examinations in Secondary School* (Norwood Report), HMSO, 1943, pp. 45–46.

36. *Secondary School Examinations Other than the G.C.E.,* HMSO, 1960.

37. See in particular: "The Certificate of Secondary Education," Fourth Report

of the Secondary School Examinations Council, HMSO, 1961; and "Scope and Standards of the Certificate of Secondary Education," Seventh Report of the Council, HMSO, 1963.

38. "Examining at 16-Plus," Schools Council, HMSO, 1960.

39. "Change and Response; the First Annual Report of the Schools Council," HMSO, 1965.

40. R. J. Montgomery, *Examinations; an Account of Their Evolution as Administrative Devices in England*, Longmans, 1965—on the whole, an excellent history.

41. The JMB, for example, recently did a study called "School Estimates and Examination Results Compared," in which schools were found to overestimate their pupils pretty consistently, at least as judged against external exams. See Occasional Publication 21, 1964. An even more recent experiment to compare the judgment of teachers of English about their pupils' abilities with the assessment of the JMB normal exams in that subject is unfortunately not yet at the point that definite conclusions can be recorded; but interim results look more promising than one might have expected. See H. A. Hewitt and D. I. Gordon, "English Language; an Experiment in School Assessing," JMB Occasional Publication 22, 1965.

42. I refer to a continuing series of publications called "Examination Bulletins" the first four numbers of which were published under the old name of the Secondary School Examinations Council, and from five onwards by the Schools Council, HMSO.

43. "Examinations Bulletin No. 1," HMSO, 1963.

44. *Secondary School Examinations Other than the G.C.E.*, HMSO, 1960, p. 32.

45. *Handbook on Examinations and Scholarships*, New York State Education Department, 1964, p. 7.

## CHAPTER V

1. "The Future Pattern of the Education and Training of Teachers" (the Council's eighth annual report), HMSO, 1962, p. 13.

2. "Scales of Salaries for Teachers in Primary and Secondary Schools," HMSO, 1965.

3. *Teachers and Youth Leaders* (McNair Report), HMSO, 1944, reprinted 1962, p. 13.

4. Stephen Wiseman, Director of the Institute of Education at the University of Manchester, in a speech delivered at the University of Hull, March 1964.

5. "The Training College Principal," *The Sociological Review*, July 1964, pp. 188–189.

6. William Taylor, "Who Teaches Education?" *Universities Quarterly*, Dec. 1965, p. 50.

7. The McNair Committee, a national investigative body, remarked in its 1944 report: "The core of the staff of any training institution must, however, consist of men and women who not only have the requisite standing in their subjects but have proved themselves as teachers. The difficulty is to ensure that some members of the staff have recent and intimate experi-

ence of current school problems and practice. On this aspect of staffing we should not be dealing faithfully with our subject if we did not record that one of the criticisms levelled against the training colleges by some of the young teachers who gave evidence to us was that those who instructed and supervised them in the arts of teaching were not always themselves sufficiently acquainted with school conditions and practice. . . . A proportion of the staff of every training college, or at any rate of every area training service, should consist of those who have been appointed fresh from the schools. The present system of recruiting the staffs of training institutions cannot ensure this." *Teachers and Youth Leaders,* HMSO, 1944, reprinted 1961, p. 72.

8. See, for example, P. Lawrence, "Advanced Level 1963 and After," a pamphlet published by the Joint Matriculation Board; Manchester, Oct. 1964, Table 27.

9. For a typical comment, see John Delvin, "Three-Tier Teacher Qualification?" *New Scientist,* Nov. 11, 1965, pp. 436–437.

10. The most detailed study done of the matter to date in Britain is: W. D. Furneaux, *The Chosen Few; an Examination of Some Aspects of University Selection in Britain,* published for the Nuffield Foundation by the Oxford University Press, 1961. Among other things on the subject of the interview, Furneaux comments (p. 99): "There appears to be no evidence that interviews, as they are at present conducted by most departments, contribute to the validity of selection, although they may perhaps have uses for purposes other than prediction. At their best they seem frequently to be an inefficient way of achieving ends which could better be reached with the aid of alternative techniques."

11. A. H. Body, in *TES,* Nov. 24, 1961, p. 462.

12. A. D. C. Peterson, in *TES,* Aug. 1964, p. 274. Interestingly enough, Peterson's predecessor as head of the Oxford Institute, writing a few years earlier in the same publication, said: "It is important that academic standards in training colleges should be raised, but this is not best done by attempting to equate their entrance requirements with those pertaining at the universities: indeed, even if this were so, the improvement would be bought at too high a price, the price of excluding from the teaching profession many candidates well qualified on grounds of intelligence, personality, wide interests, and a capacity which often amounts to a gift for teaching. To achieve the number of passes at A level necessary for admission to a university is evidence that the candidate is a good learner, but a good learner is very different from a good teacher: the universities are interested in producing the former, and the training colleges the latter." M. L. Jacks, in *TES,* Nov. 24, 1961, p. 333.

13. *Teachers and Youth Leaders* (McNair Report), HMSO, 1944, reprinted 1961, p. 65.

14. "The Future Pattern of the Education and Training of Teachers" (the Council's eighth annual report), HMSO, 1962, p. 17.

15. "Colleges of Education—The Three Year Course," National Union of Students, London, 1966, p. 27.

16. M. V. C. Jeffreys, *Revolution in Teacher-Training,* Pitman, 1961, p. 37.

17. A good example is the sixth annual report of the National Advisory Council on the Training and Supply of Teachers, which urges an increase to three years: "Scope and Content of the Three Year Course of Teacher Training," HMSO, 1957.

18. Mimeographed report of the Conference of Heads of London Comprehensive Schools, May 1, 1964, pp. 3–4. Elsewhere the report says: "The Conference agreed unanimously that the process of collaboration between schools and Teacher Training Colleges needs to be reviewed and radically altered. We felt it to be a matter of the deepest urgency and importance to schools of all kinds that plans for further extension of teacher training institutions should be preceded by a critical appraisal of the present system. We are convinced that the majority of existing courses of training can be greatly improved in certain respects; particularly in the one common feature of training courses with which we are intimately concerned: that of the students' periods of teaching practice. . . . in advocating radical changes, we were anxious not to obscure our sense of the need for immediate modifications to many schemes for teaching practice. We call for a general review, with these aims:

    a. To make the process of professional training more relevant to the needs of schools.

    b. To create a genuine relationship of collaboration between teachers in schools and lecturers in colleges, in a shared responsibility.

    c. To expand the training capacity of the existing system, by eliminating waste.

    ". . . Our advocacy of longer periods of teaching practice is, however, a preface to the major reform which we feel to be necessary: that is, the transfer of tutorial responsibility for students in schools from training colleges lecturers to practicing teachers. . . . Many young teachers emerge from their years of training without having learnt much more than the alphabet of their profession. . . . They have been left to fill the gap between theory and practice for themselves, in their first year of full professional employment. They have too often been taught by Education lecturers who are far removed from the plain realities of the day by day, week by week, term by term life of a school, its teachers and its children; who too often have forgotten (if indeed they ever knew) how to make a harmony of all the conflicting pressures in the working program of a young teacher. In our view, it is in fact only from the teacher-tutor, only in an extended period of school practice, that the student can learn the elements of his job as it really is going to be."

    The Heads' view of practice teaching and apprenticeship is also borne out, if it needs any further support, by a study reported in 1965 of the first year's experience of teachers: they consistently found their greatest help in practical matters, not from the preparatory work in the Colleges, but from informal discussions with experienced colleagues. "The Probationary Year," mimeographed report from the Institute of Education Training Colleges Research Group, University of Birmingham, 1965.

19. "A Compendium of Teacher Training Courses in England and Wales," List No. 172, HMSO, 1965, p. 2.

20. *Teachers and Youth Leaders* (McNair Report), HMSO, 1944, reprinted 1961. The heart of the committee's recommendations is on pp. 48–62.
21. William Taylor, "The University Teacher in Education; Report of a Survey Undertaken in January 1964 with the Aid of a Grant from the Nuffield Foundation," Department of Education, Oxford University, pp. 7–8.
22. Harry K. Hutton, "Compulsory Teacher Training in England," *School and Society*, Nov. 28, 1964, p. 358.
23. In the spring of 1966, the Council recommended to the Secretary that pedagogical training be made compulsory for all teachers in colleges of further education; the Secretary said he liked the idea but that the shortage of both funds and teachers made the recommendation impossible for the present.
24. "The Training of Teachers" (mimeographed evidence of the NAS submitted to the Committee of Higher Education), Oct. 1961, p. 11.
25. *Forum*, Summer 1963, p. 85.
26. "Undergraduate Attitudes to Teaching," *Trends in Education*, April 1966, p. 16.
27. Boris Ford, in *The Idea of a New University*, edited by David Daiches, André Deutsch, 1964, p. 135.
28. *The Characteristics of Teacher Education Students in the British Isles and the United States*, mimeographed document from the Research Foundation of the University of Toledo, 300 pages. It is dated 1965, but was not released until the spring of 1966.
29. David G. Ryans, *Characteristics of Teachers*, American Council on Education, 1960, pp. 366–370.
30. The following kind of statement is met with some frequency in British journals: "Teachers must be leaders of thought as well as craftsmen. And the study of education is readily comprehensible as a discipline if viewed without prejudice. Starting with the mental and physical growth of individuals, it reaches out to the social and cultural influences at work on them in home, school, neighborhood, and the wider world. It brings us all, sooner or later, face to face with profound philosophical questions. Education is demonstrably a proper subject for university study." Robin Pedley, in *TES*, April 1, 1960, p. 649.
31. *Inventory of Training Possibilities in Europe*, OECD, 1965.
32. Stephen Wiseman, *Education and Environment*, Manchester University Press, 1964, p. 2.
33. See G. E. R. Borroughs, "Co-operative Research in Institutes of Education," *British Journal of Educational Psychology*, June 1962.
34. Michael Young, *Innovation and Research in Education*, Routledge, 1965; see Appendix I, pp. 137–144.
35. "Report of the Study Group on the Government of Colleges of Education," HMSO, 1966, 29 pages.
36. Cyril Bibby, "Bachelor of Education: Retrospect and Prospect," *Universities Quarterly*, Dec. 1965, p. 30.

CHAPTER VI

1. *Report of the Committee on Higher Education* (Robbins Report); the main report and first four volumes of appendices were published, HMSO, in 1963, and the fifth appendix in 1964. Further volumes of evidence were also published in 1965.

2. "Socialism and Education," a pamphlet reprinted from the *Journal of the Socialist Educational Association,* March 1964, p. 12.

3. *Report of the Commission of Inquiry* (Franks Report), 2 vols., Oxford University Press, 1966.

4. "Memorandum of Evidence of the Committee on Higher Education," the Committee of Vice-Chancellors and Principals of the Universities of the United Kingdom (evidence to the Robbins Committee), Nov. 1961, p. 6.

5. *Access to Higher Education,* Vol. I, UNESCO, 1963, p. 3.

6. *Some Thoughts on University Education,* Cambridge University Press, 1949, p. 67.

7. Richard Lattimore, "Robbins and the Classics," the Joint Association of Classical Teachers, Pamphlet No. 1, 1964, p. 10.

8. R. V. Jones, "In Search of Scientists," *The Listener,* Sept. 23, 1965, p. 447.

9. Jasper Rose and John Ziman, *Camford Observed,* Gollancz, 1966, p. 77.

10. W. Ivor Jennings (then master of one of the Cambridge colleges) made this computation in 1964. He found that the men's colleges had taken in 2,931 students from no fewer than 685 schools but that the Public schools and direct-grant establishments predominated in numbers of successful candidates (359 of the schools involved offered only one candidate). He added: "It seems reasonable to conclude . . . that in the stern competition of the scholarship examinations the independent and direct grant schools do better, no doubt because so many of them have strong sixth forms with specialist teachers and also because many of the direct grant schools 'cream' the primary schools at 11 plus. On the other hand, the figures show that, in the process of selection by committees and tutors, the maintained schools do better. This fact is not mentioned in Robbins; but in case there is a supplement it should be said that the prejudices of dons (though admittedly most of us come from grammar schools) do not provide the explanation." "The Scholarship Examination, 1964," *The Cambridge Review,* Feb. 20, 1965, pp. 280–281.

11. Of the difficulties that Britain and all countries face in making such manpower predications, the Robbins Report thought it was uncertain enough even when only "single types of skill over long periods" are involved. "But they are still more formidable in forecasting demand for highly qualified manpower in general. This is not a matter of simple aggregation of particular forecasts: the entire future movement of the economy is involved, both internally and in relation to the almost infinite possibilities of change abroad, and the inter-relationships of the different variables are of a degree of complexity that so far has defied practical solution. It may be that, in time to come, ways may be discovered of making projections of this sort, and we hope very much that research into these difficult problems may be part of the duties of the regular machinery

that we shall propose for continuous statistical investigation." Pp. 72–73.

12. See, for example, M. H. Peston, "Some Economic Aspects," *The Technologist*, April 1964; and E. G. West, "A Counterblast to Robbins," *The Statist*, Nov. 8, 1963.

13. C. A. Moser and P. R. G. Layard, in a speech in 1964 to the Royal Statistical Society, reprinted in *Forum*, May 29, 1964. Among other things, they said: ". . . we must stress that decisions as to how much weight to put on the demand for places and how much on manpower needs cannot be made on purely technical grounds. The instruments of measurement are likely to remain too blunt to provide precise information for the eventual political decision. But if the country is moving into a period of more systematic economic planning, it may well be that manpower considerations will come to play a more important part in educational planning than hitherto. For these considerations to be at all securely based will require far better information at national level than is yet available as well as more intensive research."

14. "University of Keele Students' Union Academic Research Project," 1965, p. 5.

15. Sir John Fulton, "Experiment in Higher Education," Tavistock Pamphlet No. 8, 1964, p. 14.

16. Marjorie Reeves, "Liberal Arts Colleges," *TES*, Feb. 10, 1961, pp. 251, 301.

17. *Report of the Committee on University Teaching Methods* (Hale Report), HMSO, 1964, pp. 19, 37.

18. Quoted in "Education in Germany," published by Inter Nationes, Bonn, March 1964.

19. R. T. Berry, "Post-Graduate Research," *TES*, May 25, 1962, p. 1079.

20. R. V. Jones, "In Search of Scientists," *The Listener*, Sept. 30, 1965, p. 488.

21. J. G. Powles, in *The Guardian*, Oct. 26, 1962.

22. *Report of the Committee on University Teaching Methods* (Hale Report), HMSO, 1964, p. 104.

23. *Report of the Committee on University Teaching Methods* (Hale Report), HMSO, 1964, p. 68.

24. Jasper Rose and John Ziman, *Camford Observed*, Gollancz, 1964, p. 69.

25. Cyril Bailey, in *The Handbook of the University of Oxford*, Oxford University Press, 1965, p. 284.

26. R. I. Moore, *Spectator*, March 13, 1964, p. 12.

27. In *Encounter*, Oct. 1963, p. 92.

28. O. Meredith Wilson, in a speech to the Land-Grant Annual Meeting, 1964.

29. J. Gwyn Morgan, "What the Students Want," *New Statesman*, March 3, 1961, p. 18.

30. *Report of the Committee on University Teaching Methods* (Hale Report), HMSO, 1964, p. 45.

31. "University of Keele Students' Union Academic Research Project," 1965, p. 6.

32. "Comments on the Report to the General Board of Committee on Teaching," mimeographed document from the Student Representative Council,

Cambridge, 1964, p. 5. See also the negative comment on Cambridge lecturing in R. H. White, *Cambridge Life*, Eyre & Spottiswoode, 1960, pp. 88–90.

## CHAPTER VII

1. Sir Geoffrey Crowther, "English and American Education; Depth versus Breadth," *Atlantic Monthly*, April, 1960, p. 37.
2. Donald W. Dunnan, in a speech at the annual conference of the American Association of School Administrators, Atlantic City, February 1966.
3. Robin Pedley, *The Comprehensive School*, Penguin, 1963, pp. 27–28.
4. John N. Wales, *School of Democracy*, Michigan State University Press, 1962; all quoted matter from Chapter V, pp. 61–71.
5. *Bulletin* of the Council for Basic Education, Washington, D.C., Oct. 1964, pp. 1–4.
6. Catherine Avent, "Notes on American High School Education," memorandum to the Central Advisory Council for Education (Newsom Committee), 1962.

## CHAPTER VIII

1. J. A. Lauwerys, in *Access in Higher Education*, Vol. II, UNESCO, 1965, p. 492.
2. *Report of Commission of Inquiry*, Vol. I, Oxford University Press, 1966, p. 80.
3. See, for example, an article in its journal *The Teacher* (June 11, 1965, p. 10) entitled "Auxiliaries: 50 Points to Be Decided," most of which are trivial or irrelevant. The NUT's real concern is betrayed in this comment: "It is essential for every profession to lay down its professional principles and to limit the degree of assistance which it will allow ancillary workers to render."
4. *The Observer*, Sept. 6, 1965, p. 21.
5. As calculated by Seymour Harris, "Economics of Education," *OECD Observer*, Oct. 1963, p. 7.
6. Anthony Crosland, "The Case for Comprehension," a speech at the North of England Education Conference, Jan. 14, 1966.
7. Typical is the statement in "The Future Pattern of Education and Training of Teachers" (Eighth Report of the National Advisory Council on the Training and Supply of Teachers), HMSO, 1962, pp. 14–15.
8. Editorial in *Education*, Jan. 7, 1966, p. 2.
9. "Let Us Teach; Final Report of an Analysis of the Helpfulness of Certain Aspects of the School Program to Classroom Teaching" (A Report of the Senate Factfinding Committee on Governmental Administration), published by the Senate of the State of California, 1965, pp. 7–8.
10. *The American High School Today*, McGraw-Hill, 1959, p. 40.
11. Peter D. Moss, in *Liberal Education*, July 1964, p. 16.
12. "Socialism and Education," a reprint from the Journal of the Socialist Educational Association, March 1964, p. 14.

13. *The Guardian*, Dec. 23, 1965, p. 6.
14. C. H. Dobinson, *Schooling—1963–1970*, Harrap, 1963, pp. 14–15.
15. John Wilson, *Public Schools and Private Practice*, Allen & Unwin, 1962, pp. 127–128.
16. *Crisis in Education*, McGraw-Hill Book Company, 1949, p. 44.
17. *Life Adjustment for Every Youth*, U.S. Office of Education (1946?).
18. *Curriculum and Examinations in Secondary Schools* (Norwood Report), HMSO, 1943, reprinted 1962, p. viii.
19. John N. Wales, *Schools of Democracy*, Michigan State University Press, 1962, pp. 149–150.
20. "Are We Educating Our Children for the Wrong Future?" *Saturday Review Education Supplement*, Sept. 11, 1965, p. 83.
21. "Report of the General Sub-Committee on the Reorganization of Post-Primary Education," from the "Minutes of the Proceedings of the London County Council Education Committee," July 19, 1944, p. 462. This document, by the way, is an interesting account of the original reasoning within the LCC for going comprehensive after World War II.

## APPENDIX A

1. "The New School in Sweden," Royal Board of Education, Stockholm, 1963, p. 4.
2. *Comprehensive School and Continuation Schools in Sweden*, Royal Board of Education, Stockholm, 1962.
3. "Educational Change in Sweden," *Comparative Education*, Pergamon Press, June 1965, p. 186.
4. *Ability Grouping and Scholastic Achievement*, Almqvist & Wiksell, Uppsala, 1962.
5. Husén has discussed the Stockholm experiments and the comprehensive school in a great many places, one of the most interesting being a monograph, "Problems of Differentiation in Swedish Compulsory Schooling," Svenska Bokforlaget, 1965.
6. "The Contribution of Research to the Reform of Secondary Education," mimeographed paper given at the Quadrennial Congress of the International Association for the Advancement of Educational Research," Cambridge (England), August 9, 1965, p. 5.
7. Carl H. Lindroth, in *The Times*, Feb. 2, 1965, p. 8.
8. *Läroplan för Gymnasiet*, Royal Board of Education, Stockholm, 1965.

## APPENDIX C

1. Ronald Goldman *et al.*, "An Open Letter to L.E.A. Religious Education Advisory Committees," University of Reading, 1965.
2. Diana Dewar, *Backward Christian Soldiers*, Hutchinson, 1964, p. 59.
3. *Learning for Living; a Journal of Christian Education*, Jan. 1963, p. 4.
4. John A. T. Robinson, *The New Reformation?* SCM Press, 1965, p. 4.
5. *Fifteen to Eighteen* (Crowther Report), Vol. I, HMSO, 1959, p. 175.
6. "Some Aspects of Religious Education in Secondary Schools," NUT, 1963.

7. Lord Eccles, *Half-Way to Faith*, Geoffrey Bles, 1966, p. 60.
8. Dietrich Bonhoeffer, *Letters and Papers from Prison*, Fontana Books, 1959, 1965, p. 65.
9. *Soundings; Essays Concerning Christian Understanding*, edited by A. R. Vidler, Cambridge University Press, 1962, 1964, pp. ix, 6.
10. *New Christian*, Oct. 7, 1965, p. 1.
11. John A. T. Robinson, *The New Reformation?* SCM Press, 1965, p. 13.
12. Philip E. Jacob, *Changing Values in College*, Harper, 1957, p. 7.
13. From his essay "Modern Education and the Classics," 1932, reprinted in *Selected Prose*, edited by John Hayward, Penguin, 1953, p. 208.

# Index